N. C. EDSALL
1970

D1125922

Yale Studies in Political Science, 14

INTELLECTUALS IN POLITICS

❧ JOHN STUART MILL AND

THE PHILOSOPHIC RADICALS

JOSEPH HAMBURGER

YALE UNIVERSITY PRESS: NEW HAVEN AND LONDON

Copyright © 1965 by Yale University.
Second printing, August 1966.
Designed by John O. C. McCrillis,
set in Times Roman type,
and printed in the United States of America by
The Carl Purington Rollins Printing-Office of
the Yale University Press, New Haven, Connecticut.

Library of Congress catalog card number: 65–22320

FOR MY MOTHER

Preface

The literature on Philosophic Radicalism has usually emphasized its place in the history of ideas; its manifestations in the political activity of the day have been largely neglected, except when its influence on the making of public policy has been traced. The present study analyzes the Philosophic Radicals as politicians who sought to establish a new political party in order to upset the balance in Parliament. They failed, but in spite of their failure the enterprise was important as an episode in parliamentary politics and, even more, for what it reveals about their doctrine. I have not attempted to give a full historical narrative of their parliamentary activities nor to consider the various kinds of philosophy with which Philosophic Radicalism has been connected. I have concentrated instead on the political ideas the Philosophic Radicals thought relevant to their activities as politicians. They tried to be both philosophers and politicians; in analyzing the way in which they combined the two roles, I have placed special emphasis on one of the consequences—their doctrinairism, which is examined both from their point of view and in its relation to the broad spectrum of political opinion.

Although this is a study of a coterie of intellectuals who engaged in politics, John Stuart Mill has a special place as the leading member of the group. During this period Mill was still quite a young man and had not yet achieved the prominence that came with the publication of his *Logic, Political Economy,* and later works. Although these early years were important as a formative period when most of the ideas in the treatises were taking shape, Mill is dealt with not as a future philosopher but as a member of a group of men who were both spokesmen for a doctrine and politicians ambitious to exercise power on its behalf.

Several persons and institutions have kindly allowed me to publish extracts of manuscripts, and I would like to record my gratitude to them: Viscount Lambton; Russell Ellice; James M. Osborn; Frank Spurway and the County Branch Library, Liskeard; County Record Office, West Sussex County Council; Victoria and Albert Museum; University College, London; the Trustees of the British Museum; Public Archives of Canada; Harvard College Library; University of Illinois Library; Yale University Library; British Library of Political and Economic Science and the National Provincial Bank; Bibliothèque Publique et Universitaire, Geneva; National Library of Scotland; and the University of Durham.

I am grateful to F. E. Mineka, J. Robson, and J. Viner for having read the manuscript; their critical observations have saved me from errors, though not as often as they thought necessary. Professor Mineka and, at an earlier stage, F. A. Hayek, kindly allowed me to examine their files of unpublished Mill letters. Walter Houghton identified the authors of several articles in Victorian periodicals. I am grateful to Anne Granger for her efficient handling of the typing and even more for her considerable toleration and good humor. I owe thanks to the American Philosophical Society for a grant that allowed me to conduct some of the research; to the Rockefeller Foundation for a fellowship that provided time for writing; and to several administrative officials at Yale for generous grants of funds. I owe special debts of gratitude to the late Morton Grodzins and to Professor Hayek for stimulation, helpful criticism, and encouragement. I have been greatly aided by my wife, who became an avid reader of the press of the 1830s. I have also benefited from her keen editorial sense.

Contents

Abbreviations

Add. MSS	Additional Manuscripts, British Museum
Auto.	John Stuart Mill, *Autobiography,* ed. H. J. Laski (World's Classics ed.)
BL	British Library of Political and Economic Science, London School of Economics
BM	British Museum
BrP	Brougham Papers
CPA	Canadian Public Archives
DD	J. S. Mill, *Dissertations and Discussions* (London, 1859)
Edin. Rev.	*Edinburgh Review*
EL	*Earlier Letters of John Stuart Mill 1812–1848,* ed. Francis E. Mineka (Univ. of Toronto Press, 1963)
EP	Ellice Papers
Hansard	*Hansard's Parliamentary Debates,* third series
JPP	Joseph Parkes Papers
Lond. Rev.	*London Review*
LP	Lambton Papers
LWR	*London and Westminster Review*
Mo. Rep.	*Monthly Repository,* second series
NLS	National Library of Scotland
Pamph.P	*Pamphlets for the People,* ed. J. A. Roebuck
SRO	Sussex Record Office, West Sussex County Council
UCL	University College, London
West. Rev.	*Westminster Review*

1. *Ideological Politicians*

Bagehot said of English politicians that they are "Whigs, or Radicals, or Tories, but they are much else too. They are common Englishmen, and . . . 'hard to be worked up to the dogmatic level.'" This absence of ideological politics in England has been the occasion for foreign admiration and native pride. There has been, as Bagehot noted, "a studied and illogical moderation" and a reluctance "to press the tenets of . . . party to impossible conclusions." [1] However, there have been exceptions, and one of them is the subject of this study. The Philosophic Radicals, as both politicians and philosophers, formulated an ideology and attempted to organize a political party with a doctrinairism quite contrary to Bagehot's generalization.

The Philosophic Radicals—there were twenty or so—formed an intellectual coterie in the 1820s. John Stuart Mill was the most distinguished member, but the group also included George Grote, John Arthur Roebuck, Charles Buller, Joseph Hume, and Sir William Molesworth. These men took some of Bentham's vast and varied array of ideas and from them fashioned a rationale and a guide for reshaping a particular regime—what we would call an ideology. But they were not simply a group of politically oriented intellectuals. Many of them went into Parliament, where they formed what Namier called an "ideological group." [2] This separated them from other reformers and liberal Whigs with whom they appeared to have an affinity. The fate of this parliamentary faction was the main public concern of John Stuart Mill's life during the 1830s; his energy, most of his writing, and even his modest funds went into a journal that was meant to represent the parliamentary Radicals. Despite his partial alienation from Benthamism, he remained, as he explained

1. Walter Bagehot, *The English Constitution* (London, Oxford, 1955), pp. 126–27. The passage quoted by Bagehot was from Cardinal Newman.
2. L. B. Namier, *Conflicts* (London, Macmillan, 1942), p. 202.

in his *Autobiography*, very much a Radical so far as English politics were concerned.

The Philosophic Radicals, as their name implies, played two roles. They considered themselves both philosophers and politicians. The way they combined these roles affected both their philosophy and their political conduct. Their aspiration to be politicians led them to reshape their intellectual inheritance into an ideology that would serve their parliamentary interests. Drawing on utilitarian philosophy, this ideology initially provided a defense of democratic government. But it also defined the way in which democratic government was to be achieved—by the realignment of parties and the establishment of a new Radical party that had as its program the creation of a democratic form of government. Since they were the self-elected leaders of this party, indeed the chief instrument by which democratic government was to be achieved, their ideology, in addition to providing a defense of democracy, was a means of gratifying their ambitions as politicians. For more than a decade the Philosophic Radicals channeled into parliamentary politics the energies of the largest group of Bentham's disciples, thereby narrowing the focus and scope of Benthamite political thought. The experiences they had in politics in turn affected their judgments and values, including their response to Benthamism and to democratic politics generally.

The fact that the Philosophic Radicals were spokesmen for an ideology is a clue to much of their otherwise inexplicable role in Parliament. It is this that explains their wish to draw sharp distinctions between themselves and other reformers, whether Radicals, Liberals, or liberal Whigs. Their version of political parties was one of clearly marked boundaries and, as a result, politicians such as liberal Whigs, who appeared to be the natural allies of the Philosophic Radicals, were in fact seen as antagonists. Their ideological position also explains why their belief in the main principles of classical political economy had so little effect on their conduct as politicians. Of course, they usually did uphold the economic policies that were derived from classical economics, but such policies were at most secondary to the political goals that mainly occupied them. Thus there were fellow politicians holding liberal views on economic policy who were opposed by the Philosophic Radicals on political grounds. Affinities in the realm of economic doctrine did not necessarily smooth the path to political cooperation. The Philosophic Radicals' ideological commitment also makes it easier to understand why their political careers ended and the entire Philosophic Radical movement, after a decade or so of parliamentary activity, suddenly disappeared from the political scene.

MAKING CONVERTS

"It was my father's opinions," John Stuart Mill said, "which gave the distinguishing character to the Benthamic or utilitarian propagandism" of the time.[3] This is what James Mill intended, for he, much more than Bentham, looked forward to the formation of a movement that would effect political changes along Benthamite lines. James Mill believed himself "a most faithful and fervent disciple," indeed, his "master's favourite." He also saw himself as especially well situated to propagate the creed; this was, he reminded Bentham (who was then 66), "a very fortunate coincidence, that any man with views and propensities of such rare occurrence as mine, should happen to come in toward the close of your career to carry on the work without any intermission." So anxious was Mill to continue as the "real successor" to Bentham, that when they quarreled in 1814 it was Mill who sacrificed the feelings of the moment to the larger, impersonal cause. "I could not suddenly depart," he wrote to Bentham, "without proclaiming to the world that there was a quarrel between us; and this, I think, for the sake of both of us, and more especially the cause which has been the great bond of connexion between us, we should carefully endeavour to avoid." [4] They continued their cooperation, and Mill, who was a fiercely independent person, continued an arrangement that must have been odious to him—to rent a house from Bentham below market value and to spend the summers as Bentham's

3. John Stuart Mill, *Autobiography* (London, Oxford, 1958), p. 86 [hereafter *Auto*.].

4. James Mill to Bentham, Sept. 19, 1814; *The Works of Jeremy Bentham,* ed. John Bowring (Edinburgh, 1843), *10,* 481.

guest at Ford Abbey. This went on after 1815, although Mill was tempted to follow other impecunious Englishmen who lived in France.[5]

Mill's strong wish to be the founder of an intellectual and political movement contrasts somewhat with Bentham's attitude. Bentham, it is true, welcomed the aid and influence of disciples, particularly as he became older, and he jested about Mill being his disciple and Ricardo his grand-disciple; but rarely did he proselytize, nor did he actively engage in a search for new recruits. His was an old man's wish to have his ideas and even his name perpetuated.[6] It was James Mill who sought a widening circle of influential followers.

But those were poor days for the mobilization of a reform movement. Even after the termination of the war against France the government pursued a repressive policy against radical reformers. There were real risks attending the free expression of political opinions, and authors, editors, printers, and news vendors found themselves prosecuted for seditious or blasphemous libel and harassed even if not convicted. When the common law and old statutes were not adequate for repression, new legislation was enacted, the most notable example being the notorious "six acts" of 1819. Furthermore, the symptoms of discontent that could be seen as the first stirrings of a politically awakened populace eager for radical leadership also carried hints of danger. There were outbreaks of hostile feelings—for example, Luddism and the wild and unrealistic plots such as brought on the "Pentrich Revolution" and the Cato Street conspiracy. But these spontaneous expressions of hostility gave evidence of naiveté among the very members of the laboring classes who were most politically conscious. The disorder and the bloodshed at Peterloo also indicated the dangers of political mobilization as much as they showed a readiness for it among some of the populace; the situation was bound to make responsible reformers such as James Mill hesitate.

5. Alexander Bain, *James Mill* (London, 1882), pp. 139–40.

6. John Neal, "Notes and a Biographical Notice of Jeremy Bentham and of M. Dumont," in Bentham, *Principles of Legislation,* Eng. trans. J. Neal (Boston, 1830), p. 51. Cf. pp. 22–23 below.

In these circumstances James Mill prepared for a future when, with the spread of literacy and popular education, the populace could be more effectively and also more safely mobilized. Later in the 1820s, when there was reasonable hope that adult education would have an impact on the populace, he participated in such schemes as the Society for the Diffusion of Useful Knowledge. But meanwhile Mill wrote for educated readers; and no matter what the subject—law, India, or the press—his writings contained (though sometimes concealed) a political argument. Thus his *Encyclopaedia Brittanica* article, "Liberty of the Press," in addition to its discussion of libel law, includes a manual of tactics for reformers that points to the means by which fundamental changes in the constitution could be achieved by peaceful means. His *History of British India* can be seen as an esoteric critique of English government and society.[7] As for the famous essay "Government," Mill's closest friend, Ricardo, immediately recognized its polemical purpose when he commended Mill for not revealing his favorable opinion on the secret ballot, saying that to raise the question "would have given the article too much the appearance of an essay on Reform of Parliament which it was desirable to avoid."[8]

James Mill's preparation for the future is pointedly evident in the famous education of his first son. He made his hopes explicit when he was faced with a serious illness. His son was then six, and Mill reminded Bentham of his offer to assume responsibility for the boy's education in the event of Mill's death:

> If I were to die any time before this poor boy is a man, one of the things that would pinch me most sorely, would be, the being obliged to leave his mind unmade to the degree of excellence, of which I hope to make it. . . . the only

7. Duncan Forbes, "James Mill and India," *Cambridge Journal, 5* (Oct. 1951), 19–33. Mill said (to Ricardo, Oct. 19, 1817), "that book of mine, if it answers my expectation, or rather my wish, will make no bad introduction to the study of civil society in general. The subject afforded an opportunity of laying open the principles and laws of social order." *Works and Correspondence of David Ricardo,* eds. Piero Sraffa and M. H. Dobb (Cambridge, Univ. Press, 1952–55), *7,* 195–96.

8. Ricardo to James Mill, July 27, 1820, Ricardo, *Works, 8,* 211.

prospect which would lessen that pain, would be the leaving him in your hands. . . . then we may perhaps leave him a successor worthy of both of us.[9]

John Stuart Mill, whose varied development perhaps is the most appropriate comment on the way such paternal ambition was implemented, was keenly aware of the role his father expected him to play. He was tortured by this awareness during the early 1830s, before the death of his father, when newly acquired, heretical opinions were partly suppressed and, when expressed, were formulated in a convoluted fashion in a futile effort to obscure the deviation and blunt his father's disappointment. However mixed the results, the education of young Mill is at least an indication of the father's ambition, including his political ambition.

Yet in spite of later misgivings, John Stuart Mill was to excel in the role his father had planned for him. The years of his early manhood were to coincide with increasing political awareness among the populace and a markedly greater willingness among young members of the educated classes to engage in reform politics. Thus young Mill was to become instrumental in creating and holding together an intellectual coterie that looked to his father as a mentor. Meanwhile, the elder Mill had to be content with the conversion of but few disciples, Place, Ricardo, and Grote being the most notable. He met Francis Place (1771–1854) in 1812 and gradually introduced him into Bentham's circle of friends. By 1817 Place, like Mill and his family, spent the summer as Bentham's guest at Ford Abbey. Mill played the role of teacher, as he did with most of his acquaintances, and Place, like most of them, willingly was the pupil. Of course, Place was disposed to accept Mill's political doctrines. He was, as he put it, already a chartist in 1791 when he was persuaded "that no government could be really good nor no people in a sound and wholesome condition while there was any privileged class or person in the nation." [10] However, Mill's economic outlook, unlike his political ideas, would not ordinarily be found in

9. James Mill to Bentham, July 28, 1812, Bentham, *Works, 10*, 473.
10. Place to T. P. Thompson, Jan. 2, 1841, British Museum, Place Papers, Add. MSS 35,151, f. 289.

a person of Place's background and experience. Yet Mill was mainly responsible for Place's adoption of the entire credo of Malthusianism and political economy, even though originally Place had had little disposition to accept these doctrines. For the remainder of his life Place was often in the difficult situation of trying to overcome the skepticism of working-class leaders by explaining that the principles of Malthus and the Economists were "really," despite the appearance of harshness, in the interest of the working classes.

Mill was also responsible for bringing Ricardo (1772–1823) to reform politics. They met after the publication of Mill's pamphlet *Commerce Defended* (1808), and Ricardo was said to be Mill's most intimate friend. After making a vast fortune in government loans during the Napoleonic wars, Ricardo was strongly disposed to retire. However, Mill was determined to keep him from indolence. Just as he prodded Ricardo into writing the *Principles of Political Economy and Taxation* (1817), he also urged and cajoled him into entering Parliament. Mill brought Ricardo into contact with Brougham and Edward Wakefield, both of whom helped Ricardo arrange for the purchase of his seat.[11] During the brief period Ricardo sat in the House of Commons, from 1819 until his death in 1823, he spoke on behalf of parliamentary reform. Between the publication of his *Principles* in 1817 and his entry into Parliament Ricardo underwent nothing less than a course of training in the principles of government. He was, it is true, not so docile a pupil as Place; his correspondence with Mill shows that he voiced some skepticism and, during the Westminster election of 1818 in which Mill and Bentham supported the Radical candidate against their old Whig friend Sir Samuel Romilly, Ricardo "at first hesitated, but at length voted for Romilly." [12] His speeches in the House

11. "With very few exceptions,—perhaps with none,—Mr. Mill of all men possessed the greatest influence over him . . . his judgment, his discrimination, and his opinion had greater weight with him than any other person's": "A Memoir of David Ricardo" (1824) [By one of his brothers], in Ricardo, *Works, 10,* 9. Also see *Works, 5,* 13–19 ("Introduction to the Speeches in Parliament"); *6,* xv (Introductory Notes).

12. Lady Seymour, *The "Pope" of Holland House* (London, 1906), p. 200.

of Commons reveal, however, the measure of Mill's success in
bringing him into the Radical camp.[13]

Mill's friendship with Ricardo led to the conversion of George
Grote (1794–1871). This proved especially important, for
Grote later entered Parliament and became one of the acknowledged leaders of the Philosophic Radical group in the House of
Commons. Grote was apprenticed in his father's banking house
when he met James Mill in 1819 at Ricardo's breakfast table.
Grote, self-educated and exceedingly serious, found Mill "a very
profound thinking man" and so decided to "cultivate his acquaintance a good deal farther." Until this time Grote had been
reading widely and pondering the foundations of morals, but
his independent speculation soon ended. His wife has described
how he presently "found himself enthralled in the circle of Mill's
speculations, and after a year or two of intimate commerce there
existed but little difference, in point of opinion, between master
and pupil." Not long after, Grote put the newly acquired principles to use; in 1821 he published a long pamphlet which used
the principles of Mill's *Essay on Government* to discredit a Whig
attack on Bentham's reform pamphlet. Grote probably was
James Mill's most faithful disciple. The master's encouragement
was hardly necessary, for Grote was so inspired, "inoculated, as
it were," that James Mill's dicta "assumed the force and sanction
of duties." [14] In this mood Grote joined in the small study groups
organized by John Stuart Mill. During much of the decade preceding the Reform Bill they got up three hours before breakfast
and the day's labor in order to discuss treatises on logic and
political economy. By 1833, when the Benthamites made a stand
as a separate body in Parliament, Grote was well prepared to
assume his place as leader of their parliamentary party. His
political career as a Philosophic Radical preceded the publication
of his *History of Greece* and the reputation he earned as a
scholar, for which he is best known today.

13. Ricardo, *Works*, 5, 112–13, 283–89, 474–75, 484–512.
14. Harriet Grote, *Personal Life of George Grote* (London, 1873), pp.
21–23; [George Grote], *Statement of the Question of Parliamentary Reform; With a Reply to the Objections of the Edinburgh Review, No.
LXI* (London, 1821). This was a reply to Sir James Mackintosh's review
of Bentham's *Plan of Parliamentary Reform* (1817).

"ALL THOSE EMOTIONS AND IMPULSES WHICH DESERVE THE NAME OF RELIGIOUS."

As John Stuart Mill emerged from the extreme isolation of his youth, his growing circle of acquaintances became the most important source of recruits to the Philosophic Radical cause. Young Mill, like his father, played the role of teacher to young men attracted by his impressive intellectual achievements as well as by the opportunity to acquire a systematic, authoritative outlook.

John Stuart Mill did not assume a militant, proselytizing role as a matter of course. An experience akin to a religious conversion preceded it. In 1822 his father had given him Bentham's *Traité de Legislation*. Immediately the first pages "burst upon me with all the force of novelty." On reading Bentham's critique of the common modes of reasoning in law and morals, "the feeling rushed upon me, that all previous moralists were superseded, and that here indeed was the commencement of a new era in thought." By the time he finished the work, Mill felt he "had become a different being," and looking back on his experience it clearly appeared as "an epoch in my life; one of the turning points in my mental history." But its significance was not only intellectual, as Mill confessed in a famous passage:

> The 'principle of utility' understood as Bentham understood it . . . fell exactly into its place as the keystone which held together the detached and fragmentary component parts of my knowledge and beliefs. It gave unity to my conception of things. I now had opinions; a creed, a doctrine, a philosophy; in one among the best senses of the word, a religion; the inculcation and diffusion of which could be made the principal outward purpose of a life. . . . the vista of improvement which [Bentham] did open was sufficiently large and brilliant to light up my life, as well as to give a definite shape to my aspirations.[15]

This state of mind created intimate connections between intellect and action, and between the private and the public realms. Mill

15. *Auto.,* pp. 54, 56–57.

now had an intellectual key that seemed to explain all things; and he could follow (or recommend) a course of action secure in the belief that its rationale was readily available. He became so intensely identified with this outlook that its public manifestations were a direct reflection of an intimate personal experience.

Armed with the confidence and sense of zeal that this doctrine inspired, John Stuart Mill began to proselytize on behalf of Benthamism. His first move was to organize the Utilitarian Society. "Any young man of education who fell my way," he tells us, "and whose opinions were not incompatible with those of the Society, I endeavoured to press into its service." This brought him into contact with several such persons, "among whom," Mill modestly says, "I was for some time a sort of leader." [16]

One of the early recruits was John Arthur Roebuck (1802–79), who later had a long and stormy career in Parliament. Born in Madras where his father was an Indian civil servant, brought up in Canada where he was taken after his father's death, Roebuck arrived in London in 1824 with an introduction to Thomas Love Peacock, who, among many other things, was James Mill's colleague in the Examiner's Office at India House. Of course this brought him to John Stuart Mill, who only the year before had begun under his father's tutelage his thirty-five-year career in that establishment.

Roebuck was self-educated; he had read widely in the Quebec public library (which had been formed in accordance with the advice of Joseph Priestley), but he said "that reading had been without a plan and I without a guide." Young Mill soon introduced him to the Utilitarian Society and the "disquisition set of young men," as Peacock had described them. He also was introduced to the writings of Bentham and James Mill, and he experienced the novelty, enthusiasm, and sense of apocalypse that was to be characteristic of either personal or intellectual encounters with these men. Roebuck was "greatly struck with the works of Bentham and James Mill," and he records that he also became a pupil of John Stuart Mill, whose training, facility,

16. Ibid., p. 68.

and enthusiasm were such that Roebuck thought "he was armed at all points." With his reading now planned and guided, a "new world" was opened to him and his experience of it "was the cause of a mighty effect upon my whole life." [17]

Several other recruits, all approximately the same age as John Stuart Mill, came from Cambridge. Among them, Charles Austin and Eyton Tooke, both with personal ties to the Mills, were intermediaries. Charles Austin was a younger brother of the Benthamite jurist, John Austin, and he had known the Mills from visits to his brother who, like James Mill, rented a house on Bentham's property at Queen Square Place. Eyton Tooke, whose death in 1830 at the age of twenty-two cut short one of the few intimate friendships in John Stuart Mill's life, was the son of the economist Thomas Tooke who had joined with James Mill in 1821 to form the Political Economy Club. On coming down from Cambridge in the mid-1820s, Austin and Tooke introduced some of their liberal-minded university friends to the Mills. Among them were Edward Strutt, Charles Buller, Charles and Hyde Villiers, and John Romilly, who was the son of Bentham's friend and admirer Sir Samuel Romilly. Most of these young men had been active on the reform side in the Union debates at Cambridge.[18] As a result of their contact with the

17. Ibid., pp. 101–103; Robert E. Leader, *Life and Letters of John Arthur Roebuck* (London, 1897), pp. 8, 25–26; Roebuck, "Notes on Mill," ff. 2–3, in collection of J. M. Osborn, Yale Univ. Roebuck also said of J. S. Mill, "He pointed out the path I ought to follow. He named the books I should read, and he looked over and criticized much that I wrote. . . . the great outlines of the philosophy which has governed my life, he drew." Ibid., f. 7. "I learned that there was a *science of Government*. . . . That the true experience on which the conclusions respecting Government rested, was not derived simply or chiefly from the faulty chronicles called the History of Nations, but depended upon principles of our nature which are invariable": "A Letter to Daniel O'Connell," *Pamphlets for the People* [no. 30, Dec. 31, 1835], p. 2 [hereafter *Pamph. P*].

18. The Mills' circle included five former presidents of the Cambridge Union—Edward Strutt, Charles Austin, Charles Villiers, Eyton Tooke, and Charles Buller; and two former secretaries—T. H. Villiers and Edward Romilly. Percy Cradock, *Recollections of the Cambridge Union 1815–1939* (Cambridge, Bowes and Bowes, 1953), pp. 169–70.

Mills, their favorable disposition to reform was turned to zeal. Most of them entered Parliament during the 1830s where they became part of the Philosophic Radical group.

One of them, Charles Buller (1806–48), played an especially active part in the Philosophic Radical party. Coming from a wealthy family of the Cornish gentry, he was in London to read for the bar before taking the seat in Parliament that his family controlled through its county influence. He became a Benthamite, he explained, because "it affords the best explanation of men's opinions on morals." [19] At the time of his succession to his father's seat in Parliament he was one of the leading speakers on the Utilitarian side in the London Debating Society. Even though his grandfather, according to rumor, controlled six parliamentary seats, he voted for the Reform Bill and for the abolition of his own seat. At the election which followed, however, he was returned for another Cornish borough. Carlyle, his former tutor, abominated his politics but thought him the only Radical of genius in Parliament.[20]

Grote's wife, Harriet Lewin Grote (1792–1878), was to play an important role in the Philosophic Radical group. Although at first not favorably disposed to James Mill or the ideas adopted by her husband, she became no less devoted to the cause than her husband. She came to share his opinions and was even more vigorous in asserting them. She could construct as hostile an epithet about the Whigs or feel as much rage about the stupidity of those who withheld agreement as James Mill himself. Her strong interest in politics and her influence among Grote's friends impressed many contemporaries. Charles Sumner thought her "high minded" and "masculine" and called her "one of the most remarkable women in England." [21] She was "a great politician and 'a blue,' though," it was said, "she does not acknowledge her right to the last title." [22] Her assertive, imperious temperament

19. E. M. Wrong, *Charles Buller and Responsible Government* (Oxford, Clarendon, 1926), p. 6.

20. *Letters of Thomas Carlyle to John Stuart Mill, John Sterling and Robert Browning,* ed. Alexander Carlyle (London, Unwin, 1923), p. 49.

21. *Memoir and Letters of Charles Sumner,* ed. E. L. Pierce (Boston, 1877–93), *2,* 184.

22. Mlle. C. Wisley to F. M. Lewin, Jan. 18, 1836, *The Lewin Letters,* ed. T. H. Lewin (London, 1909), *1,* 337.

made Philosophic Radical doctrine in its most extreme form especially congenial. Appropriately she was an advocate of the extreme tactics that expressed the most dogmatic interpretation that the doctrine would allow. Her influence among the other members of the coterie was very great. Many of the Radicals' deliberations about tactics were conducted under her leadership, and her home became a political salon for the parliamentary Radicals. Cobden shrewdly observed that, "Had she been a man, she would have been the leader of a party." [23] To Sydney Smith she was "the queen of the radicals." And Place was not far wrong when he said "she *was* the philosophic radicals." [24]

Although most of the young Benthamites in the late 1820s were introduced to their new creed by John Stuart Mill and Charles Austin, the real source of inspiration continued to come from the elder Mill. Austere, demanding, confident to the point of dogmatism, yet always prepared with elaborate reasons, he was an awesome figure who did not hesitate to give direction to his son's young, liberal-minded acquaintances who now appeared in increasing numbers. Those who had been to Cambridge already had been exposed to his ideas through the reprinting of his *Encyclopaedia Brittanica* articles, for they were used as "text books" there by the young men of liberal views in the Union.[25] But his conversation was an even more important vehicle of influence. Grote especially remembered his

> colloquial fertility on philosophical subjects, his power of discussing himself, and of stimulating others to discuss . . . these accomplishments were, to those who knew him, even more impressive than that what he composed for the press. Conversation with him was not merely instructive, but provocative to the dormant intelligence. . . . When to this we add a strenuous character, earnest convictions, and single-minded devotion to truth, . . . it may be conceived

23. Jessie Buckley, *Joseph Parkes of Birmingham* (London, Methuen, 1926), p. 151.

24. *The Letters of Sydney Smith*, ed. Nowell C. Smith (Oxford, Clarendon, 1953) 2, 704. Mona Wilson, *Jane Austen and Some Contemporaries* (London, Cresset Press, 1938), p. 254.

25. James Mill to J. R. McCulloch, Aug. 18, 1825, NLS, MS 673, f. 56.

that such a man exercised powerful intellectual ascendancy over younger minds.[26]

Grote's testimony is confirmed by several others. Roebuck, despite an early quarrel with James Mill, called him his political and philosophical teacher, and said, "To him I owe greater obligations than to any other man. If I know any thing, from him I learned it." [27] Another of John Stuart Mill's young friends, William Ellis, said of his early encounter with James Mill, "he *worked a complete change* in me. He taught me how to think and what to live for." Indeed, Mill supplied him "with all those emotions and impulses which deserve the name of religious," and Ellis often spoke of James Mill "as the person to whom he was most indebted for the direction which his mind received in early life." [28] Parkes said of Henry Warburton, who was to be a prominent parliamentary member of the group, that James Mill was "his chief political instructor." [29] And Parkes himself confessed that his introduction to Bentham, Grote, and James Mill "created all the power and moral courage I have brought to bear in favour of the People." [30]

26. George Grote, *Minor Works* (London, 1873), p. 284. Mrs. Grote: "He possessed the faculty of kindling in his auditors the generous impulses towards the popular side, . . . So attractive came to be the conceptions of duty towards mankind at large, as embodied in James Mill's eloquent discourse, that the young disciples, becoming fired with patriotic ardour on the one hand and with bitter antipathies on the other, respectively braced themselves up, prepared to wage battle when the day should come, in behalf of 'the true faith,' according to Mill's 'programme' and preaching." *Life of Grote*, p. 23.

27. Roebuck to Brougham, June 29, 1836, UCL, BrP. On the quarrel, see Leader, *Roebuck*, p. 29.

28. F. F. Miller, "William Ellis and His Work as an Educationist," *Fraser's Magazine*, n.s., *25* (1882), 236; E. K. Blyth, *William Ellis* (London, 1892), p. 2. John Black also remembered "the force of his personal character. . . . Young men were particularly fond of his society; and it was always to him a source of great delight to have an opportunity of contributing to form their minds and exalt their character." "Death of Mr. James Mill," *Morning Chronicle*, June 25, 1836, p. 3.

29. Obituary, *Times*, Sept. 21, 1858, p. 7; evidence of Parkes' authorship: Parkes to Brougham, Sept. 23, 1858, UCL, BrP.

30. H. Grote, *Life of Grote*, p. 80. Henry Solly, another of John Stuart Mill's early friends, also looked up to James Mill with "hero-

Using this personal ascendancy "as an instrument for the diffusion of his opinions," James Mill emerged in the 1820s as the real leader of a coterie of intellectuals that attracted public attention by their bold and uncompromising demand for fundamental changes in the constitution of government. Not that they were the only reformers on the scene; indeed, "Liberalism seemed to be becoming the tone of the time." But here was a small group who wrote with an "air of strong conviction. . . . when scarcely any one else seemed to have an equally strong faith in as definite a creed." Thus the public eye was attracted by "the regular appearance in controversy of what seemed a new school of writers, claiming to be the legislators and theorists of this new tendency." [31]

THEIR "CHIEF POLITICAL INSTRUCTOR"

That James Mill should be credited with intellectual leadership is made even more clear by examination of Bentham's relationship to Mill and the entire group of so-called Benthamites. Contrary to general belief, Bentham personally had little direct contact with the Philosophic Radicals, and with James Mill there was enmity and estrangement during much of the decade preceding Bentham's death in 1832.

Bentham's distant connection with the young disciples in part was the result of his great age. Born in 1748, he was over seventy before he met any of those (other than the Mills and Place) who were to become Philosophic Radicals, and he was almost eighty when the group was taking shape. There was a decade before his death when he might have developed more intimate connections with the men who were to be seen by the world as spokesmen for his principles, but acrimony in his dealings with James Mill proved to be an obstacle.

The relationship had been marred by mutual irritation as far back as 1814. Living at close quarters, both in town and at Ford Abbey during the summers, there was bound to be diffi-

---

worship" and felt "admiration and wondering awe" for him. Henry Solly, *These Eighty Years* (London, 1893), *1*, 130, 145.

31. Mill, *Auto.*, pp. 84–85.

culty. Mill, with much independence of spirit ("proud as Lucifer," Bentham said), yet greatly aided by Bentham's generosity, was anything but comfortable in his subordinate position. Bentham, notorious for his eccentricity and increasingly vain with advancing age, was jealous of any disturbance of his routine, especially if the attendance of his friends and devotees was interrupted. By 1818 Mill confessed that "there are no small incompatibilities between us." [32] Mill's self-control might have allowed him to deal with Bentham's crotchets and the threat of humiliation, but at this time their lives moved in different directions. Before the publication (in 1817) of Mill's *History of British India,* the fruit of eleven years of disciplined labor, he was hardly known beyond a small circle of journalists and politicians.[33] The immediate success of the book led to his appointment in the political administration of the East India Company. Since his initial salary was £800, he was now relieved of his dependence on Bentham's financial help. Soon he became deeply involved with his new duties at the India House and was writing to Ricardo, "I must glory a little in my own virtue, for though I might procure leave of absence for the asking, there are so many despatches to answer, and the happiness and misery of so many millions are affected by what I write, that I cannot find in my heart to abstract a day from the labours of this place." [34]

32. James Mill to Place, Sept. 13, 1818, Add. MSS 35,153, f. 50; Bain, *James Mill,* pp. 136–40; Bentham, *Works, 10,* 481. Anna Jean Mill, ed., "Introduction," *John Mill's Boyhood Visit to France* (Univ. of Toronto Press, 1960), p. xiii; also see p. xxi for Bentham's reference to their "many clashes" and Mill's "unkindness" to him. Parkes described how "Old Bentham on Sunday particularly begged me to copy some verses from the Examiner *many years* back laudatory of him and signed W. C. and to make out who the initials were: The Glorious old Man like all the species has a vein of vanity." Parkes to Hone, Nov. 8, 1824, BM, Hone Papers, Add. MSS 40,120, f. 221.

33. Wakefield was "quite grieved to hear that Mill anticipates so much [illegible] to his Indian work; rely upon it he will be miserably disappointed. . . . for a long while back I have named both him and his book amongst all reading and thinking persons whom I have met, but he is quite unknown to them." Edward Wakefield to Place, Sept. 29, 1814, Add. MSS 37,949, ff. 25–26.

34. James Mill to Ricardo, Aug. 14, 1819; Ricardo, *Works, 8,* 51.

When he did gain leisure, his energies flowed into writing the other books for which he is best known. Most of the *Encyclopaedia Brittanica* articles, some of which later appeared in his *Essays,* were written during this period. *Elements of Political Economy* appeared in 1821, and he projected several other works at this time, including *Analysis of the Human Mind.* Removal from Bentham's property did not put an end to their quarrels, however. With the petty irritants removed, others, some of them more serious, were discovered.

Bentham in 1820 became acquainted with John Bowring, who soon supplanted Mill as Bentham's intellectual companion. "The intimacy strengthened from day to day. For the last ten years of his life," Bowring says, "not a thought—not a feeling of his was concealed from me." [35] Bowring was disliked and distrusted by James Mill, and this attitude later was picked up by his young friends. He was accused of seducing Bentham with flattery; Bentham's secretary observed that "no one, among his *once-numerous* friends and associates," ever flattered the old man so much as Bowring.[36] When Bentham set up the *Westminster Review* in 1824, with Bowring as editor, the Mills and their friends contributed to it, but reluctantly. James Mill, it is true, had been offered the editorship, but he refused, and his son was careful to point out that his "father was in no degree a party to setting up the Westminster Review." [37] Even before the first number went to press, Place and Mill had quarreled with Bowring, challenging his authority as editor to alter manuscripts. Place complained that he would "under the present circumstances have nothing to do with the Review nor contribute to it in any way," and he told Bentham that Mill fully approved of his intention.[38] Mrs. Grote reported that Mill felt much the same. "You must be careful," she wrote, "not to speak of Mill's doing aught in the new 'Benthamite Review,' as he is writing for it

35. Bentham, *Works, 10,* 516.

36. J. F. Colls, *Utilitarianism Unmasked* (London, 1844), see pp. 9–10.

37. Mill, *Auto.,* p. 76.

38. Place to Mill, Sept. 1823; Place to Bentham, Sept. 1823: Add. MSS 35, 145, ff. 82–85, 90.

against his inclination, having, he says, no opinion of the utility of a review conducted as he thinks it will be." [39]

The *Westminster Review* at first had a great success. The first two thousand copies were sold out and its founders were enthusiastic. The acrimonious atmosphere in which it had begun was momentarily forgotten. But the disputes with Bowring broke out once again, and the suspicion with which Bowring was held only widened the gulf between Bentham and Mill. In 1826 Bentham made Bowring his literary executor instead of Place. After his first flurry of articles, James Mill gradually withdrew from the enterprise and contributed with ever increasing reluctance and only under great pressure. After Macaulay made his famous attack on James Mill in 1829, Mill did not bother to reply in the *Westminster*. Although John Stuart Mill contributed thirteen articles, he left little doubt about his opinion of the *Review*. He said, "it is worth noting as a fact in the history of Benthamism that the periodical organ, by which it was best known, was from the first extremely unsatisfactory to those whose opinions on all subjects it was supposed specially to represent." [40] Among Bentham's disciples, those who later were called Philosophic Radicals contributed surprisingly few articles, John Stuart Mill excepted.[41]

Nor were Bentham's last years spent among the men who were to become Philosophic Radicals. The Utilitarian Society sometimes met in his house, but Bentham "never met with them, nor was it expected of him; and of their whole number not more than half perhaps had ever interchanged a word with him." [42] Bentham's main interest during the late twenties was law reform, whereas the followers of James Mill were more concerned with the movement for reform of Parliament. After 1825 Bentham courted Burdett, Brougham, and O'Connell in the hope of enlisting their aid in propagating his law reform proposals. Bentham

39. Mrs. Grote to Norman, Nov. 1823; George Grote, *Posthumous Papers*, ed. H. Grote (London, 1874), p. 29.

40. Mill, *Auto.*, p. 82.

41. G. L. Nesbitt, *Benthamite Reviewing* (New York, Columbia, 1934), pp. 137, 177–83.

42. Neal, "Biographical Notice of Jeremy Bentham," in *Principles of Legislation*, p. 24.

seems to have been preoccupied with this; not only did he urge "sending forth *preachers* of Law Reform" but his "impatience to see the splendid reforms . . . accomplished before his death" made him, according to Brougham's complaint, "regard even his most familiar friends only as instruments of reformation, and gave a very unamiable and indeed revolting aspect of callousness to his feelings towards them." [43] Along with Bowring, Edwin Chadwick became one of the men closest to Bentham. He served as Bentham's secretary, and Bentham urged him to undertake the propagation of his creed in exchange for an annuity. [44] Although he took part in some Philosophic Radical activities, Chadwick was at the periphery of their group, and he drew apart from them during the 1830s. Bentham, always a recluse, lived in even greater seclusion during his last years, "seeing none but men, who, from their talents or station, were likely to carry his principles into practical operation." [45] James Mill's visits to him were "a very unusual thing." [46] Bentham's isolation is clear

43. Bentham to O'Connell, Aug. 25, 1829; "Unpublished Correspondence of Jeremy Bentham and Daniel O'Connell," *Irish Monthly, 11* (1883), 516. Henry Brougham, *Speeches* (Edinburgh, 1838), *2,* 297. Also see Bentham, *Works, 10,* 600; R. B. McDowell, *Public Opinion and Government Policy in Ireland, 1801–1846* (London, Faber, 1952), p. 127. "J.B. is in . . . excellent spirits about law amendments writing away at the rate of 10 or 20 pages a day": George Bentham to Neal, March 1, 1828, in I. T. Richards, *The Life and Works of John Neal* (Ph.D. diss., Harvard, 1932), *3,* Appx. A.

44. Cf. S. E. Finer, *The Life and Times of Sir Edwin Chadwick* (London, Methuen, 1952), Chap. 3, where Chadwick is portrayed as a typical member of the Radical group. Although he opened a debate on the Poor Laws in the London Debating Society (Nov. 13, 1829), this was the only occasion on which he did so during the 1829–30 session; he did not address any of the 1825–26 meetings. J. S. Mill did not even mention him in that part of the *Auto.* that dealt with the Society: London Debating Society, *Laws and Transactions, with a List of the Members, Corrected up to November 1st, 1826* (London, 1826); *Fourth Supplement to the Laws and Transactions . . . 1829–1830* (London, 1831).

45. Archibald Prentice. *Historical Sketches and Personal Recollections of Manchester* (2d. ed. London, 1851), p. 379.

46. Bentham, *Works, 10,* 576. Bentham himself described "the seclusion under which I have so long been at work not admitting to personal intercourse with anybody but for some public beneficial purpose;

from James Mill's remark that the "men whom, even during this
short and last period of his life he saw with any frequency . . .
were but two or three at most." [47]

The Mills' coolness toward Bentham, and the Philosophic
Radicals' dissatisfaction with Bowring and the *Westminster
Review,* is reflected in their effort to establish a periodical more
suitable to their purpose. In 1826 they began the *Parliamentary
History and Review,* a journal which probably was more representative of Philosophic Radicalism than the *Westminster Review*
after its first numbers. Whereas the *Westminster* had contributions from a great variety of writers, but comparatively few
from those who came to be called Philosophic Radicals, articles
in the *Parliamentary History and Review,* where authorship is
known, are almost uniformly the product of those disciples who
came to be known about this time as Philosophic Radicals.

This journal was to be published annually, consisting of two
parts. First, parliamentary debates were to be reprinted, arranged not in the conventional chronological order but by topic.
All debates on such subjects as currency, Irish affairs, courts,
and parliamentary reform would appear under the appropriate
general heading. The second part was to be made up of "critical
essays," each one dealing with one of the general topics of
parliamentary discussion. The purpose was to aid the public "to
form an estimate of the amount of talent and knowledge actually
assembled in the two Houses of Parliament." This was to be
done by analyzing the arguments according to the criteria in
Bentham's *Book of Fallacies,* an abridgment of which was
printed in the first volume. Although the contributors did not
always adopt the method of analysis Bentham had prescribed, it
allowed them to expound the Radical position against both

---

at any rate some purpose in which in my view of it that property has
place." Bentham to Peel, March 28, 1830, Add. MSS 40,400, ff. 136–37.
"Every moment I give to individuals I regard as stolen from mankind":
Bentham to Neal, Jan. 5, 1830; in I. T. Richards, *Neal, 3,* Appx. A.

47. James Mill, *A Fragment on Mackintosh* (London, 1835), p. 125.
Mill reported "The old philosopher precisely the same—but little seen
by me. Writing letters is now his great occupation, on the various occasions which excite him, many of them very small ones." James Mill to
Dumont, July 31, 1828; Biblio. Publique et Univ. de Genève.

aristocratic factions whose arguments were "almost always irrelevant, but too generally delusive." [48] This disputatious approach was congenial to the Philosophic Radicals, who looked above all things to Parliament and who thrived on controversy. John Stuart Mill felt that "the best strength of the party was put forth in" the *Parliamentary History and Review,* and that "its execution did them much more credit than that of the Westminster Review had ever done." [49]

The Philosophic Radicals had not broken off their connection with the *Westminster,* but their support was desultory. However, after the *Parliamentary History and Review* came to an end in 1828 (probably for financial reasons), the Mills tried to wrest the *Westminster* from Bowring and presumably from Bentham as well. Their negotiations with Bowring were unsuccessful and led to another quarrel. Bowring complained about "unfair conspiracies" and suspected John Stuart Mill as author of a newspaper article announcing "that the writers [in the *Review*] who have hitherto been its chief contributors have in a body seceded and refused to continue their support. This will in fact render the future numbers a totally distinct work . . . distinct we mean as to the writers, whether the same principles will be maintained remains to be seen." Bentham and Joseph Hume tried to arrange a reconciliation, but it was at most a partial success. After this James Mill contributed only one article (on the ballot). His feelings were such that he did not contribute an answer to Macaulay's harsh review of his article "Government." [50]

---

48. *Parlimentary History and Review for 1825.* Advertisement (not paginated). This periodical was edited by P. Bingham, the editor of Bentham's *Book of Fallacies* (1824), and Charles Austin.

49. Mill, *Auto.,* p. 100.

50. During the negotiations, Bowring sought and gained the support of Col. T. P. Thompson, thereby attracting the Mills' charge of duplicity. Bowring to Place, Jan. 6, 7, Feb. 5, 1829, Add. MSS 37,949, ff. 226, 228, 232. Hume complained that "both the Mr. Mills should have set themselves against that Review" and that they "not only have refused to contribute . . . but, actually, say everything in their power against it . . . the Edinburgh Review . . . must soon fall to insignificance, if the Westminster R could appear in full force": Hume to Place, Sept. 16, 1829, Add. MSS 35,145, ff. 99–100.

During the later part of the 1820s James Mill could well feel that he was more in the center of the "march of intellect" than Bentham. Their estrangement continued and, though he saw Bentham, their relations were hardly cordial. They quarreled about such trivial things as books borrowed and not returned, and there was an unpleasant discussion about the financial responsibility for repairs to the house which Mill had rented from Bentham.[51] This was the time when Bentham harshly observed of Mill that "his creed of politics resulted less from love for the many, than from hatred of the few." John Stuart Mill published a defense of his father when this remark appeared, but privately he admitted that, as "there was some coldness on [Bentham's] part towards my father, it is not unlikely that he may at times have said unpleasant things of him." [52] While Bentham toward the end of his life lived amid a few disciples interested in his schemes of law and administrative reform, James Mill and his disciples felt with greater urgency the heightened excitement of the public pulse and looked to the wider field of parliamentary politics.

James Mill seemed to enjoy his role as leader of a school and sacrificed other things for it. J. L. Mallet complained in his diary that Mill had stopped attending the meetings of the Political Economy Club. Mill, he wrote, "is not enough of an oracle, among us, and does not find [in the Club] that deference, not to say adulation, which is paid him by young Utilitarians and aristocratical worshippers of talent." [53] James Mill by implication claimed to be leader of the Philosophic Radical movement when he denied it had been formed under Bentham's direct leadership. Attacking Sir James Mackintosh's contention that the "disciples of Bentham derive their opinions . . . from familiar

51. James Mill to Bentham, Feb. 22, 1827, UCL, Bentham Papers. Bentham to Mill, Feb. 23, 1827, Yale Univ. Library. On the house, see Add. MSS 37,949, ff. 250–55.

52. Bentham, *Works, 10*, 450; also see pp. 482, 571. J. S. Mill to Editor, *Edin. Rev., 79* (Jan. 1844), 267–71. J. S. Mill to Napier, Oct. 14, 1843; *The Earlier Letters of John Stuart Mill 1812–1848,* [hereafter *EL*] ed. F. E. Mineka (Univ. of Toronto Press, 1963), *2, 598.*

53. *Political Economy Club, Minutes of Proceedings, 6* (London, 1921), 224–26.

conversation with a master," he pointed out that Bentham's "accomplices" had little direct knowledge of Bentham, indeed that Bentham, toward the end of his life, regularly saw at most three persons who "professed peculiar esteem for his doctrines." [54] It was James Mill who had the intellectual allegiance of his son's circle of friends. John Stuart Mill could well say that his father was "as much the head and leader of the intellectual radicals in England, as Voltaire was of the *philosophes* of France." [55]

TURNING TO POLITICS

James Mill's initial impact on his disciples was to give a strong sense of moral purpose, but he also encouraged their political ambition and gave it focus and direction. Indeed, it was the intellectual foundation he gave to their moral aspirations which combined with their newly acquired political ambition to give a doctrinaire spirit to their conduct on the political scene. The character of their ambition is revealed in John Stuart Mill's confession that "the French *philosophes* of the eighteenth century were the example we sought to imitate," and he noted that "we hoped to accomplish no less results." This goal originated in his father's opinions, which, he said, "were seized on with youthful fanaticism by the little knot of young men of whom I was one: and we put into them a sectarian spirit, from which, in intention at least, my father was wholly free." [56]

One of the manifestations of this spirit was the adoption of language and the expression of opinions that allowed them to establish before the world their separate identity. Finding conventional language inadequate for the communication of their new truths, they used jargon. Perhaps the best example is John Stuart Mill's adoption of the term utilitarian as a banner and

54. James Mill, *Fragment on Mackintosh,* pp. 123–25.
55. *Auto.,* p. 173.
56. As it bears on the father, this statement is somewhat qualified by another observation, that "he disliked . . . a fanatic in any *bad* cause" (italics added). Ibid., pp. 42, 91. Buller called himself the "Cornish Voltaire": Buller to Carlyle, Aug. 30, 1828; NLS.

"sectarian appellation." [57] They also emphasized the importance
of those principles that would clearly distinguish them from
others, so that "to *outrer* whatever was by anybody considered
offensive in the doctrines and maxims of Benthamism, became at
one time the badge of a small coterie of youths." [58]

Such practices—young Mill later became ashamed of them
and called them "boyish vanities" [59]—attracted notice and even
ridicule and did much to establish their reputation as extremists
and doctrinaires. The motto, "greatest good for the greatest
number," a hostile critic said, "is to be effected by reducing the
numbers to a few and their pleasures to nothing." [60] And a
writer in the *Edinburgh Review* interrupted a critique of
Bentham's *Rationale of Judicial Evidence* to take note of the
Philosophic Radicals:

> The country is obliged to this great master, and his imme-
> diate disciples, for the most peremptory and proselytising
> seminary of *ipse dixitists,* (to use one of their own beautiful

57. *Auto.,* p. 67. This must be distinguished from (although it is not
entirely unrelated to) J. S. Mill's adoption (1837) of the word *bureaucracy*
and Bentham's inventions of new words, which include *international,
self-regarding, minimize, maximize, meliorability, cross-examination,* and
perhaps *dynamic, unilateral,* and *social science;* Mill, "Armand Carrel,"
LWR, 28 (Oct. 1837), 72; G. Wallas, "Notes on Jeremy Bentham's Attitude to Word-Creation," Society for Pure English, Tract No. 31 (Oxford, Clarendon, 1928), p. 334; J. H. Burns, *Jeremy Bentham and University College* (London, Athlone, 1962), p. 8. Macaulay ridiculed "the
project of mending a bad world by teaching people to give new names to
old things. . . . What society wants is a new motive—not a new cant. . . .
[One] must learn, in the schools of the Utilitarians, a new sleight of
tongue." "Westminster Reviewer's Defence of Mill," *Miscellaneous Writings of Lord Macaulay* (London, 1860), *1,* 353.

58. Mill, *Auto.,* p. 66. Whereas his father avoided using terms like
democracy and universal suffrage, J. S. Mill showed no such restraint.
For example, "Speech on the British Constitution," May 19, 1826, in
James McCrimmon, *Studies toward a Biography of John Stuart Mill*
(Ph.D. diss., Northwestern Univ., 1936), Appx. D, p. 358. For dating,
see London Debating Society, *Laws and Transactions, with a List of the
Members, Corrected up to November 1st, 1826* (London, 1826), pp.
20–21.

59. *Auto.,* p. 66.

60. Coulson, quoted in Nesbitt, *Benthamite Reviewing,* p. 59.

words,) which has ever flourished. . . . When we hear of
Mr. Such-a-one, the Benthamite, we feel a sensible satisfaction, which we can in no way account for, except in so
far as we are thus recalled to those abstract and dogmatical
times when men were principally distinguished by the
theory of morals that they might happen to profess.[61]

Macaulay, who turned the poking of fun into ridicule, probably did more than any of his contemporaries to establish their
reputation:

As to the greater part of the sect, it is, we apprehend, of
little consequence what they study or under whom. It would
be more amusing, to be sure, and more reputable, if they
would take up the old republican cant and declaim about
Brutus and Timoleon, the duty of killing tyrants and the
blessedness of dying for liberty. But, on the whole, they
might have chosen worse. They may as well be Utilitarians
as jockeys or dandies. And, though quibbling about self-
interest and motives, and objects of desire, and the greatest
happiness of the greatest number, is but a poor employment for a grown man, it certainly hurts the health less than
hard drinking and the fortune less than high play; it is not
much more laughable than phrenology, and is immeasur-
ably more humane than cockfighting.[62]

The sectarian spirit that amused and sometimes piqued their
opponents also caused some observers to discern a potentially
dangerous side of Philosophic Radicalism. Macaulay (in the
tradition of Burke) directed his famous critique of James Mill
against the rationalist insensitivity to the political function of
the fabric of social and cultural life, and he was seriously con-

61. [William Empson], "Bentham's Rationale of Evidence," *Edin. Rev.*,
48 (Dec. 1828), 463. For John Stuart Mill's use of "ipse dixit," see
"Speech on British Constitution," in McCrimmon, *Studies*, p. 346.

62. "Mill's Essay on Government," *Misc. Writings, 1,* 322. Such was
their reputation that for more than a year the *Westminster Review* was
kept out of the Oxford Union's reading room; Gladstone was among
those who arranged for this: H. A. Morrah, *The Oxford Union 1823–
1923* (London, Cassell, 1923), p. 54.

cerned by the possibility that such an orientation might be introduced into the British political system. Henry Taylor (later the author of *The Statesman*) saw John Stuart Mill's political philosophy during the 1820s as being "at heart something in the nature of political fanaticism," and in the London Debating Society Taylor spoke against the very facet of utilitarianism that elicited Macaulay's attack.[63]

These more serious criticisms of the Philosophic Radicals were provoked by the conduct of John Stuart Mill and his friends at the various debating societies which they attended, where they displayed still another aspect of their sectarian spirit. They preferred to engage in political debate with spokesmen for principles as clear, explicit, and concerned with the same issues as their own. They were eager to come into conflict with ideological opponents. As political economists they engaged the ideologies of an Owenite-inspired Cooperative Society, and as aspiring Radical politicians they (rather than liberal Whigs) provided the opposition to the Tories in the London Debating Society. The exhilaration of conflict in which one's own position is not complicated by mixed feelings or the restraint caused by responsibility is reflected in John Stuart Mill's recollection of debates with a group of Owenites who, Mill said, "naturally preferred a controversy with opponents to a tame discussion among their own body." So Ellis, Roebuck, Mill, and others, apparently not content with tame discussions in the Utilitarian Society, sought out the Owenites for "general battle. . . . It was a *lutte corps à corps* between Owenites and political economists, whom the Owenites regarded as their most inveterate opponents." A similar alignment emerged in the London Debating Society where "almost every debate was a *bataille rangée* between the 'philosophic Radicals' and the Tory lawyers." [64]

63. *Autobiography of Henry Taylor* (London, 1885), *1*, 77–79; also see (pp. 90–95) extracts from one of Taylor's anti-utilitarian speeches. Macaulay professed to see no danger in the utilitarians (*Misc. Writings, 1*, 357), but this is belied by his argument and his persistence in criticizing them. Also see Leveson Smith, *Remarks upon An Essay on Government by James Mill, Esq.*, ed. C. M. Smith (London, 1827).

64. Mill, *Auto.*, pp. 104–05, 108. Mill must have had these debates in mind when he wrote, "I acknowledge that the tendency of all opinions

One of the consequences of this outlook was an indifference to moderates whose position was not easily defined in terms of a single principle because it was shaped by prudential consideration of special circumstances and the conflict of several principles. A doctrinaire insistence that politics should be a battle of principled extremes left no place for such moderates, though it did guarantee a place, and an important one, to those making the extremist claim. Thus, even though Mill was at first disappointed by the desertion of liberal Whigs such as Macaulay, Lord Howick, and C. P. Thomson from the London Debating Society after the fiasco of its first meeting, it is noteworthy that he and Roebuck, with great persistence in the face of continued failure, kept the organization alive until at last it attracted enough speakers to allow the sort of alignment they wanted: the Philosophic Radicals attacking and a group of Tories providing the defense of "the side of existing opinions and institutions." Mill wrote, "our doctrines were fairly pitted against their opposites," and this made the London Debating Society unique.

> At least our debates were very different from those of common debating societies, for they habitually consisted of the strongest arguments and most philosophic principles which either side was able to produce, thrown often into close and *serré* confutations of one another.[65]

---

to become sectarian is not cured by the freest discussion, but is often heightened and exacerbated thereby; the truth which ought to have been, but was not, seen, being rejected all the more violently because proclaimed by persons regarded as opponents": *On Liberty* (London, Everyman, 1947) p. 111. Of the 12 debates during the 1825–26 session, Mill spoke in 7, and one or another of the Philosophic Radicals spoke in 11 of them. Among the questions were the influence of the aristocracy, primogeniture, and the merits of the English universities. London Debating Society, *Laws and Transactions* (1826), passim. In 1828 Mill spoke on questions of church establishments, perfectability, and the benefits to posterity of the Constituent Assembly: Henry Cole, Diary, 1828, Victoria and Albert Museum.

65. *The Early Draft of John Stuart Mill's Autobiography,* ed. Jack Stillinger (Urbana, Univ. of Illinois, 1961), pp. 114–15. The latter of these two passages appears in the later version of the *Auto.,* but not in the immediate context of Tory opposition, in which it was placed in the

In noting that it was "the only arena" in which such an alignment was to be found, Mill was making an allusion to the defects of Parliament itself as well as giving a hint of the worldly ambitions which were linked to their political speculations.[66]

Devoted as they were to the cause of reform, and with an ambition that arose from their confessedly fanatical attachment to a doctrine, they naturally looked forward to careers in Parliament where they could attempt to implement that doctrine. Not all of them went into Parliament, but those who did not usually wished they were there and became publicists identified with the Philosophic Radical cause. For John Stuart Mill it was a mere fit of depression in 1837 that brought him to remark, "for the first time these ten years I have no wish to be in Parliament." Through his journalism, however, Mill tried to lead the Philosophic Radical party—"to put ideas into their heads and purpose into their hearts." [67] Of course there were some, like Buller and Molesworth, whose family circumstances would have led them anyway to a parliamentary career. But regardless of the source of their parliamentary ambitions, many of those who had submitted to the intellectual and moral leadership of James Mill in the 1820s became devoted servants of the Radical cause during the decade that followed. Several, though trained as barristers, gave up the law for politics. Roebuck, recalling the quickened pace and encouraging developments in reform politics in 1829–30, said, "we all threw ourselves into the torrent, and were as mad and ardent as youth, energy and sincere belief in our

---

early draft. Henry Taylor felt driven to adopt "the language . . . of an ardent Conservative" when he attempted to refute the Philosophic Radical position: *Auto., 1,* 89.

66. *Early Draft,* p. 114, n. 324. Another member said "our proceedings were conducted with all the forms that prevailed in the House of Commons, and with all the decorum and solemnity you would wish. We had even opposition and ministerial sides": John Neal, *Wandering Recollections of a Somewhat Busy Life* (Boston, 1869), pp. 59–60.

67. Mill, *Auto.,* p. 166; Mill to Robertson, Aug. 6, 1837, *EL, 1,* 345. He probably would have sought a parliamentary career had he not been prevented by his employment with the East India Company. Parkes also was not an M.P. but wished to be one: Parkes to Durham, May 1, 1836, LP.

opinions could make us." [68] Their devotion was such that to an outside observer it seemed that "no monk ever adhered with more ascetic severity to the discipline of a monastery than did these Benthamites to the one purpose of their lives . . . the reform of the world." [69] Buller, writing to Carlyle, his former tutor, confessed to having a wish "to acquire distinction in Politics"; and once in Parliament, with the Reform Bill already introduced, he exultingly announced, "Great days are these for those who have long in sorrow and almost in solitude held firm the true Radical faith: and great even for those who like myself have embraced that faith just in time to share in its triumph." [70]

68. "Notes," f. 4; in collection of James M. Osborn, Yale Univ.
69. [Henry Reeve], "Autobiography of John Stuart Mill," *Edin. Rev., 139* (1874), 99.
70. Buller to Carlyle, Aug. 30, 1828, March 14, 1831, NLS, MS 665, nos. 26–27, 31, 33.

2. Philosophic Radical Doctrine

James Mill and his disciples thought of themselves as unique and not merely as part of a general Radical movement. They were educated, responsible, even scientific, a far cry from the demagogue Henry Hunt, romantic eulogist of the countryside William Cobbett, or such leaders of working-class groups as Cleave or Lovett, whose radicalism ignored the truths of Malthus and political economy. Yet there was a striking, if superficial, similarity in the political programs endorsed by the Philosophic Radicals and many other prominent Radical politicians of the 1820s and 1830s. There were disagreements, it is true, about private property and free trade. Yet James Mill and his followers agreed even with the socialists of this period in their endorsement of essentially democratic reform for the British constitution. On certain measures they also stood with such Radicals as Cobbett, Major Cartwright, and Henry Hunt, all of whom advocated universal suffrage, annual parliaments, and secret ballot.[1] In response to practical considerations some of the Radicals, including James Mill and his disciples, moderated their demands. Thus universal suffrage would be changed to suffrage for all men above forty years (as in James Mill's *Essay on Government*) or to household suffrage; and annual parliaments would be changed to triennial. But a near democratic suffrage, secret ballot, and short duration of parliamentary sessions was the common ground of the otherwise varied groups of Radical politicians during this period.[2]

1. For example, cf. *Cobbett's Political Register,* (Jan. 31, 1818), *33*, 140, 146–47, and passim.
2. On James Mill, see pp. 37–38. Roebuck, acknowledging Mill's article "Government" as his authority, confessed that he adopted "the so-much dreaded doctrine of *universal suffrage*": "Of What Use is the House of Lords?," in *Pamph. P* [No. 9, Aug. 6, 1835], pp. 1 n., 4 n. When working-class leaders insisted on universal suffrage, Hume said, "I subscribe

The similarity among the various groups of Radicals went farther. The Philosophic Radicals were antiaristocratic, and in one way or another most other Radicals shared this sentiment. Some were explicitly opposed to the aristocracy, whereas others directed their attacks against such things as tithes, the patronage system, the Corn Laws, the Church Establishment, and the power of the local magistracy, whether in the judicial machinery, Poor Law administration, or in municipal corporations. Whatever particular grievance moved them, they all expressed hostility to aristocratic privilege—a hostility that was part of the ethos among politically conscious but electorally disqualified persons at that time. The appeal of this sentiment is indicated by the continued popularity of John Wade's *Extraordinary Black Book,* first published in 1820 and at frequent intervals into the 1830s, both as a serial and in complete volumes. Wade presented lists of titled persons and their numerous relations who were on the public payroll, in order to support his charge that the aristocratic domination of government was corrupt and costly.

In view of these similarities in program and rhetoric, in what way were the Philosophic Radicals different? It was their rationale for their program that gave them a distinctive position. Whereas most other Radicals had particular grievances directed at various aristocratic privileges, the Philosophic Radicals were mainly concerned with the first principles of government and therefore with the proper role of an aristocracy. Thus, other Radicals were concerned with high taxes and their source in aristocratic nepotism, or with the cost of bread and the way the Corn Laws gave monopoly prices to aristocratic landlords, or with tithes and thus with the constitutional status of the Established Church. The Philosophic Radicals shared these views, but they saw the immediate targets of other Radicals merely as secondary fortresses of the main enemy. They meant to carry their attack to the source of these varied privileges—to the

---

to the doctrine as the only . . . principle on which to stand for permanent good to the Community: But that I could not pledge myself to bring it forward until the public mind was better prepared": Hume to Place, Nov. 18, 1837, Add. MSS 35,151, ff. 35–36.

foundation of aristocratic power. They were concerned with the principle that underlay the numerous and varied discontents with aristocratic privilege. In John Stuart Mill's words, they tried "to give principle and philosophy to the Liberalism which was growing into importance." [3]

Despite the affinity, therefore, between the Philosophic and other Radicals in their opposition to the aristocracy, the Philosophic Radicals differed from most others with regard to their goals. Whereas most other Radicals would have been satisfied with achieving their immediate targets, such as reducing tariffs on grains, or rationalizing the law, or abolishing disabilities of religious dissenters, the Philosophic Radicals saw this as winning battles but not the war, and in their view the important thing was to achieve total political victory, i.e. to destroy aristocratic power. Hence they had mixed feelings at the achievement of small liberal victories. Not that they were displeased by such reforms as Catholic Emancipation or partial reforms of the electoral system, but on such occasions they were more concerned about the distance still to be traveled than appreciative of the ground already gained. And their evaluation of reform in the offing was always based on calculations of its contribution to their ultimate goal; this led to their being disparaging even if not totally indifferent to most partial reforms. Their difference from other Radicals with regard to political goals thus approached being a difference in kind, especially when they were in their most extreme doctrinaire moods.

This difference was related to the origins of political goals. For most other Radicals, the formulation of goals and the motives for pursuing them were linked to a personal identification with the fears, aspirations, hostilities, and interests of particular classes of persons. In contrast, the Philosophic Radicals' outlook was not a reflection of the aspirations and fears of a particular social and economic class. They were not nostalgic for the self-sufficient, ordered, agrarian society that inspired Cobbett's dislike of the emerging nineteenth-century social system. And although they felt sympathy for the various seg-

3. Stillinger, *Early Draft*, p. 114.

ments of the population that experienced economic distress, this did not bring them to personal hatred of landowners or stockjobbers or any other class that might be held responsible.[4] The remedies that they proposed for problems were designed in accordance with impersonal standards, and the design was not affected by the wish to gratify any particular group of citizens. Nor was their doctrine justified as the genuine expression of needs, interests, hostilities, or aspirations of any class suffering from injustice. Thus John Mill said, "My zeal [for the good of mankind] was as yet little else . . . than zeal for speculative opinions. It had not its root in . . . sympathy with mankind."[5] The only legitimate social category, in their view, was "the People," a term that was meant to comprehend the entire society; furthermore, it was used in an abstract way, without reference to any group of particular persons who shared a sense of identification with one another. Unlike the ideas of the Manchester School, Chartism, the Tory radicalism of the factory reformers, or Cobbett, Philosophic Radicalism was not an expression of the feelings of any significant group in the society, not even (as has often been held) of the middle class.

The Philosophic Radicals approached being pure intellectuals in politics. Because they felt no close identification with any of the established parties, classes, or other groupings of society, their conduct as politicians could be guided by their speculations without being restrained by the sympathies, hostilities, and attachments to which most politicians were subjected. Therefore, the doctrine that they looked to as the sole source of guidance and justification for their political conduct is of particular importance.[6]

4. Occasionally James Mill said things that make him an exception to this statement. See pp. 40–41.

5. *Auto.*, p. 92.

6. It is not being claimed that they were completely alienated intellectuals, such as Mannheim described, whose values and conduct were fully autonomous. But they did aspire to this situation and they adopted a philosophic position that assumed it possible to achieve such a status. Furthermore, their specific political doctrine denied legitimacy to politicians and parties that represented the interests or wishes of any segment of the populace. See pp. 47, 55.

JAMES MILL'S PRINCIPLES OF POLITICS

Philosophic Radical doctrine was based on James Mill's political ideas, and these owed a great deal to Jeremy Bentham.[7] It can be seen as a three-generation development, with each new generation selecting some ideas and rejecting or ignoring others. This sifting and reinterpretation took place in response to the purposes and ambitions of each new generation. The main principle of selection was dictated by each generation's conception of the way in which philosophy could be adapted to politics. As a new generation became more concerned with parliamentary and party politics, the ideas increasingly were adapted to their needs as politicians. Thus Bentham's varied legal, ethical, and political ideas were more narrowly conceived and more sharply focused by James Mill; and Mill's disciples carried this process still farther. The development was accompanied by shifts in the direction of greater and more immediate concern with the institutions, parties, and issues of the day.

John Stuart Mill supported his father's claim to intellectual leadership of the Philosophic Radicals. In doing so he did not deny all influence to Bentham. On the contrary, he acknowledged Bentham's indirect influence on their mode of thinking. Nor would he have denied that the Philosophic Radicals shared and even acquired from Bentham various opinions on law reform, judicial administration, and political economy. But James Mill's opinions "were the principal element which gave its colour and character to the little group of young men who were the

7. But Mill's political speculations were also shaped by the Physiocrats, especially Gournay and Quesnay. Although he rejected their argument for the absolute authority of a single man, he endorsed several of their beliefs and commended their approach to politics (the same as his own and Bentham's), which was "to point out the mode of combining the various springs of social action in a more liberal and beneficent system than had yet been recommended to the world." This was the portion of their outlook that was worth preserving, though it had been obscured by their economic principles which, in any case, were erroneous, as Adam Smith had shown. Mill acknowledged the Hobbsian background from which this outlook (like his own) was derived. "Economists," *Supplement to the Fourth, Fifth, and Sixth Editions of the Encyclopaedia Brittanica*, vol. 3, pp. 708, 712–13, 719–23.

first propagators of what was afterwards called 'Philosophic Radicalism,' " and John Stuart Mill evidently thought their doctrine novel, not merely a reaffirmation of radical ideas as found in Bentham's writings or elsewhere in the literature of radicalism.[8]

Since Philosophic Radical doctrine had its immediate origin in the ideas of James Mill, naturally there is a similarity between their outlook and his. The differences are not so much in the language used as in the arguments developed to support the general position they shared with him. These differences had their origin in the way they tried to relate their ideas to active politics and in their expectations as to the possibility of playing an active political role. James Mill was primarily the critic of established institutions; most of his writing was done before reformers could reasonably entertain high hopes of achieving fundamental changes. However, by the time most of his disciples were in their early twenties, political events could stir the imagination and stimulate the hopes of reformers. Catholic Emancipation, the July Revolution in Paris, the split in the Tory party, and the stirring reform agitation all went to create this mood. For those old enough to recall the decade following Napoleon's fall, the new developments appeared even more novel when contrasted to the repression and, among large segments of society, the quiescence of the recent past. As a result, the disciples nourished not only hopes but ambitions, and these were reinforced by an extreme enthusiasm. As John Stuart Mill said, those of his father's ideas which they adopted were given a "sectarian spirit." By adapting James Mill's ideas to their own goals, the disciples emphasized certain parts of their intellectual inheritance and altered the meaning of other aspects of it. The result was not inconsistent with James Mill's earlier view; indeed, in some cases it is implied in his position. But there is a difference in emphasis. Whereas James Mill mainly sought to provide the intellectual foundation for an attack on the established political system, his followers, while sharing his outlook, developed a rationale for a political party that was to engage in political combat within that system.

8. Mill, *Auto.*, p. 88.

James Mill's political ideas are best known through the famous *Essay on Government,* which first appeared in 1820 as an article in the *Supplement* to the *Encyclopaedia Brittanica.* Its prominence, however, was achieved a few years later when it was reprinted with other articles for circulation among friends and disciples. In some ways the *Essay* has been the means of spreading misconceptions about Mill's political ideas; it appears to be a theoretical treatise, and this impression is encouraged by its style and its mode of argument. An axiom about human nature is related to political conduct, and Mill, on this basis, judges alternative ways of defining qualifications for the electorate and thus of distributing political power. And this is done with a minimum of reference to the particular institutions found in Britain at that time. Macaulay, in his famous critique, emphasized its theoretical defects, arguing that Mill's method of reasoning was inadequate, as "it is utterly impossible to deduce the science of government from the principles of human nature." [9] Once more the theoretical aspect of the *Essay* was emphasized, and this is the impression that has remained.

Yet Mill did not consider the *Essay* exclusively a theoretical or scientific treatise. He did allude to the need "to lay a foundation for the science of government," but he went on to say that this "is not compatible with the present design." [10] Actually the essay was a tract; like most things Mill wrote, its purpose was polemical. His closest friend, Ricardo, assumed that this was the case; it was "well calculated," he said, "to serve the good cause" and, noting Mill's suppression of views that would have antagonized his audience, Ricardo commended this silence on the ground that the essay otherwise would have had the appearance of a reform pamphlet.[11]

There is more than one reason for the misleading impression that the *Essay* creates. For one thing, Mill was fond of abstrac-

9. Macaulay, "Mill's Essay on Government," *Misc. Writings, 1,* 317.

10. *An Essay on Government,* ed. C. V. Shields (New York, Liberal Arts Press, 1955), p. 48. The essay was first published as an article in *Suppl.,* . . . *Encyclopaedia Britannica* (Edinburgh, 1824), *4,* 491–505. The various parts (half-volumes) were issued separately between 1815 and 1824, and the part containing this article of Mill's appeared in Sept. 1820.

11. Ricardo, *Works, 8,* 211.

tion and syllogistic reasoning. It also was useful since it allowed him to avoid mentioning particular institutions and officials, which would have made him vulnerable to prosecution for seditious libel. But the main reason was rhetorical. By giving the article an appearance of abstraction and by hinting at theoretical problems, Mill disguised his concern with the form of government in England of the 1820s and the pressing need for its reform. His son noted that James Mill was well aware of opinions that "could not prudently be avowed to the world," as frankness "would either risk the loss of means of subsistence, or would amount to exclusion from some sphere of usefulness peculiarly suitable to the capacities of the individual." [12] He had this in mind as he wrote the *Essay*. To the editor of the *Encyclopaedia* where it first appeared, he wrote, "You need be under no alarm about my article Government. I shall say nothing capable of alarming even a whig." [13]

It cannot be said that James Mill totally failed. The *Essay* was an argument for a democratic suffrage. Yet generations of commentators, including Dicey, have concluded from Mill's few vague but prominently placed references to the middle ranks that he was defending a restricted, middle-class electorate.[14] They were encouraged to do this by Mill's use of equivocal statements and vague words and by his practice of developing arguments but avoiding conclusions. For example, he discussed alternative ways of defining "the pecuniary qualification"; but finally, without making his preference explicit, he pointed to the need for an electorate unrestricted by such qualifications.[15] In-

---

12. Mill, *Auto.*, pp. 36–37; also see pp. 17–18, 74.
13. James Mill to Napier, Sept. 10, 1819, Add. MSS 34,612, f. 287.
14. See pp. 48–53.
15. He discussed four ways by which electoral qualifications could be defined: property, age, sex, and intellectual qualities. A high property qualification would produce an "aristocracy of wealth," which was evil. A low property qualification, if it created a majority electorate, would not be evil; but "it can hardly be said . . . that there would be any good" in it, for "if the whole mass of the people who have some property would make a good choice [it being their interest to do so], it will hardly be pretended that, added to them, the comparatively small number of those who have none . . . would be able to make the choice a bad one." He acknowledged that "without inconvenience" men under

deed, his argument for nearly universal suffrage is so fragmented and convoluted, it is difficult to avoid concluding that he deliberately presented it in this way.

Of course, James Mill's disciples had no difficulty seeing through the disguise. In addition to their conversations with him, they saw the full import of his views in various articles (c. 1824–35) in which discussion of questions of immediate concern required that abstract principles be related to particular institutions.[16] Thus John Stuart Mill could say that this essay and the others were "mere outlines to be filled up"; and he added, "The Essay on Government, in particular, has been almost a text-book to many of those who may be termed the Philosophic Radicals." [17]

Sinister interests and the aristocracy

Bentham adopted a psychological theory to help him analyze the conduct of officials responsible for the administration of

---

forty and women could be excluded; but this was not defended as desirable, and these concessions were peripheral to serious consideration of the suffrage as a political question. Regarding "mental qualities," Mill held that exclusion on this ground would create a minority electorate and thus be evil "by design"; whereas if the allegedly incapable populace votes, evils may be produced "by mistake." Since evil is invariable in the former case, uncertain in the latter, incapacity was to be risked. Futhermore, the latter is "not incurable": *Essay*, pp. 72–86; "James Mill on Universal Suffrage and the Middle Class," *Journal of Politics, 24* (1962), 172–77.

16. Mill was able to deal with particular English institutions more and more during the years following the *Essay on Government,* because of liberalization in the enforcement of the libel laws. Prosecutions were frequent in 1816–24 but there were comparatively few after that time, so that authors and editors were able to feel that the government was becoming quite permissive (news vendors' experiences were altogether different).

17. [J. S. Mill], "Mr. Mill," in Edward Lytton Bulwer, *England and the English* (London, 1836 [1st ed. 1833]), *2,* 326. His son also said the essays were "more read than any other of Mr. Mill's writings." With regard to his conversation, one witness said it "was so energetic and complete in thought, so succinct . . . in expression, that if reported as uttered, his colloquial observations or arguments would have been perfect compositions": *Examiner,* June 26, 1836, p. 403.

justice and of citizens as they responded to the law. Interests were the basis of action; this category was essential for the analysis of human conduct, for interest was defined as concern for the maximization of pleasure and the minimization of pain. Bentham did not rule out that men would have as much interest in the happiness of their fellows as in their own, but this was not a necessary consequence of an individual's action. Given the opportunity to maximize pleasure or minimize pain at another's expense, it would be exploited. It was the function of the law to deny men such opportunities.

With the application of Bentham's method of analysis to political institutions, the concept of sinister interest was developed. Bentham's increased concern with politics during the early decades of the nineteenth century, which was greatly reinforced by James Mill, facilitated this development, for the concept of sinister interest was peculiarly well adapted to an analysis of politics that emphasized the difference, and even the conflict, between rulers and ruled. Although Bentham used the concept as a category of analysis that was applicable to many kinds of situations, under James Mill's aegis it soon became tied to political analysis, and even to one particular political group (the ruling elite). Bentham used the category less narrowly. He held that it was not confined to one particular species of interest, such as the political, for he saw the possibility of sinister interest in any situation. Its existence depended on circumstances: thus an interest might move in a sinister or evil direction; by its force "a man is prompted or excited to engage in some evil line of conduct." Circumstances might also move a man in the opposite, favorable direction. Just as in heraldry, "every scutcheon has a *dexter* side as well as a *sinister* side," so every interest had both aspects. He added, with some bitterness, that "the language of psychology, though a science rather more useful than heraldry, is not equally well provided." [18]

The concept of sinister interest, however, came to be used as a political weapon. With attention directed to the one species of interest that could be sought by rulers when political institutions

18. Bentham, *Works,* 6, 258.

did not adequately check or limit their exercise of political power, the concept was increasingly used to describe the conduct of a ruling elite seeking private gain incompatible with public good. Like other men, politicians would seek "the allurements of pleasure, the aversion to pain, the desire of wealth, power, reputation" in the absence of the obstacles that would protect their fellow citizens from such predatory conduct.[19] If not deterred, a ruling elite would be predatory. The result was *"separate,* and consequently with reference to the public service, . . . *sinister* interests."[20] Both Mill and Bentham thought of sinecures, places, and money as the fruits of sinister interests; the result was corruption. Many of the activities and expenses of the government were the result of sinister interests and thus brought the perversion of the true end of government. "Think of the end," Mill suggests, "as it really is, in its own nature. Think next of the facility of the means—justice, police, and security from foreign invaders. And then think of the oppression practiced upon the people of England under the pretext of providing them."[21]

Although the concept of sinister interest might have been exemplified by any species of interest—political, legal, economic, or any other—it increasingly was used, by both Bentham and Mill, in the analysis of political elites. James Mill went farther and connected it with one particular group, the aristocracy. Although Benthamite analysis, in combination with the undercurrent of opposition to aristocracy in the radical tradition, must have led him to this, James Mill's personal suspicion of the aristocracy also contributed. In Mill's case it would have been surprising, given the circumstances of his life, if he had not felt some resentment toward the aristocracy. Not that he freely expressed it; on the contrary, he usually argued as if his opposition to the aristocracy was an entirely philosophical rather than

19. James Mill, "Summary Review of the Conduct and Measures of the Seventh Imperial Parliament," *Parliamentary Review for 1826* (London, 1826), p. 772.

20. Bentham, *Plan of Parliamentary Reform* (London, 1817), p. 223 (Preface).

21. "Summary Review," p. 776.

emotional matter. Aristocratic venality and corruption, he said, were nothing more than the product of "the steady operation of the law of human nature." [22] But sometimes the intensity of his feeling slipped out. He saw reform politics as an effort "to emancipate lowborn men from the highborn," and his distaste for social relationships dominated by the highborn occasionally came out in formal writings. In his article "Education," he complained that "the political machine is such that the grand objects of desire are seen to be the reward, not of virtue, not of talent, but of subservience to the will . . . of the ruling few." [23] It was this personal hostility to the aristocracy that Bentham alluded to when he said of Mill, "He argues against oppression, less because he loves the oppressed many, than because he hates the oppressing few. He fights for the people—not that he cares for the suffering people, but that he cannot tolerate the suffering-creating rulers." [24]

James Mill became so preoccupied with the overthrow of aristocratic government in England that he came to look upon the aristocracy as the only important example of a sinister interest. He associated the two concepts so closely that his statements about the aristocracy assumed its sinister interest. The term aristocracy, he wrote, was no longer used "in the mere sense of a titled nobility"; it became for him synonymous with bad government. "This body, sharing among them the powers of government, and sharing among themselves the profits of misrule, we denominate the aristocratical body." Since such a

22. James Mill to Ricardo, Oct. 10, 1815; Ricardo, *Works, 6*, 307–08.
23. James Mill to Brougham, n.d. [1835], UCL, BrP. "Education," *Suppl., Encyclopaedia Brittanica, 4,* 33.
24. Bentham, *Works, 10*, 482. But Mill put the shoe on the other foot: "that the aristocracy hate the people is manifested by their language. Why do they abuse them with every epithet of hatred and contempt? . . . How reluctantly is anything yielded to, that will do them any good?": BL, Mill-Taylor Collection; *59*, f. 17v. Place also showed of personal hostility to the aristocracy. Lord Durham asked, "why will he always wear a coat of bristles when he is in company with those who are by the *accident of station* his superiors in society? . . . he seems to think himself always called upon to evince his sturdy independence and his contempt for artificial distinctions." Durham to Parkes, Dec. 16, 1833, LP.

class had a sinister interest in resisting reform, any obstacle to reform was seen exclusively as an appendage to the aristocracy. Thus his perceptions of other institutions were shaped and, perhaps, in part, distorted by this preoccupation. The church and the legal profession were "props" to the aristocracy, and the universities were but a subdivision of the church.[25] Any political or social problem was traced to its source in some aristocratic benefit. The desire for colonies arose from the sinister interest of the aristocracy: "There is not one of the colonies but what augments the number of places. There are governorships and judgeships, and a long train of *et ceteras;* and above all . . . there are generalships and colonelships, and captainships, and lieutenantships." The theory even explains unnecessary wars, for war not only augments the proportion of the national wealth at the command of the government but also increases the number of dependents subject to it.[26]

The struggle between the aristocracy and the people was the most important political issue. The government of England was "an aristocratical engine, wielded by the aristocracy for their own benefit."

> Till now [1819] the people never saw this, or not clearly. Now they do see it pretty clearly, and are going on to see it more and more clearly. They are inclined therefore to say that government must no longer be a mere engine of the aristocracy. The aristocracy of England are inclined to say, it shall continue to be, as it always has been, that engine. Hence the collision, which must go on till one of the parties gives way.[27]

This point of view, which gave Mill's practical judgment of English government greater prominence than the analytical category (sinister interest) on which it was based, was passed on to his disciples. John Stuart Mill, arguing in debating societies

25. James Mill, "Edinburgh Review," *West. Rev., 1* (Jan. 1824), 211, 213.

26. James Mill, "Colony," *Suppl., Ency. Brit., 3,* 272.

27. James Mill to Dumont, Dec. 13, 1819, Biblio. Publique et Univ. de Genève.

against the view that England had a mixed government, held that "a great majority in the House of Commons is returned by two hundred families." These families "therefore possess absolute control over the government: and if a government controlled by two hundred families is not an aristocracy, then such a thing as an aristocracy cannot be said to exist." Since such a government is controlled and administered by a few, he concluded "that it is conducted wholly for the benefit of a few." [28] Francis Place also considered the aristocracy essentially selfish. Government, he said, was "conducted by and for the aristocracy, almost solely with a view to their separate advantage; the people being nothing—their order being everything." [29]

This preoccupation with the aristocracy as the sole cause of bad government led to a narrowing of the focus of Bentham's political philosophy. Bentham had found the justification for government, exercising its power through the law, in the need to protect individuals from injuring one another, and he was concerned with this in varied contexts, judicial and administrative as well as legislative. James Mill and his disciples, accepting this principle, found the chief danger in one class of individuals, the legislators. Although they did not abandon Bentham's concern with law as a protection of all persons from all others, they concentrated their interest on the problem of one kind of injury inflicted by one set of citizens upon all the others. They were primarily concerned with the injuries done by rulers to the ruled. This is exemplified in James Mill's *Essay on Government*. Although he defines the end of government as the protection of individuals against the universal tendency of each man "to take from any other man who is weaker than himself," in his application of the principle he considers only the need to protect the people from the injuries that can be inflicted by the "small number" to whom power is necessarily delegated for the original purpose of government.[30] Furthermore, since he was mainly

28. "Speech on Parliamentary Reform at the Mutual Improvement Society, 1823 or 1824," *Realist*, 1 (Sept. 1929), 54–55.

29. [Francis Place,] *National Political Union. Proceedings at the Second Annual Meeting* (London, 1833), p. 7.

30. *Essay*, Section 1.

concerned with his own society, for the term rulers he substituted the term aristocracy. To Mill, society consisted of two fundamental classes—aristocracy and people: " 'the Few' . . . that governs; 'the Many' . . . that is governed." [31] From Bentham's point of view Mill was dealing with just one aspect of the broad field of law—the legal controls in the realm of constitutional law. But for most of the disciples, more under James Mill's influence than Bentham's, political speculation was at least initially confined to this restricted area. Grote in 1821 narrowly defined political philosophy as "that science which professes to arrange the relations between the rulers and the governed." [32] The other disciples came to look on politics in the same light, and this shaped their judgment about the relative importance of various issues, the goals that had priority, and even about the proper alignment of parliamentary parties.

There is still another aspect to this narrowing of the scope of political thought for which James Mill was responsible. Most of his examples of the aristocracy's sinister interest involved venality, with avarice as the motive. Politics was a struggle between two classes—the avaricious rulers and their intended victims. "The first class, *Ceux qui pillent,* are the small number. They are the ruling Few. The second class, *Ceux qui sont pillés,* are the great number. They are the subject Many." To take away the power "by which the class *qui pillent* succeed in carrying on their vocation," Mill said, "has ever been the great problem of Government." [33] The wish for power was seen as a means to better gratify avarice. If there was no scarcity, he said, there would be no need for government.

This emphasis meant that he ignored the problem of oppression that is independent of simple venality. Mill was aware of it; in the *Essay on Government* there are allusions to the boundlessness of the wish for power, and he quotes Montesquieu to the effect that all men are inclined to abuse power to the utmost.

31. "Colony," *Suppl., Ency. Brit., 3,* 272.
32. Grote, *Statement of the Question of Parliamentary Reform* (London, 1821), p. 5.
33. James Mill, "The State of the Nation," *Lond. Rev., 1* (April 1835), 6, 14; also see "Summary Review" pp. 775–76.

But for all the defects of the constitution, England was not a place where the danger of tyranny or even oppressiveness loomed too ominously. And since English politics was Mill's main concern, he de-emphasized and almost ignored the problem of libertarian government. Mill was able to do this only because special circumstances allowed aristocratic sinister interest to operate without resorting to oppression. He pointed to the example of the English gentleman, who seemed to be "a favourable specimen of civilization . . . [and] all the qualities . . . that make human nature estimable." Yet in the West Indies, circumstances led English gentlemen to violate libertarian values; there they made "property of their fellow creatures [and were led] to treat them with a degree of cruelty the very description of which froze the blood." [34] If in England there were fewer infringements of individual liberty, it was not because the English gentleman was an exception to the principles of human nature. Circumstances did not require it; aristocratic greed was satisfied without going so far; there also was the fear of potential resistance that prudently restrained the rulers. Perhaps because England was an exceptional case, Mill, as Macaulay noted, gave the impression of being concerned with corruption rather than oppression, and this contributed to the narrowing of the scope of his political thought.

The numerous classes and the middle classes

Another fundamental category in Philosophic Radical doctrine had its origin in the effort to find a remedy for the corruption caused by aristocratic domination of government. The people, or the "subject Many," were the intended beneficiaries of reform. Not that Mill or Bentham was moved by any conviction about the natural rights of the people or of individuals, nor was it an ethically founded claim that was made on their behalf. They did not share Cobbett's inclination to find special virtues in the unspoiled, uncorrupted populace; they did not subscribe to the natural rights doctrine that was popular among reformers of the 1780s and 1790s; and they rejected claims, such as Thomas

34. *Essay,* pp. 57, 60.

Attwood's, based on a belief in an original contract that had
established the people's rights. In contrast to such notions, their
propositions about the people did not originate in historical
reconstructions or moral assumptions, but in the logic of
Benthamite analysis of bad government.

Mill's special use of the category "the People" had its origin
in his (and Bentham's) definition of a sinister interest. Sinister
interests were a compound of human nature and opportunity,
and therefore any man was prone to them. The problem was to
create political situations in which the rulers could perform their
duties only as members of the whole community, not of any
segment of it. Anything partial was sinister; anything that did
not deny the whole interest was not sinister (or was "wholesome"). By definition, the nonpartial category was the entire
community or the people. How are the rulers to be prevented
from abusing their power? Having posed the question, Mill
replied: "The people must appoint watchmen"; and, "Who are
to watch the watchmen?" Again he replied: "The people themselves. There is no other resource; and without this ultimate
safeguard, the ruling Few will be for ever the scourge and
oppression of the subject many." It was his purpose, then, to
make the people the means by which control over government
was to be achieved. "We know but one way of accomplishing our
object," Mill said, "which is to grant the people the entire and
complete choice of their representatives." [35]

The demand for popular government, and thus the importance
of "the people," had its origin in the fact that they were a
numerous body. The political function of the populace was only
an incidental by-product of its existence. Being a large group,
the whole by definition, it had no partial or sinister interest.

> The People, that is, the Mass of the community, are some-
> times called a class; but that is only to distinguish them,
> like the term Lower Orders, from the aristocratical class.
> In the proper meaning of the term class, it is not applicable
> to the People. No interest is in common to them, which is
> not in common to the rest of the community. There is

35. James Mill, "State of the Nation," pp. 14–15.

nothing which can operate as a cause of benefit to them exclusively. Whatever operates as a cause of benefit to them in common, operates equally as a cause of benefit to every part of the community, saving and excepting those who are in possession of some mischievous power.[36]

Extension of the suffrage was to be a means of achieving popular control. The people, in James Mill's revealing phrase, were merely the "numerous classes." [37]

This view of the political role of the numerous classes (the vast majority and ideally the whole populace) meant that James Mill and his disciples could not consistently act as spokesmen for any particular class, for any segment of the populace would have had sinister interests. The reforms they sought were justified as being equally in the interest of all individuals as citizens. This was especially true of such constitutional reforms as near-universal suffrage and the secret ballot, but it held also, at least in their eyes, for the changes in economic policy which they advocated. They were not unaware of the class cleavages that did exist; but they held that conflict between the middle and working classes was based on ignorance and fear and that in fact these two classes could have shared interests. (This was also an assumption of the political economy doctrine that they supported.[38]) When they acted as politicians they tried to avoid associating with any organization or movement that represented one particular class. For example, during the Reform Bill agitation, Place, with Mill's blessing, was instrumental in establishing the National Political Union in which strong emphasis was given to class cooperation. In contrast to the National Union of Working Classes, which claimed to represent the working classes alone

36. James Mill, *Analysis of the Phenomena of the Human Mind* (London, 1829), 2, 187. Also (p. 188), "There is no Love of Class, therefore, but in a Privileged Order." "Whom do I call the people? All but the Aristocracy, and the clergy of the established church": BL, Mill-Taylor Collection, *59*, f. 19v.

37. James Mill, "Edinburgh Review," *West. Rev., 1,* 209, 210; Grote, *Statement of the Question,* pp. 18–19.

38. R. K. Webb, *The British Working Class Reader 1790–1848; Literacy and Social Tension* (London, Allen and Unwin, 1955), p. 99.

and where the language of class conflict was used, Place's organization was to be "a Union of all classes." One of its placards
stated its position:

> This is not a Union of the Working Classes, nor of the
> Middle Classes, nor of any other Class, but of all Reform-
> ers, of the masses and the millions.

> The National Political Union is essentially a Union of the
> People, and is the first instance on record of the Nation
> breaking through the trammels of caste, to associate for
> the Common Interest in a Common Cause.[39]

The belief in the basic similarity of interests among working and
middle classes, which is reflected in this statement, also shaped
the Philosophic Radicals' attitudes to other organizations and
movements during the decade that followed.

There is a widely held belief that the Philosophic Radicals
were spokesmen for the middle class and its interest, and this can
hardly be reconciled with the above analysis. Dicey, for example, said "James Mill in reality advocates the political supremacy of the Middle Class." [40] Mill was said to have "favored
the middle class"; or, "it was in the interest of emancipating the
middle class that the Benthamites demanded extensive reform
in British life, . . . Mill actually took great pains to justify limit-
ing political rights to the 'wise and virtuous members of society,
the middle rank.' " [41] Such views are given credence by the
Philosophic Radicals' association with the political economists
and the laissez-faire ideas that have been assumed to be pecul-

39. [Francis Place], "National Political Union. Resolutions . . . October 31, 1831"; and *Report of a Committee Appointed . . . October 14,
1831* (London, 1831), p. 2.

40. A. V. Dicey, *Law and Opinion* (2d ed.) p. 160.

41. Francis Wilson, "Public Opinion and the Middle Class," *Review
of Politics, 17* (Oct. 1955), 493; C. V. Shields, "The Political Thought of
the British Utilitarians" (editor's introduction), in James Mill, *Essay,* p.
33. For other examples see G. H. Sabine, *A History of Political Theory,*
p. 662; J. S. Schapiro, *Liberalism: Its Meaning and History,* p. 42; R. P.
Anschutz, *The Philosophy of J. S. Mill* (Oxford, Clarendon, 1953), pp.
33–34, 43.

iarly middle-class doctrines; by the Benthamite support of the
Reform Bill of 1832; and by James Mill's famous eulogy of the
middle class in his *Essay on Government*.

The eulogy appeared near the end of the essay. It is the middle
class (actually, he avoids this phrase, referring instead to the
middle rank) that is "the most wise and the most virtuous part
of the community." [42]

> The opinions of that class of people who are below the
> middle rank are formed, and their minds are directed by
> that intelligent, that virtuous rank who come the most im-
> mediately in contact with them, to whom they fly for advice
> and assistance in all their numerous difficulties, upon whom
> they feel an immediate and daily dependence in health and
> in sickness, in infancy and in old age; to whom their chil-
> dren look up as models for their imitation, whose opinions
> they hear daily repeated and account it their honor to adopt.
> There can be no doubt that the middle rank, which gives to
> science, to art, and to legislation itself their most distin-
> guished ornaments, and is the chief source of all that has
> exalted and refined human nature, is that portion of the
> community of which, if the basis of representation were
> ever so far extended, the opinion would ultimately decide.
> Of the people beneath them a vast majority would be sure
> to be guided by their advice and example.[43]

These are the statements that have been used to justify the claim
that Mill was a spokesman for the middle class.

The middle class was relevant to Mill's analysis because of
the function it had in shaping the opinions of those in lower
ranks. Mill intended his observations as a factual description of
the way working-class opinions were formed in the England of
his time. Two inferences as to who should have the right to vote
can be drawn from the description. It can be argued that, since
the middle class shapes the views of those beneath them, the
vote may as well be restricted to the middle class, for those

42. *Essay*, pp. 89–90.
43. Ibid., p. 90

beneath them add nothing to the electoral decision. On the other hand, it can be argued that, since the lower ranks imitate those above them, nothing is gained by excluding them. Many of Mill's critics have adopted the first of these alternatives, leading to the conclusion that the suffrage should be restricted to the middle class. The only evidence supporting this is to be found in the flattering terms Mill used to describe this class. Not only does this contradict Mill's revealed preference for universal suffrage, but the context in which these words were used shows that Mill, in spite of all the rhetoric, favored the second interpretation, which argued that those beneath the middle rank should be allowed to vote.[44]

The entire discussion of the middle rank takes place against the background of Mill's awareness of an objection that could be made to his thesis—it could be argued that people are not capable of acting agreeably to their interests. Mill introduces the middle rank in response to this hypothetical objection. His observations about the rank can be reduced to two propositions, both intended to be statements of fact. First, the lower ranks form their opinions (and presumably their votes) by imitating the middle rank; and second, most of the educated intelligence in the nation is in the middle class, not in the aristocracy.[45] Mill used these two propositions in order to invalidate the argument that the people are incapable of satisfactorily exercising electoral privileges. Therefore, far from indicating a preference for a middle-class electorate, his description of the middle class was intended to reinforce his defense of a practically universal suffrage.[46]

44. Mill acquired the reputation for being a spokesman for the middle class only after his death. Macaulay recognized that he was "in favor of pure democracy" (July 10, 1833). *Speeches by Lord Macaulay*, ed. G. M. Young (London, Oxford, 1952), p. 126.

45. The middle rank is "wholly included in that part of the community which is not the aristocratical"; and "there is not only as great a proportion of the wise men in that part of the community which is not the aristocracy as in that which is, but . . . there is a much greater." *Essay*, pp. 84, 89.

46. Although Mill saw some use in the "bourgeoisification" of the working class, he was not seeking a democratic society in which middle

Mill's references to the middle rank, then, did not form part of the structure of his argument. They appear in connection with his effort to dispose of an anticipated objection. They also allowed him to add a rhetorical flourish that could only reassure his readers at a time when the values associated with "middle class" were rising in prestige, not only, as Mill argued, among the populace but also among the aristocracy itself. Mill is often taken to be a bold and almost unique spokesman for the middle class when, in fact, flattering allusions to this group were commonplace. Early in the century the middle class already was "eulogized" and given "paeans of praise," and it was often thought to be "the most important opinion-making group in a changing society." [47] Such eulogies were so commonplace that a conservative pamphleteer in 1831 expressed annoyance with the "frequent panegyrics of the independence and intelligence of the middle ranks." [48] Indeed, Mill's most outspoken critic was

---

class values were predominant. What he admired most was a society in which intellectual eminence was esteemed and encouraged. "Think what a society must be, in which all that is respectable in intellect and correct in conduct is the object of display . . . And where such is the style . . . in the leading class—a class not separated from, but initimately mixed with, the rest of the community, the imitation of it is inevitable." "Aristocracy," *Lond. Rev., 2* (Jan. 1836), 290–91. Also see "Ballot," *West. Rev., 13* (July 1830), 37–38.

47. Asa Briggs, "Middle-Class Consciousness in English Politics, 1780–1846," *Past and Present*, no. 9 (April 1956), pp. 68–69. James Mill noted: "The value of the middle classes of this country, their growing numbers and importance, are acknowledged by all. These classes have long been spoken of, and not grudgingly by their superiors themselves, as the glory of England"; "State of the Nation," *West. Rev., 6* (Oct. 1826), 269.

48. Sir John Walsh, *Popular Opinions on Parliamentary Reform, Considered* (3d ed. London, 1831), pp. 103–04. Many illustrations can be found. When the talents of two "middling class" persons were being discussed in 1818, they were taken as "proof of the intelligence now spread through that rank of Englishmen." Lord John Russell, ed., *Memoirs, Journal, and Correspondence of Thomas Moore* (1853–56), *2,* 244; quoted in Uno Philipson, *Political Slang 1750–1850* (Lund Studies in English, *9,* 1941), p. 41, n. 1. Lord Grey spoke of "the middle classes—of the great mass of intelligence and property throughout the country;" the conservative Lord Tenterden protested that "he entertained as great a respect as any man" for the middle classes: *Hansard 8* (Oct. 7, 1831),

a more effective spokesman for the middle class than was Mill.
It was Macaulay who said that his "fervent wish and . . . sanguine
hope, is that we may see such a reform of the House of Commons
as may render its votes the express image of the opinion of the
middle orders of Britain." [49] The prevalence of such views made
it possible for Mill to exploit for rhetorical purposes the high
esteem in which the middle classes were already held. Whereas
the *Essay* advocated universal suffrage without using the words,
his prominent references to the middle class have obscured his
genuine beliefs and misled readers into assuming that he wished
that class to have special privileges. This is especially worthy of
notice, inasmuch as most middle-class persons, according to
more than one contemporary observer, were markedly and uncompromisingly hostile to universal suffrage.[50]

Regardless of appearance and reputation, James Mill was not
a spokesman for the middle classes. On the contrary, his conception of the "numerous classes" (or the People) and "sinister
interests"—two categories at the heart of his political thinking
—were defined and used in a way that made middle-class government (or any privileges for the middle classes) illegitimate.
The disciples took over these beliefs and, although they modi-

---

301, 323; also see 265, 306, and *12, 356–57*; and W. A. Mackinnon, *On
the Rise, Progress, and Present State of Public Opinion in Great Britain*
(London, 1828), p. 15. Other examples are given by Briggs, "The Language of 'Class' in Early Nineteenth Century England," in Asa Briggs
and John Saville, eds., *Essays in Labour History* (1960), pp. 54–60.

49. "Utilitarian Theory of Government," *Misc. Writings, 1*, 395. This
view was widely held by prominent Whig-aristocratic politicians; see N.
Gash, *Politics in the Age of Peel* (London, Longman's, 1953), pp. 14–17.

50. "The middle classes, with hardly an exception are indisposed to
such a sweeping measure [as universal suffrage]." [John Wade] *The Extraordinary Black Book* (London, 1831), p. 562. J. S. Mill said that "to
propose Universal Suffrage would be to bid adieu to all support from
the middle class. Most of the Reformers who belong to that class at
present, deem Universal Suffrage objectionable in principle." "Reorganization of the Reform Party." *LWR, 32* (April 1839), 492–93. The other
circumstances that have given credence to the belief that Mill and his
disciples were spokesmen for the middle class—their views on economic
policy and on the Reform Bill—will be discussed elsewhere; see pp. 71–
74, 120–22.

fied them in some ways, they retained James Mill's attitude to the middle classes and, indeed, as politicians pursued a course that alienated the middle classes.

DOCTRINE OF A PARTY

The Philosophic Radicals' goal was to establish a new political party that would be one of two parties in Parliament. This involved the transformation of the party system and the elimination of the Whigs as an independent party. James Mill's disciples developed a rationale for the new party's claim to existence and for its hope of ultimate domination. Toward this end they reshaped their intellectual inheritance. The change, which took place gradually, began in the mid-twenties when they first experienced hopes for political careers, and they continued to develop the theoretical basis of their party after several of them entered Parliament in 1833. The doctrine that emerged was not the work of one or even a few persons, though some, especially John Stuart Mill, played a more active part than others in elaborating it. In the elucidation of the doctrine that follows, the evidence is drawn from the writings and statements of various members of the group.

The People

One alteration introduced by the disciples concerned the use of the term "People"; for James Mill, as for Bentham, this was but a synonym for populace or "numerous classes." It referred to all who were not rulers and who therefore had no sinister interest but rather a shared interest in preventing the high costs of government for which the aristocracy was presumed to be responsible. The interest of the people was necessarily the same as the universal interest. "No interest is in common to them, which is not in common to the rest of the community. There is nothing which can operate as a cause of benefit to them exclusively." Radical reforms, Bentham had said, express the "demands of the *universal interest*—of the interest of the whole people." Thus universal suffrage would allow the people to serve as a "checking body" against the sinister interest of any ruling group. Without any sense of identification with the populace as a deprived or underprivileged body of persons, it was recognized that the people, by virtue only of its size, could perform a useful function. It was the means of establishing "efficient checks," "effectual securities," and "popular control." Through certain contrivances in the electoral system the people could be the means of assuring good government.[51]

The numerous classes, a phrase that was defined only in terms of numbers, reflected this meaning. However, James Mill's followers neglected this usage. Instead, "the People" was a phrase used very often, not only in the sense of a numerous checking body but even more often as a distinguishable part of the society with group solidarity and self-consciousness. As such, it became the body on whose behalf the Philosophic Radicals acted. It was set up as the other significant force which, together with the aristocracy, made up political reality. The disciples continued to be concerned with the need for good government. But the concept of the people took on an importance in their thinking and conduct much greater than it would have had if the achievement of good government, with which it was originally associated, had been their only purpose.

This shift, which led to the reification of the concept, began with James Mill; at least he made it easy for his disciples to proceed in this way. Hs assumed, of course, that men would act rationally to exploit any advantages given them by the electoral system. This appeared to have been the case, at least for the minority electorate of his time. Supported by this example, he argued that "the interest of the body is the ruling principle of action [for individual members]," and that men's "sympathies are with one another, not with those exterior parties whose interests come in competition with theirs." [52] Even if this proposi-

51. James Mill, *Analysis of the Phenomena of the Human Mind, 2,* 187; Bentham, *Plan of Parliamentary Reform,* p. 306 (Preface). "Representative government is a contrivance by which those who pay taxes may have a control over those who levy taxes": [James Mill] *An Abridgement of the Article on the Ballot* (London, [1831]), p. 6.

52. James Mill, "Summary Review," *Parliamentary Review for 1826,* p. 773. For another formulation, see J. S. Mill, "Speech on Perfectability" (1828), in *Auto.,* pp. 298–99. This conception of the People and its interest is described in S. H. Beer, "Representation of Interests in British Government," *American Political Science Review, 51* (Sept. 1957), 633.

tion correctly described the conduct of the minority electorate of his time, it is questionable when applied to a majority electorate or to an entire populace. Yet Mill assumed that a majority electorate created by a democratic suffrage would behave in the same manner—that its individual members would have sympathies with one another that would make them indifferent to the "exterior parties" whose interests were partial (i.e. sinister). This meant that Mill expected men to ignore all the influences of tradition and sentiment associated with social class, party, or family once they had an opportunity to act as members of the whole community. This made it possible, by a process of easy translation, for the people, originally considered an aggregate of individuals, to be seen as a solidary group which, with the establishment of a democratic electorate, would be called into being and then would actively implement the universal interest. As they turned to parliamentary politics Mill, and even more emphatically his disciples, tended to invest this idea with reality. They thought of the people as a functioning group in politics.

Their alteration in the meaning of the term People was important to them as politicians. As the body in which the universal interest reposed, the People became the only group on behalf of which politicians could legitimately act. Not that they had any sense of personal identification with the populace. Most of them (Place and Roebuck are exceptions) had no connection with working-class political or educational organizations. Henry Reeve, who knew several of the young Philosophic Radicals, said none of them "had any personal sympathy or acquaintance with the people . . . they felt and expressed the utmost contempt for what they regarded as the gross prejudices and ignorance of the class in whose name they fought." [53] There is a marked disparity between the great importance they gave the People in their thinking and their meager involvement with the actual populace. Like Bentham and James Mill, they were convinced that the reforms they proposed would truly benefit them, but the People (frequently capitalized) had additional significance for them. As active politicians in the radical cause, but without any great involvement in popular organizations, invocation of

53. "Personal Memoir of Mr. Grote," *Edin. Rev., 138* (July 1873), 230.

the People gave confidence and a sense of legitimacy to their bold and zealous efforts on behalf of reform. This concept justified their effort to set up a Radical party and it gave plausibility to their fantasy of gaining power in its name.

The party system of aristocratic government

The disciples adopted in its entirety James Mill's and Bentham's analysis of parties in relation to the aristocracy, and from this proceeded to develop their argument for the transformation of the party system.[54]

Bentham's theory of law and government, before the doctrine of sinister interests became a prominent part of it, was not directly concerned with parties. Though he made no direct attack on them during this early period, his ideal legislature was hardly one in which parties could be prominent. Ideally, the lawmaker would consult utilitarian principles in order to construct laws that would comprehend the universal interest. Men who pursued the lesser ends of party interest had no place in such a rational system. Furthermore, Bentham's notions of the proper scope of government also limited the functions of political parties. Since so many of the nation's collective decisions were to be left to the market and the private sphere, there would be little need for parties, each advocating a general policy, to compete for the support of the populace.

With the development of the idea of sinister interests, both the major parties were accused of harboring them, for the way in which parties were in fact organized made it easy to establish a direct connection. The prevailing conception of government did not promote binding allegiance to party. Government was still looked upon as "the administration" and not as a group of men seeking to legislate in accordance with a broadly defined social and economic policy that would affect all facets of the way men lived. On most questions, Members of Parliament who felt ideologically bound to any specific policy were in the minority.

54. It should be acknowledged that during this period there was no party "system" in the modern sense. However, James Mill thought the relation of parties had the characteristics of a system. My use of the term party only reflects the Philosophic Radicals' usage and does not assume that disciplined, cohesive parties in fact existed.

This facilitated the process by which those in control of the administration used patronage to identify the interest of Members of Parliament with the ministry. Sinecures, pensions, and appointments in the civil, military, and diplomatic service all were used for this purpose. In this way ministers contrived to maintain a parliamentary majority.[55] Most politicians felt little guilt in engaging in these practices, which were accepted as normal. Brougham, for example, in an attack upon the Philosophic Radicals, accused them of falling "into the ordinary error of forgetting, that whether we please or not, one party always exists, held together by the ties of place, and paid out of the public purse—namely, the government and its supporters." [56]

Bentham and his followers at first looked upon these practices merely as obstacles to the legislator's rational attempt to construct laws in the light of utilitarian principles. To pursue party interests was to neglect "utility and reason." Bentham ridiculed these practices as a method to "secure fidelity at the expense of sincerity in parliament." [57] Francis Place saw in politicians "the bane of all good legislation; they are the panders to party." [58] And according to James Mill, "Party is only necessary for concert in evil, and never did exist for any other purpose." [59] As the doctrine of sinister interest became more prominent, and as the aristocracy came to be seen as the sole significant obstacle to political good, the Whigs and Tories as the two aristocratic parties came to be regarded as the embodiment of the evils of the existing system. They were no longer merely an obstacle to rational political conduct; they became the main enemy of reformers.

The fact that the two major parties were engaged in continuous conflict did not seriously challenge the analysis of the aristocracy as a single class that dominated the government and exploited

55. L. B. Namier, *Conflicts* (London, Macmillan, 1942), pp. 199–201, 210–211; *Monarchy and the Party System* (Oxford, Clarendon, 1952), *passim*.

56. "Parliamentary History," *Edin. Rev., 44* (Sept. 1826), 489.

57. Bentham, *Works, 10,* 511; *5,* 291.

58. Place, "A Repeal of the Stamp Duty on Newspapers," in *Pamph. P* [No. 29, Dec. 24, 1835], pp. 2–3.

59. Common Place Book, BL, Mill-Taylor Collection, *59,* f. 111.

the people. For the two parties, though different in small ways, were considered equally aristocratic. They were but two factions of the aristocratic oligarchy and the protectors of the same sinister interests. The difference between them were not important, for "whatsoever may be the hostility of the two sinister interests to one another, the hostility of both to the only right and proper interest is much more extensive and unchangeable." [60] For Place, this view was confirmed by the Westminster election of 1819. He managed the campaign for the Radical candidate (Hobhouse), who was opposed by a single candidate who received the combined support of both Whigs and Tories. After Hobhouse's defeat, Place observed that "the two Aristocratical factions . . . have once more laid aside their disgraceful squabbles for power and plunder, and have united to prevent Reform." [61] Nor was this analysis embarrassed by the fact that the Whigs enjoyed (and cultivated) a reputation for liberalism and reform. Their occasional advocacy of reform measures and their historical claim to an alliance with the people seemed to substantiate this reputation. James Mill dealt with this by acknowledging the facts and discounting the claim. The Whigs, he said, advocated "petty reforms" so as to gain the favor of the people while at the same time not antagonizing the rest of the aristocracy. Their only purpose was "to effect a change of the hands by which the distribution of the advantages is made—to obtain hands through which their share will be enlarged." Bentham in 1817 had used a similar argument: the only difference between the parties was that what "the Tories have in *possession* . . . the Whigs have before them in *prospect,* and *expectancy."* Both had "the same separate and sinister interest:—an interest completely and unchangeably opposite to that of the whole uncorrupt portion of the people." James Mill concluded that the Whigs were "the opposition section of the aristocracy." [62]

60. Bentham, *Works, 1,* 254.
61. [Place], *An Authentic Narrative of the Events of the Westminster Election . . . 1819* (London, 1819), p. 116.
62. James Mill, "Summary Review," *Parliamentary Review for 1826,* p. 778; "Edinburgh Review," *West. Rev., 1,* 217, 221. Bentham, *Plan of Parliamentary Reform,* pp. 306–07 (Preface).

This view was adopted by the disciples for whom it became a foundation stone supporting their belief in the need for an antiaristocratic Radical party. With the resignation of the Wellington government, the Tory party, the open advocate of sinister interests, prudently deferred to the democratic spirit of the age: it "deputed its power to a certain go-between party, offsets of the aristocracy, namely the Whigs." In this role—as mediators between the people and the aristocracy—the Whigs passed the Reform Bill, and by this means "the aristocratic party was saved from the destruction with which it was threatened." But Whig reformism was not genuine: when aristocratic privilege and good government come into conflict, the Whigs then reveal their highest loyalty to the aristocracy. Circumstances made the Whigs assume a popular pose: "Today they are liberal; tomorrow the reverse. Aristocratic in principle; democratic in pretence." There was "a constant see-saw between hostile principles," as James Mill liked to put it. Or, as Place said, "the peculiar character of the Whigs is their see-sawing dawdling mode of proceeding." Thus Whig "words have been many, their works have been few"; they were "no better than the Tories"; they "were of use only for evil, and as far as the people were concerned were only mischievous." [63]

Since the Whigs, in this view, were not really different from the Tories, the disciples found it easy to adopt James Mill's conclusion that Whigs and Tories were "the two aristocratic factions." [64] The quarreling between them was "a dirty conflict between two sets of scramble-mongers, one to grasp and the other to keep the victuals of office." [65] According to Place, "the Tories are split under the names of Whig and Tory," but in reality they were two sections of the same aristocratic party.[66]

63. *Hansard, 36* (Jan. 31, 1837), 30, 32; *38* (June 9, 1837), 1339, 1341, 1344, 1348. Place to Parkes, Dec. 8, 1835, Add. MSS 35, 150, ff. 100–01.

64. Leader, *Hansard, 39* (Nov. 21, 1837), 92.

65. C. P. Villiers, Nov. 17, 1836, in Sir Herbert Maxwell, *Life and Letters of George William Frederick Fourth Earl of Clarendon* (London, 1913), *1*, 126.

66. Place to Parkes, Jan. 27, 1837, Add. MSS 35, 150, f. 233. Also, according to John Stuart Mill, "the doctrine that the working bees

Realignment of parties

The establishment of a Radical party required a transformation of the party system, and the Philosophic Radicals looked for a realignment of parties as the means of achieving this. This hope was based on the belief that political conflict and therefore political parties ought to reflect the fundamental interests in society. When they did, the issues that divided parties would cease to be trivial.

Since Whigs and Tories were but two factions of the aristocracy, it was easy to conclude that they ought to merge into a single aristocratic party. An analogous line of thought led to the belief that there ought to be a party representing the universal interest. And here their tendency to reify the idea of the "numerous classes" came into play. Just as the sinister interest of the aristocracy was an interest shared by an identifiable group in the society, so it was assumed that the universal interest resided in "the People." Thus the antagonism between the universal and one particular sinister interest came to be seen as a conflict between the People and the Aristocracy. These became the most important and the most frequently used categories of analysis for the Philosophic Radicals. Having begun with a firm belief in the reality of the two kinds of interests and the great importance of the conflict between them, the Philosophic Radicals developed a doctrine based on the assumption that, analogous to conflict of universal and sinister interests, the conflict between People and Aristocracy and between the parties representing each was the only proper model for political activity. Once parties were aligned in this fashion they would reflect the basic political struggle. Then, Roebuck said, "parties will be divided by one broad line of distinction. Aristocracy and Democracy will be fairly arrayed against each other; no middle party will exist, and no middle course will be pursued." [67] This,

should be governed by the drones" is part of "the theoretic foundation both of Toryism and Whiggism": "Notes on the Newspapers," *Mo. Rep.*, *8*, (April 1834), 244.

67. "Prospects of the Coming Session," in *Pamph. P* [no. 23, Nov. 12, 1835], p. 6. Molesworth said realignment would "alter the constitution

John Stuart Mill said, would make party conflict reflect the "contest . . . between the two principles which divide the world, the aristocratic principle and the democratic." Politicians would be obliged to choose between these principles. "The problem will then be reduced to its simplest terms: Who is for the aristocracy and who for the people, will be the plain question." [68]

The first step was for the two aristocratic factions to unite into a single party. Second, the party representing the universal interest of the people (alternatively called the Popular, Radical, or People's party) had to be formed. The Philosophic Radicals' parliamentary efforts and their journalism were designed to encourage these developments. They did not consider that they were starting from scratch, for they had a firm confidence that their image of political conflict was an accurate reflection of the underlying reality; therefore they looked for an unfolding of that reality and acted on the assumption that, given a reasonable opportunity, party relationships could be reshaped.

This faith made them confident that the Whigs and Tories would soon unite. Not that they expected all supporters of the Whig governments of the 1830s to take on the Tory label. They saw such supporters as being themselves divided into true Whigs and therefore aristocrats and what John Stuart Mill called "nominal Whigs," who, as representatives of new towns and religious Dissent, basically were (or should have been) hostile to the aristocracy. It was assumed that the Whig government's supporters could be provoked to split. "One portion," Molesworth said, "that in which the aristocratic feelings are predominant, will join the Tories, whilst the other will amalgamate itself with the Radicals." After such a split, John Stuart Mill said,

---

[so] that the distribution of constitutional power may no longer be different from that of real power": "Terms of Alliance between Radicals and Whigs," *LWR, 26* (Jan. 1837), 311.

68. "Parliamentary Proceedings of the Session," *Lond. Rev., 1* (July 1835), 516. Also Place: "Things will come round 'ere long to . . . coalition of the best whigs and the best tories, and the sooner this happens the better, we shall then have, Reformers and Anti-reformers, and shall come to a clear understanding." Place to Parkes, Jan. 27, 1837, Add. MSS 35,150, f. 233.

"the whole of the Whig aristocracy will combine with the Tories in a determined resistance to all further extension of popular influences." Molesworth believed that "most of the ancient Whigs, with Sir Robert Peel at their head," belonged to such an aristocratic party. He explained that "the fear of being accused of apostasy has as yet held most of them aloof," but "it is an undoubted fact that all their sympathies are secretly in his favour." [69] Place thought that "there will be a coalition of Whigs and Tories whether the reformers [i.e. Philosophic Radicals] support [Whig] ministers or oppose them." [70]

Holding these beliefs, they also thought it reasonable to expect the appearance of an antiaristocratic party that would complete the realignment. Once the Whig aristocrats joined their Tory brethren in an aristocratic party, then the antiaristocratic supporters of the Whig ministers (the "nominal Whigs") would combine with the Radicals to form the Popular party "resting upon the people." Molesworth thought these processes were silently taking place: "The nation is in the act of dividing itself into two great parties, those of aristocracy and democracy," and, ignoring much evidence, he asserted that "aristocratic and democratic parties" were the only ones "into which . . . this country, though not openly, is yet in reality divided." [71] C. P. Villiers shared this outlook:

> If there comes a dissolution, a great many timid, half-and-half, glory-of-the-British-constitution, rally-round-the-throne people would get returned; but there would also be a larger number than usual of independent, general-happi-

63. J. S. Mill, "Parliamentary Proceedings," *Lond. Rev., 1,* 516; Molesworth, "Terms of Alliance," *LWR, 26* (Jan. 1837), 291–92.

70. Place to Hume, Nov. 7, 1836, Add. MSS 35,150, f. 173.

71. "Parliamentary Proceedings," *Lond. Rev., 1,* 516; "Terms of Alliance," *LWR, 26,* 287–88, 292. Roebuck saw politics as "a fearful struggle between two great principles of government, that which endeavoured to make the many dominant, and the other which endeavoured to maintain the domination of the few": *Hansard, 36* (Jan. 31, 1837), 29. Also, "Former disputes and contests in politics were between various sections of the Aristocracy: the contest that is now going on is between the *Aristocracy* and the *People*": Roebuck, "Trades' Unions: Their Advantages to the Working Classes," *Pamph. P* [no. 7, July 23, 1835], p. 1.

ness, things-to-be-measured-by-their-utility people returned. What would never appear again would be the good old Whig. That cannot exist again, and its component parts will take different directions—some to make a Tory, some a Radical.[72]

This expectation was shared by Fonblanque, editor of the *Examiner:*

> It is clear that the trimming milieu system is drawing to a close; a precipitation is in process and opinions are tending to settle according to their affinities. Men must soon take up their positions either with the Retrograde or the Movement division of the country. As the conflict of the two sets of principles approaches, the stragglers between the two hosts must disappear, and fall into the ranks of the one or the ranks of the other, and leave a clear open space between the opposed forces. When the powers maintaining the adverse principles are marshalled, the victory will be won without a blow.[73]

In the same vein, J. T. Leader claimed that the populace would assert its rights and "prove to the aristocratic factions that there is a power above them—the power of the great majority of the people," and he made the prophecy that "the line will soon be drawn between the aristocratic and the popular parties." [74]

Once realignment was achieved, the Radical party would be established in Parliament. Since Philosophic Radical doctrine justified the formation of this party, it came into apparent conflict with Bentham's and James Mill's condemnation of party politics. However, the two positions were not incompatible. As Roebuck said, "The object we have in view is to establish a National Government. . . . We seek to take away *all* power from every sect and party." However, before this situation could prevail, aristocratic resistance to democracy had to be overcome. By trying to make the conflict between aristocracy and democ-

72. Maxwell, *Clarendon, 1,* 108.
73. *Examiner,* June 22, 1834, p. 387.
74. *Hansard,* 39 (Nov. 21, 1837), 92.

racy the central issue of politics, Philosophic Radicalism pointed the way to Bentham's ultimate goal. But in doing so it justified party politics and thus made it possible for John Mill and the other disciples to visualize a political world in which they could play an active role in parliamentary politics and at the same time maintain their commitment to the general principles enunciated by Bentham and James Mill.

The use of the label Philosophic Radical can be explained by the disciples' views on the need for realignment. The phrase "Philosophic Radical" has been widely used to identify almost any position adopted by Bentham and his varied associates— the aspiration for a science of law, the rationale for the Poor Law of 1834, Chadwick's vision of bureaucracy, laissez-faire economics, and the entire intellectual foundation of utilitarianism.[75] Among the persons who acknowledged it as a label identifying themselves it was used rather infrequently because, as John Stuart Mill explained, "This designation too often repeated gave a *coterie* air which it was felt to be objectionable." [76] But when it was used by these persons, in contrast to the various definitions given the phrase by historians, it had a precise meaning that had its source in the belief that the conflict between People and Aristocracy was the most significant characteristic of the social structure.

The term "radical" was used in political discussion, initially, as an adjective that referred to remedies that went to the root of the matter and thus were fundamental; and later as a noun to identify those persons who advocated such fundamental rem-

75. For example, Elie Halevy, *The Growth of Philosophic Radicalism* (London, Faber and Gwyer, 1928), part 3; Sidney Webb, "The Basis of Socialism—Historic," in G. B. Shaw, ed. *Fabian Essays in Socialism* (London, 1889), pp. 44–45, 58; J. P. Plamenatz, "The Legacy of Philosophical Radicalism," in *Law and Opinion in England in the 20th Century,* ed. M. Ginsberg (London, Stevens, 1959), pp. 27–41.

76. Mill to Fonblanque, Jan. 30, 1838, *EL,* p. 370. Among the other places where the phrase is used, see [J. S. Mill], "Death of Jeremy Bentham," *Examiner,* June 10, 1832, p. 371; *Auto.,* p. 181; *Mo. Rep., 8,* 173–74, 309, 369; *LWR, 27,* 67; *Spectator, 9,* 1951; *11,* 233, 894; *12,* 34; *Hansard, 40,* 398–99, 1169. Among the synonyms were complete, instructed, thorough, and enlightened reformers.

edies as universal suffrage.[77] John Stuart Mill's circle of friends saw themselves as Radicals in this latter sense. They also shared with the numerous other Radicals the democratic wish to reduce the influence of the aristocracy and enhance the interest of the populace. But their Radicalism was philosophic by virtue of the particular way they viewed the connection between democratic reform and the conflict between Aristocracy and People. The conflicting interests of the antagonists could be defended by a principle of government. Thus there was a parallel between the intellectual conflict of principles and the political conflict of interests. When the connection between these two facets of the contest was discerned, the contestants could engage in the struggle more realistically and more effectively. Engaging in politics on behalf of such principles—whether on the aristocratic or the popular side—entitled one to be considered philosophic. Thus a party could have a philosophic basis by self-consciously taking one of the two possible positions with regard to the distribution of power in society. In this sense the Philosophic Radicals justified their adoption of the title and distinguished themselves from other Radicals and reformers.

One party that clearly did not qualify was the Whigs. Really a party of aristocrats, yet claiming to be reformers and friends of the people, it evaded the central issue of aristocracy versus democracy. This evasiveness was evident to the Philosophic Radicals when during the 1830s the Whigs named themselves the "Reform Ministry" and yet avoided proposing the reforms that would oblige politicians to define their position with regard

77. Cobbett, 1822: "The word radical. . . . It means something belonging to or appertaining to the root; and if we have an evil to remove, is it not necessary to go to the root of it?" Quoted in L. G. Johnson, *General T. Perronet Thompson* (London, Allen and Unwin, 1957), p. 115, n. 1; "If a man has a fever, he must be cured *radically*, not *partially* or *moderately*. On the same principle the honest political physician will prescribe a course of medicine which will go to the *radix*, or root of the national disease. He will physic, purge, bleed,—he will ERADICATE,— he will be a RADICAL": *The Radical* ([London], Hetherington), no. 1, Aug. 20, 1831; Elie Halevy, *A History of the English People in the Nineteenth Century* (London, Benn, 1949–50), 2, 67, n. 6; Philipson, *Political Slang 1750–1850*, pp. 97–100.

to the issue of aristocracy versus democracy. Because of this
equivocal, ambiguous position, the Whigs were, as Parkes put
it, "between two fires of ultra opposite parties." This meant they
were "founded upon no principles, but standing between two
principles." [78] Their conduct, Roebuck said, was "vacillating,
inconsistent, contradictory, and wholly undirected by any guiding
principle." [79] Furthermore, this status, neither wholeheartedly
reformers, nor identified with an extreme aristocratic position,
gave them (in Roebuck's words) a "strange and anomalous
position." Parkes said they were "an unnatural party standing
between the People and the Tory aristocracy." In these circumstances the Radicals held that the Whigs were doomed—they
"must, in a contest of principles, cease ere long to exist," Molesworth said; and Parkes announced that "their hearse is ordered." [80] Once parties were properly aligned, individual Whigs
would have to "join the one party or the other, and be content
with that subordinate position befitting their power and
intellect." [81]

In contrast to the Whigs, many Tories, since they took a clear
and definite position on this fundamental issue, were credited
with acting from principle. Roebuck said of them, that although
they are "the avowed enemies of popular government," at least
"there is no doubt or mystery about their intentions or their
principles." They took a "hostile but honest" position with respect to the "democratic party." [82] John Stuart Mill remarked
that it is possible to give "to Toryism (what can be given to it,

78. Parkes to Durham, July 19, 1836, LP; Molesworth, "Terms of
Alliance," *LWR, 26*, 291. J. S. Mill said "They are afraid of principles.
. . . They are men of shifts and expedients": *Examiner*, Sept. 22, 1833,
p. 593. Place said a Whig "is necessarily a shuffler": Place to Parkes,
July 17, 1834, Add. MSS 35,149, unfol.

79. "Prospects of the Coming Session," *Pamph. P* [no. 23, Nov. 12,
1835], p. 5.

80. Roebuck to Papineau, Sept. 4, 1836, CPA, Roebuck Papers, no.
11; Parkes to Place, Jan. 2, 1836, Add. MSS 35,150, f. 100; Molesworth,
"Terms of Alliance," p. 291.

81. Roebuck, "Prospects of the Coming Session," *Pamph. P* [no. 23,
Nov. 12, 1835], p. 6.

82. Ibid., p. 5; *Hansard, 36*, 29.

though not to Whiggism) something like a philosophic basis."
And in an otherwise severely critical review of the Tory Sir John
Walsh, Mill calls him "more rational" for recognizing that the
really significant struggle was between Conservatives and Radicals, in contrast to the Whigs, a "middle party," that would soon
be "rather an appearance than a reality." [83]

Just as Toryism had a "philosophic basis," and the Whigs had
none, so the Radicals thought of themselves as philosophic because they took a position on the fundamental question. They
claimed to be "liberals in consequence of a true sympathy with
the people, and a thorough understanding of the science of
political government"; thus they were "truly of the party of the
people." [84] There was then a sense of identification with the
People, but it was an identification with an abstraction for, as
mentioned, there is very little evidence that the actual populace
was anything but remote from their daily lives and even from
their thoughts. All the same, this sense of identification allowed
them to think of their party as "resting upon the people." This
connection with the people and thus with the fundamental
question of politics led them to look upon an extremist aristo-

83. J. S. Mill, "Tories, Whigs, and Radicals," *LWR, 25* (July 1836),
285, 292. Mill was reviewing Sir John Walsh, *Chapters of Contemporary
History* (London, 1836). Also, "Toryism is a creed easily understood;
Radicalism is a doctrine whose truths cannot be questioned. . . . Whiggism
alone is undefined and inexplicable": *Constitutional,* Sept. 17, 1836, p. 2.
Like Walsh, other doctrinaire conservatives held similar views; for example, the Radical or Utilitarian party was called "a more shrewd, intelligent, and philosophical class of men than the Whigs, accustomed to a
closer method of reasoning": James B. Bernard, *Theory of the Constitution* (London, 1834), p. 5. Also see Disraeli: "A Tory and a Radical,
I understand; a Whig—a democratic aristocrat, I cannot comprehend":
Whigs and Whiggism; Political Writings, ed. William Hutcheon (London,
1913), p. 19. Francis Jeffrey explained the hostility of ideological extremes for middle parties: "The real reason of the animosity with which
we [Whigs] are honoured by the more eager of the two extreme parties,
is, that we . . . impede the assault they are impatient mutually to make
on each other, and take away from them the means of that direct onset,
by which the sanguine in both hosts imagine they might at once achieve
a decisive victory": "Moore's *Life of Sheridan," Edin. Rev., 45* (Dec.
1826), 35.

84. Roebuck to Papineau, Sept. 4, 1836, CPA, Roebuck Papers, no. 11.

cratic party as their ideal antagonist, and it was such an opponent that they usually sought.[85]

The rationale for organic reform

With the growth of their ambition to form a parliamentary party, there was a shift in emphasis in the Philosophic Radicals' rationale for the parliamentary reforms they advocated. For Bentham and James Mill, annual parliaments, secret ballot, and universal suffrage were the means of implementing representation and thus protecting all individuals from sinister interests. These reforms were the most efficient means to good government. For James Mill a democratic suffrage was "the most essential of 'securities for good government.' " Bentham favored "democratic ascendancy" for this purpose alone, to oppose the oligarchy "acting in a state of corrupt dependency." The secret ballot was to give "security against spuriousness," so that the people's nonsinister interest would be genuinely recorded. It was a device that was meant to prevent coercion of tenants by landlords and of shopkeepers by their customers, as well as the more overt forms of bribery. Like the ballot and extended suffrage, short parliaments were also meant to give effective popular control of government. Bentham and James Mill reasoned that, if a representative were obliged to submit frequently and regularly to popular review of his conduct, he would not be tempted to pursue a sinister interest. The "perfect power of choice," as James Mill put it, "implies the power of speedy removal." [86]

The disciples continued to use these arguments throughout the 1830s, but they sometimes formulated the arguments in a way that reflected their primary concern with their particular struggle against a particular aristocracy. As a result, extensive parliamentary reform was justified as a way of rearranging the party system so that it would reflect the basic categories of social

85. Thus Mill defined Philosophic Radicalism as "enmity to the aristocratical principle": "Fonblanque's England Under Seven Administrations," *LWR, 27* (April 1837), 67.

86. J. S. Mill, *Auto.,* p. 90; Bentham, *Plan of Parliamentary Reform,* pp. 175, 268 (Preface); James Mill, "State of the Nation," *Lond. Rev., 1,* 14–15.

structure, i.e. aristocracy and people. An extended suffrage and the ballot especially would elicit electoral responses that would naturally group all nonaristocrats, regardless of other social and economic characteristics, into "the People." They would also force the two aristocratic factions to coalesce into the single party into which they naturally belonged. Thus organic reforms, in addition to being useful as devices for achieving good government (as Bentham had argued), became for the disciples the levers for the emergence of the Radical party.

The added twist given to their rationale for fundamental reforms is especially evident in their advocacy of the ballot, which was particularly important to them, more so even than an extended suffrage. It was "the key that will unlock, to all those that are excluded, the portals of the constitution." [87] On practical grounds they had good reason to want it, for they were acquainted with the effects of bribery, which they hoped the ballot would eliminate. Place complained that the two great parties always tried to make the elections in Westminster "contests of the purse." Grote, with experience as a candidate, thought that no matter how large the constituency, if the vote is cast openly, "the victory in an election contest must depend upon hard and well-organized canvassing and upon the force of private obligation actively and unscrupulously put forth," so that "the most unprincipled intimidators" achieve the greatest success.[88] In addition to this conventional argument for the

87. Ward, quoted in *Fraser's Magazine, 17* (Jan. 1838), 132.
88. Place to J. W. Unett and Parkes, Jan. 8, 1828, Add. MSS 35,148, f. 22; Grote to Brougham, July 31, 1837, UCL, BrP. This does not mean that the Radicals never became involved with bribery. Parkes claimed that he never was a party to it, but he admitted that his "profession necessitates my occasional attack upon and defence of it." His correspondence with E. J. Stanley, a Secretary of the Treasury, contains several allusions to his involvement. It also describes Warburton's complicity: Parkes to Cobden, Nov. 18, 1843, SRO, Cobden Papers; Parkes-Stanley correspondence (typed copies), passim, but esp. Sept. 7, 8, 1841, May 8, 1842, UCL, JPP. Parkes (referring to Stafford): "of course I had too much good sense to pay any single person myself. . . . We were so far implicated, that though we did not know exactly how it was paid, or by whom the money was drawn . . . we had a knowledge therefore,

secret ballot, they also held that it would be the means of re-aligning parties. Assuming, as John Stuart Mill put it, that there was "a great deal of passive radicalism in the electoral body," it was only necessary to allow it free expression in order to give birth to a Radical party that would, presently if not immediately, overwhelm the aristocracy. Let the ballot be established, "then reform will have finally triumphed: the aristocratic principle will be completely annihilated, and we shall enter into a new era of government." [89] Grote, too, saw the ballot in this context; the public "were at least a reforming public," but it was necessary to establish a system of fairly collecting its sentiments.

> [He wanted] a system which would express the opinions, he did not say of an extended, but of the existing con-stituency; and if they did that . . . the parties in Parliament would be very different from what they were at that moment.[90]

Furthermore, the ballot as an issue, even before it was made part of the electoral procedure, was intended to be a means of promoting the establishment of a Radical party. Since secret voting was inimical to aristocratic power, it was assumed that the aristocratic parties would be compelled by self-interest to resist it. Therefore, by making an issue of it, it was hoped that all politicians could be made to take a stand with regard to the central question of democratic versus aristocratic power. For this reason the attitude to the ballot among other politicians was made a criterion for judging them. Throughout the thirties the size of the minority supporting Grote's frequent motions on the ballot was taken as a measure of the number of liberal supporters of Whig governments ("nominal Whigs") that "really" belonged in the Radical party. And for this reason John Stuart Mill could say, "[Buller] is half mad about it, and is for throwing overboard

though participation in the offense could not be traced home to us": *Parliamentary Papers. Report from the Select Committee on Bribery at Elections,* 1835 (547). VIII, ques. 1603.

89. Mill to Fonblanque, Feb. 3, 1838; Mill to Tocqueville, Jan. 7, 1837, *EL,* pp. 317, 374.

90. *Hansard, 39* (Nov. 20, 1837), 60.

Reform of the Lords and everything else and pushing for the ballot and the ballot only." Mill himself held that "opposition to the ballot is interpreted as opposition to all radicalism." [91]

The Philosophic Radicals were not indifferent to other reforms, but even where they approved, their concern with them was abated by their feeling that such other reforms would not alter the distribution of power. James Mill had taught them that the Whigs would approve of reforms such as the abolition of slavery or Catholic Emancipation because the "hold possessed by the aristocracy upon the powers of government, was not likely to be weakened, by any opinions propagated on the subjects of political economy, and the slave trade; not even on that of Catholic emancipation." [92] Even the Whig Reform Bill was seen in this light. The Whigs of 1831–32 were unwilling reformers who made concessions from a fear of revolution combined with a desire to retain office. Since they remained aristocratic, Roebuck said, Whig reform "will be inadequate for the purpose of the People, while it will serve the turn of its proposers." [93] Thus it was only organic reforms that were fundamental, for only they could alter the distribution of power; and only by making an issue of them could politicians be classified as either radical or aristocratic. In contrast, other reform proposals divided Whig from Tory, and thus allowed for a distinction where there was no important difference. They were irrelevant to the fundamental issue, ephemeral if not trivial. Such proposals, generally considered reforms, were ridiculed as "half-measures," "small meas-

91. Mill also said, "As for Ministers—I have advised Molesworth and shall advise every radical I know, to be guided in his tone and conduct about the ministry, mainly by the part they take on Grote's [ballot] motion": Mill to Fonblanque, n.d. [Feb. 13 (?), 1837]; Mill to Kemble, Oct. 14, 1839, *EL*, pp. 327, 410.

92. James Mill, "Edinburgh Review," *West. Rev., 1*, 234. Place, referring to the so-called liberal measures promoted by Huskisson and Canning, said they "took from the Government no portion of its power, destroyed none of its influence for evil, and hence the endeavours they made to a very limited extent to promote free trade": Place to Hobhouse, June 4, 1828, Add. MSS 35,148, f. 28.

93. Roebuck to Papineau, Sept. 4, 1836, CPA, Roebuck Papers; Roebuck, "Prospects," p. 6.

ures," and "petty reforms," and their sponsors, "half-and-half
reformers." In contrast, the Philosophic Radicals, advocating
the organic reforms that were antiaristocratic, and which were,
in fact, opposed by Whigs and Tories alike, called themselves
"real reformers," "complete reformers," indeed, "philosophic
reformers." [94]

The Philosophic Radicals' preoccupation with organic reform
of the constitution reduced what otherwise might have been
marked concern with economic policy. Yet Philosophic Radicalism has been historically associated with the demand for the New
Poor Law and free trade—with the rise of the middle class as a
social and economic group that had an interest in laissez-faire
doctrine. But to trace the prominence of certain questions of
economic policy to Philosophic Radicalism is to ignore the emphatically political character of that doctrine. Not that the Philosophic Radicals were indifferent to the Poor Law of 1834 or the
cause of free trade. They supported both; but so long as they
continued to entertain hope for the fulfillment of their specifically
political vision, economic questions had in their eyes only secondary importance.[95]

94. *Lond. Rev., 1,* 11; *LWR, 26,* 280, 286; *Parliamentary Review for
1826,* p. 778; Parkes to Durham, Oct. 10, 1836, LP.

95. Their participation in the Political Economy Club can be taken as
an indication of the degree of their interest in economic questions. Grote,
an original member, resigned in 1831; Warburton, also an original member, remained in the Club, but attended only once during the period
1832–40; T. P. Thompson was elected in 1831 and resigned in 1835;
Hume was an unsuccessful candidate for membership; Buller, having entered the Club in 1835, attended fairly often, but did not initiate discussion until 1842; J. S. Mill entered in 1836 and attended frequently, but
he proposed none of the questions discussed in the Club until Feb. 6,
1840, whereas after this he was responsible for the questions at 2
meetings each year (out of 7 held) during several of the years following;
James Mill attended only 3 times after 1826: *Political Economy Club.
Minutes of Proceedings, 1821–1882, Roll of Members, and Questions
Discussed,* (London, 1882), *4,* 95–142; ibid., *6,* xiii, 43–60, 220, 357–67.
Michael Packe, *The Life of John Stuart Mill,* p. 310. J. S. Mill's essays,
later published as *Unsettled Questions of Political Economy* (1844), were
completed sometime before 1833 and were the result of discussions that
took place during the late 1820s; the article on political economy
published in *LWR, 26* (Oct. 1836), 1–29, was a product of this earlier
period: *EL,* pp. 79, 178.

Most questions of economic policy provoked discussion in terms of segments of the populace like working class, artisans, or middle class. Since this disturbed the image of the People as comprehending all groups and as a category from which the Philosophic Radicals derived the legitimacy of their position, such discussion was deplored and generally avoided. Economic questions, they thought, invited incorrect answers from all sorts of persons whose ignorance or prejudice prevented them from arriving at the correct answers that the science of political economy could provide. Too great an attachment to erroneous views only divided those who should have been political allies— whom John Stuart Mill called "natural Radicals." Thus Mill, after acknowledging considerable disagreement with W. J. Fox about the Poor Law, expressed the hope that it would be "an 'open question' both among radicals and among London reviewers." However, with regard to political questions he was not so tolerant. When an article involved "directly and comprehensively all the political principles of the review," he was reluctant to have contributions "written at a distance from the conductors of the review and by contributors not in daily intercourse with them and with the details of whose opinions they are not conversant." [96]

The Philosophic Radicals' wish to subordinate economic to political questions is evident in their response to the agitation for free trade, with which they are often associated. They watched the growing interest in repeal of the Corn Laws with mixed feelings. On the one hand, they approved of the goal; indeed, they helped organize the Metropolitan Anti-Corn Law Association in 1836, though this organization contributed little to the ultimate success of the free trade movement.[97] On the other hand, they did not eagerly endorse the Anti-Corn Law League's agitation organized by Cobden, for it had a divisive and a dampening effect on the political aspirations they entertained. For one thing, the League avoided affiliation with either political party and also with agitation for parliamentary reform.

96. Mill to J. B. White, April 15, May 19, 1835; Mill to W. J. Fox, n.d. [Jan. 27, 1837]: *EL*, pp. 258, 263, 320.
97. Norman McCord, *The Anti-Corn Law League* (London, Allen and Unwin, 1958), pp. 16, 75–77, 178.

Thus it did not appear to be an effective means of promoting the political objects sought by the parliamentary Radicals. (This is not to say that in the long run it would not affect the political power of the aristocracy, as they recognized.) In fact, they seem to have been somewhat fearful that it would supersede their own favorite issue. In response to the way the League side-tracked the question of political reform, Roebuck indignantly complained of "the bigots of the league" and "these rabid Leaguers." [98] There also was disappointment at the hostility between Chartists and Leaguers, especially as it evoked a good deal of the rhetoric of class conflict between middle- and working-class spokesmen. They felt that the goals of the Chartists and of the League were not really incompatible. If obliged to choose between them, however, without being sympathetic to the Chartists, the Philosophic Radicals would have opted against the League and its emphasis on the economic issue. Place saw the organic political reforms, such as were embodied in the Charter, as the means of achieving all reforms, economic among others. For him the Charter was "the general and all comprehensive measure," whereas Corn Law repeal was a "very momentous measure though only one of detail." [99] John Stuart Mill took the same line: if manufacturers and merchants, he said, want to get rid of the Corn Laws, "they must combine to agitate, not against the Corn Laws, but against the source of the Corn Laws, as well as of every other grievance—the vicious constitution of the legislature." [100]

Although the basic categories of Philosophic Radical doctrine —aristocracy, sinister interest, "the People," realignment of

98. Roebuck to Brougham, Feb. 27, 1842, UCL, BrP.

99. Place to Lovett, n.d. [1838], Add. MSS 35,151, f. 86. When Place made this statement he had not yet become bitterly hostile to the Chartists; but that hostility was with the Chartists (not with Chartism) and did not alter this view (see pp. 252–60).

100. J. S. Mill, "Reorganization of the Reform Party," *LWR, 32* (April 1839), 485. Parkes had a somewhat different view. He also held that a change in the composition of Parliament must precede repeal of the Corn Laws; but he acknowledged that anti-Corn Law agitation would contribute to this result: Parkes to Cobden, March 23, 1839, May 31, 1841, SRO, Cobden Papers.

parties, organic reform—can all be traced to James Mill and Bentham, they had in most cases a different status in the disciples' political thinking. The differences between the Philosophic Radicals' intellectual inheritance and their own rendering of it are not great, but they are important. Some facets of the doctrine were de-emphasized, others were made more prominent; some categories were redefined; and even where opinions were unchanged, the rationale offered in their support was altered. What was clearly not theoretical for Bentham (and for James Mill, too, though he blurred somewhat the distinction between theory and practice) was incorporated into the disciples' theorizing about politics. The changes were the result of the expectations of reform developed during the late 1820s in response to a new political atmosphere. Such expectations could not reasonably have been held a decade earlier. To this was added the cultivation of personal political ambition that led them to think of themselves as eligible for the role of politician as well as philosopher. In addition, these expectations were heightened and the ambitions were greatly reinforced by the sectarian enthusiasm that John Stuart Mill described in his *Autobiography*. This fanaticism, as he called it, had still another consequence. It led to a confusion of the two roles. What they sought as politicians had a marked effect on their speculations about politics; and their claim to be philosophers affected their performance as politicians. As a result, their intellectual inheritance was altered so that the doctrine was not only a rationale for certain constitutional changes, as it had been for James Mill and Bentham, but simultaneously an instrument for the fulfillment of their political ambition, that is, for the establishment of a Radical party.

3. *John Stuart Mill as a Philosophic Radical*

> [Mill] talked about his own personal character which he
> bore with other people. With utilitarians, said he, he was
> a mystic—with mystics a Utilitarian—with Logicians a
> sentimentalist and with the latter a Logician.[1]

John Stuart Mill's education had been designed so that he would
become a philosopher of reform and thus a worthy successor to
Bentham and his father. He was to pursue the truth, not for its
own sake, but as an instrument for the improvement of mankind.
However, soon after young Mill was released from his father's
immediate supervision he diverted from the path James Mill
had hoped he would follow, and soon he was flirting with ideas
that were diametrically opposed to the most cherished tenets of
his teachers. This diversion began with the mental depression
that reflected the deficiencies of the educational process he had
endured. The sense of purpose that had come with his conversion to Benthamite reform suddenly (in 1826 at the age of
twenty) left him and he discovered that "the fountains of vanity
and ambition seemed to have dried up within me, as completely
as those of benevolence." He no longer cared whether all the
reforms that had been the object of his life were realized or not.
Lacking genuine sympathy with the people on whom the benefits
of those reforms were to have been conferred, he felt incomplete as a person.[2]

1. Henry Cole's Diary, 1827–1834, entry of Nov. 23, 1831, Victoria
and Albert Museum.
2. *Auto.*, pp. 113, 118. Also (p. 115), "My education, which was
wholly his [James Mill's] work, had been conducted without any regard
to the possibility of its ending in this result . . . his plans had failed . . .
the failure was probably irremediable, and, at all events, beyond the
power of *his* remedies." Also see the insightful account in Ruth Borchard,
John Stuart Mill—the Man (London, Watts, 1957), Chap. 4.

After a year or so he recovered (though in circumstances that revealed to posterity if not to Mill himself that he was not whole-heartedly grateful to his father for his education).[3] But he also had changed. Among the consequences of this experience was the discovery that "the internal culture of the individual" was one of the prime necessities of well-being. He therefore "ceased to attach almost exclusive importance to . . . the training of the human being for speculation and for action," i.e. to the role for which he had been trained.[4] Mill now emphasized the emotional component of thought as a necessary complement to the rational, and he acknowledged that poetry, as something that "acts upon the feelings and awakens the sympathies," and which has for its "sole object . . . to produce emotion," was a significant kind of literature distinct from but not inferior to science and philos-ophy.[5] He opened the door to new experiences, emotional as well as intellectual. As a result he was to welcome the impact of a variety of influences which for most other persons would have been bewildering. Wordsworth, Comte, Mrs. Taylor, Car-lyle, Tocqueville, and Coleridge all contributed to his intellectual and emotional adventures during these years, and they provided

3. "I was reading, accidentally, Marmontel's 'Memoires,' and came to the passage which relates his father's death, the . . . sudden inspira-tion by which he, then a mere boy, felt . . . that he . . . would supply the place of all that they had lost. A vivid conception of the scene and its feelings came over me, and I was moved to tears. From this moment my burden grew lighter." Ibid., p. 119; also see A. W. Levi, "The 'Mental Crisis' of John Stuart Mill," *Psychoanalytic Review, 32* (1945), 97–101.

4. *Auto.,* p. 121.

5. "On the Applications of the Terms Poetry, Science, and Phi-losophy," *Mo. Rep.,* 8 (May 1834), 324. For Mill's authorship, see Fran-cis Mineka, *The Dissidence of Dissent* (Chapel Hill, Univ. of N. Carolina Press, 1944), p. 419. He also expressed these views in conversation: "The uncertainty of conviction from Reason alone unless accompanied with an influence upon the emotions, which Poetry in its full extent, effects"; "our talk turned on the comparative value of scientific or poetical views . . . the latter . . . was equally worthy of (being?) known": Henry Cole's Diary, Oct. 6, 1831; May 16, 1832, Victoria and Albert Museum. Mill met Southey, Wordsworth, and Coleridge at this time: Packe, *Mill,* p. 107. Cole reported (July 3, 1833), "We met Alfred Tennyson. Mill was asked but came not."

his intellectual legacy from James Mill with some stiff competition.

As a result of these new influences John Mill (as he was known to his contemporaries during this early period) became aware of deficiencies in utilitarianism—in its psychology, its view of history, and above all in its political philosophy. More than deficiencies, Mill found defects, and initially he rejected Benthamism and identified himself with an alternative outlook that in large part was derived from the writings of the St. Simonians. Rejection of his intellectual inheritance went so far that he saw it as an "important transformation in my opinions and character." Mill's own testimony, his occasional criticisms of Bentham during these years, his outspoken admiration for such anti-Benthamites as Carlyle and Coleridge, and especially his adoption of certain St. Simonian ideas have created an impression that he now disassociated himself from the Philosophic Radical movement.[6] Certainly if Mill had not managed to reconcile the new influences with the old Benthamism, he could not have played his part as a Philosophic Radical. However, by using certain intellectual devices he achieved a reconciliation that allowed him to cooperate with the other Radicals. But there is a good deal of ambiguity in his relationship to Philosophic Radicalism. Even after Mill resumed his place as a Philosophic Radical, he retained unorthodox ideas and values which he tried to combine with that doctrine. This intellectual process affected the way he was to play his part as the most significant spokesman for Philosophic Radicalism.

THE SOURCES OF HERESY—MACAULAY AND THE SAINT SIMONIANS

Mill's dissatisfaction with his intellectual inheritance was brought to the surface by Macaulay's critique (1829) of James Mill's article "Government." The grounds and disposition for this dissatisfaction had been laid during his mental crisis in

6. *Auto.*, p. 112; Edward Lytton Bulwer, England and the English (London, 1833), Appx. B, "Remarks on Bentham's Philosophy"; Appx. C, "A Few Observations on Mr. Mill" (both written from notes supplied by J. S. Mill).

1826–27, and since that time he had been considering alternative philosophies, particularly the St. Simonian. Macaulay's attack served as a catalyst that led Mill to focus his doubts on particular facets of Benthamite doctrine. The new beliefs that were soon to emerge, though expressed in the language of the St. Simonians, were in response to deficiencies in the doctrines of James Mill that Macaulay's articles now suggested. The new speculations covered a wide range of topics, including a theory of history, psychological doctrine, and political theory.

It was in regard to political theory, of course, that skepticism most directly affected John Mill's status as a Philosophic Radical. First of all Macaulay cast doubt on James Mill's epistemology. The position in the article "Government," Macaulay charged, was based on a priori reasoning that was not appropriate to politics.

> The style which the Utilitarians admire suits only those subjects on which it is possible to reason *a priori*. . . . Mr. Mill . . . is an Aristotelian of the fifteenth century, born out of due season. We have here an elaborate treatise on Government, from which, but for two or three passing allusions, it would not appear that the author was aware that any governments actually existed among men. Certain propensities of human nature are assumed; and from these premises the whole science of politics is synthetically deduced! [7]

This was not all. Macaulay went on to claim that James Mill, having adopted the wrong method, compounded his error by proceeding from premises about human nature that were too narrowly defined to comprehend the full range of motivations by which men are moved.

> The fact is, that, when men, in treating of things that cannot be circumscribed by precise definitions, adopt this mode of reasoning, when once they begin to talk of power, happiness, misery, pain, pleasure, motives, objects of desire, as they talk of lines and numbers, there is no end to

7. Macaulay, "Mill on Government," *Misc. Writings, 1,* 284–85.

the contradictions and absurdities into which they fall. . . . Mr. Mill has chosen to look only at one-half of human nature, and to reason on the motives which impel men to oppress and despoil others, as if they were the only motives by which men could possibly be influenced.[8]

These criticisms hit home. John Mill "could not help feeling that there was truth in several of his strictures on my father's treatment of the subject; that my father's premises were really too narrow, and included but a small part of the general truths on which, in politics, the important consequences depend."[9] The blow was made more severe by his father's failure to publish a reply and by the way his father dealt (apparently in conversation) with Macaulay's criticisms.[10]

The reflections on epistemology that were stimulated by this controversy made an important contribution to the *Logic* (1843).[11] But their immediate effect was to give credence to Macaulay's criticism of James Mill's political doctrine which provided for good government by means of democratic conditions of election that were to create an identity of interest between government and populace. Macaulay questioned James Mill's democratic prescription in two ways, both involving a

8. Ibid., pp. 294–95.

9. *Early Draft*, p. 134. This view was also expressed soon after Macaulay's critique appeared: for example, in *The Spirit of the Age* [1831], ed. F. A. Hayek (Univ. of Chicago Press, 1942), p. 47; "Writings of Junius Redivivus," *Mo. Rep.*, 7 (April 1833), 269; Mill to d'Eichthal, Oct. 8, 1829, *EL*, pp. 35–36 and n. 5.

10. *Auto.*, p. 134. James Mill's quarrel with Bowring made it difficult but not impossible to reply in the *Westminster Review*. James Mill's silence caused consternation among some of the Radicals: see Add. MSS 35,145, f. 104. A portion of *Fragment on Mackintosh* (pp. 277–92), written about 1830 but not published until 1835, was meant to be a reply to Macaulay: J. S. Mill, "Rationale of Representation," *Lond. Rev.*, *1* (July 1835), 346. Of course, replies were published in the *West. Rev.*, *11* (July, Oct. 1829), *12* (Jan. 1830) but they were not written by James Mill.

11. *Auto.*, pp. 135–36; O. A. Kubitz, *Development of John Stuart Mill's System of Logic* (Urbana, Illinois Studies in the Social Sciences, 1932), pp. 31–37.

demonstration that it was unworkable on Mill's own assumptions. First, he suggested that democratic controls would not provide security against abuses. Assuming that even democratically elected representatives could be moved by the rapacious human nature that Mill attributed to all men, he asked, "Is it not clear that the representatives, as soon as they are elected, are an aristocracy, with an interest opposed to the interest of the community?" Macaulay concluded that an absolute identity of interest could not be achieved.

Having questioned James Mill's remedy for rapacious rulers, Macaulay turned to his image of the populace in order to question Mill's assumption that the preferences of a majority necessarily coincided with the universal interest. Macaulay pointed out, again on Mill's assumption regarding human nature, that the majority might well have preferences that involved a sacrifice of the interests of succeeding generations. He also conjured up the familiar image of plunder by an enfranchised but poverty-stricken majority.[12] Persuaded that the populace might well be indifferent and even destructive to the permanent interests of society, John Mill now decided that "identity of interest between the governing body and the community at large is not . . . the only thing on which good government depends." Nor could identity of interests be achieved through "the mere conditions of election." [13]

Disillusioned with James Mill's image of the populace and his rationale for democratic institutions, John Mill found a substitute in St. Simonian writings, particularly in the elitism he found there. Since his father's democratic checks were no longer adequate, he was looking for some other device through which the universal interest could be ascertained and sought. Young Mill tried to satisfy both these requirements with the St. Simonian conception of an elite whose intellectual qualities provided assurance that the universal interest would be discovered and whose moral qualities guaranteed that no sinister interest would divert it from fulfilling its function. However, this cannot be

12. Macaulay, "Mill on Government," pp. 304, 306, 311–12.
13. *Auto.*, p. 134.

seen as a case of simple influence upon a *tabula rasa;* the ground had been prepared by Macaulay, and Mill read with questions in mind that made him especially sensitive to certain parts of St. Simonian writings and resistant to others. Thus he could say, "I had much changed from what I was, before I read any of their publications; but it was their works which gave order and system to the ideas which I had already imbibed from intercourse with others, and derived from my own reflections." [14]

John Mill discovered the possibility of adopting an elitist solution to the problems created by Macaulay's critique when reading one of Comte's early writings, in which there is an account of the natural succession of the theological, metaphysical, and positive stages through which knowledge progresses. Mill already looked upon the methods of physical science as the proper models for the study of politics.

> But one important point in the parallelism much insisted on by M. Comte, had not before occurred to me. In mathematics and physics what is called the liberty of conscience . . . is merely nominal . . . those who have studied the subject are all of the same opinion; . . . those who have not studied these sciences take their conclusions on trust from those who have, and the practical world goes on . . . applying . . . conclusions of reasoning which it receives on the faith not of its own reason but of the authority of the instructed. [15]

Mill now wondered why the same authority might not be established in morals and politics. Yet he had always "identified

14. Mill to d'Eichthal, Feb. 9, 1830, *EL*, p. 45; on his resistance to St. Simonianism, see *EL*, pp. 36–37, 47, 73, 109, 120; F. A. Hayek, "John Stuart Mill at the Age of Twenty-Five," pp. xviii–xxiii, in J. S. Mill, *The Spirit of the Age* (Univ. of Chicago Press, 1942). He also described himself "an Englishman, himself no St. Simonian, and agreeing with the St. Simonians though partially on almost all points, entirely perhaps on none": "Comparison of the Tendencies of French and English Intellect," *Mo. Rep.*, 7 (Nov. 1833), 800.

15. *Early Draft*, pp. 187–88 (rejected leaves). Comte's book presumably was *Système de Politique Positive*, vol. 1, part 1, *Plan des Travaux scientifiques nécessaires pour réorganiser la societé* (Paris, 1824).

deference to authority with mental slavery and the repression of individual thought." However, Mill now ceased to see this as a necessary obstacle, for he observed that this repression was used only in those cases in which "adherence is enforced to opinions from which . . . instructed persons dissent." When this condition did not prevail, "when all such [instructed] persons are as nearly unanimous, as they are in the more advanced of the physical Sciences, their authority will have an ascendancy which will be increased, not diminished, by the intellectual and scientific cultivation of the multitude, who, after learning all which their circumstances permit, can do nothing wiser than rely for all beyond on the knowledge of the more highly instructed." The consequence of this new understanding for his view of politics was immediately evident.

> I no longer believed that the fate of mankind depended on the possibility of making all of them competent judges of questions of government and legislation. From this time my hopes of improvement rested less on the reason of the multitude, than on the possibility of effecting such an improvement in the methods of political and social philosophy, as should enable all thinking and instructed persons who have no sinister interest to be so nearly of one mind on these subjects, as to carry the multitude with them by their united authority.

This view, Mill explained, "had been overlooked, or its importance not seen, by my first instructors." [16]

16. *Early Draft,* pp. 188–89. These views were expressed in *Spirit of the Age,* pp. 17–21, 24–31, passim. Cf. I. W. Mueller, *John Stuart Mill and French Thought* (Urbana, Univ. of Illinois Press, 1956), Chap. 3, where St. Simonian influence on Mill is considered without reference to the way Macaulay's critique and other experiences had made him vulnerable. Mill is seen as a passive agent who was shaped by exposure to various books (e.g. pp. 51, 57, 69), whereas actually his sensitivity to new ideas was limited and shaped by the particular problems and goals with which he was preoccupied at the time. Furthermore, "influences" were established only after he engaged in a silent debate that determined whether the new idea was to be rejected or combined with his previous position. See p. 96.

This outlook involved Mill in many deviations from orthodox Benthamism. Whereas his father had proposed making institutionalized distrust of any segment of the populace the basis of the constitution, John Mill now wanted to give a special status to one particular group. Rather than distrust the governing class, "the people, i.e., the uninstructed, shall entertain the same feelings of deference and submission to the authority of the instructed, in morals and politics, as they at present do in the physical sciences." [17] But it was not expected that this deference would be based on rational appreciation. Moral more than intellectual qualities were to give the elite the authority that would evoke deference from the populace. The elite was to have "a *pouvoir spirituel* capable of commanding the faith of the majority, who must and do believe on authority." [18] Not only would this have amended James Mill's psychology but it was incompatible with the Benthamite axiom that each man is the best judge of his own interests. Finally, and most important, young Mill altered his judgment about organic reform. Since the people could not be trusted with a sovereign role in politics, he came to doubt the wisdom of those organic reforms that were meant to establish popular control of government. The ideal relation of ruler and ruled could not be achieved, he decided, merely by regulating the conditions of election.[19]

In their extreme form these new attitudes were only to be temporary; but they had the effect of removing John Mill from Benthamite political activities just as the Reform Bill agitation was being intensified. Since nonrational attitudes were to be as important as purely intellectual judgments, Mill thought it was "utterly hopeless and chimerical to suppose that the regeneration of mankind can ever be wrought by means of working on their

17. Mill to Gustave d'Eichthal, Nov. 7, 1829, *EL*, p. 40.
18. Mill to G. d'Eichthal, Feb. 9, 1830, *EL*, p. 48.
19. Mill also said "it was partly by [St. Simonian] writings that my eyes were opened to the very limited and temporary value of the old political economy": *Auto.*, p. 141. Thus in 1833 he wrote of the *laissez faire* system, "that principle like other negative ones has work to do yet, work, namely, of a destroying kind . . . peace be with its ashes when it does expire, for I doubt much if it will reach the resurrection." Mill to Carlyle, April 11—12, 1833, *EL*, p. 152.

opinions." [20] With this attitude to public opinion and education generally, it is not surprising that during this period he "wrote very little, and nothing regularly, for publication." He dropped out of the London Debating Society in 1829, explaining that he had "a great dislike of controversy, and am persuaded that discussion, *as* discussion, seldom did any good. . . . I object to placing myself in the situation of an advocate, for or against a cause." [21] He also asked "whether our 'march of intellect' be not rather a march towards doing without intellect." [22] When he did write on domestic politics, he revealed his disagreements with orthodox Benthamite radicalism. When Place and others were urging the electorate to demand pledges of support for reform from candidates, Mill was opposed on the ground that, if leadership is to be with "the wisest and best men in the nation . . . why set the smaller wisdom to instruct the greater." [23] He also stood aside when his father and all his friends eagerly took part in the extraparliamentary politics that accompanied the passing of the Reform Bill; but he was "often surprised how little I really care about them. The time is not yet come when a calm and impartial person can intermeddle with advantage in the questions and contests of the day." Apart from infrequent

20. Mill to G. d'Eichthal, Feb. 9, 1830, *EL,* p. 47. "An opinion suggests hardly anything to an uninformed mind. . . . Words, or anything which can be stated in words, benefit none but those minds to whom the words suggest an ample store of correct and clear ideas, and sound and accurate knowledge previously acquired concerning the things which are meant by the words. It is therefore of little use altering men's opinions": Mill to G. d'Eichthal, Nov. 7, 1829, *EL,* p. 42.

21. *Auto.,* pp. 112, 132; Mill to d'Eichthal, Feb. 9, 1830, *EL,* pp. 45–46. Cole recorded his fear that the London Debating Society was "in a bad way, doubtless owing to the secession of Mill and his friends" (entry of Feb. 19, 1830); and that when Goldsmid introduced the question, "that the Utilitarian system of philosophy is pernicious and absurd," there was no debate, but only "a satyrical reply from C. Buller he being the only disciple of that system present" (entry of Jan. 8, 1830); however, a year later Mill appeared again to speak on the French Revolution (entry of Feb. 18, 1831): Henry Cole's Diary, 1827–1834, Victoria and Albert Museum.

22. "On Genius," *Mo. Rep.,* 6 (Oct. 1832), 650.

23. "Pledges," *Examiner,* July 1, 1832, p. 417; [F. Place], *On Pledges to be Given by Candidates* (London, 1832), pp. 1–8.

and unenthusiastic token support of his friends, he remained aloof from politics at a time when popular demand for an extended suffrage was becoming so intense that many aristocratic politicians were persuaded that some reform was necessary. Indeed, he scoffed at "Constitution-mongering" and confessed that he "ceased to feel interested in politics." [24]

JAMES MILL AND SAINT SIMON RECONCILED

John Mill's wish to gain "worldly power" for an intellectual elite was to remain a prominent feature of his political thought. Yet Philosophic Radicalism required a commitment to a program of democratic reform. How was he to reconcile his elitism with a program of democratic controls so as to take his place as a Philosophic Radical?

Within a few years after his initial rejection of democratic reform he began struggling with this problem.

> The grand difficulty in politics will for a long time be, how best to conciliate the two great elements on which good government depends; to combine the greatest amount of the advantage derived from the independent judgment of a specially instructed few, with the greatest degree of the security for rectitude of purpose derived from rendering those few responsible to the Many.[25]

Mill was disposed to find a reconciliation, and by 1835 (at the latest), after three to four years when he could no longer accept the Benthamite rationale for democracy, he tentatively was able to outline the way he would reconcile that rationale with the claim for educated leadership that he derived from Comte and the other St. Simonians. (This had permanent significance, for

24. Mill to Sterling, Oct. 20–22, 1831; Mill to Carlyle, March 9, 1833: *EL*, pp. 78, 145. His token support included attendance at the organizational meeting of the Parliamentary Candidates Society, March 14, 1831, and a contribution of £1; another contribution of £1 to the National Political Union; and a newspaper article recommending several friends as parliamentary candidates: Place to Bentham, March 18, 1831, UCL, Bentham Papers; BM, Place Collection of Newscuttings, Set 63, *1*, f. 276; *Examiner*, Sept. 2, 1832, p. 569.

25. "Rationale of Representation," *Lond. Rev., 1* (July 1835), 348.

a search for the means of reconciling democracy with enlightened leadership remained a feature of his political reflections, and the solution he outlined at this time, though altered in details, was used in his *Representative Government* [1861].)

In 1835, under the stimulation of two books—Samuel Bailey's *The Rationale of Political Representation* and the first part of Tocqueville's *Democracy in America*—he began to formulate a solution, and he undertook the task believing that "what was good in the influences of aristocracy, is compatible if we really wish to find it so, with a well-regulated democracy." [26] Mill's attempt at reconciliation incorporated both the democratic checks on government that made up the Radical program and the St. Simonian insistence that government be of the wisest and therefore by the Few. He tried to visualize a system in which the people would "choose for their rulers the most instructed and the ablest persons who can be found, and having done so, [would proceed] to allow them to exercise their knowledge and ability for the good of the people freely, or with the least possible control—as long as it *is* the good of the people, and not some private end, that they are aiming at." At the same time, control would be necessary: "in no government will the interests of the people be the object, except where the people are able to dismiss their rulers as soon as the devotion of those rulers to the interests of the people becomes questionable." This would be "true" or "rational democracy," for the people themselves do not govern, but they have security for good government. "A democracy thus administered, would unite all the good qualities ever possessed by any government . . . the omnipotence of the majority would be exercised through the agency and at the discretion of an enlightened minority, accountable to the majority in the last resort." [27]

The reconciliation was not based on a mechanical combination of two goals. In order for Mill to visualize a political order

---

26. "De Tocqueville on Democracy in America," *Lond. Rev., 2* (Oct. 1835), 91. Also see "Blakey's History of Moral Science," *Mo. Rep., 7* (Oct. 1833), 669, for an earlier indication of the disposition to see reconciliation as easily accessible.

27. "De Tocqueville," pp. 109–11.

with all the democratic checks, yet ruled by an intellectual aristocracy, he had to persuade himself that it was at least possible that the multitude would defer to the enlightened minority. This did not mean that such deference would necessarily exist, but it did require that he see it as something that could exist, not accidentally, but normally.

The reconciliation, then, was based on the assumption that the populace normally would acknowledge that legislation was "a profession: the study and the occupation of a laborious life," just as it acknowledged the professional status of a physician:

> The parallel holds exactly between the legislator and the physician. The people themselves, whether in the high or the low classes, are, or might be, sufficiently qualified to judge, by the evidence which might be brought before them, of the merits of different physicians, whether for the body politic or natural; but it is utterly impossible that they should be competent judges of different modes of treatment. They can tell that they are ill; and that is as much as can be rationally expected from them. Intellects specially educated for the task are necessary to discover and apply the remedy. . . . the principle that electors are to judge of men, and representatives of measures (as a king or a minister appoints a general, but does not instruct him when and how to fight) is of the very essence of a representative government.[28]

The analogy allowed Mill to provide for enlightened leadership, yet without denying the people a political role. This arrangement would "not render the control of the people nugatory. The

28. "Rationale of Representation," pp. 360, 365–66. Mill gave the following example: "Many of the truths of politics (in political economy for instance) are the result of a concatenation of propositions, the very first steps of which no one who has not gone through a course of study is prepared to concede. . . . How will philosophers bring these home to the perceptions of the multitude? Can they enable common sense to judge of science, or inexperience of experience? . . . The multitude will never believe these truths, until tendered to them from an authority in which they have as unlimited confidence as they have in the unanimous voice of astronomers on a question of astronomy": "De Tocqueville," p. 111, n.

control of a government over the commander of its army is not nugatory. A man's control over his physician is not nugatory, although he does not direct his physician what medicine to administer. He either obeys the prescription of his physician, or, if dissatisfied with him, takes another. In that consists his security. In that consists also the people's security." [29]

This view of the people's role allowed Mill to maintain a measure of his earlier skepticism about the capabilities of the populace. He no longer held that the populace must show "deference and submission"; now they could judge "the evidence . . . of the merits" of rival political doctors, a role that required only modest capabilities.

> It is not necessary that the Many should themselves be perfectly wise; it is sufficient, if they be duly sensible of the value of superior wisdom. It is sufficient if they be aware, that the majority of political questions turn upon considerations of which they, and all persons not trained for the purpose, must necessarily be very imperfect judges; and that their judgment must in general be exercised rather upon the characters and talents of the persons whom they appoint to decide these questions for them, than upon the questions themselves. They would then select as their representatives those whom the general voice of the instructed pointed out as the *most* instructed; and would retain them, so long as no symptom was manifested in their conduct of being under the influence of interests or of feelings at variance with the public welfare.

This involved only "very ordinary wisdom." [30]

Could such ordinary wisdom be found under conditions of

---

29. Ibid., p. 110.

30. "Rationale of Representation," pp. 348–49. Cf. Joseph A. Schumpeter, *Capitalism, Socialism, and Democracy* (2d ed. New York, Harper, 1947), Chaps. 21, 22. Although they reject the classical theory of democracy for different reasons, there are similarities in Mill's and Schumpeter's alternatives, especially in their emphasis on the choice and acceptance of leadership as the main role of the populace.

universal suffrage? Whether the people would play their proper role—judging politicians as they did doctors—was the crucial point which would "constitute, in reality, the test whether a people be ripe for the sound exercise of the power of complete control over their governors, or not." [31] In practice, then, it depended on the particular nation at a particular time. However, as a theoretical question he unequivocally subscribed to universal suffrage. His theoretical position was based on orthodox Benthamism. "A governing class not accountable to the people are sure, in the main, to sacrifice the people to the pursuit of separate interests and inclinations of their own." [32] This, of course, is the result of the operation of sinister interests. The remedy is equally orthodox: "Not only must the interest of the representatives be made, so far as possible, coincident with that of the electors, but the interest of the electors must be made coincident with the interest of the whole people," a principle, as Mill points out, that leads to universal suffrage.[33]

Mill was uncertain and therefore hesitant when it came to judging whether England in 1835 was ready for universal suffrage, but he avoided identifying himself with a variety of arguments against it. Various authorities, he pointed out, held that the electorate might be restricted to a portion of the whole people whose interest could be assumed to be identical with that of the whole; but he denied that such an electorate would always provide security against abuse. Nor did Mill accept Bailey's suggestion that a property qualification be used as an approximate test of that minimum level of intelligence required for the suffrage: "If the bulk of our operative manufacturers are to be excluded from the suffrage, it must be, we suspect, on quite other grounds than inferiority of intelligence to those who are permitted to exercise it." Mill described but did not endorse tests that might be used *if* the real object was the exclusion of those disqualified by ignorance or vice. For example, inability

31. "Rationale of Representation," pp. 349, 365.
32. "De Tocqueville," p. 110. Also (p. 116): "The only steadiness which aristocracy *never* fails to manifest, is tenacity in clinging to its own privileges."
33. "Rationale of Representation," p. 352.

to read, write, and cipher, or having been seen drunk during the previous year, might serve as indications of ignorance or vice, instead of poverty "which is a mere presumption of their existence." Mill then turned to another argument that might be used to disqualify the unpropertied classes, but again, without endorsing it. Instead of trying to show their inferiority in intelligence, their disqualification might possibly be founded "on difference in apparent interest." Here he had in mind "mischievous opinions and feelings" that undermine the foundations of the social order. Mill put this as the most rational argument against universal suffrage. As an abstract argument, he did not subscribe to it; but he did think it relevant as "a question not of argument, but of fact; and as such we think the question of universal suffrage ought always to be considered." When he made his own assessment of the facts, he admitted uncertainty. When he examined other persons' fearful assessments he found them "vastly exaggerated," and he believed that "almost all persons of what are called the educated classes, if they have any opinion on the point, have it without evidence." [34]

Even though Mill avoided endorsing any of these arguments against universal suffrage, his hesitation is evident. All his statements on the practicality of universal suffrage for the English were either conditional or equivocal. Thus it is not surprising that he closed the discussion with the statement (one senses the relief he seems to have felt), "Happily there is no necessity for a speedy decision of the question." Although it was theoretically possible, in view of the circumstances of 1835, he was not con-

---

34. Ibid., pp. 352, 354–57. That Mill was not seriously concerned about opinions incompatible with the social order is clear in his statement, "we can anticipate nothing in the present age but good, from the severest, from even the most hostile scrutiny of the first principles of the social union. . . . our fear is lest (the old creeds . . . having become obsolete) the fabric should mechanically hold together by . . . personal interests, without any basis of moral conviction at all. Rather than see this we should prefer to see the whole of the working classes speculatively Owenites or Saint Simonians. We have no fear that [anti-property doctrines] should ever prevail so extensively as to be dangerous": "The Monster Trial," *Mo. Rep.*, 9 (June 1835), 394 (quoting his own article in *Examiner*, Jan. 26, 1834, pp. 56–57).

vinced that universal suffrage and mass deference to the enlightened Few could be made to co-exist.[35]

This uncertainty (which has a bearing only on Mill's practical judgment of immediate circumstances) is especially evident in the article reviewing Bailey's *Rationale of Political Representation*. By the time he wrote his first review of Tocqueville—a few months later—his doubts had greatly diminished. Whereas he had been assuming that democratic institutions discouraged the development of government by the enlightened Few, he now claimed that these two variables were unconnected. Since the cause of this shift is not revealed in the review or in his correspondence, it is tempting to speculate about Tocqueville's influence. Tocqueville began with the assumption that the growth of democracy was inevitable; in his view, all events conspired to promote the development of equality, and from this came the predominance of the majority in government and extraparliamentary spheres alike. However, this did not allow Tocqueville to predict the kind of regime that would prevail in the future—whether democracy would be combined with liberty or tyranny. If liberty rather than tyranny was to be combined with democracy, certain social conditions would have to exist (such as secondary powers, decentralization, widespread religious belief) —conditions which conceivably could, but would not inevitably, coexist with democracy.

Mill's problem was different, but he appears to have used Tocqueville's approach as a model. Indeed, Mill seems to have adopted the structure, but not the content, of Tocqueville's argument. Unlike Tocqueville, Mill was not at this time primarily concerned with liberty. But like Tocqueville, he was concerned to combine democracy with another value, in his case, rule by an intellectual elite. He also thought democracy was inevitable; thus he spoke of a "moral revolution" during which

35. "Rationale of Representation," p. 357. For additional evidence of this uncertainty also see p. 347: "expediency may require that we . . . content ourselves with a somewhat less approximation to [identity of interest] than might possibly be attainable, for the sake of some other ends." Also see "Writings of Junius Redivivus," *Mo., Rep.,* 7 (April 1833), 268.

"power has passed from the few into the hands of the many." And he also saw it as being either dangerous or benign, depending on whether or not it was combined with deference to the enlightened few.[36] Whereas previously he had thought that the existence of democracy might be incompatible with the other value that he hoped to actualize, now, following the pattern of Tocqueville's argument, Mill held that rule by the enlightened few depended on conditions that existed independently of democracy itself. Thus the capacity of the people to choose the wisest among them and the willingness to submit to their rule, which made the "difference between the true and the false idea of a representative democracy," depended on the level of civilization, i.e. on the moral, educational, and cultural qualities of the people (and, of course, their leaders). Therefore, "it is not possible that the constitution of democracy itself should provide adequate security for its being understood and administered in this spirit [of true democracy], and not according to the erroneous notion of democracy. This rests with the good sense of the people themselves." Far from assuming that deference to the enlightened Few could not be found in democracy, Mill said "it would be difficult for democracy to exhibit less of this willingness than has been shown by the English aristocracy in all periods of their history, or less than is shown by them at this moment."[37]

Now (after the Tocqueville article) that he had persuaded himself that the people could select and defer to an elite even in

36. "Notes on the Newspapers," *Mo. Rep., 8* (March 1834), 164.
37. "De Tocqueville," pp. 109–11, 117. Also, see "Armand Carrel," *LWR, 28* (Oct. 1837), 80–81. In adopting the structure of Tocqueville's argument Mill was in part rejecting its substance. Tocqueville held that the people in a democracy are unlikely to select the wisest among them as leaders. But Mill disagreed: that was a "false idea of democracy propagated by its enemies, and by some of its injudicious friends," and he announced that "this source of evil tells for very little with us in the comparison between democracy and aristocracy" (pp. 112–17). Also see *DD, 2,* 32–36. Cf. Mueller, *Mill and French Thought,* p. 144, where it is stated that at this time Mill still had "illusions" about democracy and that he believed "talent was unnecessary in a democratic government."

a democracy, he reasserted his hostility to aristocracy with renewed vigor. Indeed, Mill decided that if any political order
discouraged rule by an intellectual elite, it was an aristocracy.
On this question his St. Simonian doctrines and his father's
teaching combined to persuade him that the aristocratic ethos
was hostile to the emergence of an intellectual elite. It would
discourage intellectuals and it would corrupt the tastes of the
masses, thus preventing the development of attitudes of deference to an intellectual elite. James Mill consistently complained
that the circumstances of an aristocracy prevented them from
encouraging intellectual preeminence:

> What motive have they to cultivate intellectual virtues?
> Their business is pleasure. Distinction is created for them.
> . . . Not acquiring the intellectual virtues it is their interest
> to profess contempt for them, and to the utmost of their
> power to prevent the esteem of them from rising in the
> community. . . . The effect of this is very great in keeping
> down the value of intellectual acquirements in the nation
> —lessening the motive to the acquisition of them, and
> diminishing the number of those who reach them; for this
> class have the power of setting the fashion, and their
> example forms the general taste.[38]

John Mill expressed identical sentiments before his recon-
sideration of his father's doctrines, and the same attitude survived
his adoption of St. Simonian ideas, though the language was
altered. Under St. Simonian influence, he saw his own time as a
transitional period during which the aristocracy still enjoyed
political power, though they ceased to possess that virtue and
intelligence that could give "moral ascendancy" and gain the
confidence of the populace. He complained that they lacked
talent and that they were "enervated by lazy enjoyment." Their
"power and fitness for power have altogether ceased to correspond"; consequently, "they must . . . be divested of the
monopoly of worldly power" and so yield to the "most virtuous
and best-instructed of the nation." [39] With this view of the

38. James Mill, "Aristocracy," *Lond. Rev.*, 2 (Jan. 1836), 286.
39. *Spirit of the Age*, pp. 44, 90–91, 93. Also see "Civilization," *LWR*,
25 (April 1836), 10, 12–13; "Democracy in America" (1840), *DD*, 2,

aristocracy's influence, instead of having democratic reform wait for intellectual improvement of the public, Mill wondered "whether the people are likely ever to be made better, morally or intellectually, without a *previous* change in the government." [40] And with regard to the need to encourage intellectual attainments, he argued that it was a recommendation for democracy, since it was the kind of polity that would "put an end to every kind of unearned distinction, and let the only road open to honour and ascendancy be that of personal qualities." [41]

Mill wrestled with the problem of reconciling the claims of democracy and an intellectual aristocracy many times throughout his career. However, for the present he had accommodated them. It is remarkable that, after having rejected much of his intellectual inheritance, he was able to recover so much of it and that he could combine it with his newly acquired beliefs. On the other hand, it also would have been remarkable if, after the education he had received, his early intellectual attachments could have been completely severed. The result was intellectual struggle, of which he was aware. (There also was emotional struggle, both while learning and while rejecting what he had learned, which is not surprising in view of the fact that his teacher also was his father.)

---

17. Mill admitted that "some aristocracies" were exceptions, most notably "the government of Prussia—a most powerfully and skilfully organized aristocracy of all the most highly educated men in the kingdom." The British government in India, Mill added, "partakes (with considerable modifications) of the same character." Prussia was exceptional in another way; since "The popularity of government [was] almost a necessary condition of its security, a very considerable degree of good government has occasionally been produced, even without any express accountability to the people." But Prussia was no precedent for Mill; "Such fortunate circumstances, however, are seldom to be reckoned upon": "Rationale of Representation," p. 348.

40. "The French Revolution," *Mo. Rev., 7* (Aug. 1833), 515. "Power, and whatever confers power, have been in all ages the great objects of the admiration of mankind . . . and according as that is obtained by rank, the favourable sentiments of mankind will attach themselves, and their ambition will be directed to one or another of these attributes": "Writings of Junius Redivivus," ibid., p. 267.

41. "Civilization," *LWR, 25,* 28.

I found the fabric of my old and taught opinions giving way
in many fresh places, and I never allowed it to fall to
pieces, but was incessantly occupied in weaving it anew:
I never, in the course of my transition, suffered myself to
remain confused and unsettled. When I had taken in any
new idea I could not rest till I had adjusted its relation to
all my old opinions.[42]

This process of weaving and adjusting allowed him to hang on to
much of his father's position, even after he conceded the correctness of arguments that challenged it. His newly acquired beliefs
were placed "in some new light by which they were reconciled
with, and served to confirm even while they modified, the truths
. . . contained in my early opinions and in no essential part of
which I at any time wavered. All my thinking only rendered the
foundation of these deeper and stronger." [43]

RADICALISM REAFFIRMED

After a few years (c. 1829–33) of hostility to Benthamism
and withdrawal from political propagandizing on its behalf, John
Mill resumed his old role as spokesman for Radicalism as a
political program. At least some of his former opinions had been
retained, even during the period of rebellion; but his initial
rejection of his father's *Essay on Government* as a complete
political philosophy prevented him from voicing with confidence
or vigor even that part of the old creed that he had retained;
and of course there were parts that he had ceased to believe in.
However, once he accommodated, at the theoretical level, his

42. *Early Draft,* p. 133. Mill also (p. 35) described himself as having
"a mind which was always pressing forward, equally ready to learn and
to unlearn either from its own thoughts or from those of others."

43. Ibid., p. 140. Mill also described how "an individual mind, when,
after having been taught to think . . . by teachers of some particular
school, and having for a time exercised the power only in the path
shown to it by its first teachers, it begins, without abandoning that, to
tread also in other paths; learns to see with its naked eyes, and not
through the eye-glasses of its teachers." He was discussing the change in
French national intellect "from the stage of adolescence to that of
early maturity," but was clearly drawing a parallel that was autobio-
graphical: "Armand Carrel," *LWR, 28* (Oct. 1837), 79.

old creed and the new ideas, he could again join the other Philosophic Radicals in energetically promoting their shared goals as party politicians. An extended suffrage, shorter parliaments, and the ballot, which, during his few years of extreme reaction he thought of as "mere conditions of election," he now advocated even more ardently than the other Philosophic Radicals. Of course, with his new ideas, he was more sensitive than his father had been to the problem of combining enlightened leadership with popular democracy; and he now held that the identity of interest between rulers and ruled was only one of the ingredients of good government. But for Mill these were additional, not contradictory, concerns; the new and the old could be made compatible by enlarging the scope of the philosophic foundations.[44]

Once again Mill used the Philosophic Radicals' rationale for democratic reforms. Repeating the argument of his father's article "Government," Mill asserted that there is a "need of popular representation, because, without it, those who wielded the powers of government would oppress the rest." This he called a fundamental truth, which he now (1835) defended against Macaulay's attack of 1829. He quoted and endorsed the replies to Macaulay that had recently appeared—Bailey's and his father's (in the *Fragment on Mackintosh*). In addition, using language quite close to James Mill's, he defended his father's position as one of prudence and common sense.[45] Furthermore, Mill once more adopted language and arguments that sounded like a Philosophic Radical's. He opposed "the sordid sinister interests," especially the aristocracy and the House of Lords.[46] Whereas he had op-

---

44. *Early Draft*, p. 140. However, see A. Seth Pringle-Pattison, *The Philosophical Radicals and Other Essays* (Edinburgh, 1907), p. 31: "His method of incessantly weaving the new into the fabric of the old . . . made . . . a thorough revision impossible. The old groundwork remained, and the new elements appeared as incongruous patches."

45. "Rationale of Representation," pp. 343–47. He also referred to his father as authority against the victims of his reviews: "Blakey's History of Moral Science," *Mo. Rep., 7*, (Oct. 1833), 664; "Professor Sedgwick's Discourse—State of Philosophy in England," *Lond. Rev., 1* (April 1835), p. 109 n.; also see pp. 117–18, 120–21, 132–33.

46. "Postscript. The Close of the Session." *Lond. Rev., 2* (Oct. 1835), 271–72, 277; "De Tocqueville," p. 116.

posed the "pledgemania" of the other Radicals in 1832, on the
ground that the exaction of pledges was an obstacle to the realization of a political system in which the electorate would defer to
an intellectually superior elite, now in 1835 he reverted to the
orthodox Radical position that justified pledges as a means of
achieving a degree of popular control of a representative.[47] Also,
after having ridiculed the "march of intellect" in 1831, Mill
again became an advocate of popular education, and he even had
a kind word to say for the Society for the Diffusion of Useful
Knowledge.[48] And he again defended, as his father and Grote
had done, the doctrine of universal interest against "the master
fallacy of all, the theory of *class-representation*." [49] Thus Mill
could say of this period:

> change in the premises of my political philosophy did not
> alter my practical political creed as to the requirements of
> my own time and country. I was as much as ever a Radical
> and Democrat for Europe, and especially for England. I
> thought the predominance of the aristocratic classes, the
> noble and the rich, in the English Constitution, an evil
> worth any struggle to get rid of.[50]

In keeping with this statement, Mill saw himself as having no
less than the other Philosophic Radicals an obligation to enter
the political arena. Since he was excluded from a parliamentary
career by reason of his appointment with the East India Company, he elevated and perhaps exaggerated the potential political
significance of journalism. Excluded from the world of action, a
man can turn to words, for "words are deeds, and the cause of
deeds." Mill thought that "journalism is to modern Europe what
political oratory was to Athens and Rome, and that, to become
what it ought, it should be wielded by the same sort of men." [51]

47. Mill to Carlyle, Sept. 17, 1832, *EL,* p. 121; "Rationale of Representation," pp. 364–66; *Early Draft,* p. 144.
48. "Civilization," *LWR, 25* (April 1836), 20.
49. "Rationale of Representation," pp. 368–69.
50. *Auto.,* p. 145.
51. "Armand Carrel," *LWR, 28* (Oct. 1837), 69.

The great instrument of journalism was the periodical press. This made it necessary to give up the ambition to write few but great books for posterity; "but *frequent* writers are those who do good in their generation." Furthermore, it was the peculiar mission of the age to popularize and, given the circumstances of the time, "the staple of all popular writing . . . must be politics." [52] Mill wrote enviously of France where the situation allowed journalists to play this role. "There the editors of daily journals, any one of whom may be considered as individually the head, or at lowest the right hand, of a political party." There was, for example, Armand Carrel, who "made himself, without a seat in the legislature or any public station beyond the editorship of his journal, the most powerful political leader of his age and country." In England, unfortunately, "no journalist, however popular, is esteemed anything higher than the powerful and formidable but rather dangerous and disagreeable *sting in its* [a political party's] *tail*." Mill looked for a continuation of the "moral revolution" in England which would "exalt public writers to a station and consequence proportioned to their real power." [53] Mill saw himself as playing the political role created by this revolution, and he did it on behalf of the Philosophic Radicals in Parliament.

To this end Mill, in cooperation with his father and Molesworth, set up a new quarterly journal in 1835 (initially the *London Review* and, after a merger of the two in 1836, the *London and Westminster*). It was to be "a periodical organ of philosophic radicalism, to take the place which the Westminster Review had been intended to fill." One of its principal purposes

> was to stir up the educated Radicals, in and out of Parliament, to exertion, and induce them to make themselves, what I thought by using the proper means they might become—a powerful party capable of taking the government

52. "Writings of Junius Redivivus," *Mo. Rep., 7* (April 1833), 266.
53. "Fonblanque's England Under Seven Administrations," *LWR, 27* (April 1837), 98; "Letter from an Englishman to a Frenchman, on a Recent Apology in 'The Journal des Debats,' for the Faults of the English National Character," *Mo. Rep., 8* (June 1834), 393–94. Also, see "Notes on the Newspapers," ibid., March, p. 172.

of the country, or at least of dictating the terms on which they should share it with the Whigs.[54]

Mill was the real though not the nominal editor, and after Molesworth withdrew in 1837 he became the proprietor as well. He solicited contributions from the Philosophic Radicals, and Buller, Molesworth, and his father were among the frequent contributors.[55] Mill's wish to change the Radicals' reputation for narrowness led him to invoke some of the ideas to which he had been exposed during his rebellion against Benthamism, and this sometimes angered and even estranged the other Philosophic Radicals. Even in these circumstances Mill directed the political article, which was a regular feature in the *Review,* to a consideration of their parliamentary position. When he disagreed with them it was on a question of tactics. He correctly assumed that they shared his political goals.[56]

THE OLD AND THE NEW PHILOSOPHIC RADICALISM

Although Mill once more felt able to cooperate with the Philosophic Radicals, his period of doubt was to leave some traces. As a result, he was different from typical members of the group such as Grote or Molesworth. He saw politics in terms of fundamental needs. There was the need to prevent the control of government by sinister interests, which the other Philosophic Radicals took into account; there also was the need for enlightened leadership, something they had neglected.

The problem of systematically providing for both these needs became, in his mind, the main task of political theory. Accordingly, both these needs were incorporated into Mill's reconciliation of the claims of St. Simonism and Benthamism. Initial efforts at formulating the problem in this way appeared in his writings during the mid-thirties, but his better-known articles on

54. *Auto.,* pp. 168, 181. Also (p. 184), he ended his connection with the *Review* only "after the last hope of the formation of a Radical party had disappeared."

55. He began with promises of support from his father, Grote, John Austin, Bailey, Thomas Love Peacock, W. J. Fox, Buller, Roebuck, and Strutt, among others: *EL,* p. 246.

56. *Auto.,* p. 181.

Bentham (1838) and Coleridge (1840) best exemplify this view. Mill saw the two articles as complementing each other. Each took into account one of the fundamental needs: "each would find, or show the way to finding, much of what the other missed." [57]

Bentham's theory of government, according to Mill, was not so much wrong as incomplete. There were three great questions in government, and they all concerned authority. Bentham seriously considered only one of them: "By what means are the abuses of this authority to be checked?" To this question Bentham gave "the only answer it admits of"; indeed, "there must, we know, be some paramount power in society; and that the majority should be that power, is on the whole right, not as being just in itself, but as being less unjust than any other footing on which the matter can be placed." Thus Mill admitted the necessity for universal suffrage, but he was dissatisfied with Bentham's provision for enlightened leadership. He complained that Bentham "exhausted all the resources of ingenuity in devising means for riveting the yoke of public opinion closer and closer round the necks of all public functionaries, and excluding every possibility of the exercise of the slightest or most temporary influence either by a minority, or by the functionary's own notion of right." At this point the other two questions become important: "To what authority is it for the good of the people that they should be subject?"; and, "How are they to be induced to obey that authority?" Mill believed that answers to these two questions could have provided for enlightened leadership without sacrificing democratic control. If a theory of government answered all three questions, then one could see that "the power of the majority is salutary . . . as it is used defensively, not offensively—as its exertion is tempered by respect for the personality of the individual, and deference to superiority of cultivated intelligence." [58]

In Coleridge, Mill found a philosopher with an answer to the

57. "Coleridge" (1840), *DD, 1,* 395. That both articles were the result of reflection and long preparation, see Mill to Tait, Nov. 20, 1837; Mill to Sterling, Sept. 28, Nov. 4, 1839: *EL,* pp. 358, 405–06, 411.
58. "Bentham" (1838), *DD, 1,* 376–77, 380–81.

question about the authority to which people ought to submit. Coleridge provided for a class that enjoyed superiority of cultivated intelligence, the clerisy, as he called it. Mill saw it as an "organized body, set apart and endowed for the cultivation and diffusion of knowledge," and he emphasized that, despite the religious affiliation that it had in Coleridge's thinking, it performed the functions of an intellectual elite.

> The *clerisy* [according to Coleridge, as quoted by Mill] of the nation, or national church in its primary acceptation and original intention, comprehended the learned of all denominations, the sages and professors of the law and jurisprudence, of medicine and physiology, of music, of military and civic architecture, with the mathematical as the common organ of the preceding; in short, all the so-called liberal arts and sciences, the possession and application of which constitute the civilization of a country, as well as the theological.[59]

In addition, Mill found in Coleridge an answer to the other (and related) question that Bentham had neglected: how are the people to be induced to obey that authority? Deference to the superiority of cultivated intelligence was required, but the rationalism and prudent mistrust that Bentham and James Mill incorporated into their psychology prevented them from looking favorably on deference to an elite. Coleridge felt no such qualms. Not only did he assume that the pervasive authority of the clerisy would be accepted throughout society but he (and the "Germano-Coleridgian school" generally) had a philosophy of human culture and of history that allowed one to visualize the

59. "Coleridge," pp. 439–40. The passage continues: "The [theological] was, indeed, placed at the head of all; and of good right did it claim the precedence. But why? Because under the name of theology or divinity were contained . . . logic, ethics, and the determination of ethical science, in application to the rights and duties of men in all their various relations, social and civil; and lastly, the ground-knowledge, the *prima scientia*, as it was named—philosophy, or the doctrine and discipline of ideas"; Mill was quoting *On the Constitution of Church and State According to the Idea of Each,* ed. H. N. Coleridge (London, 1839), pp. 49–50.

evolution of a society in which a clerisy would achieve a position of authority that was freely deferred to by the populace.[60] Therefore, on Coleridge's assumptions, Mill was able to visualize the development of a society in which such deference to a clerisy existed, thus allowing a numerical majority to exercise its influence "defensively, not offensively." [61] On this hinged his distinction between "the true and the false idea of a representative democracy." [62]

These views are similar to those Mill developed a few years earlier (in the articles of 1835 on Bailey and Tocqueville). Actually, Coleridge's ideas had been influencing Mill since 1829, and they undoubtedly affected his accommodation of democratic and elitist views in 1835. But since at that time he was still using the language of the St. Simonians, Coleridge's contribution to his thought was obscured. Therefore, the formulation of his

60. "Coleridge," pp. 425, 427.
61. "Bentham," p. 381.
62. "De Tocqueville," *Lond. Rev.,* 2 (July 1835), 109–10. Far from fundamentally altering these views, the last half of Tocqueville's *Democracy* (Books 2, 3, 4), which appeared in 1840, at most reinforced them. Mill absorbed what supported his position and rejected what did not. Since he wished to provide for a clerisy in a democratic society, he firmly rejected Tocqueville's identification of democracy as the cause of all the social, moral, intellectual characteristics that were incompatible with deference to a clerisy. Tocqueville has "confounded the effects of Democracy with the effects of Civilization," and by this Mill meant "commercial civilization." This and its agents, "the American Many, and our middle class, [who] agree in being commercial classes,"—here was the difficulty. But this was not a necessary part of democracy, as commercial England demonstrated. On the other hand, where Tocqueville supports Mill on the need for protection of the individuality of those, including a "learned class," who give diversity to society, then Mill adopts Tocqueville's views: "Democracy in America" (1840), *DD,* 2, 39–42, 62–77. Thus Mill saw this article as "a sort of completion and winding up of . . . my present opinions and modes of thinking": Mill to Napier, Sept. 5, 1840, *EL,* p. 443. Cf. Mueller, *Mill and French Thought,* pp. 144, 162, 168, where Tocqueville's influence is exaggerated; also cf. Michael Packe, *The Life of John Stuart Mill* (London, Secker and Warburg, 1954), pp. 199–204, where Tocqueville's influence is discussed without reference to that concern with the clerisy in relation to democracy which shaped Mill's receptiveness to Tocqueville.

views, in the article on Coleridge, on the way enlightened leadership can be combined with democracy, represents a new stage in the development of his rhetoric rather than a markedly new development in his opinions.[63]

Mill did not look to Coleridge as a source of a philosophy while demoting Bentham to the realm of practice. Both were philosophers, but with incomplete philosophies. The problem was to combine them. "Whoever could master the premises and combine the methods of both, would possess the entire English philosophy of his age." This might appear to be difficult, even impossible, since Bentham was the Radical, the subversive, whereas Coleridge was acknowledged to be a Conservative. But for Mill "these two sorts of men, who seem to be, and believe themselves to be, enemies, are in reality allies. The powers they wield are opposite poles of one great force of progression. . . . Each ought to hail with rejoicing the advent of the other." Since Coleridge provided answers to questions that were necessary to complete the political philosophy that was to serve as a foundation to Mill's vision of the future, Mill decided that Coleridge was in effect a Radical: "Reformers ought to hail the man as a brother Reformer." [64]

Mill had no difficulty in finding defects in Coleridge's philosophy, just as he had in Bentham's: Coleridge's epistemology and his views on the landed interest and on political economy were unacceptable. Like Bentham, he had discovered part of the truth.[65] Mill took it upon himself to gather different truths from rival philosophies. Since he now felt that truth was "many-

63. Already in 1834 Mill had said, "Few persons have exercised more influence over my thoughts and character than Coleridge has; not much by personal knowledge of him, though I have seen and conversed with him several times, but by his works, and by the fact that several persons with whom I have been very intimate were completely trained in his school": Mill to Nichol, April 15, 1834, *EL*, p. 221.

64. "Coleridge," pp. 397, 437; also see pp. 396, 442, 444, 448.

65. Mill to Sterling, Oct. 2, 1839, *EL*, pp. 408–09; "Coleridge," p. 409, where he rejects "the central idea" of Coleridge's philosophy on empiricist grounds; p. 452, "In political economy especially he writes like an arrant driveller." Also (p. 449), "Coleridge's theory is but a mere commencement, not amounting to the first lines of a political philosophy."

sided," he became an admirer of eclecticism. "Substituting one fragment of the truth for another is not what is wanted, but combining them together so as to obtain as large a portion as possible of the whole." This he called "practical eclecticism." [66] In this spirit he could be understanding of, and on some occasions sympathetic with, the Puseyites and Carlyle as well as Coleridge and the St. Simonians. Mill felt that he was "under a special obligation to preach . . . the meaning and necessity of a catholic spirit in philosophy," and his articles on Bentham and Coleridge represent the outline of the task as he then saw it. Neither Bentham nor Coleridge comprehended all the positions that had to be taken into account, but they epitomized the two main points of view, one representing the eighteenth century and the other the nineteenth, and Mill wanted to synthesize these antithetical positions.[67] Mill saw himself as above the battle: "I never joined in the reaction against [the 18th century], but kept as firm hold of one side of the truth as I took of the other." He sought to reconcile the two outlooks.[68] Such a synthesis would have allowed him to go on being a Radical in politics while holding views the other Philosophic Radicals would not endorse, and it also allowed him to see Coleridge as an intellectual source of his radicalism. Thus it was consistent for him to look on this

66. *Auto.,* p. 136; Mill to d'Eichthal, Oct. 8, Nov. 7, 1829, *EL,* pp. 38, 42. "I applied to . . . Coleridge himself, many of Coleridge's sayings about half-truths": *Auto.,* p. 138.

67. Mill to Sterling, Nov. 4, 1839, *EL,* p. 411; "Coleridge," p. 403. His father was "the last of the eighteenth century": *Auto.,* p. 173. Referring to Bible Societies, Tract Societies, Puseyism, Socialism, Chartism, and Benthamism, though they all were deficient, "doubtless they have all some elements of truth and good in them": Mill to R. B. Fox, Dec. 19, 1842, *EL,* pp. 563–64. On the Oxford School, see *EL,* pp. 415–16. Mill's intention in the *Logic* was "to harmonize the true portions of discordant theories" (Preface to 1st ed. [1843]): *A System of Logic* (10th ed. London, 1879), *1,* v.

68. *Auto.,* p. 138; glossing over the brief but extreme reaction against Benthamism and his father's *Essay on Government,* Mill (in the sentence quoted) acknowledged that, "at one period in my progress, I for some time undervalued that great century." Also see the excellent introduction by Gertrude Himmelfarb in Mill, *Essays on Politics and Culture* (New York, Doubleday, 1962), pp. xi, xiii, xix.

synthesis as a "scheme of conciliation between the old and the new 'philosophic radicalism.' " [69]

In contrast to the "new" Philosophic Radicalism, which sought to be broadly based on a philosophic consideration of all the functions that a political system was to perform, Mill thought the "old" Philosophic Radicals were narrow. The philosophic basis of their Radicalism took into account only one of the basic functions of a political system; they acknowledged part of the truth. It was not that they were wrong, but they were only half-right, and therefore narrow. They saw *"clearly"* what they did see, though it was but little." Being narrow, he saw them as incomplete, as "half-men," though he made exceptions, as in the case of William Johnson Fox, who was "not a half-man, but three quarters of a man at least." T. P. Thompson, on the other hand, had "an understanding like a pin, going very far into a thing, but never covering a larger portion of it than the area of a pin's point." However, they were less narrow than other professed philosophers, and decidedly less so than their elders among the utilitarians. Furthermore, there were signs of improvement.[70] But the narrowness of the other Philosophic

69. *Auto.*, p. 170. Mill saw Tocqueville as playing a similar role in France, where "an 'eclectic philosophy' was formed. There was reaction against the irreligion of Diderot and d'Holbach . . . [and] against the conclusions of the political philosophy of the Constituent Assembly. . . . Thus arose the new political philosophy of the present generation. . . . [D]ifferent minds, according to their capacities or their tendencies, have struck out or appropriated to themselves different portions of it, which as yet have only been partially harmonised and fitted into one another. . . . the book, which up to the present time embodies the largest portion of the spirit [of it, is] . . . *Democracy in America*": "Carrel," *LWR, 28* (Oct. 1837), 80–81.

70. Mill to Carlyle, Oct. 22, 1832, *EL,* pp. 126–28. Grote "is a Utilitarian; in one sense I am so too, but *he* is so in rather a narrow sense. . . . with much logical and but little aesthetic culture; *narrow* therefore": Mill to Carlyle, Aug. 2, 1833, *EL,* p. 170. Molesworth "is genuine, and *is perfectly* the thing he is; complete within his limited sphere. . . . a natural tendency to be intolerant, because unappreciative of ideas and persons, unlike him and his ideas . . . I have been just like him myself": Mill to R. B. Fox, Dec. 23, 1840, *EL,* p. 453. "One-sided men commonly enforce their partial views with a vehemence and an air of strong conviction which persons of more comprehensive minds are often without, being unable to

Radicals was not an obstacle to Mill's acting with them. When he did this, he recognized that he was attempting to satisfy only part of the comprehensive doctrine that synthesized Coleridge (and all he stood for) with Bentham. Thus he said of them that he thought "sufficiently well to be able to cooperate with them in their own field of usefulness, though perhaps they would not always join me in mine." [71]

This situation was bound to lead to misunderstandings. Acting as a spokesman for two intellectual traditions, one of them shared by the Philosophic Radicals and the other quite antithetical, Mill found it difficult to avoid annoying his old associates. They could not but be aware that his strictures on narrowness and sectarianism were directed at them. They could also read Mill's articles on Tocqueville, Bailey, Bentham, and Coleridge and, despite his endorsement in these articles of the Philosophic Radical program, he attracted their opposition. Roebuck protested against Mill's belief "in the advantages to be derived from an Aristocracy of intellect." Opposed to that kind of aristocracy as to any other, Roebuck said he was "not terrified by the so-much-dreaded fickleness and vagaries of the People; nor are my suspicions to be lulled asleep by ingenious plans for giving intellect her dominance." [72] By 1837 Mrs. Grote "felt quite persuaded the Review will cease to be the engine of propagating sound and sane doctrines on Ethics and politics under J.M."; and, disappointed with Mill's alterations of an article her husband contributed to the *Review,* she complained of "that wayward intellectual deity John Mill." [73] Place also abused him. Soon after the article

---

throw their whole Souls into a part only of the Truth": "Writings of Junius Redivivus," *Mo. Rep.,* 7 (April 1833), 265. See also *Auto.,* p. 138. This also affected his attitude to political economy and its doctrines: see p. 84 n. 19.

71. Mill to Carlyle, Sept. 17, 1832, *EL,* p. 117.

72. Roebuck, "Democracy in America," *Pamph. P* [no. 20, Oct. 22, 1835], pp. 3–4. Roebuck in part misunderstood Mill's position; cf. Mill, "Rationale of Representation," *Lond. Rev., 1* (July 1835), 364–66.

73. Mrs. Grote to Roebuck, April 1837, Alexander Bain, *John Stuart Mill. A Criticism: With Personal Recollections* (London, 1882), p. 57 n.; Mrs. Grote to Place, Aug. 16, 1837, Add. MSS 35,150, f. 279. Bowring

"Bentham" appeared, he expressed the view "that [since] John
Mill has made great progress in becoming a German Metaphysical Mystic, excentricity [*sic*] and absurdity must occasionally be
the result." [74] However, these acrimonious comments, like most
of Mill's about them, did not prevent cooperation. In a few cases,
such as Roebuck's, there was estrangement as a result of Mill's
being offended by unsolicited and unwelcome advice about his
relationship with Mrs. Taylor. Yet even this did not prevent a
degree of alliance for, as Mill explained, his differences with
Roebuck "became so strongly pronounced that we ceased to be
allies either in opinion or in action except as to the immediate
objects of radicalism." [75]

(in 1840) "spoke of Mill with evident contempt as a renegade from philosophy, Anglicè—a renouncer of Bentham's creed and an expounder of
Coleridge's. . . . Mill's newly-developed 'Imagination' puzzles him not a
little": Caroline Fox, *Memories of Old Friends,* ed. H. N. Pym (3d ed.
London, 1882), *1,* 216.

74. Place to Falconer, Sept. 2, 1838, Add. MSS 35,151, f. 86. Buller
was an exception: "I have read your article on Bentham, which is ad-
mirable. I agree in your new Conservatism": Buller to Mill, Oct. 13, 1838;
Report of the Public Archives [of Canada] *for the Year 1928* (Ottawa,
1929), p. 76. The article on Bentham had appeared in August. Mill later
wrote, "the substance of this criticism I still think just, but I have much
doubted since whether it was right to publish it. I have often felt that
Bentham's philosophy as an instrument of progress has been in a great
measure discredited before it had half done its work"; regarding the
Coleridge article, "here I erred by giving undue prominence to the favourable side, as I had done in the case of Bentham to the unfavourable. In
both cases, the impetus . . . carried me too far to the opposite side":
Early Draft, p. 166.

75. Ibid., p. 127; Packe, *Mill,* pp. 153, 221; F. A. Hayek, *John Stuart
Mill and Harriet Taylor* (London, Routledge, 1951), pp. 89–90; Borchard,
Mill, Chap. 7. Mill attributed their falling out to a disagreement about the
comparative merits of Wordsworth and Byron in the London Debating
Society (Jan. 16, 30, 1829). Roebuck, after reading this account in Mill's
Autobiography, denied it: "something far more potent was required to
break up so old and warm a friendship. That potent influence was found
in a Woman": "Notes," f. 9, in collection of James M. Osborn, Yale
Univ.; *Auto.,* pp. 127–28; Roebuck contributed three articles to Mill's
Review, and his *Pamphlets for the People,* regularly received advertising
from it, published extracts (including one full article) from it, and in one
issue, after criticizing Mill's review of Tocqueville, commended the *Review*

Despite his reputation as a mystic, however, Mill was usually clear in his own mind about how he stood with regard to the "old" Philosophic Radicalism. There were moods when he disassociated himself from it, most notably in 1838 during the course of a private correspondence with Fonblanque, who, while criticizing Mill's political writings and the Radicals' parliamentary conduct, had assumed that both were part of the same target. To Fonblanque, who mainly saw the side of Mill that remained radical and democratic, this must have seemed reasonable, even obvious. But Mill was keenly aware of his recently acquired beliefs which, though accommodated to the old Philosophic Radicalism, also separated him from its other spokesmen. Thus he could with sincerity say, "my radicalism is of a school the most remote from theirs, at all points, which exists." [76] However, in the very letter where this statement appears, he gives evidence of his continued identification with the Philosophic Radicals by discussing the tactics they ought to adopt and by upholding their parliamentary position, deviating from this only to criticize them for being too timid, i.e. for not being more vigorous in their pursuit of Philosophic Radical goals.[77] The few statements in which he completely disassociated himself from the Philosophic Radicals were made at moments of marked frustration.[78] More representative was the statement, written about the same time, in which he endorsed the goals of what

---

for its "general tendency . . . [and] most of the leading doctrines"; all contributors share "a common purpose, and agree in the general principles of their moral and political system": Roebuck, "Democracy in America"; "The London Review and the Irish Church Question," *Pamph. P* [no. 20, Oct. 22, 1835], pp. 1–4, 7. Cf. F. E. Hyde, "Utility and Radicalism, 1825–1837; A note on the Mill-Roebuck Friendship," *Economic History Review, 16* (1946), 40–44.

76. Mill to Fonblanque, Jan. 30, 1838, *EL,* pp. 370–71; also see letters of Feb. 3, 6, 7, 1838, *EL,* pp. 373, 375, 376–77.

77. *EL,* pp. 371, 374, 377. Also see Mill to Fonblanque, n.d. [Feb. 1836], *EL,* p. 297. Furthermore, since during the previous year Mill had approvingly identified Fonblanque's opinions as "those of the philosophic radicals," perhaps it is understandable that Fonblanque assumed the label could be attached to Mill himself: *LWR, 27* (April 1837), 67.

78. See pp. 222–25.

Fonblanque called the "Grote conclave," not as the expression of a complete philosophy but as "one portion of important truth."

> It is very conceivable that such a doctrine [as Bentham's] should find acceptance from some of the noblest spirits, in a time of reaction against the aristocratic governments of modern Europe. . . . European reformers have been accustomed to see the numerical majority everywhere unjustly depressed. . . . To see these things, and to seek to put an end to them, by means (among other things) of giving more political power to the majority, constitutes Radicalism; and it is because so many in this age have felt this wish, and have felt that the realization of it was an object worthy of men's devoting their lives to it, that such a theory as Bentham's has found power with them.[79]

Mill leaves no doubt where he stands in relation to this movement, for he describes Bentham as one "who, in the classification which may be made of all writers into Progressive and Conservative, belongs to the same division with ourselves." [80]

Mill played two philosophic roles. Sometimes he preferred the role of Coleridgian philosopher who was broadly concerned with human culture and, within the context it provided, with "moral regeneration" as the most appropriate means for the improvement of mankind. On other occasions he gave greater prominence to a more narrowly conceived philosophic role; then he emphasized change in political institutions, instead of moral regeneration, as the means of improving mankind. In this role, as an "old" Philosophic Radical, he sought to be spokesman and intellectual guide for the parliamentary Radicals. From about 1833 he played both roles, but on some occasions one of them

79. "Bentham," DD, 1, 378–79. Also, "that small . . . glorious minority . . . The conduct of Mr. Grote, Mr. Warburton, and Mr. Hume will live in history. . . . [also] Sir William Molesworth and Mr. Leader": Mill, "Lord Durham and the Canadians," LWR, 28 (Jan. 1838), 532.

80. DD, 1, 331. Yet the following prophecy has been fulfilled: "It is my opinion that one hundred years hence Mr. Mill will be exhumed as a Conservative authority": Captain Maxse, R.N., The Causes of Social Revolt (London, 1872), p. 55, n.

would be given greater prominence while the other was pushed into the background of his thinking. Indeed, sometimes they were put into what seemed to be separate compartments of his mind; but neither one was allowed to disappear entirely. The role of Coleridgian-like philosopher was given special prominence from about 1829 to 1833 and again in the years immediately after 1840 when he was discouraged about the effectiveness of political means to human improvement. At such times progress was to be achieved by the discovery of new principles that were to be incorporated into the body politic only at some opportune period in the future. (Book VI of the *Logic* [1843] and *Principles of Political Economy* [1848] were to serve this purpose.[81]) Philosophy was to forge ahead and then wait for social evolution to catch up. "Originality in science, in theology, and even in political philosophy," Mill explained, "appreciable at first only by schools and sects of men, waits for justice till the school or the sect becomes, in numbers and intelligence, co-extensive with society at large." [82] However, during the years 1833–40, when the opportunity for reform through change in

81. "It is becoming more and more clearly evident to me that the mental regeneration of Europe must precede its social regeneration": Mill to R. B. Fox, Dec. 19, 1842, *EL*, p. 563. The *Logic* occupied him at various times throughout the thirties, but mainly when he was out of heart about politics. It is noteworthy that it was begun in 1830 and speedily brought to completion after 1839. Book VI was to determine whether moral and social phenomena could be made subject to scientific laws that could then be used to form a new "body of received doctrine" that would replace the old creeds that had decayed: *System of Logic, 1,* viii; also see Book VI, chap. 1, 3–6.

82. "On the Life, Character, and Works of Dr. Priestley," *Mo. Rep., 7* (Jan. 1833), 20. Also, "such men as Priestley or Bentham must wait the revolutions of opinion, and the regeneration of social institutions." At these times Mill also emphasized the importance of a philosophy of history. Since it allowed him to project into the future the actualization of values that were not easily harmonized with other desiderata, it allowed him to avoid acknowledging commitments to irreconcilable positions. Cf. his observations on the relation of political theory and the philosophy of history in the middle of the decade (*Lond. Rev., 1* [April 1835], 106) and at the beginning and end (*Examiner,* Feb. 5, 1832, p. 84; *Auto.,* p. 137, dealing with period 1829–30; *DD, 1,* 425 [1840]). Also see Packe, *Mill,* pp. 90–91.

political institutions seemed favorable, his Coleridgian role was allowed to recede somewhat while, without ceasing to be a philosopher, he was mainly concerned with practical politics.

Mill at this period presents a somewhat strange case of someone who shared opinions and cooperated with a group of men with whom he was associated in the public mind but for whom he had little personal sympathy. In contrast to them, he felt a strong affinity with others who took next to no part in his journalistic and political enterprises and whose opinions had little direct bearing on immediate political problems. Mill sought in Coleridge, Carlyle, Sterling, the St. Simonians, Comte, and Tocqueville, different as they were from one another, a model for the ideas he admired most, and he felt with them an affinity of spirit that was lacking in his relations with the Philosophic Radicals with whom he shared opinions that were oriented to political action.

4. Into Parliament

The appearance of several Philosophic Radicals in the House of Commons where they tried to establish a new parliamentary party was a new development in the history of Benthamism. Bentham, had he lived a couple of years longer, would have been struck by the novelty for, although he had hoped that his views would spread, he had mainly looked for influence from key administrators such as James Mill in the East India Company or Chadwick on the Poor Law Board. There had been, it is true, individual spokesmen in Parliament for particular Benthamite proposals. Romilly, Burdett, Ricardo, Brougham, and O'Connell had played this role. But they always acted independently, never as spokesmen for a parliamentary party nor even for a small faction; and their Benthamism often involved law reform. Now, however, in the first parliament following the Reform Act, Benthamite ranks swelled and became more systematic and more purposeful. And even though the Philosophic Radicals put most of their energies into the advocacy of a doctrine that was elaborated from only a part of Bentham's system, they were responsible for the first significant extension of the Benthamite movement into parliamentary politics.

The emergence of this parliamentary coterie was accompanied by another development. The apprenticeship of John Mill's circle of friends was ended, and they now came fully into view on the political stage. Old Bentham died at eighty-four with the passing of the Reform Bill, and James Mill, during the three years that were left to him, often was occupied with Indian affairs. His senior position at India House and the loss of rapport with his son, brought on by young Mill's flirtation with St. Simonian doctrines as well as the relationship with Mrs. Taylor, removed him from the coterie atmosphere in which the Philosophic Radicals carried on their deliberations. Without being estranged from them, James Mill now was on the periphery. A new generation had taken over.

Popular excitement about reform, which had been generated by the fifteen-month agitation for the Reform Bill, was responsible for the electoral success enjoyed by the Philosophic Radicals. The agitation had concealed the differences between Whigs and Benthamite Radicals; both were reformers and received the benefits of popular approval for the Reform Bill. This carried over to the elections in December 1832 and allowed many Radicals to gain access to the House of Commons. The electorate, even though only a minority of it was voting for the first time, often did not distinguish between Whig reformer and Radical reformer, with the result that Benthamites won elections with Whig support, a favor they did not often enjoy at subsequent elections. Roebuck admitted this; "the public," he said, "were very peculiarly situated as regarded the candidates. . . . They were guided in their choice chiefly by the fact of the candidates having opposed or supported the Reform Bill." [1]

Without this development in public feeling, it is uncertain that the Radicals, in some cases, would have been able to begin parliamentary careers in 1833. They would have been unwilling to enter Parliament with the aid of a patron—to become what Roebuck called the "intellectual condottieri [sic]" of the great Whig families.[2] Nor were many of them able or willing to purchase seats, though James Mill had encouraged Ricardo to do this, and it had Bentham's approval as well.[3] A few of them would have had their seats in any case—Buller's family's interest in Cornwall had brought him into Parliament in 1830, and in 1832 he was unopposed, as was Molesworth, a new recruit to the movement, whose property in Cornwall also contributed to his success. In other cases it was the pro-Reform sentiment that still prevailed late in 1832 that brought electoral victory. Only this can explain Grote's unprecedented poll of 8,412 votes in the City of London; and it also contributed to Roebuck's victory at Bath.[4]

1. "Extracts from the Diary of an M.P.," *Tait's Edinburgh Magazine, 2* (July 1833), 415.
2. *History of the Whig Ministry of 1830* (London, 1852), *1,* 205, n. 1.
3. James Mill to Ricardo, Dec. 16, 1816, *Works of Ricardo, 7,* 110; Bentham, *Plan of Parliamentary Reform* (1817), p. 170 (Preface).
4. Place (who was not a candidate) claimed that he had three invita-

In all there were at least fifty Radicals in the new Parliament
(and some estimates went up to 120).[5] Of these, there were a
dozen or so who had been associated with the London Debating
Society and the Mills; these include Buller, Grote, Roebuck,
John Romilly, Edward Romilly, Edward Strutt, and William
Ewart. In addition, there were Charles Villiers and John Leader
(who did not enter Parliament until 1835), and Molesworth,
who was introduced into the Philosophic Radical circle in 1832.
Already antiauthoritarian, religiously skeptical, and resentful toward the aristocracy, he found among his new associates "intellectual example and corroboration" for his radical tendencies,
and he was soon at home in the Philosophic Radical world.[6] This

---

tions to stand: *A Letter to the Electors of Westminster, from Francis
Place* (London, 1832), p. 4. Bowring was an unsuccessful candidate in
1832 (losing by 13 votes), but he was elected in 1835: C. R. Dod, *Electoral Facts, from 1832 to 1852* (London, 1852). Place was the organizer
of the Parliamentary Candidate Society in 1831, which was intended to
promote parliamentary careers for reformers. Among the candidates promoted by the Society were Place, John Mill, James Mill, Tooke, J.
Romilly, E. Strutt, Warburton, W. Coulson, S. Bailey, T. P. Thompson,
Hume, Grote, R. Doane, Southwood Smith, Chadwick: *Spectator*, March
13, 22, 1831.

5. Edward Lytton Bulwer said there were 50 at most: *England and the
English* (4th ed. London, 1836 [1st ed. 1833]), *2*, 261; John Wade said
there were at least 120: "Character and Composition of the First Reformed Parliament," *The Black Book* (London, 1835), Chap. 7, Appx.
According to *The Companion to the Newspaper*, Jan. 1, 1834 (no. 13), pp.
194–95, there were above 400 ministerial members, 150 Tories, and under
100 of those who "in the French Chamber would be called the Coté
Gauche, including Radicals, Ultra-Liberals, Independents, Irish Repealers,
etc." J. S. Buckingham, classifying members into Receders (Conservatives),
Halters (Whigs), and Advancers (Liberals), lists 97 Liberals: *Parliamentary Review, 1* (1833), 30–35.

6. In conversation with Mrs. Grote (1840) Molesworth traced his
political views to many sources—education, travel, a sense of injury
arising from rejection of a love suit by "certain members of the aristocratic class" and "a hatred of all constituted authorities," which he considered the result of "the unkind conduct" of his father and his expulsion
from Cambridge (for challenging his tutor to duel with pistols), all of
which were integrated and justified by the principles to which he was
exposed in the Mill circle: Harriet Grote, *The Philosophical Radicals of*

core of their parliamentary faction joined Joseph Hume and Henry Warburton, both old associates of Bentham, James Mill, and Ricardo. Together they formed a group which, though small, when reinforced by the journalism of John Mill, Molesworth, and Roebuck, and initially by Fonblanque as well, achieved prominence for representing an ideological position that appeared threatening and therefore important.

Apart from the Philosophic Radicals, other Radicals also achieved electoral success by virtue of the new enthusiasm for reformers. The only cohesive group was the Irish under O'Connell's leadership, and their radicalism originated in their opposition to the subjugation of Ireland, combined with a determination to have a block of dissident votes with which to bargain for concessions. Otherwise the Radical camp was in disarray. Although they all shared a common label, their aims were quite different, in some cases irreconcilably so. The heterogeneous Radical group as a whole neither acted nor voted together. For example, when Attwood brought in his motion on the currency and economic distress, the Philosophic Radicals, strongly opposed to his economic policy, deserted him to vote with the ministerial majority.[7] When Roebuck spoke on behalf of state support for a scheme of national education, Cobbett attacked his views in a way that clearly revealed the deep division between the different themes of the radical tradition that each represented. Cobbett's romantic vision of a nation unadulterated by any kind of modernism included little sympathy for universal education. He argued that "within the last thirty-five years . . . education had increased twenty-fold; but experience showed, that the morals of the people had not mended with the increase of education." [8] The same kind of division among the Radicals occurred on the Poor Law which was introduced by the Whig government. This measure was given strong support by the Philosophic Radicals,

---

1832, Comprising the Life of Sir William Molesworth and Some Incidents Connected with the Reform Movement from 1832 to 1842 (London, 1866), pp. 5–6, 51–53.

7. *Hansard, 17,* 586; also see *21,* 1013; and J. S. Mill, "The Currency Juggle," *Tait's Edinburgh Magazine, 2* (Jan. 1833), 461–67.

8. *Hansard, 24,* 131.

but several other Radicals, most notably Cobbett and Attwood, along with some Tories, opposed the bill.

This assortment of Radicals—Bulwer described them as "a motley confused, jarring miscellany of irreconcilable theorists" —most of them new Members and some of them from new constituencies created by the Reform Bill, had neither the organization needed to act as a party nor the traditions that might have helped them to cooperate.[9] Consequently, Hume's attempt early in the session to give leadership to the Radical body as a whole was bound to fail. His first effort came when the government proposed that Manners Sutton, a Tory, should continue as Speaker, on the ground that his experience would be useful in managing a House that was expected to be unruly. Hume objected to a Tory Speaker for a House that professed to be overwhelmingly in favor of reform. He countered with an alternative, but when the House divided, he had the support of a mere thirty-one Members, including most of the Philosophic Radicals.[10] When O'Connell, during the debate on the Address, challenged the government's proposal for Ireland, Hume again tried to organize the Radicals in opposition. But he only alienated many Radicals, one of whom called him "a coxcomb whose vanity had led him to take the line he did in his speech." Denying that he approved of the violent O'Connell, "he looked anything rather that the leader of a successful party." He was "scarcely listened to," Le Marchant reports. "The yawns of Hume's friends immediately around him were involuntary but forcible testimonies of his failure." [11]

The absence of effective leadership and the deep divisions of opinion on important subjects were noticed by sympathizers and unfriendly observers alike. To the Radical editor John Wade they were "a disorganized mass," and he lamented their "having

9. *England and the English* (1833), *2*, 268. On lack of consultation among Radicals, see for example, Hume, *Hansard, 21* (Feb. 4, 1834), 61.

10. Ibid., *15* (Jan. 29, 1833), 44, 76. The radical *Examiner* attributed the size of the minority to Hume, saying that the Radicals "will not again be found in so small a minority for never was a question worse handled than that of the Speakership": *Examiner,* Feb. 3, 1833, p. 66.

11. A. Aspinall, "Le Marchant's Reports of Debates in the House of Commons, 1833," *English Historical Review, 58* (Jan. 1943), 91.

no leader in whose superior character and ability they can ac-
quiesce," and he called them "a body without a soul." [12] John
Mill was quite impatient:

> The Radical party . . . is a rope of sand. It is not only with-
> out a head, but without members or a body. It is *not* a
> party; [they] . . . seem incapable, not merely of organized,
> but even of casual cooperation. The evil consequences of
> this incapacity display themselves most of all, in the case
> of those who aspire to be, and in some measure deserve to
> be, distinguished as the instructed and philosophical Rad-
> icals; for *they* appear to be incapable, not only of acting in
> concert, but also of acting singly. . . . They will never be
> any thing but ciphers, till they are grouped together.[13]

Roebuck also complained that there were "no guides, no rulers,
no leaders are acknowledged. Every one sets up for himself."
Greville also remarked that there was "no *party* but that of the
Government; the Irish act as a body under O'Connell to the
number of about forty; the Radicals are scattered up and down
without a leader, numerous, restless, turbulent, and bold." [14]

Amidst this dissident and inharmonious group of Radicals, the
Philosophic Radicals, consisting of no more than twenty members, usually acted together. Grote came to be acknowledged as
their leader. Although at first they were not always recognized as
a separate group united by an ideology that distinguished them
from both other Radicals and liberal Whigs, they were aware of
their special intellectual heritage. Disdainful of Cobbett and
O'Connell, they sometimes struck others as men who "did not
very willingly associate with men of less philosophic princi-

12. Wade, *Black Book* (1835), pp. 57–58. Fonblanque, though he seems
to have contradicted Wade, made the same point: "in the Radical Party
there is this peculiarity that nearly all are leaders": *Examiner*, May 19,
1833, p. 316.

13. "Notes on the Newspapers," *Mo. Rep.*, 8 (March 1934), 173–74.

14. "Extracts from the Diary of an M.P.," *Tait's Edinburgh Magazine*,
3 (July 1833), 413. *The Greville Memoirs, 1814–1860,* eds. Lytton
Strachey and Roger Fulford (London, Macmillan, 1938), (Feb. 22, 1833),
2, 361. Also see J. S. Buckingham, *Parliamentary Review*, 2 (1833),
388–89.

ples." [15] Apart from Roebuck, who quickly acquired a reputation for ungenteel vituperativeness, their respectability also became evident, and they were seen as "the better class of the montagne." [16] It was only gradually that they came to be recognized as a discrete group with an ideology and party aspiration that distinguished them from most other politicians.

THE HOSTILE GESTURE

The vague but pervasive sentiment favorable to reform that put several of the Philosophic Radicals into the House of Commons also created an expectation that the cooperation between Radicals and Whigs, which helped make the agitation for the Reform Bill effective, would be continued. After the year and a half during which many Radicals, with James Mill's associates among the most important, adopted tactics that called for popular support of the Whig government, it was not surprising that many politicians looked for a continuation of the arrangement. This was encouraged by the tendency for both to adopt the label "Reformer"; as the painter Benjamin Haydon remarked (after many conversations with Whig politicians), "to be a Reformer now is the fashion." [17] Lord Durham classified politicians into two opposing parties, Reformers and Tories, thereby assuming that the parliamentary Radicals as a matter of course would align themselves with the Whigs in opposition to the Tories (who now renamed themselves Conservatives).[18] Lord Holland, making the same assumption, gleefully welcomed the election results with the observation that in the Commons "we shall be stronger than ever." [19] In addition, there were pressures from the Radical

15. Henry Reeve, "Personal Memoir of Mr. Grote," *Edin. Rev., 138* (July 1873), 229. Reeve said their group in Parliament "never exceeded fifteen or twenty members" and that they "all regarded Mr. Grote as their chief."

16. "Le Marchant's Reports," p. 93.

17. R. B. Haydon, *Correspondence and Table-Talk,* ed. F. W. Haydon (London, 1876), *2* (Oct. 24, 1832), 351.

18. Durham to Ellice, Dec. 28, 1832, NLS, EP; also see *Examiner,* Dec. 16, 1832, pp. 802–03.

19. A. Aspinall, ed., *Three Early Nineteenth Century Diaries* (London, Williams and Norgate, 1952), p. 285, n. 4.

side in favor of continued support for the Whigs. T. P. Thompson, for example, the co-proprietor (with Bentham) of the *Westminster Review* (with which the Mills were unconnected), thought that "the Whigs should be honest, and the Radicals moderate," for, in addition to carrying the Reform Bill, "by their coalition . . . there is much future good, that will be prevented if they split." [20]

Although the cooperation in 1831–32 supported the expectation that a Whig–Radical alliance could be maintained, so far as the Philosophic Radicals were concerned, that expectation was unfounded. For one thing, James Mill, Place, Parkes, and their followers did not look on the Whigs as like-minded reformers but as men who made concessions of reform only from fear of a worse alternative. The Benthamites saw their own cooperation as a temporary arrangement required by immediate circumstances. Moreover, the Philosophic Radicals supported the Whig Ministry in 1831–32 in anticipation of the consequences of the Reform Bill, not from any great satisfaction with the provisions of the Bill itself or the principles on which it was founded. For them the required reforms were vote by ballot and a considerable extension of the suffrage so that at least all householders would be voters (ideally all adult males). They also looked for shorter parliaments, so that elections would be held at least every three years or, better still, every year. The Reform Bill ignored two of these three issues (ballot and duration of parliaments) and the enlargement of the electorate for which it provided was, from the Philosophic Radical point of view, minuscule.

Furthermore, the most important provisions of the Reform Bill had been especially condemned. The Bill provided for the disfranchisement of various small boroughs (Schedule A) and transferrence of those franchises to others, including larger boroughs and towns not previously represented (Schedule B). However, although James Mill was pleased with such concessions in 1831, on principle he had condemned this kind of change, on the ground that it "would detract nothing from the power of the

20. Thompson to Bowring, Dec. 13, 1831: L. G. Johnson, *General T. Perronet Thompson 1783–1869,* p. 178.

aristocracy, who would nominate just as many members after such a change, as before it." [21] In addition, the principles on which the Whigs based their measure were incompatible with the Philosophic Radical doctrine. Whereas the Whigs saw their Bill as restoring a balance between the varied interests that ideally ought to be represented in Parliament, the Philosophic Radicals saw all such interests as sinister. Grote, defending what in effect was a populist theory of representation, had already attacked the theory of varied interests as early as 1821. Nor could the Philosophic Radicals accept the Whig assumption that propertied interests were the foundation of representation. Macaulay had insisted that "the right of suffrage should depend on a pecuniary qualification" and defended the Reform Bill for extending the property base so that it was not confined only to those with landed property. But James Mill, in his essay *Government,* had denied the relevance of the pecuniary qualifications for the suffrage, and during the Reform Bill agitation he said property "should have nothing to do with representation" (adding, however, that this "is true, though not a truth for the present time").[22]

It was the expected consequences of the passing of the Reform Bill rather than its actual provisions that explains the Philosophic Radicals' strenuous efforts to bring success to the Whig Ministry. They thought agitation would extend the political awareness and thus the demands of the masses and that a political change would stimulate the appetite for still more. Thus James Mill held that even trivial change that did not alter the distribution of power still might *"indirectly* be of advantage: by leading the people to reflect more keenly upon the ends which are to be attained, and the means adapted to their attainment." Place held the same view. *"The Reform Bills are in themselves of little value,"* he

21. James Mill to Fonblanque, Oct. 25, 1831: BL, Mill-Taylor Collection, *49,* f. 2. James Mill, "Summary Review," *Parliamentary History and Review for 1826,* p. 783. Charles Buller also condemned this kind of change: *On the Necessity of a Radical Reform* (London, 1831), pp. 42–44.

22. Grote, *Statement,* pp. 46–58; T. B. Macaulay, *Speeches,* ed. G. M. Young (London, Oxford, 1952), pp. 4, 6, 80; James Mill, *Essay,* pp. 75–77; James Mill to Place, Oct. 25, 1831, Add. MSS 35,149, ff. 121–22.

said, "but as a commencement of the breaking up of the old rotten system they are invaluable." Thus he saw them as "a means
to an end," or, as Roebuck said, "as an installment of justice—
as . . . a stepping stone to further great improvements." Parkes
also saw the Reform Bill in this light: it was an "aristocratical"
measure, and thus "good for very little except as *precedents* of
change." [23]

Neither their evaluation of the Reform Bill nor their rationale
for supporting the Whig ministry in 1831–32 justified an expectation that the Philosophic Radicals would consider themselves
allies of the Whig party. Had the Whig leaders looked more
closely at the election campaign statements of Grote, Roebuck,
or Place, even though the language was softened, the fundamental differences would have been evident; and a recollection
of past pronouncements on the Whig party would have left no
doubt as to the Philosophic Radicals' basic hostility to the Whigs.

When the Philosophic Radicals entered the first Reformed
Parliament they expressed this long-standing doctrinal hostility
to the Whigs by taking seats on the opposition benches. Even
though they sometimes voted for ministerial measures, they sat
as opponents to the Whig government. This is revealed in the reports of debates; for example, Roebuck referred to "the noble
lord (Althorp) opposite." [24] Also, in the Hayter painting of the
first reformed Parliament the Philosophic Radicals, along with
several others, are pictured on the opposition benches.[25] In fact,

23. James Mill, "Summary Review," p. 783; Graham Wallas, *Life of
Francis Place* (London, Longmans, 1908), p. 326; Henry Jephson, *The
Platform* (London, 1892), *2*, 142; *Hansard, 36* (Jan. 31, 1837), 30;
Buckley, *Parkes*, p. 96; Parkes to Cobden, May 28, 1838, SRO, Cobden
Papers.

24. *Northcroft's Parliamentary Chronicle*, Feb. 14, 1833, p. 159; also
see *Hansard, 15* (Feb. 22, 1833), 1112; *16* (March 8, 1833), 490, where
Buller calls himself "a member of the minority"; *20* (July 26, 1833), 7; *21*
(March 4, 1834), 1104; *22* (March 13, 1834), 174–75; *24* (June 2, 1834),
19, where Hume referred to "the Conservatives sitting on his right." Also
see *Greville Memoirs, 2*, 354; John O'Connell, *Recollections and Experiences During a Parliamentary Career* (London, 1849), *1*, 5; *Annual Register* (1833), pp. 1–2; Wade, *Black Book* (1835), Chap. 7, Appx., pp. 57–58.

25. "Interior of the Old House of Commons in St. Stephen's Chapel at
Westminster during the moving of the Address to the Crown at the

there was a time when the Radicals appeared so prominently on the opposition benches that there were rumors of an organized coalition between Tories and Radicals. Of course, Peel rejected this suggestion, but there was a brief period when, because of the Radicals' presence, "Peel and others could hardly find places together"; when the Tories moved elsewhere the Radicals were left to "form the ostensible Opposition." [26]

Their taking this position was not only a consequence of hostility to the Whig party but was also an expression of the Radicals' entire ideology. Believing that aristocracy and the people were the only significant ingredients of the social structure, politics in their view could legitimately reflect only the conflict between these two interests. Since a Radical party could rightfully claim to represent the people, it was only natural that it would occupy one side of the House in opposition to an aristocratic party. The main obstacle to this, of course, had been the traditional antagonism between the two aristocratic factions that had monopolized parliamentary power. Now in 1833 the Philosophic Radicals hoped that the reform excitement would facilitate a realignment of parties so they would more accurately reflect the "reality" of social structure. "Like many other persons at the time," John Mill said, "I thought that we had had our revolution; that the way was now smooth for the advance of democracy." [27] Therefore, observing the divided, demoralized, and reduced size of the Tory party, the Philosophic Radicals thought its demise was at hand. Parkes said the elections in 1832 read "the funeral service over the Tories." [28] And John Mill said "the *present* Tory

---

Meeting of the First Reformed Parliament, 5th February 1833," painted by Sir George Hayter; in the National Portrait Gallery, London. See George Scharf, *Historical and Descriptive Catalogue of the Pictures, Busts, etc. in the National Portrait Gallery, Exhibition Road, South Kensington* (London, 1884), pp. 375–85; *A Descriptive Catalogue of the Historical Pictures of the First Reformed House of Commons . . . by Sir George Hayter* (London, 1843).

26. Thomas Raikes, *A Portion of a Journal* (London, 1858), *1*, 96–97; Charles Parker, ed., *Sir Robert Peel* (London, 1891–99), *2*, 212–13, 244, 247; Aspinall, ed., *Three Diaries*, pp. 296–97.

27. *Early Draft*, p. 144.

28. Aspinall, ed., *Three Diaries*, p. xxx, n. 5.

party is now utterly annihilated." The fact that the Whigs adopted the label "Reformers" did not deceive him. They were really aristocrats, and with the *present* Tory party eliminated, presumably the Whigs, in fact if not in name, were in future to play the role of the Tories. He saw signs of the merger of the two aristocratic factions in Wellington's willingness to sponsor the Reform Bill in May 1832; Wellington "found that if he meant to be a minister he must be a Whig"; the rest of the nominal Tories were either "in the main Whigs already" or "nothing at all." Thus Mill could believe that Whig–Radical antagonism could plausibly dominate the parliamentary stage: "There is now nothing definite and determinate in politics except radicalism; and we shall have nothing but radicals and Whigs for a long time to come." [29] Whig predominance in 1833 was seen as temporary, the result of their misrepresenting themselves as reformers. As the new session began, Grote confidently thought that although "the Whigs will have it all their own way for the present . . . their reign cannot be of long duration," for no party "can long maintain itself, resting neither upon the aristocracy nor upon the people." Fonblanque thought "the period of Radical ascendancy seems approaching with unexpected rapidity." And Roebuck felt that "the Radicals must be in power before three years are passed." [30]

That these expectations were held seriously may seem incongruous, in view of the fact that Whigs and Tories did not merge, but continued to oppose each other. However, during the early

29. Mill to Carlyle, May 29, 1832, *EL,* pp. 106–07. Fonblanque said, "on all other subjects [than the Corn Law], the contest will be solely between the stationary principle and the Progressive; between the spirit of Toryism, whether under its own or Whig colours, and the spirit of Reform": *Examiner,* Dec. 23, 1832, p. 817.

30. Grote to Parkes, Jan. 26, 1833, *Posthumous Papers,* p. 47; *Examiner,* May 19, 1833, p. 316; Roebuck, "Extracts from the Diary of an M.P.," *Tait's Edinburgh Magazine, 3* (Aug. 1833), 644. Roebuck asked his readers to consider what sort of Chancellor of the Exchequer Grote would make. *Tait's* reported that there was discussion of the possibility of a Radical government and mentioned the Philosophic Radicals as candidates for ministerial office: ibid., *4,* 133, 139. Greville reported the Radicals as being "confident and sanguine": *Memoirs, 2* (Feb. 22, 1833), 361.

1830s it was not entirely implausible for the Philosophic Radicals to believe that the aristocratic core of the Whig party would
shed the genuine though moderate reformers on its periphery
and combine with the Tories, making way for the emergence of
the Radicals as a major party. Although these expectations were
derived from Philosophic Radical doctrine, there also was evidence that supported their view. The Whigs were in fact divided.
In 1831 they were not uniformly enthusiastic about the Reform
Bill, and with the passing of the Bill the party attracted many
sincere and liberal reformers who were now grouped together
with men like Stanley, Graham, and even Melbourne, who
looked upon further reform with skepticism. The Cabinet reflected this mixture, and its cleavages were the subject of public
comment. The resignation in 1834 of Stanley and Graham encouraged the belief that the split was beginning, and the alliance
these ex-ministers formed with Peel was taken as a sign that the
Whig–Tory merger had begun. Furthermore, there was persistent talk of a Whig–Tory coalition to oppose the rising tide of
radicalism. This began during the Reform Bill crisis, and these
rumors were not without foundation. In 1833 O'Connell spoke
of "the long-rumoured coalition" of Whigs and Tories. In the
summer of 1834 the King proposed such a coalition to Peel.
Even after the dismissal of his government, Melbourne used Mrs.
Norton as a go-between to see if a coalition might be arranged
with moderate Tories. These events, and the rumors of them,
gave plausibility to the Philosophic Radicals' belief.[31]

Both Whig and Tory policy on organic reform seemed to confirm the belief that they might (and certainly ought to) merge
into a single aristocratic party in opposition to a Radical party
representing the people. Although the Whigs more than Tories
could justifiably claim to be reformers, they were as one in their
opposition to the fundamental constitutional reforms that were
crucial for the Philosophic Radicals. The official policy of the

31. Aspinall, ed. *Three Diaries,* p. xxx; "Le Marchant's Reports,"
English Historical Review, 58, (Jan. 1943), 80; Norman Gash, "Peel and
the Party System," *Transactions of the Royal Historical Society* (5th ser.),
1 (1951), 56; David Cecil, *Melbourne* (New York, Bobbs-Merrill, 1954),
p. 269.

Whig Cabinet, whatever the variety of opinions within, was opposed even to making an open question of organic reform proposals such as the ballot. When Russell opposed the ballot, speaking on Grote's motion in 1835, Peel warmly commended his position. Since the Philosophic Radicals thought of organic reform as the issue dividing the Radicals from the aristocratic parties, they could see in the united opposition to organic reform additional evidence of the underlying homogeneity of the aristocratic party. It seemed clear to the Philosophic Radicals that both parties were in agreement on questions of fundamental reform. There were even occasions when the Tories supported the Whig government if a Radical motion threatened it with defeat.[32]

MOBILIZING PUBLIC OPINION

The hopes entertained for the Radical party are revealed in the journalistic enterprises that were planned as the Reformed Parliament opened. The Philosophic Radicals had always wanted to control a daily newspaper as well as a quarterly review, for these were the normal organs of parliamentary parties. Their intense interest in journalism was also an outgrowth of their belief that fundamental changes in the social structure were taking place. These changes brought political awareness to more and more men and therefore made them not only capable of criticizing their society but expectant that it could be altered through the political process. "The multitude . . . are filled with a new spirit," Roebuck said; "their attention is intently directed towards the affairs of the state." Furthermore, the process was beyond human intervention. Francis Place saw the politicians "scoffing at the 'march of intellect' without being able to understand the great moral and intellectual changes which . . . are continually taking place," and he added, "what overjoys me is, that they cannot be stayed." [33] For John Mill, these changes were

32. Aspinall, ed., *Three Diaries*, p. xxxiv; *Hansard, 19*, 1150–54; *23*, 1085–86; *28*, 464–65.

33. Roebuck, *Hansard, 20* (July 30, 1833), 144–45; Place to Hobhouse, Dec. 19, 1827, Add. MSS 35,148, f. 5. Also, Mill: "We breathe an atmosphere of movement; and it is speeding us forward on our course. . . . the power, be it what it may, which sets itself against the spirit of the age, must fall": "The Close of the Session," *Mo. Rep., 8* (Aug. 1834), 608,

the result of the acceleration of a process that stretched from the invention of printing to the French Revolution.

> All political revolutions . . . originate in moral revolutions. The subversion of established institutions is merely one consequence of the previous subversion of established opinions. . . . The French Revolution . . . was a mere *incident* in a great change in man himself, in his belief, in his principles of conduct, and therefore in the outward arrangements of society; a change which is but half completed, and which is now in a state of more rapid progress here in England, than any where else." [34]

Because of these latent changes it was possible for newspapers to become influential, as Mill said, "much more by making themselves the organs of opinions already formed, than by influencing its formation." [35] The main purpose of their journalism, therefore, was to mobilize the sentiments of men and bring to the surface the latent political awareness. This was bound to promote radicalism for, as Parkes said, "Liberal opinions are gaining . . . as indeed must be the case with such a vast increase of locomotion and such a rapidly progressing diffusion of knowledge." From the diffusion of political information, he believed, "every ultimate public object will follow as a certain consequence." [36] Journalism, therefore, was to focus the attention of the populace

34. J. S. Mill, "French Revolution," *Mo. Rep., 7* (Aug. 1833), 513.

35. J. S. Mill, "Notes on the Newspapers," *Mo. Rep., 8* (March 1834), 172.

36. Parkes to Durham, Aug. 24, 1837, LP; Parkes to Place, Dec. 5, 1830, Add. MSS 35,148, f. 77. Roebuck: "so rapid a change in the feelings of a people, respecting any of their institutions, never took place, as that which has taken place with respect to the House of Lords . . . within the last five years": *Hansard, 34* (June 30, 1836), 1103. With this expectation of what the press could achieve, Roebuck, in any case irascible, became furious when he contemplated what the press actually did. This (among other reasons) was behind his frequent and strongly worded attacks on the press, which he called "corrupt, base, and cowardly" and guilty of "wholesale falsehood" and "thorough dishonesty." Individual editors were not spared, and twice he was challenged—by Sterling of the *Times* and Black of the *Morning Chronicle:* "The Stamped Press of London, and its Morality," *Pamph. P* [no. 3, June 25, 1835], pp. 4–6; "The London Review and the Periodical Press," ibid. [no. 22, Nov. 5, 1835], p. 8; *The History of the Times* (London, Times, 1935), *1*, 420–24.

on Radical objects and make sure there was no delay in making the Radical party the beneficiary of the underlying social
changes.

Before journalism could be used in this way it was necessary
to overcome the obstacle posed by the so-called "tax on knowledge." This was a four-penny tax on all newspapers, which increased the cost of most papers to seven pence—a prohibitive
price for large segments of the populace. As a consequence,
Radical papers like the *Examiner* and the *Spectator* were available only to the opulent classes and perhaps the better-off artisans (though these papers could be seen in reading rooms maintained by Mechanics Institutes and political clubs such as the
National Political Union). The law was evaded by some of the
Radical publishers who were militant advocates of working-class
consciousness and semi-socialist doctrines (e.g. Cleave, Hetherington, Watson). These men, and even more their news vendors,
were liable to heavy fines and imprisonment. Though willing to
violate and evade the law in certain ways, the Philosophic Radicals did not openly defy the authorities. Their policy was to agitate for repeal of the newspaper stamp tax.

The agitation, led by Place, began in 1832 with his tract on
behalf of repeal. The demand was carried into Parliament where
E. L. Bulwer, supported by the Philosophic Radicals, took the
initiative. It was assumed that the resistance to repeal was politically motivated, though the tax was defended on the ground that
it was an important source of revenue. "The progress of knowledge was feared by the English aristocracy"; [37] for, as Roebuck
said, the diffusion of political information through the press
would "teach the people to understand their rights, to stand up
for what they ought to demand, and to put down the aristocratical domination under which they had too long laboured." [38] This
logic led Place to say that if he were obliged to choose, he would
"greatly prefer the repeal . . . to the ballot, [for] a three halfpenny
daily newspaper would soon procure the ballot." [39] It was as-

37. Place, "The Taxes on Knowledge," in *Pamph. P* [no. 8, July 30,
1835], p. 3.
38. *Hansard, 34* (June 20, 1836), 654.
39. Place to Parkes, Jan. 27, 1837, Add. MSS 35,150, f. 233.

sumed that by diffusing correct information the populace could easily be made to play its part as an antiaristocratic base for a Radical party. As Place said, the working people "are the most teachable, the least swayed by sinister interests." [40]

After several efforts to gain repeal, there was partial success in 1836 when the tax was reduced to one penny—a development that led to the founding of a daily Radical paper, *The Constitutional*.[41] Before this, however, plans were made to convey information to the populace despite the law. "It is lamentable," Place said, that "there should be no remedy but by a constant violation of the law." [42] Late in 1832 plans were made to found the Society for the Diffusion of Moral and Political Knowledge, which was to publish a cheap magazine as well as tracts on which the newspaper tax was to be left unpaid. Roebuck, Place, Grote, and Warburton, with advice from James Mill, were the architects, though it was expected that articles would also be contributed by John Mill, Mrs. Grote, W. J. Fox, Charles Buller, Parkes, Fonblanque, Bowring, Bailey, Col. Thompson, and

40. Place, "Circular" (1836), Add. MSS 35,150, f. 173; also (f. 174), "Very few among [the working class] would entertain erroneous notions were both sides of every question fairly laid before them." They also wanted repeal in order to combat the false economic doctrines propagated by the militant working-class leaders who had adopted Owenite and Hodgskin's ideas. This was part of the process of educating the populace to the true principles of radicalism. It was assumed that it could be done without difficulty: "If there were no stamps on newspapers and I had only £150 a year . . . I would in no long time, teach the most intelligent and honest of the leaders of the working people . . . the true doctrine of wages and profit, and have them preaching this true and simple doctrine all over the country": Place to James Mill, Oct. 26, 1831, Add. MSS 35,149, f. 123. Also see James Mill to Brougham, Sept. 3, 1832, UCL, BrP.

41. See p. 167. The circulation of all newspapers increased as a result of the reduction, and several new liberal papers were founded, as well: Parkes to Ellice, Jan. 8, 1837, LP; Parkes to Brougham, Oct. 4, 1836, UCL, BrP. Most of the Philosophic Radicals acquiesced in the reduction, but Place was furious with them: a five-penny newspaper was still "an interdict on all the working classes, small trades men, etc. to receive any information at all": Place to Parkes, Jan. 27, 1837, Add. MSS 35,150, f. 232.

42. "Taxes on Knowledge," p. 7.

Chadwick.[43] Amidst this planning they were led to expect that
the tax on newspapers would be repealed and, consequently,
publication was delayed.[44] After a long disappointing wait, finally
in 1835, more than two years after the initial plans, Roebuck began publication of his weekly *Pamphlets for the People*. Leaving
them undated to establish the fiction that they were not newspapers and thus not subject to tax, the *Pamphlets* were published
over a period of thirty-six weeks and had a circulation of close
to 10,000. Although in the end he failed to get contributions
from several of the Philosophic Radicals, the *Pamphlets* defended the program of organic reform and vigorously attacked
the Whig government as the chief obstacle to the creation of a
predominant Radical party.[45]

In 1833 plans were also made to set up a new quarterly review, which would have paralleled the *Pamphlets for the People*,

43. J. A. Roebuck, "On the Means of Conveying Information to the
People," in *Pamph. P* [no. 1, June 11, 1835], p. 5; Place, "Project for a
Society for the Diffusion of Political and Moral Knowledge," Add. MSS
35,154, ff. 162, 169–70, 176. Both Place and Roebuck considered becoming the editor (ff. 162, 172, 175). Hume was Pres.; Warburton, Vice Pres.;
Grote, Trea.; J. Romilly, Sec'y (f. 166). Also see, Wallas, *Place*, pp.
337–39. Their organization was separate from the Society for the Diffusion of Political Knowledge: R. K. Webb, *British Working Class Reader*,
pp. 92–94. Though James Mill and Grote had been connected with the
Society for the Diffusion of Useful Knowledge since its foundation in
1826, the Philosophic Radicals thought it useless because of its avoidance
of political and religious subjects: Webb, pp. 85–87; James Mill to
Thomas Hodgskin, Aug. 4, 1829, Hollander Collection, Univ. of Illinois;
Roebuck, "Conveying Information," p. 9.

44. Place, "Project for a Society," ff. 172–73, 182. The "Society
separated, and awaited Lord Althorp's good deeds": "Conveying Information," p. 5.

45. Roebuck contemplated parts dealing with general principles (such
as essays like James Mill's on government or liberty of the press); discussions of "existing institutions, testing these by Principles already established"; and presentations of the facts related to particular problems: "Mr.
Roebuck's Sketch," in Place, "Project for a Society," ff. 180–81. By July,
1835, the project required a £200 subsidy (f. 183), even though they
were selling at the rate of 10,000 per week: J. S. Mill to Guilbert, Aug.
14, 1835, *EL*, p. 270. Also see C. D. Collet, *History of the Taxes on
Knowledge* (London, 1899), *1*, 43–44.

although, of course, aimed at a different audience. John Mill took the initiative here, aided by Roebuck and Buller, and later Molesworth, who put £4,000 into it. Plans were made in 1833, but publication was postponed, first to assemble a sufficient number of writers and then to wait for an end of the indecisiveness of politics during the brief Peel administration. Finally in April 1835 the *London Review,* with John Mill as editor, began publication. The object, Mill said, was "to rally the instructed radicals round a common standard, and induce the other radicals to follow them." [46] With a broad range of contributors, including most of the Philosophic Radicals, it soon (especially after James Mill's death in 1836) became a vehicle for the propagation of John Mill's views of Radical policy. It enlarged its circulation after a year (in 1836) by merging with the original *Westminster Review.* For Mill it was the means of giving coherence and direction to the parliamentary Radicals.

INITIAL DISAPPOINTMENTS

The Philosophic Radicals planned to write, edit, and publish as much as possible of the radical press with the expectation that an important Radical party could emerge in the near future. The immediate prospect, however, was less rosy even if not bleak. Whig aristocrats, after all, were in control. Yet, without wanting to move along the path to democracy, the Whigs might perhaps be pushed, first by the contingent of non-Whig reformers in Parliament, and then by the force of public opinion, stimulated as it was by the reform agitation of 1831–32. Therefore, there was at least the hope that the Whigs might be forced to take steps in the direction of fundamental reform.

The achievements of the first session were not sufficient to satisfy a Philosophic reformer. Slavery in the West Indies was abolished, a small step was taken toward factory regulation, the Bank Charter was renewed, the Poor Law Commission was established, and the charter of the East India Company was re-

46. Mill to Carlyle, Dec. 22, 1833; Mill to Nichol, Jan. 17, April 15, Dec. 18, 1834; Mill to d'Eichthal, Nov. 29, 1834: *EL,* pp. 201, 210, 222, 242, 245; Millicent Fawcett, *Life of Sir William Molesworth* (London, 1901), p. 64.

newed, with a new provision for free competition in the China tea trade. These were, by most standards, reforms, and even the Philosophic Radicals could not condemn them. Yet they were a far cry from the organic reforms that the Radicals demanded. Indeed, the fundamental question that would have clearly revealed whether politicians were on the aristocratic or popular side were hardly raised.

There were only two exceptions. In April 1833 Grote introduced a motion on the ballot, but Whigs and Tories combined to defeat it by a majority of 105. Even though this reaffirmed his image of the aristocratic party, made up of two factions, in opposition to the nucleus of the future Radical party (his minority consisted of 106), it was nonetheless depressing. There also was a proposal for shortening the duration of parliaments, but it had the same fate as Grote's ballot motion.[47] The usual parliamentary fare was far removed from the only issues that justified and gave hope for the Radical party as Grote and Mill and their friends conceived it. Therefore, when the Whig ministry published a pamphlet defending its record of reform achievements, John Mill complained that it "passes over three-fourths of the essentials of the case." The Whigs must be judged, he said, not only by what they have done, but "what they have opposed, and so *prevented* from being done," and also by "what they have failed in doing." [48] And Roebuck said that, "with the exception of Mr. Grote's speech on the ballot, "[he] never heard in that as-

47. *Hansard, 17,* 667; *19,* 1107–12, 1150–54; *23,* 1036, 1085–86.
48. "The Ministerial Manifesto," *Examiner,* Sept. 22, 1833, p. 593. Parkes also reviewed the pamphlet, but with less severity. He acknowledged that the government had done some good, but also emphasized "what it has *not* done, and what it *must* do, or give early place to another and an advanced government." He called for a liberalization of the composition of the House of Lords, and triennial parliaments: *Morning Chronicle,* Sept. 6, 9, 1833, p. 2 (for evidence of authorship see Parkes to Ellice, Sept. 12, 1833, NLS, EP, E38, f. 3). The pamphlet had boasted "that there is a nearer approach to wisdom and honesty in the present Parliament than in any of its predecessors," and it pointed to the government's success that was achieved despite its having faced "two hostile factions, the Tories and the Radicals": *The Reform Ministry, and the Reformed Parliament* (3d ed. London, 1833), p. 2.

sembly . . . one logical and really effective argument. All has
been passion, ignorance, and prejudice." [49]

The Whigs could not have satisfied the Philosophic Radicals.
When they did not support reform, they were, in the Radical
view, being true to character. When they did, it was mere submission to pressure. Torn between their fundamental opposition
to reform and their recognition that some concession was necessary as the price of office, their record was bound to be lukewarm. Thus John Mill, commenting on the ministerial pamphlet,
held that public opinion was "in a state which must compel any
Minister to adopt many *measures* of reform." [50] James Mill,
looking back on this period, also felt that the Whigs were "compelled to profess themselves the general friends of reform," for
public opinion would not offer "either support or reward to those
who professed themselves of a different sentiment." They were
therefore "only reformers by compulsion" who "submit to it as
a necessary evil." He concluded that they "are very unfit to have
the guidance of public affairs." [51]

As frustrating as the Whigs' rejection of organic reform was
the character of the reforms that were proposed. Although they
would neither change fundamental institutions nor alter the distribution of power in Parliament, nevertheless they did legislate
small improvements. In many cases the Philosophic Radicals
voted and sometimes spoke in support of the Whig government.[52] But such support only blurred the distinction between
what they thought was the real and important distinction between Whig and Radical. It therefore prevented their having
the satisfaction of clearly being a virtuous minority. This frustration was usually expressed in their complaint that the Whigs, ex-
ploiting the general popularity of reform, attempted to identify
all anti-Tories with themselves under the guise of their all being
reformers. Roebuck was indignant that the Whigs should usurp

49. "Extracts from the Diary of an M.P.," *Tait's Edinburgh Magazine*,
2 (July 1833), 414. Also see Tooke, Buller, *Hansard, 18* (May 22, 1833),
44–45; Fonblanque, Examiner (1833), pp. 225, 226, 259, 450.
50. "The Ministerial Manifesto," p. 593.
51. "State of the Nation," *Lond. Rev.* (April 1835), *1*, 1–2.
52. *Hansard,* e.g. *16*, 488–89; *17*, 586; *23*, 812–16; *25*, 496.

this title. They "thought such advocacy politic" but were "in
their hearts opposed to liberal measures." The result was to deceive the people, whose allegiance was diverted from the leadership most worthy of it. The disappointments accumulated. Already early in the session John Mill reported that "our Utilitarian
Radicals ‌are downcast enough." Place complained that the
" 'juste milieu Ministers' [would] . . . accommodate all parties
[and] please none." Mrs. Grote reported that her husband was in
a state of depression and felt "despair of political reform." [53]

Such despair was briefly relieved by a moment of hope during
the following year. In June 1834 two of the most conservative
members of the Cabinet (Stanley and Graham) resigned. This
was seen in the light of the belief that the Whig party consisted of
two incompatible parts—one aristocratic and opposed to reform,
the other "liberal," moderately reformist, properly belonging in
a Radical party. The resignations and rumors of liberal replace-
ments put the Radicals in "great spirits." Buller called them "a
complete triumph for the Liberal part of the Cabinet: and musι
be for good." [54] The Philosophic Radicals perhaps exaggerated
their own role in the development. The Cabinet dispute concerning the right of the government to regulate church property had
been provoked by a motion introduced by H. G. Ward, one of
their close associates, and news of the resignations reached
Althorp as Grote was speaking in support of Ward's motion.
John Mill was so hopeful that the resignations had purged the
Cabinet of aristocratic influence that he offered to revise his
judgment of the ministry. The Whigs, he said, "will now have a
new basis of popularity. If they so please, all past errors will be
considered as cancelled. . . . If their future conduct show vigour
of purpose and a strong spirit of improvement, all that they have
done ill, will be imputed to Mr. Stanley and Sir James Graham."
And he added that, "From us, and . . . all the enlightened reformers, they may expect, until they shall have had a fair trial,

53. Roebuck, "Extracts from Diary," p. 415; Mill to Carlyle, March 9,
1833, *EL*, p. 145; Place to Parkes, Nov. 8, 1833, Add. MSS 35,149, f. 236;
Mrs. Grote, Aug. 23, 1833, *Lewin Letters, 1*, 203.

54. Ibid., June 10, 1834, p. 319; Buller to B. H. Lyne (his election
agent), May 28, 1834, in County Branch Library, Liskeard, Cornwall.

not only no hostility, but the most friendly encouragement and support. They must now throw themselves upon the people." [55] Additional encouragement was derived from the ministers' apparent determination to carry the Poor Law Amendment Bill, and Grote especially gave them strong support. The Radicals' usual suspicions were again put in abeyance when the government showed itself willing to go along with Roebuck's proposal regarding a national system of education. When a few months later the Poor Law was passed, Mill was quick to praise. The ministers have "proved, that when not opposed by the interests or prejudices of any powerful class, they can . . . do good spontaneously. For this we give them due honour." Mill was pleased, but this was not unqualified support, for it remained to be seen if they would vigorously seek other important reforms, all of which could only be achieved, unlike the Poor Law, by coming into conflict with privileged groups, especially the House of Lords, and by allying themselves with the people.[56]

There was little opportunity, however, to put the Whigs to additional tests, for their term of office ended abruptly in November 1834. With Peel's accession the Whigs joined the Philosophic Radicals on the opposition side of the House. There was exultation among the Philosophic Radicals, for it was assumed that this would break up the Whig party and thus lead to realignment. John Mill felt that whatever the outcome "the Movement has gained immensely by all this, and is gaining every day." [57] Mrs. Grote thought "the 'sneaking Whigs' are *done,* as a party. They will no longer be-fog the judgments of popular minded men. We shall now classify public men into pro-reform and anti-reform partizans," and she looked forward to "ridding the country of

55. "Notes on the Newspapers," *Mo. Rep., 8* (June 1834), 455–56.

56. *Hansard, 24,* 127–30, 139. Mill, "Close of the Session," *Mo. Rep., 8* (Sept. 1834), 607. For another passage, in which the hope is combined with greater skepticism, see "Notes on the Newspapers," ibid., p. 665. It was during this midyear period when the Radicals softened somewhat in their attitude to the Whigs that most of them signed an address to Althorp requesting that he not retire and offering support to the government of which he would be a part: Denis Le Marchant, *Memoir of Viscount Althorp* (London, 1876), pp. 576–78.

57. Mill to A. N. Thibaudeau, Nov. 28, 1834, *EL,* p. 240.

trimmers and juste milieu jargon." [58] Thus neither the new proximity of Whigs to Radicals on the opposition side of the House, nor the brief relaxation in Radical criticism of the ministry earlier in the year, altered the long-standing Philosophic Radical judgment that the Whig party was pernicious and obsolete.

Late in 1834, as the Conservatives began their brief term in office, the Philosophic Radicals found it difficult to foresee exactly how the future would unfold. There were many conceivable arrangements, but whatever happened, it seemed, as John Mill put it, that the Radicals "will evidently be the supreme power in the country." [59] They were encouraged by the unsettled parliamentary situation to hope that the latent radicalism in the populace could be brought to the surface where it would be made evident in the new alignment of parties. With this confidence they renewed their journalistic efforts (the *London Review* and *Pamphlets for the People* were about to be launched) and took steps to organize a Radical caucus in the House of Commons.

58. Mrs. Grote to Parkes, Jan. 22 [1835], LP.
59. *EL*, p. 240. Mill also was encouraged by the popular excitement generated by Durham's speeches at public meetings. On the role of a possible "Durham party" in the Philosophic Radical outlook, see Chap. 8.

5. *The Unnatural Alliance*

The fall of the liberal Whig government and the accession of the Tories was a crucial event for the Philosophic Radicals. It was the occasion for the organization of a separate Radical caucus, and this brought them a step nearer to the realization of their fantasy of a separate Popular–Radical party. However, their success in organizing the parliamentary Radicals separately from the Whigs and other anti-Tories was to turn sour, for the Philosophic Radicals succumbed to the temptation to cooperate with the Whigs, and the embarrassment of this alliance was to plague them for the remainder of the decade. The organization of a Radical caucus was undertaken as part of a plan for the mobilization of the Whigs and Radicals in a coordinated opposition against the Tory government. It was successful and, after five months in office, Peel resigned. When the Whigs resumed their places on the government benches the Radicals acted on the assumption that with their newly established organization they might bargain with the Whig leadership, exchanging their block of votes for the concession of further reforms. Therefore, when the Tories returned to the opposition benches, the Philosophic Radicals for the first time crossed the floor to sit on the government side of the House. This put them in the role of apparent supporters of the Whig government and established a relationship that for them was anything but satisfying. While they would welcome the reforms that the Melbourne government might concede, they were also seeking to establish an independent Radical party, but at the very time they organized its nucleus the Philosophic Radicals began a relationship with the Whigs that obscured the sense of separate identity that they were so anxious to achieve.

A Temporary Alliance

There were three groups of "liberals"—the Irish, the Whigs, and the Radicals. During the sessions of 1833 and 1834 they often disagreed; they felt so little affinity with one another that many of the Radicals and the Irish sat on the opposition side of the House. But now, in their antipathy to the Tories in office, they discovered a temporary basis for agreement. This was not sufficient, however, for achieving unity within one party caucus. "The body of Liberals," Warburton said, "will not unite cordially under a Whig Leader." Therefore it was proposed that "the three principal sections of Liberals . . . should each have their meetings and their Chairmen." Grote, Hume, Clay, and Warburton undertook to form "a Radical Brigade" with a chairman who was to communicate with O'Connell and the Whig leaders "so as to secure cooperation for common public objects." [1] Although there was some concern that Grote was not sufficiently aggressive to head the seventy or so Radicals—Parkes said "he wants devil" —he emerged as their leader, and his wife at this time referred to him as "a chief of opposition." [2]

Parkes was described as "one of the great archimages of the scheme," [3] and although he was mainly interested in promoting Whig–Radical cooperation, most of the Philosophic Radicals saw this development against the background of their long-run expectations and hopes for the realignment of parties and not as a temporary expedient made necessary by the fall of the Whigs. Molesworth considered this organization of the Radicals, separately from the Whigs and the Irish, as "the commencement of a party which will one day or another bring destruction upon both Whigs and Tories." When Edward Baines, the Congregationalist editor of the Leeds *Mercury* and Member for Leeds, was invited to join the Radical group, he was told that the recent changes in the government represented "a desperate attempt" by the aris-

1. Warburton to O'Connell, Jan. 30, 1835: *Correspondence of Daniel O'Connell*, ed. W. J. Fitzpatrick (London, 1888), *1*, 520; *Life of Edward Baines* (London, 1851), p. 208.

2. Parkes to Durham, Jan. 26, 1835, LP; *Lewin Letters, 1*, 329. Estimates of the size of the Radical group varied; Parkes said there were 70 or 80; R. Potter said there were more than 50; T. Young said 78: T. Young to Ellice, March 3, 1835, NLS, EP, E 59, f. 182; BL, Richard Potter's Parliamentary Diaries, *8*, f. 2 (entry Feb. 18, 1835).

3. E. L. Bulwer to Durham, Feb. 2, 1835, Earl of Lytton, *Life of Edward Bulwer, First Lord Lytton* (London, 1913), *1*, 499.

tocracy "to overwhelm the democracy, and to rule the country on Tory principles." The Radicals thought that the "Whigs were diminishing in number throughout the country daily, and the tendency of party in the country was now to Tory or to Radical, the Whigs not being able to keep their ground." [4] That the Philosophic Radicals did not regard their cooperation with the Whigs as a step toward the formation of a liberal party of which the Whigs would be a part is also borne out by the fact that the *London Review* and *Pamphlets for the People* now (spring 1835) began publication as Radical, anti-Whig journals.

The cooperation among these organized groups achieved its immediate purpose. Although the votes were close, the anti-Tory combination defeated Peel, and in April 1835 the Whigs under Melbourne were again in office. Now the Philosophic Radicals were faced with the alternatives—either to resume their position of hostility to the Whigs from the opposition benches or to follow the precedent established while the Whigs were in opposition and continue cooperating with them. Although there is no record of their deliberations on this question, their justification for adopting the latter course may perhaps be inferred from the recommendations offered to them by both James and John Mill in the first number of the newly established *London Review*.

James Mill still saw Whigs and Tories as two factions, each representing the same aristocratic interests; and he still saw their antagonism as a misrepresentation of the real alignment of aristocratic and popular interests that ought to be reflected in the party system. But at this time he recognized two new develop-

4. Fawcett, *Molesworth,* p. 73; *Life of Baines,* pp. 207–08, Baines reporting (Feb. 17, 1835) a conversation with an unidentified person but almost certainly a Philosophic Radical. Roebuck said that though the Radicals, like the Whigs, "form a very small minority" in the House, "they are greater in number than the Whigs." Also, "as popular opinions gather strength, the situation of the Whig party will become more and more precarious. The inevitable consequence of the present tendency of opinions is to give to the Radicals, even with the present defective constitution of the House, a majority in the Commons [then] . . . the government must be placed in their hands": "Prospects of the Coming Session," *Pamph. P* [no. 23, Nov. 12, 1835], p. 6; "Note on the 'Globe,'" ibid. [no. 25, Nov. 26, 1835], p. 13.

ments on the parliamentary scene. For one thing, the growth of public opinion favorable to reform obliged all politicians, even Tories, to be reformers in some degree. There were, he said, "two parties of grudging reformers," or as he also labeled them, "the new Moderates [the Tories, now called Conservatives] and the Old [the Whigs]." They were approximately equal in strength, with perhaps a small preponderance on the side of the Conservatives. The second new development was the emergence, in opposition to the aristocratic factions, of the Radicals, especially that "portion who deserve the name of *Complete* Reformers." These, he said, "are not a great proportion, but a considerable body, to which time is daily making additions, to which the future time will doubtless make them rapidly." He placed great hope on this small core of Philosophic Radicals and remarked that, in the present circumstances, it "is of immense importance how this little band conduct themselves."

Although James Mill's ultimate aim was to establish the "complete reformers" as the main antagonists of the two variants of Moderates, his advice in 1835 took into account the minority status of the Radicals and the persistence of antagonism between the equally balanced aristocratic factions. "The advantages at the present moment," Mill said, "are peculiarly great. The two parties of grudging reformers, the 'now's-enough' men, are nearly balanced." Therefore, it "will be the interest of every minister to have them [the Radicals] for him, rather than against him; and if the only successful mode of courtship to them be the grant of reforms, they may extort a succession of reforms from hands the most averse to the boon." However, while he encouraged them to bargain with their as yet limited strength, he warned against any cooperation that involved coalition of Radicals with either Whig or Tory parties. While in some foreseeable circumstances, it might "become the interest of either of them [Whig or Tory] to seek an accession of strength, by admitting a portion of the complete reformers to the offices of state along with them," this, he said, "would be the death-blow to the influence of the complete reformers." Only "the most soft-tempered and flexible of the party would alone be chosen for the association in question, who could not convert their friends the moderates, but be converted by them." The result would be that the complete reformers would be broken up and discredited in the eyes of the nation. He therefore counseled against accepting office in a government formed by either aristocratic party. There were two tasks. The philosophical reformers were "to make it, as far as their weight can go, the interest of every ministry, be it what it may, to be the author of reforms"; and while awaiting the realignment of parties they were "to be the champions of the philosophical principles of government." [5]

John Mill, also seeing that the time "is not yet come for a ministry of thorough Reformers," joined his father in offering this advice. In the same number of the *Review,* indeed in a "Postscript" to his father's article, it was announced that he did "not call upon the thorough Reformers to declare enmity against [the Whig government], or to seek their downfall," but he warned, "We do implore them not to implicate themselves in the responsibility of a half-reform policy." They could support the ministry when it deserved their support "with far greater effect out of office." [6] Fonblanque gave the same advice: in "an independent station" the Radicals can "act as a corps of observation," supporting the government when right, restraining it when wrong.[7] Although the conditional support recommended by the

---

5. James Mill, "State of the Nation," *Lond. Rev., 1* (April 1835), 16–18. However, Hume thought "members of the extreme *left* must be employed to satisfy their friends out of Doors, as well as within, that the administration will meet, as (far ?) as it can, the popular views of their party." His suggestions included E. L. Bulwer, Dr. Bowring, and Buller: Hume to Ellice, April 15, 1835, NLS, EP.

6. John Mill, "Postscript," *Lond. Rev., 1* (April 1835), 254–55. He reported that "at the late change it was well understood that the radicals as a body would not consent to take office. They thought, justly, that they had more power out of office than in it. To several members of the body (but to none of the leaders) offers were made of places, which they all refused, unless the leaders came in too": Mill to Guilbert, May 8, 1835, *EL,* p. 261.

7. *Examiner,* April 26, May 3, 1835, pp. 257, 274. Roebuck later claimed that at the time of the Lichfield House compact he did not share this view: "I said at the time . . . that the Radical party were wrong to enter into any compromise with the Whigs, unless they obtained a share in the Government": *Examiner,* Dec. 10, 1837, p. 795.

Mills could have been given from the opposition side of the House, such a position would have suggested a wish to immediately bring down the government. But since this was to be postponed, it would perhaps have been inappropriate to take up that hostile position. The precedent of cooperation while in opposition probably operated as well, and now for the first time the Philosophic Radicals sat on the government side of the House, ostensibly as supporters of the Whig ministers.[8] However, still anxious to maintain their independent status, they sat below the gangway, where they offered what later was called harassing support.[9] Although to outside observers this suggested a coalescence of parties, anyone close to the scene could have recognized the Radicals' anomalous position as (in Henry Bulwer's words) "a party in a party." The Philosophic Radicals looked upon the situation as temporary. James Mill was looking forward to a time when "a higher station in the great counsel of the nation is prepared for them," and when the "powers of government will be put in their hands."[10]

The Philosophic Radicals now faced a dilemma. On the one hand, cooperation with the Whigs was called for by practical considerations. By giving the support of Radical votes and Radical rhetoric, important reforms might be gained; and even if these were not the organic reforms that would fully satisfy democratic Radicals, they were steps in that direction. On the other hand, such support gave the appearance of an affiliation with the Whigs. In their own minds, of course, they were able to maintain the sharp distinction between Whig and Radical. But this was not clear to the public, and the Whig and moderate Radical appeal for unity among reformers in opposition to the Tories further tended to obscure the distinction. The Philosophic Radicals were pulled in two directions—toward moderation of

8. John Mill thought the new arrangement resulted from a tacit understanding: "Postscript: The Close of the Session," *Lond. Rev.*, 2, 275. Fonblanque also saw it this way: *Examiner*, July 10, 1836, p. 434.

9. Henry Reeve, "Personal Memoir of Mr. Grote," *Edin. Rev.*, (July 1873) *138*, 232.

10. "State of the Nation," p. 18. Henry Bulwer, *The Lords, the Government, and the Country* (London, 1836), p. 82.

their demands, piecemeal reforms, cooperation, and thus sacrifice of their sense of mission; and toward separation from the Whigs, an act that would have involved sacrifice of immediate even if small gains, but which would have been doctrinally pure. They did not respond as their doctrine demanded, at least not immediately; neither were they eager to adopt the pragmatic course of compromise, for the impulse that drove them toward doctrinal purity made them uneasy about the use of these tactics. Already, three months after the Whigs' resumption of office, John Mill was expressing their uneasiness as he warned his parliamentary friends that support of the Whigs must be "qualified and distrustful" and that they "should be under no mistake concerning the probable duration and limits of cooperation which is practicable between themselves and the Whig Cabinet." [11]

RESISTANCE TO COMPROMISE

The conflict between these two goals—immediate though small gains and isolation as a "virtuous minority"—is evident in the Philosophic Radicals' response to the proposal for Municipal Corporation reform that was brought before Parliament in 1835. This was a measure based on a report of a Royal Commission whose work was given direction and forceful leadership by Joseph Parkes, who served as secretary. The Commission itself was packed with reformers, some Whigs and some Radicals, including Benthamites. The report, written by Parkes and the chairman (Blackburne), had "an unmistakably Benthamite ring" about it; [12] and the act that was finally passed has been called

11. "Parliamentary Proceedings of the Session," *Lond. Rev., 1* (July 1835), 513; also (p. 512): Although the Whigs, if pressed, would concede a few measures of reform, Mill "did not believe . . . that the Whigs were, less than the Tories, attached to the evils, or less terrified at the remedies."

12. G. B. A. M. Finlayson, "The Municipal Corporation Commission and Report, 1833–35," *Bulletin of the Institute of Historical Research, 36* (May 1963), 45, 50. However, the role of Benthamites on the Commission can be exaggerated. Parkes boasted that a "majority of the Commissioners are personal Radical *friends* of mine"; but years later he said, "Entre nous, all our Benthamite men: C. Austin, Bingham and Co., talked theories and shied reporting . . . and said our draft Bills were un-scientific,

the "high-water mark of Benthamite Radicalism acting through the Whig machine." [13] Although the bill was modified somewhat before its final passage, it still was a genuine reform that the Philosophic Radicals could easily have welcomed. Yet whether they should support the measure was an agonizing decision which led to an embittered outburst by those Philosophic Radicals who found the Whig alliance most uncomfortable.

The Municipal Corporation Act did not provide for democratic local government, but it went farther in that direction than any previous legislation. Its electoral provisions gave the vote to many persons not eligible to vote in parliamentary elections, allowing Parkes to call it the "Postscript to the Reform Bills." [14] It made all adult male ratepayers of three years' standing, without distinction of politics, religion, or wealth, electors of responsible Town Councils. The result, as the Webbs have noted, was that "the little oligarchies which had so long ruled over their fellow-citizens, by inherent right, were suddenly and completely disestablished." [15] Though not radicalism, it was a measure as close to it as any yet adopted by the House of Commons. Parkes thought it "a grand point to get Household Suffrage and a thorough purge of the existing Corporations." [16]

The bill was returned from the Lords with amendments. Several changes were proposed, and in the end, while some of the amendments were adopted, the most important feature of the bill—the provision for household suffrage—was left un-

---

giving us no substitutes": Parkes to Ellice, Sept. 12, 1833, NLS, EP, E 38, f. 3; Parkes to Cobden, Oct. 5, 1851, SRO, Cobden Papers. The composition of the Commission and Parkes' role on it were criticized: *Hansard*, 29 (Aug. 3, 1835), 1383–93, 1412–13; (July 20, 1835), 769–70.

13. G. M. Trevelyan, *English History in the Nineteenth Century* (New York, Longmans, 1928), p. 244.

14. Parkes to Place, Jan. 2, 1836, Add. MSS 35,150, f. 99.

15. Sidney and Beatrice Webb, *English Local Government* (Hamden, Conn., Archon Books, 1963 [first publ. 1908]), *3*, 748–49 (i.e. The Manor and the Borough, vol. 2).

16. Parkes to Durham, July 1, 1835, LP. Also see W. Ivor Jennings, "The Municipal Revolution," *A Century of Municipal Progress*, eds. H. J. Laski, W. I. Jennings, and W. A. Robson (London, Allen and Unwin, 1935), pp. 60–61.

touched. That there were amendments was no surprise to the Philosophic Radicals; indeed, it had been expected that the Lords would reject the bill in its entirety. Yet, even though the amendments proposed by the Lords did not alter the electoral provisions that initially had made the bill attractive to the Radicals, they became the occasion for Philosophic Radical doubts as to whether the bill was worth having. So tenuous was their commitment to the Whig leadership that these minor amendments threatened its continuation.

Potential conflict between Lords and Commons was a real problem recognized by both Whigs and moderate Tories. Before 1832 the Lords' influence over the Commons was much greater, and undoubtedly there were fewer problems of arranging agreement about the provisions of bills. After 1832 the Whig commitment to reform, and the diverse elements in the Commons that they had to satisfy in order to maintain their position against the Tories, made it difficult for the government at the same time to satisfy their supporters in the Commons and gain the predominantly Conservative Lords' sanction for legislation. Anticipation of this problem had been the basis of some of the more enlightened opposition to the Reform Bill. With the Lords having a veto, and a popular Commons wanting reforms the Lords would not allow, it was feared that no government could carry out a legislative program and that bitter antagonism would lead to general lack of confidence in the Constitution. Even though the reformed House of Commons retained a good deal of aristocratic influence, the danger seemed real enough. There were leading politicians, including Peel as well as Whig ministers, who were anxious to avoid open conflict with the Lords and who therefore pursued a policy of conciliation in order to avoid a destructive struggle to decide finally where legislative sovereignty resided.

The Philosophic Radicals interpreted the relationship of Lords to Commons quite differently. Looking back to the Lords' resistance to the Reform Bills in 1831–32, they hopefully saw the Commons' success as a precedent and as something of a constitutional settlement. At that time, after the Lords' rejection of the Reform Bill passed in the House of Commons (October 1831), a similar bill passed, but only after the majority in

the Lords crumbled in the face of varied threats—of conflict
between the two Houses, creation of new peers, and even civil
war. Now in 1835 Roebuck looked back to those events and
said that "the Lords yielded to the People." He thought the real
significance of the reform of 1832 was that it "provided that a
majority of the House of Commons should be elected by the
People; and it was anticipated that the wishes of the People, as
expressed by their representatives, would and could meet with
no effectual opposition." When the Lords returned the Municipal Corporations Bill, he said they "have not yet acquiesced
in this arrangement": they had not comprehended their "real
position." [17] John Mill held that allowing the Lords to amend
bills approved by the Commons was "to abandon all the ends
to which the Reform Bill was intended as a means." [18] Grote also
shared this view. He asked "What the country had gained by the
Reform Bill, which had in great measure put an end to the system of filling the House by the nominees of the Lords, if the
other House was to exercise its power in another way, by en-
abling minorities in the Commons to triumph over decided
majorities of the Representatives of the People." [19]

Having hoped that the Lords had been cautioned and chas-
tened, the Philosophic Radicals were mortified to find it once
more blocking legislation. In their disappointment they lashed
out at the upper house as an institution. Roebuck defined the
issue: "the interest of the people was one thing, the interest of
the Lords another and very different thing"; indeed these in-

17. Roebuck, "The Crisis: What Ought the Ministers to Do?," *Pamph.
P* [no. 12, Aug. 27, 1835], pp. 2, 8; "The Conduct of the Ministers Respecting the Lords' Amendments," ibid. [no. 14, Sept. 10, 1835], p. 1.

18. J. S. Mill, "Tories, Whigs, and Radicals," *LWR, 25* (July 1836),
294. Already in 1834 Mill was willing to acknowledge that, "if we could
get on passably well with [the House of Lords] we ought to keep it." But
he doubted that this could be done. "It is impossible, in an age of Movement, to get on with a legislative body which will never move except
upon compulsion; and as we knew that this would be the case with the
House of Lords, we, from the first, felt that they would render it necessary to thrust them aside.": "Notes on the Newspapers," *Mo. Rep., 8*
(Aug. 1834), 662.

19. *Hansard, 30* (Sept. 1, 1835), 1203.

terests were "hostile and irreconcilable." He called the Lords "an
irresponsible, an ignorant, and an interested oligarchy" and
announced that he would introduce a proposal that "the *veto* of
the Lords in all matters of legislation should be taken away . . .
and that the Lords should in place of it be endowed with a sus-
pensive power." [20] Outside Parliament he took the next and final
step. In his *Pamphlets for the People* he warned that the Lords
"are driving us to a war *à outrance*" and that "if it be found that
our institutions stand between the People and their well-founded
wishes, we are ready completely to remove those institutions,
and thoroughly remodel the whole of our Government." He even
suggested that no Second Chamber of any sort was needed.[21]
Molesworth, calling the Lords politically evil, took the same
view: "the period would quickly arrive (which he for one would
be glad to see) when an end would be put to the privileges of an
hereditary aristocracy—of that body which, in his solemn belief,
could never be reformed, save by being dissolved!" [22] This
warning was echoed in Parliament by Hume, Clay, O'Connell,
and a few others.[23] John Mill joined these protests against the
House of Lords. "An entire change in its constitution is cried
out for from the remotest corner of the three kingdoms; and few
would be satisfied with any change short of abolishing the
hereditary principle." He proposed an upper house chosen by
the lower. The choice was to be made from the existing peerage
supplemented with qualified persons not in the Commons who
were to be given peerages. This was not the best design he could
make, but only the "best remodel" of the present House of
Lords. Its purpose was a second chamber "unlikely to set itself
in opposition to what is good in the acts and purposes of the
First." [24]

20. Ibid. (Aug. 31, 1835), col. 1164; (Sept. 2, 1835), col. 1268–69.
21. "The Crisis," p. 8.
22. *Hansard, 30* (Sept. 7, 1835), 1435–36.
23. Ibid. (Aug. 31, 1835), 1157–58, 1178; (Sept. 2, 1835), 1266,
1269–70.
24. J. S. Mill, "The House of Lords," *Globe and Traveller*, Oct. 16,
1835, p. 2; "Postscript: Close of the Session," *Lond. Rev., 2* (Oct. 1835),
272. In addition to reflecting Mill's posture as a Radical politician–
journalist, his proposal in 1835 also shows evidence of the philosophic

Open conflict between the two Houses such as the Philosophic Radicals now advocated was the very thing the Whig leaders wished to avoid. Not all the amendments sent from the Lords were accepted, but in a series of conferences between the two Houses some of them were, and this was done in order to avoid a clash between them. Lord John Russell appealed to the desire to maintain a "tempered" government; he therefore urged that the compromise, as arranged, be accepted.[25] The Lords' amendments, had they been accepted, would have preserved the property and the parliamentary voting rights of freemen, whereas the original bill greatly restricted or abolished them; they would have established a pecuniary qualification for town councillors, whereas the original bill had provided that those eligible to vote (i.e. ratepayers, regardless of amount) would be qualified to hold such office; and they would have preserved for the town councils, including at least some of the former aldermen, the power of appointment for a variety of offices and privileges, including magistrates, charity commissioners, liquor licensees, and church patronage. The ministry rejected much of this, but they compromised on the qualification of town councillors; they provided some protection to proprietary rights of the freemen; and they made some concessions on the method of appointing magistrates and charity commissioners.[26]

It might have been expected that the Philosophic Radicals would accept the bill even after the compromise on the Lords' amendments. During the previous spring, when Roebuck was looking forward to municipal corporation reform as a major

---

quest in which he was engaged at this time (see pp. 86–96). On the one hand, the members of the upper house must not be chosen by the people, "but by some party identified in interest with the people . . . the House of Commons would be more careful and enlightened judges of the merits of philosophers and statesmen"; on the other hand, this upper house would "pursue the same ends, and act on the same general principles [as the lower]. But they would be a wiser, a more instructed and discreet body": "House of Lords."

25. *Hansard, 30* (Sept. 7, 1835), 1412.

26. On provisions of the act, see the Webbs, *Local Government, 3,* 743–47; [Joseph Parkes], "Corporation Reform," *British and Foreign Review, 1* (Oct. 1835), 537–42.

step in the progress of radicalism, he would have been satisfied with an electorate consisting of ten-pound householders. Yet even after the Lords amended the bill, the qualification for voters was much lower than this; and at a time when he could foresee the compromise on the amendments he thought the measure "will still be a good one." Place too "acknowledged the boon" that the bill, even as finally passed, provided.[27]

Yet, despite their satisfaction with the substance of the bill, they were furious with the amendments, both before some of them were rejected and after the ministry arranged a compromise between the two Houses. Had it been merely a question of this particular piece of legislation, they could have accepted it. But they focused their attention on another issue that was reflected in this one, making it especially significant for them. The real issue was the antagonism between the aristocracy and the people and the relation of political parties to it. Thus Place was "looking onwards to matters of all but infinitely more importance than the boon great as it is." The Lords had mutilated a reform measure, and the Whig ministers "put up with the kicking the Lords bestowed upon them." Place asked whether they ought to have done so; this is "what the question really was." [28]

Roebuck saw it in the same light. After the debate on the Lords' amendments he criticized Russell for having confined "all his observations to the Municipal Bill, and dealt with great emphasis, and at extraordinary length, upon each petty alteration," thus showing "that he was totally unconscious of the fact that the very nature of our future government was depending on the manner in which this question was to be settled." The real issue was being ignored. "We all know and feel," Roebuck

27. "Municipal Corporation Reform," *Lond. Rev., 1* (April 1835), 75; Leader, *Roebuck,* p. 70; Place to Parkes, Oct. 4, 1835, Add MSS 35,150, unfol. In order to promote passage of the bill, Place took the initiative in setting up a weekly newspaper, *The Corporation Reformer.* Parkes joined him in the enterprise. It first appeared June 13, 1835; there were five issues (it was intended to be temporary): Place to Parkes, May 11, 1835; "Prospectus of the Municipal Corporation Reformer," June 5, 1835, Add. MSS 35,150, ff. 45–46.

28. Place to Parkes, Sept. 30, Oct. 4, 1835, Add. MSS 35,150, f. 77 and unfol.

said, "that the Question we have now to determine is, not simply the passing of the Municipal Reform Bill, but whether the wishes of the people or of the Lords are to govern in this country. . . . Whether the Government of this country is hereafter to be an aristocratic or Democratic one, is now the great point to be determined. There is no middle course." [29]

The Whig ministry's willingness to compromise with the Lords reawakened the Philosophic Radicals' long-standing suspicion of the Whigs as aristocrats. It also seemed a foretaste of the sort of role the Whigs would play: they would not take the initiative as the leading group within the alliance of reformers. Yet that was needed if any reform program was to triumph over the Tory-dominated House of Lords. Resistance to the Lords, Hume said, "would show the country who were the parties favourable, and who were the parties unfavourable, to liberal principles." Hume now discerned a conflict between support for the ministry and "his sense of duty to the people," and he warned that if the ministry "resisted the rights of the people, if they resisted popular reform," he would be obliged to reconsider his role as a supporter. Roebuck also turned on the Whigs. "There is something ungenerous in the conduct of the Ministry towards us and the people." He had hoped that "the Ministers would not now desert and betray the people." [30]

The Cost of Cooperation

The Philosophical Radical posture of uncompromising opposition to all the Lords' amendments was challenged by Joseph Parkes. As secretary to the Commission and co-author of the report on which the bill was based, he would have been gratified by passage of the original bill, but he was willing to accept the compromise. He regretted the concessions made to the House of Lords, but he said, "our regret is diminished when we reflect on the immense importance of the improvements which the Bill

29. "Conduct of the Ministers," pp. 2–3; *Hansard, 30* (Aug. 31, 1835), 1164.

30. Ibid., *31* (Feb. 5, 1836), 128; *30* (Aug. 31, 1835), 1158, 1167. On the role of the Municipal Corporations Bill in the history of the Lords, see A. S. Turberville, *The House of Lords in the Age of Reform 1784–1837* (London, Faber, 1958), pp. 351–59.

has secured. The self-elected corporations—Tory justices—jobbing town-clerks—noble recorders—all these abuses are gone for ever; and in their stead, we have freely-chosen councils—popular magistrates—upright officers—and an improved system of civil and criminal judicature." [31] These changes were good in themselves, but he also valued them as the means of gradually eroding the sources of local conservatism. The Act will "break to pieces the Tory Cliques of the old Corporators, and in the article of patronage alone makes a great dent in the influence over the Parliamentary Elections." [32] Thus he argued that the Lords "have not effected any material reduction in the essentials of the measure." He was especially pleased by the household suffrage provision. This, he wrote to Place, "would do the trick, and must lead to a uniformity and extension of the Parliamentary Franchise." [33]

In addition to his approval of the provisions of the bill, even as altered, Parkes had other reasons for accepting the compromise. While sharing the Philosophic Radicals' outlook, he was more hopeful than they were that the Whigs would gradually shed their aristocratic leadership so that the more liberal element in the party could combine with the Radicals. He also was more patient than the Philosophic Radicals and thus could accept modest gains without thinking that they were achieved at the

31. "Corporation Reform," p. 542. He enumerated other improvements: The church patronage of the corporations will be sold; an effective police under popular control; corporate lands will be disposed of by open competition to highest bidder; accounts will be submitted to audit and publication; licenses will not be given as reward of political services; juries will be impartially selected. *"Municipally* it is injured," he admitted; but he argued that as "the bill as a whole is more than we had any right to expect to obtain this year," it was "more than an equivalent I think for the discount [i.e. concession] and better have such a bird in the hand than a better in the bush": Parkes to E. J. Stanley, Sept. 6, 1835, UCL, JPP.

32. Parkes to Durham, Oct. 23, 1835, LP. Thus, "the Municipal Reform is the life of what the 1832 measures was only the body": Parkes to Durham, Jan. 5, 1836, LP.

33. "Corporation Reform," pp. 542–43; Parkes to Place, Jan. 2, 1836, Add. MSS 35,150, f. 99. Parkes' judgment probably was affected by his knowledge of opposition within the Cabinet to the household suffrage provision: Parkes to Durham, Oct. 10, 1836, LP.

sacrifice of principle or at the cost of ultimate victory. When faced with the Lords' amendments, he defended the compromise, for rejection of it by the Radicals would drive a wedge between them and the Whigs, whereas "the great point now is to preserve that *national union* of Reformers which the Tories so dread." [34]

His moderation was also based on a desire to avoid open collision between the two Houses of Parliament. Ultimately, he thought, the Lords, by their blind resistance to popularly demanded reforms, would "commit suicide or prove the cause of irremediable evil to the Constitution"—which was, no doubt, the reason for his calling them Noble Destructives. It would be preferable, of course, if they submitted to the demands of public opinion, and there were some persons who expected that they would. One way or another, compliance with increasing democratic demands was necessary. However, for the present, public opinion was not ready to play this role: "There is as yet no fulcrum for a lever against the House of Lords—no practicable proposition, nor a unanimous opinion on the *present* necessity of forcing its doors." The middle-class Liberals in particular, Parkes said, were *"not* instructed in political science" and thus were not ready to join in a demand for an organic reform such as alteration of the status of the House of Lords. Therefore, there being "no *practical* present means of legislatively curing the evil of the Torified constitution of the Upper House," Parkes was disposed to be content with the compromise.[35]

With these views Parkes urged a course of moderation on the Philosophic Radicals, several of whom were for rejecting any compromise. Roebuck, Molesworth, Ewart, and Hume spoke vigorously against the amendments and the very idea of compromise, and some of them proposed withholding supplies until the Lords accepted the bill.[36] Even Grote, not usually given to mili-

34. Parkes to Stanley, Sept. 6, 1835, UCL, JPP.

35. Parkes to Stanley, Oct. 11, 1835, UCL, JPP; Parkes to Brougham, March 21, 1836, UCL, BrP; Parkes to Durham, Oct. 23, 1835, LP.

36. *Hansard, 30* (Aug. 25, 1835), 1094; (Aug. 31, 1835), 1161, 1168. James Mill complained that the Bill was "hacked and hewn" and "murder[ed] by the Lords": Bain, *James Mill,* pp. 390–91, 394. Regarding supplies, see *Hansard, 30* (Aug. 21, 1835), 822–30.

tancy, was reported to be "in a great rage, and . . . against all concession." Only Parkes, Roebuck said, was "preaching peace, but that was not popular." [37] To Stanley (a Whig whip) Parkes referred to the Philosophic Radicals as perfectability men, Purists and Fanatics, who lacked practical judgment. He lobbied among them and other Radicals and tried to reach them through the press to "show that Lunatics only would reject [the Bill] as it now is." Mrs. Grote later complained of "the vehement railing of Joseph Parkes, who wanted to *muzzle*" her husband at this time.[38]

In the end, the Philosophic Radicals submitted. They might have pressed for a division in order to identify those who wished to reject the compromise arranged by a conference with the Lords, but they did not. For one thing, Peel's acceptance of the compromise made it clear that there would be an overwhelming majority against the uncompromising Radicals. In addition, the Radicals faced parliamentary colleagues who shared their opinion on the impropriety of the Lords' veto, yet who rejected their all-or-nothing tactics. Like Parkes, and in some cases, perhaps, persuaded by him, they settled for the bill as altered rather than risk losing even that.[39] Among members close to the Philosophic Radicals there were desertions from the uncompromising position—including Buller, Ward, Clay, and, in the end, Grote.[40]

Thus the tenuous alliance between Whigs and Radicals was preserved. Although the Philosophic Radicals made clear that they were acquiescing with reluctance, to the world at large it appeared that they were but part of the Whig party. More

37. Leader, *Roebuck*, p. 70.
38. Parkes to Stanley, Sept. 6, 1835, UCL, JPP; Mrs. Grote to Place, May 26, 1836, Add. MSS 35,144, f. 374.
39. For example, D. W. Harvey, Beauclerk, M. Philips, Tennyson, D'Eynecourt, Hawes: *Hansard, 30*, 1204–05, 1207–08, 1426, 1434–35.
40. Ibid., col. 1181, 1196–97. There was one division on an amendment proposed by Roebuck; it received 37 votes: ibid., col. 1208. Mill criticized the Radicals for not forcing more divisions, "not to carry their propositions, but to force public attention to the subject": "Parliamentary Proceedings of the Session," *Lond. Rev., 1* (July 1835), 524 n. (evidently written and published in Sept. at the earliest).

significant, they appeared this way in their own eyes. They had aimed to establish a Radical party independent of the Whigs. Their doctrine provided a rationale for this, but now they followed a course of action based on "prudence," and in doing so they felt that their principles had been compromised and the people betrayed. Place had never doubted the correctness of the uncompromising course, and now that the Philosophic Radicals failed to fight the compromise to the full he said they suffered "degradation and disgrace"—they were "sham reformers." [41] Mrs. Grote thought the Radicals had failed the people by "bow[ing] to the Whig compromise." Even Parkes, the advocate of prudent tactics who had ridiculed the Philosophic Radicals as Perfectability men, now felt uncertain about the rightness of the course he had advocated. While still defending the compromise as a considerable gain, he complained of the physical and mental drain of the work he had done in connection with the Municipal Corporation Act. It involved, he said, "as much anxiety and responsibility and *trial to integrity* and *political principle* as most *young* men ever went thro.' " [42]

Those who had been urging uncompromising tactics had a clear vision of the benefits that might have been gained. Even if these uncompromising tactics had led to defeat of the bill, Place felt that at least "the country would be alive in a truly wholesome state of excitement," and popular attention would have been focused on the Lords as an aristocratic obstacle to reform. Had the bill been enacted without Philosophic Radical votes, then "the people might be assured there was a body of men in whom they ought and would place confidence." This would have put the Philosophic Radicals into the proper relationship to the people. But "the poor creatures could not see this; they could not understand their own position." Consequently, "The People will see that they are abandoned" now that the Radicals were "merged with the Whigs." In pointing to

41. Place, "The Peers and the People," *Pamph. P* [no. 13, Sept. 3, 1835], p. 11; Mrs. Grote to Place, May 26, 1836, Add. MSS 35,144, f. 374.
42. Mrs. Grote to Place, May 26, 1836, Add. MSS 35,144, f. 374; Parkes to Place, Jan. 2, 1836, Add. MSS 35,150, f. 99.

these consequences, Place saw himself as taking "large views," in contrast to those like Parkes who were "acting on narrow views." [43]

Although the connection with the Whigs was preserved, its continuation threatened the Philosophic Radicals' sense of their own integrity. Their experience with the Municipal Corporation Bill aggravated doubts about the propriety of continuing in the role of supporters and apparent allies. Parkes was well aware of their restiveness and doubted that the Whigs would succeed in keeping peace with the Radicals. Even he seems to have considered the possibility of throwing over the Whig alliance, and he wrote to Durham: "If we cant effect [the] natural and necessary consequence of the partial Reform of the Representation in 1832 by means of the 'Liberal Party' [i.e. Whigs plus Radicals] . . . we must 'een do it by having the courage to begin again a virtuous minority." [44]

For the remaining years of the decade the Philosophic Radicals attempted to resolve the dilemma of which they were now acutely aware. Were they to cooperate with the Whigs as a "Liberal party" (or as a "Reform party," as it was also called), or were they to assert their independence and try to set up a Radical party separate from the Whigs? When James and John Mill sanctioned cooperation with the Whig government, they had assumed that, because the government would be dependent on Radical votes, it would be possible to gain concessions of reform and also maintain the independent existence of the Radical section while awaiting better opportunities. Experience had now shown that it might not be so easy to gain both objectives. Mill complained that the Radicals' quiescence—the result of the bad bargain they seem to have tacitly made with the govern-

43. Place to Parkes, Sept. 30, Oct. 4, 1835; Jan. 3, 1836: Add. MSS 35,150, ff. 78, 102; Oct. 4 letter, unfol., Place to Mrs. Grote, Jan. 7, 1836, Add. MSS 35,144, ff. 356–57; Place, "Peers and the People," p. 9; Roebuck, "Conduct of the Ministers," p. 11.

44. Parkes to Durham, Aug. 7, 1836, LP; also, letter to Durham, Oct. 10, 1836: "If the Ministry try to stop us out the lesser evil is to let the Tories in, and begin de novo. . . . These are the general sentiments of Grote . . . and our best men."

ment—involved their "yoking themselves to the ministerial car, abdicating all independent action, and leaving nothing to distinguish them from the mere Whig coterie, except the memory of their former professions." They lost their separate identity, and with what result?—there were only "niggardly measures of reform." [45] If concessions were to be meager, why not at least maintain the independence of the Radical body and the sense of integrity that came with it? The problem was not merely one of achieving organic reforms—the very identity and future existence of their party seemed in question.

45. John Mill, "Postscript: The Close of the Session," *Lond. Rev.*, 2 (Oct. 1835), 275.

6. The Rationale for Aggressive Tactics

To many of their contemporaries, the Philosophic Radicals' expectation that realignment and the establishment of a new party could actually take place seemed unreasonable, even bizarre. After all, most of the old alignments and antagonisms survived, despite the basic changes that accompanied such developments as Catholic Emancipation and the Reform Bill. Yet the Radicals had a solid confidence that their ambitious plans could be realized.

One source of this confidence was a belief that beneath the familiar surface of events fundamental changes were quietly yet incessantly taking place. The old sentiments and allegiances that supported the existing framework of society were disintegrating. This was part of the "intellectual anarchy" that for John Mill characterized the spirit of the age in a transitional era. There was a new "spirit of questioning every institution, a habit of bringing back society to its first principles." [1] With the undermining of the old order, men were becoming more and more impatient and therefore ready to try radical, democratic remedies. John Mill contrasted the time when he first took an interest in public affairs with the present (1835). There was then an "adoration of everything which existed in England—church, law, judges, . . . monopolies, rotten boroughs and all—[it] was, to appearance, as deeply rooted in the national mind, as at any former period of history." Since that time, however, discontent had led to protest and demand for change—and Mill pointed to the concessions made to such demand over the previous decade—in the realms of commerce, law, religion, and government. But these changes were only surface manifestations of underlying change. Discerning persons who looked beneath the

1. Mill, *Spirit of the Age*, p. 12; Roebuck, "Jean Jacques Rousseau," *Tait's Edinburgh Magazine, 1* (June 1832), 338.

surface saw signs of decay in the foundations of the old order
and a shifting social basis for men's allegiances. He said they
would see "the silent progress of opinion" that accompanied and
was more important than the great, visible changes; all this had
the effect of "bring[ing] up the rear-guard of civilization, and
awaken[ing] the inert mass who had [previously] slept." [2]

These changes in men's minds all pointed to democratization,
and they prepared the way for great legislative reform. Ultimately the party system and institutions would correspond to
such sentiments and opinions, and change could be hastened,
even if only a few politicians took the proper course of action.
Those few could precipitate the changes in parties and institutions that were made possible by the silent revolution in opinions.
John Mill considered the Philosophic Radicals peculiarly well
fitted to play this role, and those of his associates who also advocated aggressive tactics shared this view. The Philosophic Radicals were "the visible instruments and the only apparent agents
in this great change." Since they understood the underlying
trend, and since there was a parallel between that development
and their principles, they could serve as a catalytic agent. Mill
said there is "a vitality in the principles, there is that in them
both of absolute truth and of adaptation to the particular wants
of the time, which will not suffer that in Parliament two or three
shall be gathered together in their name, proclaiming the purpose to stand or fall by them, and to go to what lengths soever
they may lead, and that those two or three shall not soon yield
a force before which ministries and aristocracies shall quail."
He felt they had been "given such a golden harvest," they ought
not leave it to be reaped by others.[3]

2. Mill, "Postscript: Close of the Session," *Lond. Rev., 2* (Oct. 1835),
270–72.
3. Ibid., p. 273; Mill, "Parties and the Ministry" *LWR, 28* (Oct. 1837),
18–19. Also, "the effects of individual exertion, though sure, are usually
slow. Not so in the present state of politics. Every well-directed attempt,
even by a solitary individual . . . is sure of a certain measure of immediate success": Mill, "Notes on the Newspapers," *Mo. Rep. 8* (April
1834), 310.

MODERATES—WHIGS OR RADICALS?

In order to carry out their plans, the Philosophic Radicals had to induce a split in the Whig-led ministerial party which they regarded as a loose affiliation of groups that sat and often voted together without belonging together. Among these groups the Whigs were a minority, a mere "coterie." The Whig leaders tried to conceal the cleavage between themselves and the reformers who supported them, and to this end they appealed for unity among all reformers. But the Philosophic Radicals saw through this; to them the Whigs' purpose was the "saving as much as they could of the aristocracy," to say nothing of the fruits of office that they personally enjoyed. To these ends they tried "to palm themselves upon the public as Reformers." Thus they tried to govern "with liberal professions [but] Tory principles," leading Roebuck to urge them to be honest and not to pretend to be liberals when in fact they were aristocrats.[4]

Some of the supporters of the Whig Leaders (apart from the Irish and the Philosophic Radicals themselves) were liberally disposed, independent members who, unlike the Philosophic Radicals, defended the Whig government as the best means for achieving additional reforms. These men were occasionally called Radicals, more often Liberals, most frequently Moderates or moderate Reformers. The Philosophic Radicals insisted that these men were not Whigs and therefore not necessarily a part of a Whig-led party. They thought the moderates were non-intellectual but well-intentioned men who were disposed to support democratic reforms, though uncertain and timid in doing so. These were the "partial" or "half-and-half" reformers, in contrast to themselves, the "complete" or "thorough" reformers (or, to their enemies, Ultras). The moderates could be separated from the Whigs, their support being based on the Whig argument that the only alternative to Whig leadership was a

4. *Hansard*, *36* (Jan. 31, 1837), 31–32; *35* (July 19, 1836), 352; *38* (June 9, 1837), 1344. On minority status of Whigs: Roebuck, "Note on the 'Globe,'" *Pamph. P* [no. 25, Nov. 26, 1835], p. 13; Molesworth, ibid. [no. 35, Feb. 4, 1836], p. 8.

Tory government under which even less reform would be achieved. This argument, as the Philosophic Radicals saw it, ignored the possibility of a party of reformers that excluded the Whigs and combined the moderates with the complete reformers in opposition to an anti-Reform aristocratic party.[5]

This was a situation in which a few politicians could turn a latent cleavage into open conflict by proposing basic constitutional reforms which were to be the wedge that would split the Whig party and create the possibility of realignment. Since the fundamental issues of constitutional reform could be used to divide politicians into aristocrats and democratic parties, they were especially important to the Philosophic Radicals as party politicians. Molesworth, for example, said of one such issue (abolition of property qualifications for Members of Parliament) that it was "a question of . . . principle, and, consequently, a better test of the real sentiments of those who voted on it, than any measure which would have been followed by more decided practical consequences." When he applied this test he found that large numbers of the Whig government's usual supporters —the moderates—joined the Radicals in opposition to the Whig government in combination with the Tories.[6]

This alignment was especially evident on Grote's motions on behalf of the ballot. The support he attracted increased throughout the decade. There were 106 votes in 1833, 146 in 1835, 155 in 1837, 200 in 1838, and by 1839 there were 216. Even though they were always minority votes, they were encouraging, for they divided members of Parliament into two opposed groups that appeared as a microcosm of the party system as the Philosophic Radicals wished to see it. Grote in 1833 had said that the ballot

5. There was a variation on this argument. Molesworth pointed out that, while some Whigs would go over to join the Tories, others "might be expected to join the Radicals in determined opposition to the aristocratic coalition—not however as leaders of the Reform party, for that day is past, but as fellow-labourers in the cause of popular principles": "Terms of Alliance," *LWR, 26* (Jan. 1837), 280.

6. Molesworth, "Parliamentary Conduct of the Radicals," *LWR, 27* (April 1837), 272, 279–80. The vote was 133 to 104, the majority consisting of 101 Tories, 11 members of the government, and 21 of their followers.

"will become the standing mark of separation between Whigs and Radicals," and the fairly large and increasing number of "nominal Whigs" that supported his motions was taken as evidence that a large portion of the Whig supporters really consisted of reformers who belonged in a popular party. In 1835 John Mill thought the "considerable increase . . . of the avowed supporters of the ballot" was an "encouraging symptom" which should give the Philosophic Radicals a sense of "confidence in their strength." By 1837 Molesworth felt that the tone of the ballot debate was such that it was a defeat "which amounted to a victory." [7]

Encouraged by the way these results confirmed the expectations derived from their doctrine, the advocates of aggressive tactics among the Philosophic Radicals gave notice of motions that were to split the Whigs and drive their moderate supporters into the Radical camp. These motions included the abolition of property qualifications for Members of Parliament; removal of bishops from Parliament; repeal of the Septennial Act; the ballot; repeal of the rate-paying clauses in the Reform Act; and reform of the House of Lords. These were the fundamental issues that would oblige politicians to identify themselves with one of the two basic principles—aristocracy or democracy. When faced with such issues, the Whigs, as a party "founded upon no principles, but standing between two principles . . . must, in [such] a contest of principles, cease ere long to exist." [8]

7. Grote to Parkes, Jan. 26, 1833, *Posthumous Papers,* p. 46; Mill, "Parliamentary Proceedings of the Session," *Lond. Rev., 1* (July 1835), 516–17; Molesworth, "Parliamentary Conduct," pp. 279–80. Also see Warburton, *Hansard, 47* (June 4, 1839), col. 1355; and James: "The ballot . . . was supported . . . not only by the philosophical Radicals, but by the unphilosophical Radicals, and by a few stray Whigs and Whig–Radicals": ibid., *40* (Feb. 15, 1838), 1169. T. P. Thompson noted in 1836 that "the relative majority against the Ballot has in a single year come down by more than one-half": *Letters of a Representative to His Constituents during the Session of 1836* (London, 1836), p. 77.

8. Molesworth, "Parliamentary Conduct," p. 272; "Terms of Alliance," *LWR, 26* (Jan. 1837) 291. The Philosophic Radicals' position on church questions was influenced by similar considerations. If the Whigs defended the Established Church, it was hoped that moderate reformers affiliated

Given the Philosophic Radicals' assumptions, the promotion of fundamental, organic reform—what they called acting on principle—was rational, for it was based on calculations of the consequences of such tactics on the Whig party and realignment. But there also was a nonrational component, for such tactics also appealed to the doctrinaire temperament of several Philosophic Radicals. Molesworth did not wish to stay in Parliament if he could represent only a constituency in which he would "be hampered in the free expression of [his] political principles." Mrs. Grote characterized her husband (though it was more true of herself) as one for whom "speaking out, aye! and acting out, are far more to his taste than half and half 'sayings' or 'doings.' " There was a sense of satisfaction, even exhilaration, when standing on their principles and a sense of malaise when they did not. When there was a prospect of doing so Molesworth was "in great glee because he hoped for a row." When denied such an opportunity he wondered if he was "to continue aimless and purposeless doing nothing." Supporting the Whigs was "servile" and "slavish." It was, as Mrs. Grote complained, for the timid who "dare not look at the great field of politics with anything like philosophical views." [9]

With such an outlook, uncompromising, "principled" positions had still another attraction. Such positions often provoked opposition from ultra-Tories and thereby brought the Radicals into open conflict with their most extreme ideological opponents, thus bypassing Whigs and moderates on both sides of the House.

---

with Dissent would be alienated from the Whigs, thereby drawing them to the Radical standard, while leaving the Whigs to coalesce with the Tories in defense of the Church as an aristocratic institution.

9. Molesworth to Place, Sept. 5, 1836; Mrs. Grote to Place, June 7, 1835: Add. MSS 35,150, ff. 52, 145–46. Mrs. Grote to Place, Oct. 19, 1831, Add. MSS 35,149, f. 107. Leader, *Roebuck,* p. 70; Fawcett, *Molesworth,* p. 124; Roebuck, "The Radicals and the Ministers," *Pamph. P* [no. 35, Feb. 4, 1836], p. 4. Also, "Is the honest portion of sincere and zealous Reformers to be disgusted . . . by seeing their leaders . . . inactive and silently following in the train of the Whigs at the moment when they expect from them the sincere and unmodified assertion of their principles?": Falconer to Mrs. Grote, Dec. 31, 1836; H. Grote, *Philosophical Radicals of 1832,* pp. 26–27.

This kind of confrontation emerged as a result of Philosophic Radical attacks on the Orange Lodges and primogeniture, and it was one prominent ingredient in the debates occasioned by the several motions on behalf of organic reforms. Such an alignment was a realization of their vision of what politics ought to be like, for it engaged spokesmen for the opposing principles on the most fundamental issues. John Mill had already experienced the gratification of engaging the spokesmen for the ideological Right in the London Debating Society, and in 1836 he justified a long review article of a pamphlet written by an extreme Tory on the ground that it at least allowed for political debate in terms of philosophical principles. Molesworth elevated to a new status the Tory leaders who "have, as Conservatives, become the representatives of a principle—the defenders of the aristocracy"; whereas previously they "had merely been the chiefs of a faction," now they were (unlike the Whigs) "the heads of a great party in the nation." Engaging the ideological Right allowed the Philosophic Radicals to address themselves to the only issue to which their doctrine was relevant. And when they provoked opposition from the ultra-Tories they at least received, by implication, acknowledgment of the existence and indeed the dangerous character of their small party.[10]

Mobilizing the Moderates

Although the Philosophic Radicals emphasized the importance of aggressive tactics as a means of attracting the moderate, liberal supporters of the government to Radical rather than Whig leadership, organizational and journalistic devices were not neglected. The planning of the Reform Club and the establish-

10. Mill, "Tories, Whigs, and Radicals," *LWR, 25* (July 1836), 285. Molesworth, "Terms of Alliance," *LWR, 26* (Jan. 1837) 291. *Hansard, 32* (April 12, 1836), 898–914; *36* (Feb. 14, 1837), 524, 552. Roebuck was especially contemptuous of Peel, as he shunned the ultra-Tories and sought to lead "the moderates as they are called—the men of no principle as I call them": Roebuck to Brougham, Aug. 9, 1837, UCL, BrP. Extreme Tories often acknowledged the Philosophic Radicals as their ideological opposition; for example, *Fraser's Magazine, 17* (Jan. 1838), 132, where the Grotes, Warburton, and Ward are called "the accredited leaders of the Radical party."

ment of *The Constitutional,* a daily newspaper, should be seen in this light.

The initiative for the formation of the Reform Club came from the Philosophic Radicals. In early 1836, in anticipation of the meeting of Parliament, "a dozen of us of the movement," Parkes said, met to set the plan on foot. Molesworth, Grote, Hume, and Ewart took the lead. Molesworth said they wanted in the Club "the best of the Radicals and no Whigs," a wish that was reflected in the exclusion of Whigs from the first committee set up to plan the organization.[11] It was hoped that by setting up a body committed to reform, the Whig party would be split, with the aristocratic leadership opposed to reform refusing to join, leaving the large body of "nominal Whigs" to join a party in which all would have affinity of principle.

The Whigs were not pleased with this sign of initiative by the Philosophic Radicals, for such a club would provide an opportunity for the organization of a Radical–Liberal caucus independent of Whig leadership. Ellice, a Whig whip, tried to discourage the effort, alleging that it would lead to a split between the moderate supporters of the ministry and the more extreme Radicals. He warned Parkes that he "would have half our Whigs quarrelling in the club with O'Connell and Roebuck"; and, reminding him that not all the liberals were radically inclined, he asked if "a division [between Liberals and Radicals] is a good thing, or tends to give the enemy a more wholesome opinion, or apprehension of our strength?" His concern was expressed candidly, even bluntly, in conversation ("not one of the most courteous description") with Molesworth. He asked "if the Radicals intended to lead the Whigs," and warned that such

11. Parkes to Durham, March 1, 1836; Parkes and Molesworth, Memorandum [on the origin of the Reform Club], 7 Feb. 1836; E. J. Stanley to Durham, Dec. 18, 1835, Feb. 2, 1836; Yates to Durham, Feb. 3, 6, 1836: LP. Some accounts of the origin of the Reform Club suffer from a tendency to see it only in the light of its later development; for example, M. Ostrogorski, *Democracy and the Organization of Political Parties,* Eng. trans. F. Clarke (New York, 1908), *1,* 145; Louis Fagan, *The Reform Club, 1836–1886* (London, 1887), pp. 34–35. For a full, accurate account see Gash, *Politics in the Age of Peel,* pp. 403–11.

conduct would "break up the party"; Molesworth in reply told Ellice that if he "thought the Whigs were to lead us as they thought proper, he was quite mistaken; we would have a club." [12]

Molesworth was resolute and, with Hume and Parkes, he set up an organizing committee and prepared to unite Liberals and Radicals but exclude Whigs. In response to this, Stanley, a Treasury Secretary and whip, told Ellice, "that whether the Whigs would sanction it or not [a club] would be formed . . . it was not now a question of whether he would like the establishment of such a club or not, but whether he would direct and guide it or be obliged to follow after, or break up the unity of the party." Believing that the Radicals would succeed without the Whigs, Ellice hastened to join. He and Stanley negotiated with Molesworth and Parkes. In an "angry" discussion they agreed to a new committee which included Whigs as well as Radicals. This guaranteed success. It began to operate in the spring of 1836 with 1,500 members, including most of the non-Tory M.P.s and many notables as well. Ellice and Liberal Whigs were indeed, as Parkes said, "forced in," but Ellice saw it as "work[ing] with the mass—if only to be able to [quiet?] it." [13]

Molesworth confessed that he was delighted with the outcome even though Whigs were to be included. He would have been pleased with either a Radical–Liberal but non-Whig club or with a club that included Whigs, provided it was not dominated by them. In either case the Radicals could achieve independent status and have an opportunity of mobilizing the moderates. Molesworth's pleasure might be explained by his belief that the club could not have been organized without Whig assistance; he did not see the inclusion of the Whigs as an obstacle to his purpose. "I don't fear their influence," he said; "some few [of the

12. Parkes to Durham, Feb. 2, 1836, LP; Ellice to Parkes, Dec. 25, 1835, and n.d. [1836]; Ellice to Russell, Dec. 22, 1836: NLS, EP, E41, ff. 21, 23; Fawcett, *Molesworth*, pp. 76–77.

13. Ibid.; Stanley to Durham, Feb. 2, 1836; Memo., 7 Feb. 1836; Parkes to Durham, March 1, 1836; Ellice to Parkes, n.d. [1836]. "Now Ellice having taken it up pets the child (the *adopted*) as if begat by himself"; Parkes to Durham, Feb. 2, 1836.

moderates] they may seduce, but very few, whilst we shall gain
many of them, for in all arguments we are their superiors." He
saw the club as providing an opportunity to organize Radicals
and Moderates, an opportunity that previously had not existed.
Thus he enthusiastically thought its "effect will be to break up
the Whig party by joining the best of them to the Radicals, and
the club will be the political centre of the Empire, and augment
our power immensely." [14]

With a firm belief that there was a good deal of latent radicalism in the populace, the Philosophic Radicals promoted the
establishment of a daily morning newspaper that was to help
mobilize public opinion in support of the Radicals and moderate
reformers in Parliament. In contrast to 1831–32, they no longer
had easy access to leading dailies. The *Times* had ceased to be
sympathetic to the Radical cause. Fonblanque's *Examiner* had
once been considered a radical paper, but during the mid-thirties
Fonblanque became increasingly critical of the Philosophic Radicals' inflexible attitude toward the Whig ministers. Believing
that the Whigs deserved Radical support in order to keep the
Tories from office, Fonblanque approved of the moderate reformers (he called them Radicals) who supported the ministry,
and he became sharply critical of those he named Ultra-Radicals,
i.e. Mill, Molesworth, Roebuck, and the "Grote conclave." With
this apostasy from the Philosophic Radical cause it became, in
Place's words, "the Renegade Examiner." [15] Even the *Morning
Chronicle,* a paper once influenced by the Benthamites, came to
"an understanding with the Whig administration, and became
as ridiculously whiggish as the Times had become Tory-ish."
There even was some uncertainty about the usually ultra-Radical
Spectator. There were, it is true, other papers, like the *True Sun*
(now edited by W. J. Fox), that advocated radical reforms; but

14. Fawcett, *Molesworth,* pp. 77–79. Also, "Ten Radical M.P.'s were
never to be found together except in the House, consequently no one
knew what his neighbor was about. This disorganization the Whigs desired, and on this account they have always in secret been opposed to
a club."

15. Place to Roebuck, Sept. 10, 1837, Add. MSS 35,151, f. 16; see
pp. 201–05, 224–25.

they were not under Philosophic Radical control. Therefore plans were made to establish a new daily newspaper.[16]

Early in 1836 plans were made for setting up *The Constitutional*. The reduction of the newspaper stamp (the "tax on knowledge") from fourpence to a penny gave hope that the paper might be a financial success, and thus, just as the Reform Club was being established, this ambitious enterprise also was launched. Place, Grote, Molesworth, Hume, Buller, Roebuck, Ewart, and Richard Potter were among the chief architects, and although a few of them purchased shares in the joint-stock company that was set up, much of the financing came from Thackeray's stepfather, Major Carmichael-Smyth, "a fervent republican" and extreme Radical who sought an opportunity both to promote his principles and to recoup some of Thackeray's fortune which had diminished considerably during his trusteeship. £60,000 was raised. Thackeray was the Paris correspondent; Buller was to be one of the writers. The paper began publication May 23, 1836.[17]

The Constitutional aspired to be "an entirely independent, a thoroughly Radical" paper. It advocated organic reforms, especially the ballot, shorter parliaments, and an extension of the suffrage. On behalf of such reforms it was to be an "organ of un-

16. Place, "Project for the Establishment of a Daily Morning Newspaper, 1836," Add. MSS 35,145, ff. 249–54; Roebuck, "The Stamped Press of London," *Pamph. P* [no. 3, June 25, 1835], pp. 7–8. The *Morning Chronicle* had been purchased by Easthope in 1834; Parkes contemplated buying a quarter share in the paper before negotiating the transaction on behalf of Easthope instead. For doubts about the *Spectator:* H. S. Chapman in *Pamph. P* [no. 11, Aug. 20, 1835], p. 9; [no. 17, Oct. 1, 1835], pp. 14–15. When the *Spectator* was in financial difficulties in 1837, Grote and Warburton considered purchasing it: Mrs. Grote to Place, Aug. 16, 1837, Add. MSS 35,150, f. 280.

17. H. R. Fox Bourne, *English Newspapers* (London, 1887), *2*, 100; Gordon N. Ray, *The Buried Life; A Study of the Relation Between Thackeray's Fiction and His Personal History* (Cambridge, Harvard, 1952), pp. 104–06; also see *The Letters and Private Papers of William Makepeace Thackeray*, ed. G. N. Ray (Cambridge, Harvard, 1945), *1*, 301–15; on the role of the *Constitutional* in Thackeray's life, see Gordon N. Ray, *Thackeray, The Uses of Adversity, 1811–1846* (New York, McGraw-Hill, 1955), *1*, 184–93.

compromising liberal principles," and its prospectus promised
that it would "never sanction expediency at the cost of principle." [18] Although it was unostentatious in its defense of radicalism, it lived up to this promise. It never ceased to be critical
of the Whigs and it urged the Radicals to put pressure on the
government.[19] Conventionally tasteful in format and content,
it was well designed to appeal to respectable but radical opinion.

At the same time an effort was made to consolidate the reading
public of the two quarterlies that claimed to be radical. The old
Westminster continued publication under Col. Thompson's direction even after Mill and Molesworth had established the
London Review in 1835 to represent the Philosophic Radicals.
Now in March 1836, after a year of publication, Molesworth
put up £1,000 to purchase the *Westminster,* and the two reviews
were combined to be called the *London and Westminster.* The
purpose, Mill said, was to stir up radical opinion and, even more
important, to induce the parliamentary radicals to form an independent party that would have a claim on public office.[20] With
the two reviews combined, John Mill felt that, "as the sole radical
review we shall surely now have a good chance of success." The
merger, along with the establishment of *The Constitutional* and
the Reform Club, and the new spirit of revolt among the Philosophic Radicals in Parliament, led Mill to say that the "time is
evidently approaching when the radicals will once more be a
distinct party." [21]

18. *Mr. Thackeray's Writings in the National Standard and Constitutional,* ed. Sebastian Evans (London, 1899), p. 293; Add. MSS 35,150,
f. 212; "Constitutional [a printed advertisement, April 18, 1836]," BM,
Place Collection of Newscuttings, Set 70, f. 527; Fox Bourne, *2,* 196–99.

19. Esp. see *Constitutional,* Nov. 19, 1836, p. 2. It tried "not merely
at gratifying the tastes of the few, but at advocating the interests of all":
ibid., July 1, 1837, p. 3.

20. *Auto.,* pp. 169, 181.

21. Mill to Fonblanque, n.d. (Feb. 1836); Mill to E. L. Bulwer, Nov.
23, 1836: *EL,* pp. 297, 313. With Mill's encouragement, Henry Cole
brought out a weekly newspaper, *The Guide,* in support of radical reform.
It modeled itself on the *Examiner* and the *Spectator.* It began publication
April 22, 1837. Despite its financial losses, Mill (May 16, 1837) tried to
encourage Cole, and "lectured about puffing [a] rising sale of 30,000," but
by mid-June Cole had given it up: Cole, "Diary 1837–1838"; "Miscel-
lanies, 1834–1838," f. 210, Victoria and Albert Museum.

AGGRESSIVE TACTICS

Although the Reform Club and *The Constitutional* were intended to give cohesion to the "nominal" Whigs and thus prepare the way for realignment, a more direct approach to this goal was increasingly urged by the more aggressive of the Philosophic Radicals during the two years or so following the passage of the compromised Municipal Corporations Act. This involved an attempt at bargaining by the Philosophic Radicals and their allies, variously labeled the "decided" or "out-and-out" Radicals —a group, since it excluded the moderates, that consisted of perhaps twenty or thirty. It was now proposed that the Radicals should communicate directly with the Whig leaders and insist on concessions of organic reform, particularly the ballot; and if concessions were not made, they were to withdraw their support and so threaten to bring on the fall of the government. Roebuck advocated this in a pamphlet written as the session opened in February 1836. The Whigs "could not retain office one single day," he wrote, "were they not supported by the Radical party. . . . It so happens, that a dozen men may turn the scale of parties." In these circumstances, he thought a small number of determined Radicals ought to insist on concessions as the price of continued support. "If they refuse, then I propose to inform the Ministers that we shall at once proceed to the House of Commons, and publicly declare that, if the Tories should move a resolution expressing that the House had no confidence in the present Ministers, *we should be absent when the division took place.*" [22] This was not the expression of a momentary irritation; he was urging an even harder bargain later in the year:

> we (i.e. *radicals*) must take up a new position.—I shall propose to all my friends, and have no doubt of being successful, to come to a direct and definite understanding with the Whig ministry.—*Our support* is no longer to be had on past conditions—contempt and disregard have been our portion though we have been the very breath in their

22. "The Radicals and the Ministers," *Pamph. P* [no. 35, Feb. 4, 1836], pp. 1–3.

nostrils. . . . Now then we must, we will say—our opinions
must be respected our advice listened [page torn, two words
missing] our plans adopted—*or we desert you* [word miss-
ing] *once and completely.*[23]

Whereas earlier he suggested abstention, now he advocated that
the Radicals threaten to go into opposition.

The opportunity to use such tactics seemed to be especially
propitious in view of the nearly even balance between Whig and
Tory parties, a cirmumstance that could have made the Whigs
dependent on Radical support whenever opposed by the Tories.
In 1836 Melbourne's majority, including the Radicals and Irish,
consisted of perhaps fifty or sixty. Given absentees and the
lack of modern party discipline, even a small group of Radicals
could be a serious threat. John Mill supported his plea for
tougher tactics with the assertion that "without the systematic
support of the Radicals, [the Ministry] could not exist for a
day." [24] This situation gave the Philosophic Radicals, despite
their small numbers, a sense of power. "A broken pitcher kept
together by a string," Roebuck said, "is no bad representation
of the present ministry and the rads. The ministry are the
broken pitcher, the rads the string." [25]

Given the nearly even balance between the ministry and the
Tory opposition, a Radical threat to withdraw support was supposed to present the Whig leadership with a dilemma. On the one
hand, if they met Radical demands, they would become more
genuinely liberal, but this would involve a dilution of aristocratic
power and the loss of some of their traditional supporters. On
the other hand, if they refused to meet Radical demands, the
moderates might join the Radicals in separating from the Whigs.
The Whig leadership with its most loyal followers would then
be isolated and in all likelihood would coalesce with the Tories

23. Roebuck to Brougham, Sept. 7, 1836, UCL, BrP.
24. "Tories, Whigs, and Radicals," *LWR, 25* (July 1836), 296.
25. Roebuck to Place, Jan. 4, 1837, Add. MSS 35,150, f. 198; also see
Roebuck, *Hansard, 38* (June 9, 1837), 1339; Hume, ibid. (June 23, 1837),
col. 1593; Molesworth, "Parliamentary Conduct of the Radicals" *LWR,
27* (April 1837), 275, 279.

into an aristocratic, anti-Radical party. According to this argument, the alternatives facing the Whigs were concession or merger with the Tories. As Molesworth warned, the Whigs would "be driven into the arms of the Tories; or, on the other hand, led to take some decided step towards the popular side." Grote agreed: "I do not see how one of the two alternatives can be avoided—either a coalition of some sort between Whigs and Tories, or else a farther reform of the Representative system." In either case, the results would include the dilution and ultimately the end of the Whigs; and for the Radicals, an increase in stature and perhaps even an independent existence.[26]

The more aggressive tacticians among the Philosophic Radicals voiced their indifference to the possibility that a Tory government would step into the Whigs' place. Molesworth felt that "as little positive good, as far as legislative measures are concerned, can be expected from the continuance in office of the Whigs as from a Tory administration"; and Roebuck asked, "What have we to dread from the Tories?—what to hope from the Whigs?" [27] John Mill, holding that "the whole conduct of the Whigs tends to *amortir l'esprit public,"* said "it would be a good thing for invigorating and consolidating the reform party

26. As another alternative, Molesworth said they would be obliged "to concede the principle of open questions": ibid., pp. 271–72; on open questions, see pp. 174, 179. Grote to Brougham, July 31, 1837, UCL, BrP. "The Whigs have three courses . . . to join the Conservatives . . . to [reform the Reform Bill] . . . or to remain in office, pursuing neither of these courses . . . till . . . they fall the victims of a compromising policy": W. Ewart, *The Reform of the Reform Bill, and Its Anticipated Results* (London, 1837), pp. 15–16.

27. Molesworth, "Terms of Alliance," *LWR, 26* (Jan. 1837) 304; Roebuck, "Radical Support to a Whig Ministry," *Pamph. P* [no. 32, Jan. 14, 1836], p. 1. Molesworth: "If . . . every concession is to be made to the Aristocracy, and none to the People, I, for one, must confess that I should care but little for how short a time such a feeble and nerveless Administration may retain power": "Speech . . . at Birmingham," *Pamph. P* [no. 35, Feb. 4, 1836], pp. 9–10. On the other hand, T. P. Thompson, while praising Roebuck's aggressiveness, was unwilling to "construe too literally [Roebuck's] intimations that it would make no difference if the Tories were in office": *Letters of a Representative to His Constituents during the Session of 1837. Second Series* (London, 1837), p. 1.

. . . if the Tories were to come in." [28] Even Grote was "quite prepared to throw them [the Whigs] overboard," for, as his wife said, "we can do as well in opposition without being hampered with our allies." [29]

The resignation by the Whig ministry and thus a temporary defeat for the reform cause was meant to give radicalism a new status. Since the resignation would have been provoked by the withdrawal of Radical support, there would have been a permanent split between Whigs and Radicals. When this happened, that portion of the ministerial supporters "in which the aristocratic feelings are predominant, will join the Tories, whilst the other will amalgamate itself with the Radicals." They also recognized that some few of the Whigs, aristocrats though they were, would also join the Radicals. But the result would be to "destroy the Whig party by dividing it into Whigs and Radicals"; and then, as Place said, politics would be a contest of "only reformers and Tories." [30]

With the Whigs as a party destroyed, the Radicals, as the only remaining organized body of professed reformers, would have a claim on the opposition front benches. "We [Radicals, Roebuck said] then shall take up our position at the *head* of the opposition to the Tory administration, and fight the fight of the people by ourselves; *we* shall be the leaders." [31] Thus they were willing to

28. Mill to Guilbert, June 19, 1837, *EL,* p. 338.

29. Mrs. Grote to Place, May 26, June 2, 1836; Add. MSS 35,144, ff. 374, 378. "Men who think the resignation of the Whigs a reason for deserting the people are of no use to the people": Place to Roebuck, Oct. 3, 1836; Add. MSS 35,150, f. 160. On the feeling that the session of 1836 accomplished nothing, see *Spectator, 9* (June 18, 1836), 582: "This year, Reform has come to a dead stand-still"; also, *Hansard, 35* (Aug. 9, 1836), 1042, 1046, 1051.

30. Molesworth, "Terms of Alliance," p. 291; Molesworth to Mrs. Grote, Oct. 24, 1836: Fawcett, *Molesworth,* p. 123; Place to Mrs. Grote, n.d. [1837], Add. MSS 35,150, f. 281. At the Bath dinner (Jan. 5, 1837) Molesworth said he would be "most sorry" to see the Tories in office; but that if to keep the Whigs in office it was necessary that "the Popular party should cooperate with them in doing nothing—should . . . shrink from attempting to carry out their principles . . . the sacrifice is too great a one; for it is a sacrifice of principle": *Spectator,* Jan. 7, 1837, p. 5.

31. Roebuck to Brougham, Sept. 7, 1836, UCL, BrP.

see a Tory government and with it a split in the Whig–Radical alliance that had produced varied reforms since 1832, provided that an independent though minority status for the Radicals would be established. Mill and Roebuck, in conversation with Tocqueville, also emphasized the importance of independent status to the Radicals. By "hiding behind the Whigs," they said, "letting themselves get forgotten, and, in a word, not giving a lead to the passions and opinions of those who sent them to Parliament, [the Radicals] risked losing their identity." There was a feeling that "they must submit to be extinguished, or take a bolder lead than they have done." Of course it was assumed that in the long run the Radicals "shall have conquered (which victory time will surely give us) [and then] *we* shall govern." [32] As a condition of achieving this ultimate victory, it was necessary in the short run to maintain the independent status of the Radical party.

All this was to result from the Whig government's resignation in the face of the Radical threat to withdraw support. However, there was another alternative—the Whigs might choose to make concessions. These would have involved organic reform, especially the ballot. The Philosophic Radicals indicated in very general terms that this was the price for their continued support. Such a bargain was not considered a compromise of principles or integrity for it was believed that such a change in the constitution would ultimately bring victory. Complete organic reform, including universal suffrage, was not even necessary; the ballot alone would be sufficient, for they thought even the existing limited electorate "were inclined to good sound Radicalism." If only electoral choices reflected the real preferences of the voters, Grote argued, "the parties in Parliament would be very different from what they were at that moment." [33] Once the ballot was

---

32. Entry of May 29, 1835: Tocqueville, *Journeys to England and Ireland,* Eng. trans. G. Lawrence and K. P. Mayer (London, Faber, 1958), pp. 85–86. For Tocqueville's response see below, Chap. 7, n. 14 and p. 285. Falconer to Mrs. Grote, Dec. 31, 1836; H. Grote, *Philosophical Radicals of 1832,* p. 26. Roebuck to Brougham, Sept. 7, 1836.

33. *Hansard, 39* (Nov. 20, 1837), 50, 60. On the inherent radicalism of the people, see *Constitutional,* Oct. 15, 1836, p. 2: "Radicalism is now

established, "the inevitable consequence would be to get all the others [i.e. short parliaments and universal suffrage]." So emphatic was their renewed emphasis on the ballot at this time that Parkes dubbed them "The Ballot-eers." [34]

The concession actually demanded of the Whigs did not go so far as to require their support as a government for the ballot. The Philosophic Radicals would have exchanged their support for the ministry's willingness to make the ballot an open question—one on which Cabinet unanimity was not required. They thought the ballot issue, even in this form, would be sufficient.[35] It was known that some Whigs would have voted for the ballot but were restrained from doing so by strong opposition from some of the party leaders. Since Grote's motions on behalf of the ballot attracted large and increasing support, it was felt that once it was an open question its ultimate passage would be hastened. Even short of this, they counted on the ballot as an open question to drive some of the more aristocratic Whigs out of the Cabinet, perhaps even out of the party. It was assumed that the democratic implications of the question would be seen and that at least some of the Whigs would refuse to make a concession to democracy, even for the sake of office. As for the rest of the Whig party, its willingness to make the ballot an open question would in effect be a sign of greater responsiveness to its supporters, and this would give the Radicals a part in party deliberations, indeed,

---

inseparably inetrwoven with the political faith of the British people. . . . it has grown at length into a position, not of their dreams, but of their daily thoughts and abiding convictions. . . . [It] has acquired, among the poor, the sacredness of a religion. . . . [It] is the principle of more than two-thirds of the whole people." The outcome of the municipal elections in 1836 would have confirmed this belief.

34. Warburton, quoted by *Fraser's Magazine*, 17 (Jan. 1838), 132; Parkes to Ellice, Jan. 8, 1837, LP. Molesworth: "The Ballot . . . will be the grand means of overturning the unjust and undue political influence of the Aristocracy": "Speech . . . at Birmingham," p. 8. Also see, *Objections to the Ballot, answered from the Writings and Speeches of Mill, Grote, etc.* (London, 1837); [H. G. Ward], *An Apology for the Ballot* (London, 1837).

35. Molesworth, "Terms of Alliance," pp. 313, 317; also see *Spectator*, 9 (Oct. 8, 1836), 964.

it would make way for Whig–Radical cooperation within a party devoted to goals that were as much Radical as Whig.

John Mill speculated about this possibility. If the Whigs, facing the two alternatives, "did *not* choose a coalition with the Tories," the Radicals, Mill said, should join them in voting down the Tories. In this case, by "ordinary good management on the part of the Radicals . . . the only Ministry which could then be formed, would be one in the formation of which the Whigs and the Radicals would have an equal voice." If Russell and "any others who may consider themselves pledged against the Ballot" were left out, then "the Radicals would have gained a victory. They would have asserted their share of influence, as a portion, and at least an equal portion, of the majority. They would have shaken off the character of a mere *tail*." And this was to be only the beginning. Once they increased their stature in this fashion, they would, Mill said, "rally public confidence round them, and rouse the Ministry which they had called into existence." The result would be that such a ministry "would either itself be, or would prepare the way for, that of which the time will soon come, a Ministry of moderate Radicals." [36]

Regardless of which alternative the Whigs chose—coalition with the Tories in an aristocratic party or concession to the Radicals within a liberalized reform party—the consequences for the Philosophic Radicals were similar. In either case, they could establish their identity once again as a body that would potentially be one of the major parties. Until they gave up the role of being a "tail" or merely the "cote gauche of the Whig party" there would be a frustrating discrepancy between the role as visualized in their doctrine and their actual position. The bold tactics would lead to the establishment of the independent party that their doctrine envisaged.

Independent status for the Radicals—this was the very least the advocates of aggressive tactics had in mind. However, in their more buoyant moments some saw themselves as responsible for the government. Roebuck, in a letter already quoted, was

36. Mill, "Lord Durham and the Canadians," *LWR, 28* (Jan. 1838), 508–10.

fairly explicit: "we then shall take up our position at the *head* of the opposition . . . *we* shall govern." The *Spectator* revealed that it shared the Radicals' fantasy of power by its account of what a Radical cabinet might be like. Headed by Durham, it included Grote (Exchequer), Hume (Home Secretary), C. P. Villiers (Foreign Secretary), Buller (Colonies), Strutt (Admiralty), Warburton (Board of Trade), H. G. Ward (War), Molesworth (Board of Control), John Romilly (Solicitor-general); and, without specifying the offices they might have, it also mentioned Ewart, Roebuck, Col. Thompson, Charles Austin, and—Mr. John Mill.[37] There were other occasions when the Philosophic Radicals revealed this ambition, and their antagonists did not always fail to discern the implications of their remarks. When Molesworth asked if "the liberal party has been so degraded and weakened by its submission to the Tories, that her Majesty would find it impossible to form a vigorous and self-relying liberal administration, if the present Ministers were to let go their grasp of power," Palmerston discerned the bitter voice of frustrated ambition. He asked if it "might be inferred from something which had fallen from him" whether Molesworth proposed to come into office with his own followers. In response to Molesworth's denial, Palmerston then speculated about the possibility that Molesworth sought to join the Tories in "a government of fusion" and he advised Molesworth, "if he meant to be the leader of a party, to improve his knowledge of Parliamentary strategy." [38] There were other occasions. Greville described the distant Radical hope that, after the Tory party was allowed into office as a result of Radical tactics, it would fail, and "after its failure, that recourse must be had to them." [39] Lord John Russell taunted the Radicals with the problems they and the country would have if Grote were Chancellor of the Ex-

37. *Spectator,* Dec. 9, 1837, pp. 1164, 1166; also see ibid., Dec. 16, 1837, p. 1192. For another of Roebuck's allusions to the possibility that the Radicals could come into office, see *Examiner,* Dec. 17, 1837, p. 810, reporting his speech at a public meeting.

38. *Hansard, 41* (March 6, 1838), 489, 521–23.

39. *Memoirs, 4,* 106.

chequer and leader of the House of Commons. And he asked if "Sir William Molesworth's administration" could command a majority of the house.[40]

40. *Letters to the Electors of Stroud, on the Principles of the Reform Act, by Lord John Russell* (6th ed. London, 1839), pp. 32, 35. Also see Russell, *Recollections and Suggestions, 1813–1873* (London, 1875), p. 230.

7. *Doctrinaire's Dilemma*

The bold talk on behalf of aggressive tactics was in part a product of a fantasy that was nourished by a combination of doctrine and ambition. But these tactics were not altogether fanciful. The government in fact did have a reduced majority in 1835–36, and this majority diminished still more after the elections in 1837. Its difficulties were accentuated by the Tory majority in the House of Lords, which was quick to veto any reforms that were at all far-reaching. Yet the ministry, identifying itself with reform, was under some obligation to introduce and carry reform measures in order to sustain this image. In these circumstances, passivity on the back benches would have been welcomed for it would allow for the engineering of broadly based consent for those modest measures that the Lords might be persuaded to accept. Caught between the demands of reformers speaking in the name of the populace and the resistance of the Lords, the Whigs' dilemma was characterized by Edward Bulwer (quoting Machiavelli) as having "to content the people, and to manage the nobles." [1]

In these circumstances the aggressive tactics urged by some of the Philosophic Radicals were bound to be disturbing to the ministry, which recognized Molesworth, Roebuck, Mill, and the Grotes as the source of the threat. The annoyance was greatest toward the end of 1836, with the approach of several ceremonial dinners at which the Whigs hoped to have an affirmation and demonstration of that "unity among reformers" on which their majority depended. Molesworth, Leader, and Roebuck expressed their restiveness at a reform dinner at Bath, and the *Spectator,* which during the previous months had been predicting a dissolution of the Whig–Radical alliance, now announced that the " 'philosophical Radicals' have resolved to eschew mere philosophy or speculation, and to become men of action; to rely no longer upon the Whigs." At this time (January 1837) Moles-

1. *England and the English, 2,* 271.

worth's article (edited and in part rewritten by Mill), "Terms of Alliance between Whigs and Radicals," appeared in the *London and Westminster Review*. It advocated aggressive tactics: there would be no Radical support unless the ministry allowed Radical proposals to be open questions, and in any case the Radicals were "to assume an independent attitude, and pursue their ends without reference to the existence or non-existence of the Whig ministry." Mill called it "*a coup de parti,* a manifesto as we say of the radicals (or rather *for* the radicals)." [2] Stanley, a Whig whip, calling it the Molesworth explosion, expressed a fear that "the enlightened Transcendentals will kick up a row at the Mdx. dinner [Jan. 1837]." Observing the signs of Radical impatience, he thought "nothing can well have been more mischievous and injurious" than their rebellious tactics.[3] The annoyance caused by the Philosophic Radical threats is also revealed in Melbourne's reaction to the Westminster by-election result in early 1837. Leader, a close friend of Molesworth's, resigned his seat for Bridgewater in 1837 in order to become a Radical candidate in the Westminster by-election against Sir Francis Burdett, who had just undergone a conversion to Toryism. On learning of the Tory victory, Melbourne said he "was not very sorry that Burdett had got in; . . . [as] the Ultras were already hard to manage, and . . . if Leader had won, there would be no doing anything with them." [4]

2. Mill to Tocqueville, Jan. 7, 1837, *EL*, p. 316. "Terms of Alliance," pp. 312–13, 317; *Spectator, 9* (Dec. 31, 1836), 1251; also see *10* (Jan. 7, 1837), 13; on the Bath dinner, ibid., pp. 4–5; on the predictions of dissolution, *9*, 678, 701, 941, 989, 1178. Molesworth's article "was regarded . . . as the manifesto of his party. . . . It made a good deal of noise at the time": [James Grant], *The British Senate* (Philadelphia, 1838), *2*, 130. The aggressive stance was endorsed by the *Constitutional,* Dec. 8, 19, 1836; Jan. 7, 9, 1837.

3. Stanley to Parkes, Jan. 20, 1837, UCL, JPP. Stanley to Durham, Dec. 11, 1836, LP; he added, "Molesworth is a very vain . . . young man, but clever, and from his position . . . as a man of property and elevated much above his natural position by the singularity of a landed Baronet being an Ultra Radical. The Radicals worship him most humbly and glorify him as their golden calf."

4. Torrens, *Melbourne, 2,* 228. Leader was returned at the general election later in the year.

THE OPPOSITION TO AGGRESSIVE TACTICS

The spokesmen for aggressive tactics provoked opposition within the Philosophic Radical group. As in most parties and sects, there were different approaches to the goal that all professed to serve, with a doctrinaire wing meeting resistance from a group of moderates nearer the center. However, in the small Philosophic Radical group the doctrinaire wing was by no means a clear minority. The opposition to the doctrinaire wing was led by, and sometimes seemed to consist of, Joseph Parkes. As often happens to persons playing this role, Parkes became the object of suspicion and hostility. For urging moderation he was suspected of apostasy to the Whig enemy, yet he was not a Whig, and even though he differed from his allies within the Radical movement in temperament and sense of urgency, his plea that they proceed more cautiously was made from a position compatible with Philosophic Radical doctrine.

Parkes' political outlook originated in Birmingham Nonconformity. He was born into a Unitarian family, and he was proud that his wife was Dr. Joseph Priestley's granddaughter. This outlook was sharpened by his exposure to the writings and personal influence of the Benthamites. He always identified himself as a Radical, even to his Whig associates.[5] Bentham, Grote, and James Mill, he said, were the source of "all the power and moral courage I have brought to bear in favour of the People." [6] Like the other Philosophic Radicals, he advocated organic reform, especially the ballot, triennial parliaments, a greatly extended suffrage, and reform of the House of Lords. Throughout the thirties he never tired of raging against the "mis-representative system." Above all, he satisfied an important criterion of Philosophic Radicalism by seeing the Whigs as but one faction of the aristocracy. As a party, he said, they "are cold, selfish, factioning men." [7] He admitted, furthermore, to Charles Sumner that he

5. For example, Parkes to Ellice, Sept. 12, 1833, NLS, EP, E 38, f. 3; Parkes to Stanley, Oct. 9, 1836, UCL, JPP.

6. Parkes to Mrs. Grote, May 1832; H. Grote, *Life of Grote*, p. 80.

7. Parkes to Place, March 19, 1839, Add. MSS 37,949, f. 397; Parkes to Durham, Dec. 13, 1834, LP; also see Parkes to Stanley, Sept. 24, 1837, UCL, JPP.

was a republican, which perhaps explains why the coronation of Queen Victoria gave him, as he complained, a bellyache. Referring to the "epidemic of loyalty" and the "Queen mania" that seized the country, he consoled himself with the thought that "nations recover as quick from fits of loyalty as unhappily they do from Reforming agitation such as 1832." [8]

Parkes also shared the general Philosophic Radical view on the conflict between aristocracy and democracy as the most important facet of politics. Like Molesworth, Place, and the Mills, he believed that "the real political contest has been rapidly coming on some years, viz. that between the two great antagonist principles of aristocracy and Democracy." [9] He also thought that one outcome of the democratization taking place could well be a coalition of Whigs and Tories into an aristocratic, anti-Reform party. On the other hand, like the other Philosophic Radicals, he realized that, while the diehard aristocrats among the Whigs might join the Tories, many Whigs might be disposed to liberalize their party and commit themselves to a broadly based coalition that included the Radicals. At this point he deviated from the position taken by the advocates of aggressive tactics, who sometimes claimed that they were indifferent as to which alternative the Whigs adopted. Parkes was clear in his own mind that one of those alternatives, if adopted in the immediate future, would be dangerous. While wishing to enlarge the contribution of radicalism to both the policy and personnel of the ministry, Parkes was most anxious to avoid any split in the Whig–Radical coalition, as it would *immediately* bring a Tory-dominated aristocratic party into conflict with a "liberal" party from which the Whigs would be excluded. This would bring class conflict—in itself destructive—and it would also accentuate the difficulties, already great, of working the constitution.

Parkes looked forward to the ultimate success of democratic reform and thus the nullification of aristocratic privilege, and he recognized that conflict between aristocracy and the populace

8. Parkes to Charles Sumner, June 2, 1840, Harvard Coll. Library, Sumner Papers; Parkes to Cobden, July 7, 10, 1838, SRO, Cobden Papers. Also, "Last week was 'Passion week,' the whole country Coronation mad": Parkes to Durham, July 9, 1838, LP.

9. Parkes to Stanley, April 8, 1839, UCL, JPP.

was in fact taking place. For the moment, however, the sharp edge of the conflict was blunted because the aristocracy was divided, and large portions of the populace were usually apathetic. (The Chartist movement, which brought an increase in political consciousness, was only just getting under way.) His concern about the immediate confrontation of aristocracy and populace was based on his estimate of the way it would arouse the people from apathy and lead them to the opposite extreme. There might then be an extreme demand for democratic inroads on aristocratic privilege, and this would be rejected by the aristocratic politicians, Whigs as well as Tories, and perhaps by liberal, radically disposed politicians as well. In these circumstances, if the democratic movement succeeded, it would be by forcing a solution on the established classes; and even if it were not successful, there would be a gulf between the politicians and the populace that would make governing next to impossible.

Parkes assumed that a split in the Whig–Radical alliance would lead to a Tory government which, whether or not it was joined by Whigs, would resist even moderate reform. Toryism in itself was not a problem; he called it "a bugaboo except only its endangering the opposite extreme." He was disposed to "laugh at any idea of Toryism being dominant." But, he said, were it to gain a brief tenure of office, "I see in the vista an endless avenue of agitation, of unnecessary and evil tending agitation." To a man of Parkes' experience and tastes, agitation in itself was not an evil, but this particular agitation, he told Durham, would result in "the Mass go[ing] to the well again with the pitcher [and] they will break it. The most democratic claims will continue to be made out of doors; and your and my specific—Triennial Parliaments Household Suffrage and Ballot, with an equitable division of the constituencies—will be scorned as no radical cure for the cancer of mis-representation. In short if we are to have a *Stand-still* or a *Tory* government our fears in a very few years will be changed into fear of extreme Democracy not of Toryism." [10]

10. Parkes to Ellice, Jan. 8, Aug. 24, 1837; Parkes to Durham, Aug. 26, 1837: LP. Parkes believed that the Tories would turn extremist: "Wellington is overlaid by the Ultra Tory Peers and you will have heard has had

The problem as Parkes saw it was accentuated by the way the Constitution had been affected by the Reform Bill and the general increase in demand for democratic reform. The old parties were fragmented, and there was conflict between a Tory-dominated House of Lords and a reformist majority in the Commons. "The 'Constitution' is *gone*; that is to say it must be re-modelled, as far as regards the Hereditary Peerage. It cannot work, thus shattered, much longer." The conflict between the two Houses in 1831–32 and in 1835 could become a permanent condition. This meant that the Tory defenders of aristocratic privileges would have a permanent veto even though they could not (so Parkes thought) establish a government except for brief spells such as Peel enjoyed in 1834–35.[11] Apart from the constitutional problem this caused, Parkes was worried by the way it created the possibility of destructive political conflict. For if the aggressive tactics proposed by some Philosophic Radicals were successful and realignment immediately took place, the conflict between the two houses would then parallel a cleavage in the social structure. If that were to occur, what previously had been a cleavage would become an open conflict, for then the political institutions, once they provided an arena for the waging of class warfare, would bring the heretofore latent conflict to the surface. It was for this reason that Parkes thought "there is palpably no other game on the cards, but to keep the two sections of the Hereditary Peerage poised against each other," which meant maintaining in some form a coalition between Whigs and Radicals.[12]

The condition that created the danger was ignorance—not only lack of knowledge but immaturity of political judgment that reflected the inexperience of a populace not fully integrated into

---

great difficulty to keep his party together, and indeed has only done so by giving way to their furor": Parkes to Durham, Aug. 16, 1838, LP.

11. Parkes to Durham, July 19, 1836, LP. Also, "I can't see my way out of that place [Lords]. . . . No one (of sense) seems to pretend to discern a cure, except in a re-model when accident or unforeseen political circumstances may give the means of reconstruction": Parkes to Durham, May 1, 1836, LP.

12. Parkes to Ellice, Jan. 8, 1837, LP.

the political system. He told Molesworth and other Philosophic Radicals "that they always over-rate the intelligence and power (for good) of the 'masses,' " and he felt that only those "who have lived in the Provinces know how little sound stuff there is at present to ground political improvements upon." This deficiency was not confined to the working classes, since he also complained about the "as yet limited political illumination of the Middle Classes." Complete democracy must therefore "wait awhile before the ignorant Public and the unenlightened 'Middle Classes' can see the light." He therefore condemned the Philosophic Radicals for thinking it "opportune at this moment . . . [for] raising the *real* issue." [13]

This outlook provided justification for his gradualism. If too much organic reform was demanded, it would drive the Whigs from the "liberal" party into the arms of the Tories, and then politics would be defined in class terms and be extremist as well. On the other hand, if too little organic reform was offered, the populace, as their political consciousness increased, would turn to extremist solutions such as Chartism. Both these roads led to the same undesirable alignment. Gradualism, however, would maintain the political division in the aristocracy, prevent the emergence of an extremist democratic movement, and ultimately gain the aristocracy's consent to democratic innovation. The alternative to this would be a "country divided into 2 great classes —democratic and anti-democratic," and all that that entailed.[14]

13. Parkes to Place, Dec. 14, 1838, Add. MSS 35,151, f. 114; Parkes to Cobden, Jan. 17, 1838, SRO, Cobden Papers. Also, "our present confused and contending state—class arrayed against class—and the mass of the People ill educated, objectless, and misled, alienated from government—is at once melancholy and fearful": Parkes to Cobden, Dec. 30, 1839, SRO, Cobden Papers.

14. Parkes to Ellice, Aug. 24, 1837, LP. Tocqueville shared Parkes' view. In conversation with Mill and Roebuck (see p. 173), he disagreed with their defense of aggressive tactics: "the reformers ought to feel that it was an unhoped-for piece of luck to find allies within those very classes [all those "above the simple people"], who help on the work of destruction without wishing to bring things down. . . . To try to carry through a radical revolution with the aid of the people only against a united front of all the rich and enlightened classes, is an almost impossible undertaking whose results have been disastrous. So I consider the union of the Re-

Given Parkes' gradualism, and the interests and commitments of the parties, the only arrangement that could satisfy Parkes was a liberal party consisting of Whigs and Radicals. But such a party would face difficulties in maintaining a majority in the House of Commons. If it went too fast, it would invite inevitable veto by the House of Lords and lose even liberal Whig support as well. On the other hand, if such a party went too slowly, the Radical component would be alienated. Moderate reform that might be pushed through the Lords and which would still satisfy the Radicals—this was the goal dictated by prudence. Success in striking this balance was exemplified by Whig–Radical cooperation in 1835 when the Municipal Corporation Act was passed, for in Parkes' view it was a substantial reform that ought to have satisfied the Radicals, and it probably was as extensive a reform as the Lords could have been made to accept.

Since 1835, however, the Whig–Radical alliance barely approximated Parkes' image of what the liberal party ought to be. Faced with impatient Radicals calling for concession, the Whigs were restrained by conviction as well as practical consideration of the consequence of concession on both their anti-Radical support and on the Lords. In the circumstances Parkes blamed both Radicals and Whigs for their short-sightedness.

> The only danger I see is *disunion* in the House of Commons. If by bad judgment, diluted Reform measures, or truckling to the Tories, Ministers quarrel with the Radicals —or, if by bad judgment and extreme movement Motions of the Radicals in Parliament *they* unjustly quarrel with Ministers all is *pro tempore* up; the last Whig Ministry will be dissolved; Peel would come in, with a mixed cheating Cabinet.[15]

Thus he thought the Philosophic Radicals should show restraint

---

former with a section of the conservatives as greatly favouring the slow but steady progress of the former, and I think that Reform would almost certainly be delayed if Whigs and Tories joined forces [immediately]": Tocqueville, *Journey to England*, p. 85 (entry May 29, 1835).

15. Parkes to Durham, Oct. 23, 1835, LP.

and the Whigs a willingness to liberalize, if a split, with all that entailed, was to be avoided.

Parkes hoped to maintain the alliance by means of a Durham-led liberal party, which meant that his position was not based on a desire to see the Whigs continue indefinitely. The possibility of such a party emerged in 1834 when Durham attracted a good deal of popular applause for urging further organic reform—specifically, household suffrage, ballot, and triennial parliaments. Durham had already earned a reputation as the most liberal of the Whigs, having held out for the strongest measure both in the Cabinet committee that drafted the first Reform Bill and during the period when the Reform Bills were under consideration. He seemed to qualify as leader of a moderate Radical party, especially as his stand earned him the enmity of many Whigs, an enmity that probably sent him as ambassador at St. Petersburgh (what Parkes called his "honourable exile").[16]

Parkes could not foresee when the opportunity for the emergence of a Durham party would arise, though he was confident that the time would come. He usually thought it a good thing that Durham was not present to be "tarnished by participation in their [Whigs'] want of principle and policy, and that [he] would remain a 'clean animal' for a future more honest Ministry." Durham was being "reserved for possible better opportunities of future public life." Parkes also wanted to make certain that, when the opportunity did come, the Durham party would not merely be a reconstituted Whig party. Parkes feared that the Whigs, with their fortunes declining, might try to use Durham, and he warned him that they "will want you to splice a broken mast. Now I hope you will not be *used* thus, to cork a sinking vessel unless you clearly see your way to serve your *real* friends the Reformers." The Whigs, Parkes held, would inevitably fall. Meanwhile, Durham was to wait in the wings for the opportunity to "effect a real resurrection of Liberal Supremacy." [17]

16. Parkes to Durham, May 1, 1836, LP.
17. Parkes to Durham, May 1, Aug. 7, 1836, LP; also, "The Politician who will not take *time* into his calculation is a miserable arithmetician in Political Science." Parkes' vision of Durham's future did not exclude the possibility that Durham would be leader of a reform party that began in opposition.

With this long-run aim of establishing a Durham-led liberal–radical party, Parkes wished to maintain Whig–Radical cooperation as a necessary stepping-stone. It was the material from which the Durham party would be made; and he saw it as the bulwark against the breakup of parties that would lead to political warfare along class lines. Therefore he played a conciliatory role, urging restraint on the Radicals and liberalization on the Whigs. His purpose, he explained, was "to keep the peace," to "conciliate all Reformers and so greatly serve the Cause now in no little peril—or rather in a Crisis." Given the state of parties and the Lords' hostility to reform, he saw compromise as a necessity while awaiting the unforeseeable opportunity for progressing further. He depended on "men of common sense" in both parties to heal the breach.[18] When some of the Philosophic Radicals called for aggressive tactics, he ridiculed them as Perfectability men. As for their practical judgment, he said, "many of our really honest Radicals in Parliament are not fit to be even abbots of a Monastery." [19]

While pleading with the Philosophic Radicals to be moderate, Parkes tried to convince the Whigs that they ought to make concessions to Radical demand. He thought the government was losing favor with its friends, and losing ground to the Tories, and he warned that "a *Juste Milieu* Ministry thus situated could only be a temporary government. None such could or can for any time maintain itself, between two fires of ultra opposite parties." In these circumstances he thought Melbourne "had to choose between a junction with the Conservatives or better Radicals." The way to achieve this was, at the very least, to make some of the favored organic reforms open questions. In an interview with Melbourne, Parkes reports, "I told him *uncompromisingly* my sentiments . . . I told him the Ballot and Duration of Parliament *must* be *honestly* and *immediately* on the opening of Parliament stated by the Leader of the House of Commons to be Open Questions." Without such open questions "as a concession to the

18. Parkes to Durham, July 26, 1836, LP. Parkes to Brougham, Oct. 4, 1836, UCL, BrP. His estimate of the likelihood of an open split varied from time to time.

19. Parkes to Stanley, Sept. 6, 1835, UCL, JPP. Parkes to Place, Dec. 14, 1838, Add. MSS 35,151, ff. 114–15.

Radicals, the whole concern must go to pieces." Of course, he would have preferred even greater concessions, but realistically he saw that Melbourne, who was willing to concede the ballot, having been converted by an article of James Mill's, faced conservative colleagues who would have resigned before agreeing to such a move.[20]

The real difference between Parkes and the advocates of aggressive tactics among the Philosophic Radicals was temperament; they were doctrinaire, he was flexible. He was often critical of doctrinaires, the Philosophic Radicals among others. "Truly men of your opinions and mine," he wrote to Cobden, "ought to have the stomachs of pigs to digest the political humbug of our times. I am often nearly vomiting in the trough. What between Humanity-mongers, Anti-Slavery, anti-poor law, and Currency fanatics politics just now [1838] make one as sick as a dog." [21] Having written this to Cobden, he was soon complaining that the Leaguers were "men with one idea" whose bigotry threatened "the general Liberal Cause [by] . . . sacrificing it at the shrine of their single question. A one eyed horse can see better than these Manchester gents." Such persons were Purists and Fanatics—men who were "highly useful to keep up the Standard of Value, but I value not their practical *judgment* a rush." The best argument against ultras, he thought, was *"more sense and less Logic."* [22]

Doctrinairism, however, is not a matter of temperament alone. There is an intellectual component that defines the number and variety of goals being sought. The doctrinaire Philosophic Radical sought the realignment of parties as a means of establishing radicalism in opposition to aristocracy. Parkes sought this too, but not immediately, for he had other goals. He wished to avoid class conflict that threatened public order; and he was sensitive

20. Parkes to Durham, July 19, 26, Oct. 10, 1836, LP.

21. Parkes to Cobden, May 28, 1838, SRO, Cobden Papers. Attwood was "a man of Genius; an honest fanatic . . . He mistook his forte . . . to invent and propagandi[ze] a new Religion"; Parkes to Cobden, Dec. 30, 1839, SRO, Cobden Papers.

22. Parkes to Stanley, Jan. 1, 1841; Sept. 9, 1835: UCL, JPP. Parkes to Ellice, Sept. 12, 1833, NLS, EP, E 38, f. 3.

to the need for institutions that would allow for effective government and that would have legitimacy in the eyes of all, including the declining aristocracy, while also satisfying the democratic demands of populace and the Radical leaders who were its spokesmen. His tactics would have frustrated the direct expression of Philosophic Radical hostility to the Whigs; but they would not have prevented the achievement of independent status for the Radicals, at first within a greatly liberalized coalition, and later as a separate party. With this goal, and in view of his manipulative attitude to the Whigs, who in any case he considered on their last legs, Parkes always denied being a Whig. "I have always promoted union [between Whigs and Radicals] and been much blagguarded and nicknamed 'Whig' for doing so among my Movement brethren." [23] To Place, who reported hearing "bad accounts" of his "Whig-iring," Parkes irritably replied:

> It is the *usual* practice in England to hear a man before he is condemned, and to inform him of the offence for which he is to be tried. What did you ever see, know, or hear of me (with your personal experience of me, now of many years standing and some test in times very different from these) justly to entitle you to suspect me of Whiggism; much less to arraign me for that offence? I can give you *Evidence* that I am what I always was, anxiously and disinterestedly acting to promote the Popular Cause against the Aristocracy and to further extend "Parliamentary Reform."

The only difference was that he did "not exactly agree . . . in the means of obtaining our common end," and he admitted that he did "*not* want to drive the Ministry *out*. [But] I want if possible to drive them *on*," hardly, Parkes thought, justification "to call me names." [24]

23. Parkes to Stanley, April 8, 1839, UCL, JPP; also, after having written often for the *Morning Chronicle* in 1835, he "declined to do any Press work; and especially on the Chronicle because I can't do Ministerial articles, and was annoyed . . . by articles being falsely attributed to me I never did." His reputation was partly based on his having professionally served Whig candidates.

24. Parkes to Place, Jan. 8, 1837, Add. MSS 35,150, ff. 216–17, 219.

AMBIVALENCE

As the parliamentary recess came to an end in early 1837 the question of tactics was especially pressing for the Philosophic Radicals. It also became a public question, and it attracted considerable attention in view of the importance of Radical votes to the life of the Melbourne government. In early January the *London and Westminster Review* appeared with Molesworth's article, "Terms of Alliance between Whigs and Radicals," and later in the month the Radical position was once more publicly stated when a dinner of the Middlesex Reform Association gave both Whigs and Radicals opportunities to express their feelings about one another.

In these circumstances, Parkes, with his moderate position, found himself engaged in a dispute about Radical tactics with several of the Philosophic Radicals—especially Place, and Mrs. Grote, who played a leading role among those who favored aggressive tactics. Temperamentally, Mrs. Grote was well qualified. She had a reputation for being self-assertive—for what James Mill called "piquant sauciness and masculine imperative moods." Cobden also recognized this character (apparently it could not be ignored) when he met Mrs. and Mr. Grote: "I use the words Mrs. and Mr. because she is the greater politician of the two." [25] As a leading member of the coterie, and with her husband the most esteemed Radical in Parliament, she attracted many of the Radicals to her house where she cultivated a salon-like atmosphere. Here she was able to give encouragement to the latent doctrinairism of some of her husband's colleagues. Parkes claimed that the bold tactics were "her contriving," and Molesworth (according to Fonblanque) was "instigated by Mrs.

However, he was willing to accept government patronage: Parkes to Brougham, Feb. 24, 1833, UCL, BrP. Yet he expresses radical views and quotes James Mill in support of them in his "Dedication [to Lord Melbourne]," pp. viii–ix, xi–xii, signed "Philo-Bentham," in *Emancipate Your Colonies! An Unpublished Argument, by Jeremy Bentham* (London, 1838). Also see above, p. 155.

25. Henry Solly, *These Eighty Years, 1,* 149; John Morley, *The Life of Richard Cobden* (13th ed. London, 1906), pp. 136–37.

Grote, who is unfortunately more of a man, but not a better man than her husband." [26] She was easily moved to adopt the feeling and language of doctrinairism. She saw herself as fighting a "holy war" against Parkes, and her allies were a band of "sacred devoted heroes." For her, cooperation with the Whigs was "a shuffling dirty compromise" and its defense was "expediency gabble." [27]

With such an outlook Mrs. Grote was at the center of a struggle "as to the true play of the Rads." [28] She was strongly supported by Place, Molesworth, and Roebuck. Others, most notably Grote, Buller, Warburton, and Hume, were sympathetic to her view but more cautious, and therefore uncertain, and thus it was to these that Parkes appealed. John Mill reported the Radicals to be much divided; some of them for giving more, and others less, support to the ministry; and he added, "as for me I am with the extreme party; though I would not always go so far as Roebuck." It is a sign of the importance Mill attached to these discussions that he thought "the approaching session will be next to that of 1830–1831, the most important since 1688," and he was sufficiently hopeful of the result that he predicted that "parties will stand quite differently at the commencement and at the close of it." [29]

Deliberation about tactics intensified with the approach of the Middlesex dinner, which was to include both Whigs and Radicals; attendance in itself would indicate approval of their continued cooperation. Yet it was just such cooperation that was at issue. Indeed, those urging bold tactics were especially sensitive to the appeal for unity among reformers of all shades, for they felt that the Whigs were disingenuously using that appeal in order to prevent the organization of a genuine reform party.

26. Parkes to Ellice, Jan. 8, 1837; Fonblanque to Durham, Jan. 2, 1837: LP.

27. Mrs. Grote to Place, Jan. 28 [1837]; Molesworth to Roebuck, Sept. 4, 1836: Add. MSS 35,150, ff. 150, 235. Mrs. Grote to Place, June 2, 1836, Add. MSS 35,144, ff. 377–78.

28. Mrs. Grote to Place, Jan. 28 [1837], Add. MSS 35,150, f. 235.

29. Mill to Guilbert, June 19, 1837; Mill to Tocqueville, Jan. 7, 1837: EL, pp. 317, 338.

Lord John Russell had made a plea for unity among all reformers back in 1835 in order to appease Radical disappointment over the compromise of the Municipal Corporations Bill.[30]
However, to the Philosophic Radicals, a Whig commitment to
reform was not an expression of conviction but a necessary condition of governing required by the spirit of the times. The Philosophic Radicals, feeling that they were the true reformers and
the true liberals, were indignant about the debasement implied
in this use of the word reformer.[31] Molesworth said of the Whigs
that they "had been placed in power by the cry of union of reformers; and upon the repetition of that cry they have relied for
existence." The result for the Radicals was a feeling that they
had lost their separate identity by the apparent merger of Whigs
and Radicals in the alliance of reformers. "If I were merely to
state that I am a Reformer," Molesworth said, "I should use a
denomination which now embraces all political parties." He
warned that as a result popular "indifference will extend itself to
all who call themselves reformers, if a different course be not
adopted." He wrote to Mrs. Grote that at the first opportunity
he would "tear to pieces that accursed cry of 'Union amongst
Reformers!' by which they [the Whigs] have disgraced the Radicals into the dishonoured followers of their debasing policy." He
asked her to "influence . . . our friends not again to raise the cry
of 'Union amongst Reformers.' So far from its producing union,"
he said, "it will produce disunion as destroying all unity of purpose." [32]

The Middlesex Reform Club dinner was nominally for the
purpose of honoring the two Members for Middlesex, Hume and
Byng—one a moderate Radical, the other a liberal Whig. But
there was a suspicion that the real purpose was to encourage a
show of Whig–Radical unity, which perhaps explains why such
outspoken militants as Molesworth and Roebuck were not in-

---

30. *Hansard, 30,* 1418.
31. James Mill, "State of the Nation," *Lond. Rev., 1,* 3; Roebuck to
Papineau, Sept. 4, 1836, CPA, Roebuck Papers.
32. "Terms of Alliance," LWR, *26* (Jan. 1837) 283, 286, 301; Molesworth to Mrs. Grote, Oct. 15, 24, 1836: Fawcett, *Molesworth,* pp. 57,
122; Mrs. Grote, *Philosophical Radicals of 1832,* pp. 24–25. Also see
Spectator, 10 (Sept. 16, 1837), 879; *Constitutional,* Nov. 8, 1836, p. 2.

vited. Place, like Parkes, was asked to be a steward, but he refused, for he thought he would only hear "fulsome praises of the administration, and resolutions ambiguously worded in the true whig stile to secure the assent of those who may be committed by being present in supporting ministers, in breaking down as far as they can, the energies of the people, in causing them to have no confidence in public men, thus sinking them into a state of apathy. . . . This is the *sole* tendency of the meeting." He also urged Hume to disappoint the managers of the dinner by speaking out on behalf of radicalism.[33]

The dispute about tactics primarily involved Mrs. Grote and Place on one side, and Parkes on the other, with the *Spectator* (edited by Rintoul) supporting the extremist position, and the *Examiner* (edited by Fonblanque) supporting Parkes. "We have all—the Radical sections—been quarreling heartily," Parkes reported. He attacked Mrs. Grote, Place, and Rintoul as the instigators of the revolt. "With Mother Grote, Old Place, and others I have been carrying on an incessant Epistoly [sic] War, writing bang at them." He denied Place's accusation that he had arranged the dinner. "I don't believe a word of any design of '*a Whig Feast.*' I know of no 'degradation' or 'mean submission' intended; nor have *I* ever dreamt of any being successfully perpetrated." He also reported that "Mrs. Grote and I have been clawing like wild beasts," and that he had gone "to Grote's house purposely to predict to them the inevitable consequences—the complete split with the Whigs" and "to ask them whether they were awake to the folly, part of *her* contriving." Parkes also directed his fire at Rintoul, who was urging Radicals to take a strong line with the ministry.[34] He was also "going about to the several papers where he has influence endeavouring to get the

33. Place to Hume, Dec. 30, 1836, Add. MSS 35,150, ff. 186–87; also, "Show the people that there are four men deserving their support and you will soon be forty. . . . This meeting will be a crisis of great importance to the nation. . . . [Be] as staunch and good as were the leaders in the commons house in the time of the first James and the first Charles." Parkes agreed to be a steward.

34. Parkes to Ellice, Jan. 8, 1837; Parkes to Durham, Jan. 24, 1837: LP. Parkes to Place, Jan. 8, 1837, Add. MSS 35,150, f. 217. *Spectator, 10* (Jan. 14, 1837), 25; on the *Examiner, ibid., 9* (Oct. 1, 15, 22, Dec. 3, 1836), 941, 989, 1013–14, 1159.

thorough-radicals denounced as a small and uninfluential clique."
For all this he was accused of "playing trumpeter to the
Whigs" [35] and of "being under the Whig petticoats." [36]

Parkes felt his arguments had some effect. He had alarmed
Mrs. Grote and had persuaded Warburton, who previously had
flirted with the aggressive tactics, to write her "an excellent common sense letter taking just the same view, and as boldly expressed as my remonstrances." The Grotes also decided to attend
the Middlesex dinner, leading Place to complain that while "she
is by far the best of the party, . . . she is so surrounded by the
dawdlers that her own strong understanding gives way, and she
is blinded to the fact that to compromise as she calls it is to
submit." As the Middlesex dinner approached, Mrs. Grote wrote
to Parkes, "hoping we should never split," and Parkes was satisfied that the Grote coterie "are all drawing their brewing milder,
and [are] aware of the insanity of kicking over the milk pail." He
thought the danger of a split diminished, but he still regarded
concessions as essential—"Lord M. must *come on* a little and
draw the Session liquor strong." [37]

At first it seemed "the stout Radicals" would not attend, but
in the end they did show up, all except Place, and Molesworth
and Roebuck, both uninvited. As Place explained, they "were
especially excluded from any invitation, and a character not to
be mistaken given to the meeting." [38] Those who did attend,
despite their hostility to the Whigs, settled into a compromise
position in which they felt quite uneasy. Their position, which
was in effect an abdication from their anti-Whig posture, was ex-

35. Chapman to Place, n.d. [*c.* Jan. 1837], Add. MSS 35,150, f. 221;
also, Parkes was "in a furious rage with our friends. . . . he denounced the
London and Westminster review policy in the most unmeasured terms."

36. Mrs. Grote to Place, Jan. 28 [1837], Add. MSS 35,150, f. 235.

37. Parkes to Ellice, Jan. 8, 1837, LP; Place to Roebuck, Jan. 5, 1837,
Add. MSS 35,150, f. 201; Parkes to Stanley, Jan. 20, 1837, UCL, JPP.

38. Hume to Ellice, Jan. 17, 1837, NLS, EP, E 25, f. 136. Place to
Hume, Jan. 16, 1837; Leader, *Roebuck,* p. 89. "The *bête noire* of Down-
ing Street, Siir William Molesworth, was by some *accident* not to be one of
the party; Mr. Leader . . . who had been invited, withdrew; and . . .
[Roebuck] was, of course, out of the question": *Spectator, 10* (Jan. 28,
1837), 73.

pressed in the speeches they gave at the dinner. Hume, for example, said,

> I believe a gross misunderstanding has gone abroad as to the differences between Reformers. I know no Reformer, however ultra he may be, who is not determined to keep out the Tories if he can. . . . We have nothing to expect from [the Tories] but evil—while we can have nothing from a liberal government but good. You may have that good in different degrees, but the system must go on.

And Grote said:

> the Radicals have much to lose, and nothing to gain, by countenancing or abetting the Tories. . . . If Lord Melbourne wishes to be considered as the Minister of the entire Reform party, and not of one section of it only, he will consent to make the great and vital questions on which that party is divided, matter of open debate and fair discussion. . . . I will not now inquire whether his Cabinet have always acted up to the exigencies of their position; but I cannot be mistaken in believing that their interest lies distinctly in favour of progressive reform, and the interest of the Tories no less distinctly against it; and this is sufficient to command my hearty efforts on behalf of Whigs against Tories.[39]

Warburton, Buller, and Ward also made speeches containing the same mixture of feeble assertion of Radical principles combined with an affirmation of support for the Whig government and a statement of hope (not demand) that concessions would be forthcoming.

The ministers could only be pleased with this result. Melbourne had to contend with the uncertain support of the Irish and the King, as well as the Radicals. "It would try the patience of an ass," he had said, and he contemplated resigning. After the

39. *Examiner,* Jan. 29, 1837, pp. 65–66. The *Constitutional,* Jan. 24, 1837, p. 3, also attributed the following words to Hume: "I am gratified by the progress we have made during the last few years . . . but is that any reason why we should not obtain more? . . . [I] entreat all Reformers to join with me in supporting a liberal government against the Tories."

Middlesex dinner, however, Creevy was pleased to report "that
the mischievous crew—Sir Wm. Molesworth, Roebuck, . . .
are becoming quite blown upon by their brother Radicals, which
will be a monstrous relief to the Government in the approaching
session." [40]

There were two reactions among Radicals to the dinner.
The doctrinaires felt they had been humiliated; the others saw
the display of unity as a step forward. Speaking for the former
group, Place called the dinner "nothing but Glitter and Gabble." [41] Even the Grotes, who had refused Molesworth's invitation to attend the Bath dinner, where a militantly Radical demonstration took place, now regretted their conduct at the Middlesex dinner.

> It may be some (malicious) satisfaction to you to learn
> [Mrs. Grote wrote to Place], that Geo. and I tossed in our
> beds *every hour* of that night, a prey to mortification, and
> degraded in our own eyes; that we shut ourselves up all
> next day and evening, covered, as it were, in 'sack cloth and
> ashes,' groaning in the spirit; in short I cd hardly command
> my tears all that day. Never have I seen *him* so ashamed
> and contrite.

The sense of humiliation was acute. The Radicals contributed
to "a whole night's glorification of Whigs," yet no members of
the Cabinet acknowledged the eulogies or expressed their sense
of obligation to the Radicals. This, Mrs. Grote said, made the
Radical role "a vile office." [42]

40. Cecil, *Melbourne*, pp. 291–92, 361, 371; *The Creevy Papers*, ed.
H. Maxwell (London, 1904), *2*, 316 (entry of Jan. 20, 1837).

41. Place to Parkes, Jan. 27, 1837, Add. MSS 35,150, f. 232. The
Constitutional tried to assuage the Radicals' self-esteem: "No one . . .
must infer from any Whig chaunt in the Ministerial journals . . . that the
Whigs triumphed last night at the Radical expense. . . . It is true, the mere
Ministerialist has a ground of triumph . . . [but] it cannot be denied, in-
deed, that the feeling of the evening was decidedly Radical": *Constitu-
tional,* Jan. 24, 1837, p. 2. The *Spectator* noted that some persons
"contrived to give the affair a Ministerial tinge" by excluding the militant
Radicals. It claimed that Grote remained independent but complained that
Hume and Clay were too conciliatory: *Spectator, 10* (Jan. 28, 1837), 73.

42. Mrs. Grote to Place, Jan. 28 [1837]. Mrs. Grote's comment did
not take into account the presence of Lord John Russell, who was chair-

The fact was that the Philosophic Radicals were ambivalent. Their doctrine called for aggressive tactics, and it led them to expect that those tactics would bring either realignment or a considerably liberalized Radical–Whig party (with the Whigs soon subordinated). Yet they were drawn in the opposite direction by realistic observation. This ambivalence was evident in the discrepancy between their performance at and their subsequent reaction to the Middlesex dinner; and it was to be displayed again in the combination of hostile rhetoric and supporting votes that they directed to the government during the remaining years of the decade.

Their ambivalence reflected a dilemma that they were unwilling to resolve. They wanted to see continued progress of liberal reform; but they also wanted (as the core of the Radical party) to be the agents through which this reform would be achieved. They were forced by circumstances to choose between these two goals. If they preserved the integrity and independence of the Philosophic Radical faction so that it could be the agent of further reform, it meant letting the Tories gain office and thus sacrificing even the possibility of small reforms. On the other hand, if they were to assure themselves of at least the possibility of further though small reform, it would be necessary to support the Whig government on its terms, which meant sacrificing the independence of the Philosophic Radical group and therefore the possibility that it would be the agent of progress in the future. Faced with these alternatives, they were ambivalent. They gratified their wish to guarantee the independent status of Philosophic Radicalism by hostile rhetoric and demands for the adoption of aggressive tactics. On the other side, they gratified their wish for the continued progress of reform, no matter how slow and regardless of who was the agent of its achievement, by supporting the Whig government. In the circumstances, this support could hardly be anything but reluctant and grudging.

Even the most doctrinaire of the Philosophic Radicals (Fran-

---

man but did not address the meeting, except to introduce the speakers. Byng was the only "thoroughly Whig" M.P. present: *Spectator, 10* (Jan. 28, 1837), 73. Clay toasted Melbourne and the ministry; it was not acknowledged: *Constitutional,* Jan. 24, 1837, p. 3.

cis Place excepted) shared this ambivalence. Roebuck, for example, in urging the adoption of aggressive tactics, often said that it made no difference if the Tories came in; for the Whigs, as but one section of the aristocracy, were the same as the Tories. Yet such assertions were not made with full conviction. Even he confessed that the Philosophic Radicals supported the Whig government "because the tories would be still worse. More mischief . . . would result, if the true liberals were to secede from the majority than now occurs under the present government." The Whigs, he added, "are not so bad as the Tories who would be industriously mischievous active and sagacious in the production of evil." In addition, a Tory government "would bring on a rebellion in Ireland." These were the considerations, Roebuck admitted, that "have hereto tied the hands and cramped the action of the friends of the people, and made them temporize with an evil they were not strong enough to subdue." [43] Therefore, with his hands so tied, Roebuck, in his first speech after the Middlesex dinner, sadly announced that he felt "compelled" to give the government "a very guarded and jealous support." He, "in conjunction with other Gentlemen who sat on that side of the House," would give "such a degree of support as should be sufficient to maintain them [Whigs] in their places, although he did not approve either of their general policy or of the principles upon which their Government was conducted." [44]

Hume also alternated between attacks on and apologies for the government. On the one hand, the ministry had lost support as a result of its timidity; however, it did face difficulties—"he could not shut his eyes to the fact" that there were 300 Tories in the opposition. Yet he also thought the opposition was not so strong that it should have prevented the government from taking a bolder course. Still, "he could never agree . . . that the country had not derived great advantage from their administration," for

43. Roebuck to Papineau, Sept. 4, 1836, CPA, Roebuck Papers.
44. *Hansard, 36* (Jan. 31, 1837), 28–29. The *Constitutional,* Oct. 17, 1836, p. 2, recognized ambivalence in the "paradoxical Whig–Radical"—one who is critical of the government yet supports it. "Now we all do this . . . the absurdity is the natural consequence of the conviction into which we are forced."

he could cite liberal measures they had introduced. Hume therefore "could not agree in the opinion that it would be beneficial to
the country to have Gentlemen on the opposite side vested with
the Government." [45]

John Mill showed the same mixed feelings. He had identified
himself with the "extreme party" and entirely agreed with those
who said "that it would be a good thing for invigorati[ng] and
consolidating the reform party if the Tories were to come in."

> But [he explained] the country does not go with us in this
> and therefore it will not do for the radicals to aid in turning
> out the ministry; by doing so they would create so much
> hostility in their own party, that there would be no hope of
> a real united reform party with the country at its back, for
> many years. So we must linger on, each man doing for the
> present such good work as lies nearer his hand.[46]

He therefore felt obliged to admit that the Radicals should at
least support the Whigs as a way of keeping out the Tories. The
Melbourne government "is entitled, against the Tories, to as
much support from the radicals as can be reconciled with the unqualified and energetic pursuit of their separate objects *as* Radicals." [47] And he agreed that the ministry should retain office.[48]

The Philosophic Radicals thus continued in what Mill had
called a "false position." [49] Their doctrine called for one line of
conduct; circumstances required that they adopt another. They
found their "hands tied," and therefore they "lingered on." In
this situation they were bound to be, as Greville described them,

---

45. *Hansard 38* (June 9, 1837), 1361–62. Perhaps additional evidence
of ambivalence might be found in Buller's slip, in which he said he opposed dividing on an amendment to an address to the "Government, to
which he was hostile—to which he was not hostile [laughter.]": ibid., *45*
(Feb. 5, 1839), 124. The Philosophic Radicals' mixed feelings were also
revealed in the debate on the English Church Bill: ibid., *35*, 532, 534,
536, 545–47, 795, 799–802 (July 25, Aug. 2, 1836).

46. Mill to Guilbert, June 19, 1837, *EL*, p. 338.

47. "Fonblanque's England," *LWR*, 27 (April 1837), 96–97.

48. Henry Cole, "Diary 1837–1838" (entry Sept. 16, 1837), Victoria
and Albert Museum.

49. Mill to Tocqueville, Jan. 7, 1837, *EL*, p. 317.

"very irate and sulky." However, he also noted that "as they still think that there is a better chance of their views being promoted by the Whigs remaining in, they continue to vote with them in cases of need." [50]

ISOLATION OF THE PHILOSOPHIC RADICALS FROM THE MODERATE REFORMERS

In the Philosophic Radicals' calculation of their political future the moderate radicals—the liberals, "half and half men," "nominal Whigs," who were neither Whig nor fully Radical—played a crucial role. Whether this group would turn to Whig or Radical leadership would determine the future status of the Philosophic Radicals—whether they were to fulfill their aspirations to leadership or disappear in backbench obscurity of a Whig-led party.

Both Whigs and Philosophic Radicals thought they could claim the loyalty of the moderate reformers. For those moderates provided the bulk of the support enjoyed by both the ministry and by Grote when he introduced his motions for the ballot. Many favored organic reforms, but this was not their exclusive concern. They looked for at least a move in the direction of free trade; and they also had welcomed the Dissenters Marriage Bill, the abolition of slavery, the ending of the East India Company's trading monopoly, and the Municipal Corporations Act, even as amended, as reforms equal in importance to organic reforms. They had some pride in the record of the Whig government and hope for its future. Whig ministers did not hesitate to appeal to this record, including the passage of the Reform Acts.[51] Therefore, the moderates were above all anti-Tory and, as the position of the Melbourne government became increasingly precarious, their ties to it strengthened and they were "now very anxious to come to some amicable understanding with the Government, and, if possible, to prop up the concern." [52] The Philosophic Radicals only gradually became aware of the resistance of the

50. *Memoirs, 3,* 401 (entry of June 25, 1837).
51. For example, Russell, *Hansard, 38* (June 9, 1837), 1369–70.
52. Greville, *Memoirs, 4,* 154–55.

moderates to their plans. They continued to look on the moderates (as Mill put it) as "persons calling themselves Whigs [but] who are real Liberals"; [53] but the signs of resistance reduced their confidence that the moderates would desert the Whigs to become part of a Radical party.

One of the most serious signs of equivocation among those moderates who "really" were Radicals came from the *Examiner*. The Philosophic Radicals had looked on it as their paper. When Fonblanque acquired it in 1829 they gave up a plan to establish a newspaper of their own. Now in the midst of public discussion of tactics it became especially important as it was considered to speak to (and for) the moderate reformers in the House of Commons.

The Philosophic Radicals had good reason to expect help from Fonblanque, for he was enough of a Radical to have named a son after Bentham.[54] He looked forward to the ultimate achievement of universal suffrage, though for the present he advocated household suffrage, triennial parliaments, and the ballot; and he wanted a party of reformers led by Lord Durham as the means of accomplishing these goals.[55] However, his radicalism was combined with a flexibility about the pace of reform and the agency by which it was to be achieved. In his view, the Whigs could still serve the Radical cause. Therefore, recognizing that "the notion of Mrs. Grote's little party seems to be that the perfection of Radicalism is the fiercest hostility to the Whigs," he criticized the Philosophic Radicals' arguments and ridiculed their aggressive tactics.[56] When they argued that, since neither Whig nor Tory would concede organic reform, the Tories were no worse than the Whigs, Fonblanque denied their conclusion. He admitted that both parties were wrong on some questions; but he insisted that there were many questions on which the Whigs took a liberal position, whereas one could not say this for the Tories. Furthermore, the progress of public opinion was

53. Mill, "Reorganization of the Reform Party," *LWR, 32,* 476.

54. *The Life and Labours of Albany Fonblanque,* ed. E. B. de Fonblanque (London, 1874), p. 45, n. 1.

55. *Examiner,* June 25, 1837, p. 402; July 2, 1837, p. 417.

56. Fonblanque to Durham, Jan. 2, 1837, LP.

liberalizing the Whigs, and he pointed as evidence to the increasing number of converts to the ballot. He also noted that, even if the Whig government was prevented from doing little positive good, nevertheless, "it can do the good of preventing the evils which a Tory Ministry would inflict." [57] Therefore, while still thinking of himself as a Radical, he tried to prevent the moderate reformers from shifting their loyalty from Whig to extreme Radical leadership.

Since the aggressive tactics advocated by some of the Philosophic Radicals might have led to such a shift and to a Tory government, he found himself criticizing many of his old friends. He labeled them the Ultras to distinguish them from the moderate reformers, for whom he saved the honorific label "Radical." They also were called fanatical Radicals, and pseudo-Liberals; [58] and since their tactics would have led to a Tory government, they also were the Tory Radicals.

> They are of the whimsical opinion that, as the present Ministry has moved too slowly in the right direction, more good can be extracted from a Ministry whose course must lie in the wrong direction. So fond are these folks of movement that, if they cannot get forward fast enough, they will rather go backward in company with the Tories than plod with the Whigs. [59]

57. *Examiner,* Aug. 27, 1837, p. 545; Aug. 13, 1837, p. 513; Feb. 5, 1837, p. 81. Also, "in the views of the more impetuous Reformers . . . it appears to be imagined that the Liberal forces, *minus* the Whigs . . . will be of undiminished strength, and able to cope with the Tories": ibid., Dec. 21, 1837, p. 817.

58. Fonblanque to Durham, Jan. 2, 1837, LP; *Examiner,* Aug. 6, 1837, p. 497.

59. Ibid., Aug. 27, 1837, p. 545; on the Philosophic Radicals as Tory Radicals also see ibid., Sept. 3, 10, 17, 1837, pp. 563, 581, 595; Fonblanque also quoted the *Globe* on this usage, and carried on a controversy with the *Spectator,* accusing it of Tory radicalism. Of course, to the extent that their ambivalence prevented several Philosophic Radicals from consistently advocating aggressive tactics, they were exempted from Fonblanque's charge. " 'Tory Radicals' though we be—as it has been the recent fashion to call us—it is not our party that is seen *voting with the Tories*": *Constitutional,* Feb. 18, 1837, p. 2.

There were but half a dozen of "these madcaps," he said, but their number would be greatly enlarged if Melbourne did not make concessions in order to appease the large number of moderate reformers who filled the government's backbenches. Recognizing the doctrinairism of the Philosophic Radicals, he realized that appeasement would not alter their position. However, with concessions—for example, making the ballot an open question—the few ultra-Radicals could be isolated from the large body of reformers and denied any influence over them. Like Parkes, Fonblanque was an antidoctrinaire Radical; thus he was dissatisfied with the Whig government, yet also impatient with the Ultra Radicals. He saw himself, as he saw Durham, as "distinguished from both the men who never carry their views beyond the emergency of the instant, and those opposite geniuses who stumble in the path before them while they gaze at the guiding star." [60]

The Philosophic Radicals were angered by Fonblanque. It was difficult to believe that their old associate could differ so, for, as John Mill said, "Mr. Fonblanque's opinions, it need scarcely be said, are those of the philosophic radicals. . . . [His] career as a public writer is coeval with the birth of this party. He was the first journalist who unfurled their banner." [61] Thus Mill rather hopefully thought Fonblanque's present position (1837) was a "temporary, and in a great measure only apparent, separation . . . between [him], and that more active and vigorous section of the thorough reformers" for which Mill spoke. However, sharp criticism of ultra-radicalism was one of Fonblanque's main editorial themes in the *Examiner* during the late 1830s; and it brought Mill to complain that since 1835 Fonblanque "acted as if his first object was to support and glorify the ministers and [as if] the assertion of his own political doctrines [was] only the

60. *Exam.*, July 16, 1837, pp. 449–50. This belief that his position was midway between the center and the left perhaps explains the change in the epigraph that usually appeared on the first page of each issue. When he was unequivocally radical he used a passage from Pope: "Party is the madness of many for the gain of a few"; since 1834 he often quoted Defoe: "expect martyrdom on both sides."

61. Mill, "Fonblanque's England," *LWR, 27* (April 1837), 67.

second." [62] Molesworth also complained that Fonblanque encouraged the moderate reformers in their docile course of acceptance of Whig leadership. Such men, Molesworth said, were "sincerely anxious to push forward reform, yet unwilling in any way to endanger the Whig administration. With Radicals they avow Radical doctrines, and are offended at being called Whigs. Their plea is—the time is not yet arrived . . . and the Examiner has of late become their organ." [63]

There was much other evidence of the moderates' reluctance to join a mutiny against the ministry. Another paper, the *Morning Chronicle,* a daily that had once been identified with extremely liberal reform if not radicalism, also rejected the aggressive tactics. Place, accusing it of Whiggishness, in 1836, after thirty years as a regular reader, gave it up for *The Constitutional.* Mill asked, "who thinks of it in any other light than that of a mere ministerial hack writer panegyrist?" [64]

There also was a spate of pamphlets reflecting nervousness about the loyalty of the moderate reformers to the ministry. One, *Domestic Prospects of the Country,* particularly aroused the Philosophic Radicals' resentment. It argued that all reformers— whether organic reformers seeking the ballot and an extended suffrage, or Dissenters seeking abolition of church rates, or Irish liberals—should recognize that all such questions were

> secondary to the great object of maintaining Lord Melbourne's Cabinet as the great agent of future improvement free from every species of present embarrassment. There is no measure necessary to the perfection of the Reform system, either in Church or State, which will not be eventu-

62. Ibid., pp. 96–97; also, "it was an unpleasant surprise to us, that . . . [Fonblanque] would so soon fall behind those whom he formerly ran so far before. The change is not in *them,* it is in *him.*"

63. "Terms of Alliance," *LWR, 26* (Jan. 1837), 283. There was a continuing dispute between the *Examiner* and the *Spectator,* with the *Constitutional* joining in during its brief period of publication. For examples of criticisms of or answers to the *Examiner,* see *Spectator, 9* (Oct. 29, 1836), 1038–39; *Constitutional,* Oct. 31, Nov. 7, 21, Dec. 6, 19, 1836, p. 2 in each issue; n. 34.

64. "Fonblanque's England," *LWR, 27* (April 1837), 97.

ally carried, if that system be permitted—permitted by *its friends*—to develop itself in the order of reasonable progress. It is now in a condition to withstand the efforts of its enemies, but not without forbearance, temper, and good management, on the part of those who profess to be its friends.[65]

Place thought it "cleverly worded and will take with nine out of ten of those who think themselves liberals. It will please . . . every one indeed who takes a short view of the matter, and has not studied the principles of government," especially as "the Morning Chronicle and the Renegade Examiner, who are running a race of scoundrelism, are both praising the pamphlet for its wisdom." [66]

The Philosophic Radicals were also reminded by the *Edinburgh Review* that the moderate reformers accurately reflected public opinion and that they by far out-numbered the small group of ultras. This had greater credibility than other statements in that Whig journal, for Edward Lytton Bulwer was the author. If Bulwer's authorship was known, it would have been particularly damaging to the Radicals' hopes, for Bulwer in their eyes epitomized the moderate reformer who supported the Whigs but who really belonged in a Radical party. Yet Bulwer argued that for the Radicals "the only practical course open . . . at present is, to support the Administration of Lord Melbourne to the utmost of their power. In doing so," he continued, "they will be advancing their own opinions as far as their opinion can be advanced by legislation and discussion, while the contemporary opinions of the vast majority of their fellow-citizens are opposed to them." [67] In still another case, a pamphleteer who

65. *Domestic Prospects of the Country under the New Parliament* (3d ed. London, 1837), p. 41.

66. Place to Roebuck, Sept. 10, 1837, Add. MSS 35,151, ff. 15–16. Place thought Hobhouse the author.

67. "State of Parties," *Edin. Rev.*, 65 (July 1837), 271. When offering to do the article, Bulwer said he would "undertake not to make it too radical . . . [and would adopt] a conciliatory tone to all our side—whether lukewarm whig or violent radical": E. L. Bulwer to Napier, May 20, 1837, BM, Napier Papers, Add. MSS 34,618, f. 135.

clearly identified himself as a reformer warned against those Radicals who, "in their pursuit of, perhaps, useful theories, [ought] not to imitate the unwise dog in the fable, who lost the substance in snatching at the shadow; and, above all, keep your eyes on those high-flying Patriots, who, in the excess of their love of Reform, are seeking to promote Reform by upsetting a Reform Government in order to make room for those most approved reformers—the Tories!" [68]

Signs of the moderate reformers' loyalty to the Whig government could also be observed in Parliament. Various independent members expressed their appreciation for the reforms achieved under Whig leadership and their wish to see it maintained. Amongst these were Dissenters, exemplified by Edward Baines, who, like the Philosophic Radicals, advocated organic reforms, including the ballot and an extended suffrage, yet who resisted their efforts to persuade him to adopt aggressive tactics. After attending a caucus at Molesworth's house in 1838, Baines felt he saw "clearly what was the object of the meeting," and said he would do nothing that "might have an injurious effect upon the Administration generally, to whom," he said, "I thought the country under great obligations, and that I could do nothing either directly or indirectly to displace them." As a Dissenter he felt a greater stake in the Whig alternative to Toryism than in radicalism as an alternative to both. [69] In addition, O'Connell,

68. *What Next? Or The Peers and the Third Time of Asking* (3d ed. London, 1837), p. 82. Also see Henry Lytton Bulwer, *The Lords, the Government, and the Country* (5th ed. London, 1836), esp. pp. 78–82. Even H. G. Ward denied being a Radical and looked for the growth of "a new power . . . composed of men attached to neither extreme": *An Apology for the Ballot* (1837), p. 2.

69. *Life of Baines,* p. 244; also see *Hansard, 35* (July 25, 1836), 539, for Baines' public affirmation of support to the Whigs; also see ibid., *36,* 42. At a dinner of the Religious Freedom Society Baines said his maxim was, "Put in whom you like, but keep out the Tories": *Spectator, 12,* (May 18, 1839), 461. The *Constitutional,* Sept. 27, 1836, p. 2, complained that men like Baines went only a step at a time and would not deal with great grievances except as a matter of extremity; thus he was "a legitimate specimen of a moderate." Gash says that in his loyalty to the Whigs, Baines "was typical of many dissenters in the electorate": *Politics in the Age of Peel,* pp. 110–11.

leading a bloc of Irish members, rejected aggressive tactics and supported the government. To this was added occasional desertion from their own ranks, such as that of Edward Strutt, whom Mill castigated as an "apostate radical." [70] Moreover, the Reform Club, which was to have been an instrument for separating the moderates from Whig leadership, quickly came to be dominated by the Whigs and thus gave additional evidence of the ties between the moderates and the ministry.

As the Philosophic Radicals became aware of the moderates' resistance to the role assigned them, they recognized their own isolation. Mrs. Grote noted in her diary that her husband and about five others "find themselves left to sustain the Radical opinions" in the House of Commons. Roebuck acknowledged that the democratic party in Parliament was a *"miserable* minority"; and Buller made the often-quoted witticism, "I see what we are coming to, Grote, in no very long time . . . you and I shall be left to 'tell' Molesworth!" [71] The Philosophic Radicals were forced to realize that realignment would have to be postponed. If the bulk of the moderates had been less loyal to the Whigs, the Philosophic Radicals could simultaneously have sought to promote reform and adopt the aggressive tactics which were intended to provide an independent existence for the Radical party. Then they would have satisfied themselves as both reformers and party politicians. But as it was, they had to choose between being part of the Whig-led reform party, which meant accepting at most minor reforms, or striving for the independence of the Radical body at the risk of losing all.

70. *Hansard, 38* (June 9, 1837), 1360; *Examiner,* Nov. 25, 1838, p. 738; Dec. 2, 1838, p. 755, for O'Connell's account of a dispute with Grote. Mill to Sarah Austin, April 26, 1837, *EL,* p. 333.

71. H. Grote, *Life of Grote,* p. 111; *Spectator, 10* (Feb. 4, 1837), 97. Fonblanque poked fun at them, saying that it was "certainly the smallest minority that ever gave itself party airs, or struck up a party tune. . . . We suppose they scarcely require a whipper-in, but it would puzzle them to form a Ministry. Two such parties would be necessary to make a whist party. . . . Party cannot in this instance be called 'madness of many,' but it may justly be termed the eccentricity of two": *Examiner,* June 18, 1837, p. 386. See n. 60.

THE DILEMMA RESOLVED

Toward the end of 1837 the Philosophic Radicals' relationship to the Whigs reached a crisis. Lord John Russell, as the government's leading spokesman in the House of Commons, expressed his views on the finality of the Reform Bill. In the debate on the Address, at the opening of the first Parliament of the Victorian reign, Wakley deplored the absence in the Address of any proposals for constitutional reform. Reminding the ministry "that they have some Radical supporters in this House," he moved three amendments to the Address, providing that the House consider an extension of the suffrage, the ballot, and the duration of parliaments. These were seconded by Sir William Molesworth and supported in speeches by Hume and Grote. The general tenor of their complaints was the government's refusal, from fear of the Tory opposition, even to consider reform. "Was it not notorious," Grote asked, "that no measure . . . could be passed if not approved of and countersigned by [Peel] and the Gentlemen who acted with him?" He concluded that the Tories "had the power of defeating any projects of reform" that might be proposed; in effect Peel had been given "a veto upon any measure which her Majesty's Ministers might propose of a reforming character." It was "a painful conclusion," he said; but in fact, the "Conservative principle was really predominant in Parliament, and when he said Conservative he meant the negation of all substantial reform." [72]

Wakley's amendments, and the Radicals' charges made in support, brought Russell to take the position on reform that gave him the name "Finality Jack." Wakley had expressed the hope that Russell "will make some manifestations that will tend to relieve us from the deep gloom which all Radical Reformers are under from the reading of the Speech." But Russell did no such thing. The questions raised in the amendments were, he said, "nothing else, but a repeal of the Reform Act," and to accept them would be "placing the representation on a different

72. *Hansard, 39* (Nov. 20, 1837), 37–48, 58–60. In view of Grote's surprise, it would seem that these were not concerted moves.

footing. . . . Am I then prepared to do this? I say certainly not
. . . having now only five years ago reformed the representation
. . . it would be a most unwise and unsound experiment now
to begin the process again." Russell went on to say that the
Reform Bill was deliberately made "a large and extensive measure" so that it "might have a prospect of being a final measure."
He admitted that the people have a right to reconsider the terms
of the Reform Bill, but it would be "quite impossible for me," he
said, "to take any part in these large measures of re-construction,
or to consent to the repeal of the Reform Act." [73]

The first amendment, for an extension of the suffrage, was
brought to a division. It received only 20 ayes, against 509
noes.[74] In view of this result Wakley did not even bother to
divide the House on the other two. The small support, combined
with Russell's statement, added to the Radicals' depressed mood.
The next night Leader said that, owing to Russell's declaration,
"the last hope of obtaining really popular measures from the
present Government has been taken from us." Now that the
Whigs have "made common cause with the opponents of Reform" they may depend on the Tories for support; they "can
expect no confidence from the popular party." Therefore, "their
fate is decided—their tenure of office can last but for a short
time longer." Buller added his expression of disappointment.
The Radicals wanted "to have the Reform Bill carried out to its
legitimate results," but if Russell "felt tired of the support which
he received from the decided Reformers, he was perfectly right
in saying so candidly and at once—if after he had sucked the
orange he felt disposed to throw it away, the sooner they knew
that the better." Grote got up to announce the epitaph of radical
hopes. Russell's declaration, he said, "would diffuse sadness

73. Ibid., col. 46, 69–70; during the next evening's debate Russell
emphasized that he had not made his declaration on an impulse of the
moment.
74. Among the 20 were Attwood, Dunscombe, Grote, Hume, Leader,
H. G. Ward; Wakley and Molesworth were tellers. Buller explained that
his vote for the government implied no approval of finality but disapproval of Wakley's tactics: ibid., col. 81, 99–102.

through the bosoms of all Reformers"; whatever hopes the Reformers had "entertained of his Lordship's Government would be destroyed by that declaration." [75]

These sentiments were shared by the Philosophic Radicals outside Parliament. Roebuck (recently defeated when seeking re-election) remarked that "the finality of Lord John Russell is the Toryism of Sir Robert Peel with a newfangled name, and to support him and his colleagues is to support Toryism in reality." And Mrs. Grote wrote to Place that "now we know what to expect from a liberal (?) [sic] cabinet—viz. '0'—as you and I knew all along but which we could never persuade people to see." [76] Mill urged the Philosophic Radicals to go into opposition. [77]

There was, according to Greville, general speculation at this time about the possibility that Radical indignation would break up the government, but a couple of weeks later he was able to report that the "notion of a break-up of the Government had gradually faded away." "Though the Radicals have not forgiven John Russell for his speech, they appear to have no intention of altering their conduct towards the Government." Although some of them thought they might have embarrassed and perhaps overthrown the government, "wiser heads of the party [according to Greville] know that these notions are quite chimerical, and are for trusting to the chapter of accidents and letting the present Cabinet remain in." [78]

75. Ibid., col. 92–93, 98–101, 109.
76. Leader, *Roebuck,* p. 123; Mrs. Grote to Place, Nov. 21, 1837, Add. MSS 35,151, ff. 43–44.
77. Mill to G. C. Lewis, Nov. 24, 1837, *EL*, p. 360; "Lord Durham and the Canadians," *LWR, 28* (Jan. 1838), 508–09. Roebuck, joined by Warburton and Leader, also called on the Radicals to "throw off the Whigs and act an independent part" (Westminster meeting, Dec. 4, 1837): *Examiner,* Dec. 10, 1837, p. 795. Wakley pointed out that the Radicals were equally out of place on either side of the House and called upon the Speaker to provide "a few cross benches . . . for their accommodation": *Hansard, 39* (Dec. 19, 1837), 1323.
78. *Memoirs, 3,* 401–02; *4,* 106 (entries of Nov. 26, Dec. 8, 1837, and Dec. 10, 1838). Throughout, Fonblanque regretted the finality declaration but urged the reformers to support the government all the same. He

They were, in most cases, depressed more than indignant. (All but Mill and Molesworth, who soon began plotting some bold moves of their own.) Although they continued to make sniping observations about the government, now (1838) a new tone of resignation appeared. Instead of hostility, which implied a confident belief that a Radical or near-Radical alternative could be engineered, they now professed indifference, as if no efforts of theirs could alter the conservative, anti-Reform character of the government, whether Whig or Tory. Almost in unison, and much more boldly than before, the Radicals asserted that Whig and Tory were but different names for the same thing. "There was a Whig government acting on Tory principles" (Leader). The Whig ministry "adopts Tory principles in order to retain office" (Molesworth). "Little now remains either in principle or in act between the Tories and Whigs" (Hume). Grote, who had been one of those disposed to compromise during the discussions of Radical policy between 1835 and 1837, now felt it was "not at all worth while to undergo the fatigue of a nightly attendance in Parliament for the simple purpose of sustaining *Whig* conservatism against *Tory* conservatism." [79]

Their dejection reflected an awareness of their lack of support within Parliament and among the electorate. They already had evidence of the reluctance of the moderate reformers to join their cause. Most of the 200 ballot men, when pressed to choose, preferred to support the government rather than stand by Radical principle. A sign of the absence of public support could be found in the failure, after about one year, of the *Constitutional*. The elections of August 1837 (required by the death of William IV) provided additional evidence. Roebuck, Joseph Hume, and Thompson were defeated, and Grote was the last of four suc-

---

praised Buller, Clay, and Strutt for voting against Wakley's amendment, and expressed satisfaction that "the Radicals did not allow it to make a breach in the Liberal ranks through which the Tories would have marched into power": *Examiner*, Nov. 26, 1837, p. 753; Dec. 3, 1837, p. 769; Dec. 10, 1837, p. 785; Dec. 30, 1838, p. 818.

79. *Hansard*, 41 (March 6, 7, 1838), 488–89, 577; also see *44* (July 16, 1838), 235, 348. Hume to Place, Jan. 1, 1838, Add. MSS 35,151, f. 48. Grote to John Austin, Feb. 1838: H. Grote, *Life of Grote*, p. 127.

cessful candidates in the City, winning by only six votes. (He had led the poll in 1832.) [80] From Switzerland, where she had gone with her husband after the election, Mrs. Grote surveyed the results. "I don't see how we Radicals are to make head this coming Parliament at all. Our ranks," she wrote to Molesworth, "are indeed properly thinned out. . . . The brunt of the battle will have to be sustained by Grote and you, aided by Buller, Leader, Charles Villiers, and a few more. I really feel astounded when I hear of Radical after Radical losing." The results of the elections only accentuated her exasperation with English politics "by testifying to the canker which devours the national sense of citizenship." [81] Even if some of the electoral results were discounted on the ground that open voting distorted the outcome, there still was evidence of rejection or at least indifference. This left only the nonvoting populace to whom they could appeal as the source of support. But since the demand for universal suffrage was given primacy by the politically conscious among the working classes, an appeal to them would have had the effect of reinforcing the Philosophic Radicals' isolation within the context of parliamentary politics. Therefore, such an appeal would not remedy their parliamentary isolation, which was the immediate source of their weakness.

Before the "final" rejection of further organic reform by the Whigs, the Philosophic Radicals had faced a dilemma; they felt

80. Hume was soon returned for Kilkenny. Referring to a by-election (St. Marylebone) in 1838, Fonblanque said, "In this example must be marked . . . the wide chasm that now separates the main body of the Radicals from the extreme section; . . . In the thousands for Mr. Ewart [3,762] to the hundreds for Colonel Thompson [186], [note] how few the Ultras are compared with the . . . moderate Radicals": *Examiner*, March 4, 1838, p. 130. Ewart was also unsuccessful, however.

81. Mrs. Grote to Molesworth, Aug. 13, 1837: H. Grote, *Life of Grote*, p. 120; Mrs. Grote to Place, Aug. 16, 1837, Add. MSS 35,150, f. 179. Molesworth's reply: "Your political gloom I don't share in . . . I have a firm faith in the progress of the human mind and in the steady advance of democracy": Fawcett, *Molesworth*, p. 134. After his defeat at Maidstone (where Disraeli was successful), Thompson said, "The hateful compost of vice and pollution called the constitution, decrees that the seats in our representation shall be won and lost by money": *Letters of a Representative . . . Second Series*, p. 105.

obliged to choose between piecemeal reform under Whig leadership and the independent status of the Radical party. This was a painful choice, for as reformers and Radical party politicians their primary hope was for success in both roles. The circumstances of reform politics between 1835 and 1838 made it necessary to postpone the establishment of a separate party, but their ultimate hopes for this were not abandoned, and meanwhile they consoled themselves with expectations of piecemeal reforms from the Whigs. Although it was not a satisfactory situation, neither was it hopeless. But now, after the finality declaration, there was a basic change. With the government turning its back on reform, they could not expect even piecemeal changes; and this was not all. For the other alternative posed in their dilemma was no longer open to them. After the elections of 1837, the minority of twenty in November 1837, and the other varied indications of Whig loyalties among the moderate reformers, it was now not possible to visualize the mobilization of the moderates into a Radical party. The result was that both horns of their dilemma, so to speak, had been eliminated. It no longer was open to them to support the Whig government in the hope of achieving at least some reform, for the government refused to play the role of reformer. Nor was it open to them to adopt the aggressive tactics with the hope of achieving independent, even if minority, status for a Radical party.

8. John Stuart Mill — The Last Spokesman for Philosophic Radicalism

John Mill's commitment to Philosophic Radicalism was such that after most of his associates succumbed to disillusionment he clung to his faith in the possibility of imminent success. This allowed him to recognize late in 1838 an opportunity "for a bold and successful stroke for Radicalism," [1] which Mill almost single-handedly attempted to use on behalf of the Radical party. The opportunity arose from the repercussions in England of the rebellion in Canada.

MILL'S IMMUNITY TO DISILLUSIONMENT

Mill, like the other Philosophic Radicals, had since 1835 combined sharp hostility with reluctant support for the Whig government. In his case the hostility was especially severe. In the deliberations over tactics he had identified himself with the "extreme party" and he commended Molesworth for his aggressive stand in January 1837. When Molesworth was joined by some of the other spokesmen for aggressive tactics Mill was pleased: "I have been driving them these four years to what they have now at last done, and done most successfully." [2]

The strength of Mill's commitment to the doctrine and the degree of confidence he had in the possibility of its successful implementation is revealed in his reactions to the situations that brought disappointment to the other Radicals. His confidence survived the elections of 1837, which reduced the ranks of the Radicals and were considered by many to reflect a conservative reaction. [3] In November 1837, after the government announced

1. *Auto.*, p. 182.
2. Mill to Mrs. Austin, April 26, 1837, *EL*, p. 335.
3. "The Radicals *seem* to have lost most only because they have lost some of their most leading men, but those will come in again for some other place very soon; and a great number of the new members are very

the Finality doctrine that led the other Radicals to contemplate retirement from politics, Mill responded by vigorously urging the reassertion of Radical independence from the Whig ministry. Of course, he too was angered by Russell's rejection of further reform, but he also had the satisfaction of finding his worst suspicions confirmed: "To have got rid of a delusion which made us torpid and cowardly . . . is a gain." Having decided that a "completely new tone must now . . . be taken, since the suicidal declaration of the Whigs against the reform of the reform bill," he attended a meeting at Molesworth's house in order to rouse the others. Mill held that "the time is come when all temporizing—all delicacy towards the Whigs—all fear of disuniting Reformers, or of embarrassing Ministers by pressing forward reforms, must be at an end." He became outspoken in his advocacy of complete separation from the Whigs, urging the Philosophic Radicals to "assume the precise position towards Lord Melbourne which they occupied in the first Reformed Parliament towards Lord Grey. Let them separate from the Ministry and go into declared opposition." [4]

Although he succeeded with a few—Molesworth, Leader, Harvey, and Wakley—he confessed "failure of our attempt to

---

decided Radicals": Mill to Robertson, Aug. 6, 1837, *EL*, p. 345. Also, "The late election enables us . . . to say, England is moderate-Radical": "Parties and the Ministry," *LWR, 28* (Oct. 1837), 8.

4. Mill to G. C. Lewis, Nov. 24, 1837, *EL*, p. 360; [Mill], "To the Electors of Leeds," in *Morning Chronicle,* Dec. 4, 1837, p. 1 (advertisements); "Lord Durham and the Canadians," *LWR, 28,* 506, 508–09. It is assumed that at the meeting Mill took the same position that he adopted in writing at that time. The address to the electors of Leeds was nominally by Molesworth, actually by Mill (except for a few words at the beginning and end): Mill, *Bibliography,* ed. MacMinn et al., pp. 49–50. It also appeared in *Spectator,* Dec. 2, 1837, p. 1149. The editors of Mill's *Bibliography* incorrectly identified this item as an article on page 3 of the *Morning Chronicle* of Dec. 4. However, the article on page 3 is an adverse criticism of Molesworth's address, and such a view is inconsistent with Mill's position stated elsewhere at this time. Furthermore, the Address on page 1 is the only article that appeared, as Mill in his *Bibliography* indicated, in both the *Morning Chronicle,* Dec. 4, and the *Spectator,* Dec. 2 (Mill mistakenly said Dec. 3, a Sunday, whereas the weekly *Spectator* was published on Saturdays).

obtain a collective demonstration." Indeed, he "raved and stormed with no effect, but that of being thought an impracticable enthusiast." He persisted, however, and a month later others, including Grote and Warburton, "showed a good deal of spirit" and seemed to come over to his views, for they "resolved to form a party and quitting the Ministerial benches, take up a separate position in the House." Actually, most of the Radicals soon thought their efforts were futile; yet Mill, unabashed, announced that the "Ministers are now understood. The alliance between them and the Radicals is broken, never more to be reunited. . . . The Radicals are organizing themselves as a separate party." He took the fact of Whig dependence on Tory votes and Tory support of Russell's finality doctrine as a hopeful sign that both "are studiously preparing the way for a coalition." He also foresaw "in another session, if not Sir Robert Peel and Lord Russell, Sir Robert Peel's and Lord John Russell's followers, seated on the same benches, and enthusiastically supporting the same Ministry; while the opposition benches will be occupied by the Radical party, and by thirty or forty rabid Orangemen, the offscouring of the House." [5]

The refusal to be daunted by evidence is also to be found in an ambitious article Mill had prepared for publication in January 1838, but which was held back because of the effect of the Canadian rebellion on radicalism. In it he presented a new version of the party that had been the goal of Philosophic Radical efforts for a decade. He indicated which politicians would belong in it, he defined its policy and principles, and he pointed to the social basis from which it would draw its support. In doing this, Mill gave a more detailed and concrete exposition than he or the other Radicals had previously offered. The purpose of the article was "to review and characterize the various divisions of the multitudinous and widely scattered Radical party . . . to point out to them the common ground on which they may meet and cooperate." [6]

5. Mill to Nichol, Dec. 21, 1837, *EL,* p. 365; "Lord Durham and the Canadians," *LWR, 28* (Jan. 1838), 504–06, 508.
6. Ibid., pp. 503–04; Mill thought the article was to be postponed only until the next issue; it did not appear until April 1839: see n. 7 below.

Mill held to his faith that the Radical party could be established, and that this was prevented only by a failure of statesmanship to bring the party system into alignment with the realities of the social structure. He complained that the Radicals' "whole strength in the country has never been called forth." The country in fact was divided into Conservative and Radical feeling, and it was the task of Radical leadership to call forth the "Radical feeling which already existed, from a passive state into an active." A radical Reform party was briefly and informally activated in order to pass the Reform Bill, and Mill now wanted "this great party reconstructed." To the argument that it was not practical, Mill replied that such a judgment was based on the false assumption that the Reform party of 1831–32 would be the model. Radical sentiment existed then as now, at least latently. The problem was to discover the means of bringing it into the open, and that was the purpose of the article, which was appropriately entitled "Reorganization of the Reform Party." What was needed was "singleness of purpose, and the energy of a strong will, aided by sufficient knowledge of the state of opinions in Great Britain and Ireland, and of the peculiarities of the different classes of society." [7]

Mill's article analyzed the relation of political opinion to social structure as a means of determining who were the "natural Radicals" and their "natural opponents." He traced the social foundations of these two parties in the interests and class feelings

7. "Reorganization of the Reform Party," *LWR, 32* (April 1839), 475–77. It is a sign of Mill's confidence that Radical sentiment existed, though latently, in large sections of the populace that he was willing to test this assumption. Thus he included in the speech written for Molesworth several pleas for the activation of public opinion on behalf of the ballot. The Ministers claimed the people were "Apathetic . . . indifferent to Reform. . . . The reason for this quiet, deferential . . . course . . . has now ended. . . . If you wish for [organic reform] . . . *you* must say it in the teeth of both the Aristocratic Factions. . . . Nothing can now be done for you within the walls of the House." Using language reminiscent of the agitation of 1831–32, he also called for a "simultaneous demonstration" and even parish-level organization that was meant to create "the terror of your voices": "To the Electors of Leeds," *Morn. Chr.,* Dec. 4, 1837, p. 1.

that placed men either in the privileged or in the disqualified classes. The Privileged classes consisted of those "contented with their position; who think that the institutions of the country work well for them." An inventory began with the landed interest, at least the great landed proprietors who, despite the Reform Act, still enjoyed near-control of government. To these were added the rich, the church, and the heads of the army, navy, and the bar. In all cases they either derived from the landed class or had a vested interest in the perpetuation of the privileges of that class. These were the groups that "thrive under existing institutions better than they would hope to thrive under any probable change, and who are, therefore, the natural Conservatives of the country."

In contrast to the natural Conservatives, there were "the classes who are dissatisfied with their position, and who compose the natural Radicals." They included, first, the middle classes, both small capitalists and persons in trade. Their dissatisfaction arose from the restrictive effects of protection to agriculture, which curtailed foreign demand for English manufactures. Next came the Dissenters, a group which, of course, included many of the middle classes. They were naturally Radical, for conscience as well as interest drove them into opposition to the aristocracy and the established church. In addition, there were "almost all the skilled employments, those which require talent and education but confer no rank." This group, which also included many Dissenters, was naturally Radical, as "the men of active and aspiring talent . . . are Radicals everywhere; for what is Radicalism, but the claim of pre-eminence for personal qualities above conventional or accidental advantages?" Finally, there was "the whole effective political strength of the working classes: classes deeply and increasingly discontented." [8]

Mill acknowledged that each of these varied groups had particular interests not shared with the others. Thus there would be disagreements about the policy to be pursued, but fundamentally they all shared in the general interest. "In calling upon all these sections to knit themselves together into one compact body, we

8. "Reorganization of the Reform Party," pp. 477–79, 483–88.

are not seeking to build a party on a mere combination of classes for the promotion of separate interests, however legitimate. We are appealing in behalf of the general interest of all, to those whose particular interests have opened their eyes. It is not for themselves, it is for principle, that we would summon them into the field." Thus, despite their disagreements, all these groups stood to gain by first pressing for a change in the distribution of political power. On this they could agree, even though they might differ on the amount or pace of change: "but as to the *kind* of change there is no disagreement: it must be by diminishing the power of those who are unjustly favoured, and giving more to those who are unjustly depressed." On the basis of this agreement Mill hoped to reconstruct the Reform party. It was to include "the whole Liberal party, not some mere section of it,—a combination which shall exclude no shade of opinion in which one sober or practical man can be found." It was to be "a phalanx, stretching from the Whig–Radicals at one extremity (if we may so term those among the persons calling themselves Whigs who are real Liberals) to the Ultra-Radicals and the Working Classes on the other."

This vision was still based on Philosophic Radical doctrine; and it still pointed to the realization of that doctrine in a party system in which a Radical party representing the people confronted the party of the aristocracy. This would make politics a confrontation "between the representatives of the two great principles," in contrast to the present situation in which party conflict was "between two men [i.e. party leaders] whose politics differ from one another only by the shadow of a shade." [9]

Mill considered it to be his duty, particularly after his father's death in 1836, to promote the Radical party. "I often wish I were among them [i.e. in Parliament]," he wrote; "now would be the time for knitting together a powerful party, and nobody holds the scattered threads of it in his hands except me." It was with this aspiration and this sense of duty that he assumed proprietorship of the *London and Westminster Review* in 1837 when Molesworth wished to give it up because of its losses

9. Ibid., pp. 488, 476, 508.

and his disagreements with some of its contributors. He proceeded to use the *Review* as a means of enlisting the support of a broad range of reformers.[10]

Mill thought that one major obstacle to the formation of a Radical party was the Philosophic Radicals' reputation for being narrow, doctrinaire Benthamites, indifferent to literary culture and intolerant of those with whom they disagreed. Already a decade earlier Macaulay had warned against the utilitarians. "We dread the odium and discredit of their alliance," he had written. "There is not . . . a party so unpopular. They have already made the science of political economy—a science of vast importance to the welfare of nations—an object of disgust to the majority of the community. The question of parliamentary reform will share the same fate if once an association is formed in the public mind between Reform and Utilitarianism." Mill himself had contributed to this reputation, first by example and then, in reaction to it, by providing the information for the unsympathetic characterizations of his father and Bentham that were included in Bulwer's widely read *England and the English*.[11] It seemed especially important to change this image of the Benthamites, for it was held by such men as Bulwer and Fonblanque, themselves (in Mill's view) only nominally Whig, and intellectual leaders of the moderate reformers as well.

Mill used the *Review* in order "to free philosophic radicalism from the reproach of sectarian Benthamism . . . [and] to give a wider basis and a more free and genial character to Radical speculation." Mill was oversensitive to the necessity of doing this as a result of his own personal sense of the inadequacies of Benthamism. But he also thought a change in the Benthamites' reputation was necessary in order to attract the moderates to his position. Thus when explaining what he hoped to achieve with the *Review* he coupled these two objects—to alter the

10. Mill to Nichol, Jan. 29, Dec. 21, 1837, *EL*, pp. 324, 364. Mill did not describe the disagreement; on political questions Molesworth was in close agreement with Mill, even after the transfer.

11. Macaulay, *Misc. Writings, 1*, 357–58. Bulwer drew a hostile caricature of the Benthamite Sam Square: *England and the English, 1*, 113–15.

Benthamites' reputation and to form "a powerful party." [12] His father—"the only one to whose opinions the editors were obliged to defer"—died in 1836, and that "event has made it far easier to . . . soften the harder and sterner features of its radicalism and utilitarianism." He now tried to "draw together a body of writers resembling the old school of Radicals only in being on the movement side, in philosophy, morality, and art as well as in politics and socialities, and to keep the remnant of the old school (it is dying out) in their proper place." The *Review* would then represent what he called "neo-radicalism." In this manner he tried to induce Bulwer and Fonblanque to write for the *Review* and to lend their support to the Radical party.[13]

In the course of trying to persuade men like Bulwer to join the newly organizing party, Mill attempted to give them the impression that neo-radicalism was neither narrow nor doctrinaire. In doing this he sometimes made apologetic and sometimes bitter statements about the other Philosophic Radicals, and this has created an impression of self-contradiction in his opinions of them. To Bulwer he tried to tone down the significance of Molesworth's defense of aggressive tactics. "Molesworth has not measured his words very scrupulously, but the object was to act upon the radicals, who are people not easily moved. He wanted to give them a violent shake, in order to set them going. You will not find him at all intemperate *now,* or in the least desirous of turning out the Ministry." [14] Yet at this period he himself was defending aggressive tactics and commending Molesworth's views to Mrs.

12. *Auto.*, p. 181. Mill's attempt to engage Bulwer's aid may seem inappropriate in view of Bulwer's criticisms of the Radicals (see pp. 205–06). However, Bulwer's position was not unequivocally hostile. It combined an endorsement of the moderate Radical program and criticism of the Whigs with hesitation about organizing a separate Radical party: E. L. Bulwer, *A Letter to a Late Cabinet Minister on the Present Crisis* (10th ed. London, 1834), pp. 3–5, 17, 40–43; *England and the English, 1,* xv; *2,* 274. Also, Mill's attempt preceded Bulwer's most severe criticism.

13. Mill to E. L. Bulwer, Nov. 23, 1836, *EL*, pp. 312–13.

14. Mill to E. L. Bulwer, n.d. [Jan. 1837], *EL*, p. 319. At this time Mill also personally called on Fonblanque "to make a pacification between him [Fonblanque] and Molesworth": Henry Cole, "Dairy, 1837–1838" (entry of Jan. 1, 1837), Victoria and Albert Museum.

Austin. To her he said the high reputation of the Radicals "is all owing to Molesworth, and to what he wrote and did." [15] Also, while indignantly denying, in a letter to Fonblanque, any association with the "Grote conclave," he was seeking to form a party in which the Philosophic Radicals were to play a key role. Indeed, he wanted to impress Bulwer and the moderate Radicals with the power he wielded through the *Review*—"the power . . . to begin preparing the radicals to support and even to call for their ministry." Whether this would be done was to depend on the moderate Radicals making the right choice of leaders and on "their embracing the policy which we think suitable to rally the body of moderate radicals round them, who are to be *our* party whoever is minister." [16]

THE CANADIAN REBELLION AS A THREAT TO MILL'S PLANS

John Mill was ambitiously planning on behalf of the Radical party when trouble in Canada brought discouragement. He was preparing the article "Reorganization of the Reform Party," intending to publish it in January 1838, when the rebellion broke out (December 1837) and narrowed the boundary around the Radical party.[17] That article was put aside and was replaced by one dealing with the Canadian question. Before the Canadian episode was over it gave Mill a brief period of high hopes, but he first spent ten depressed months regretting the unhappy effects of the Canadian rebellion on the Radical party.

He had reason for his concern, for events in Canada widened the gulf between the Philosophic Radicals and other reformers in Parliament. Whereas most of the reformers supported the government's Canadian policy, the Radicals opposed it. There were several reasons for this. For one thing, the Radicals were quick to oppose the ministry, especially in this case when they

15. Mill to Mrs. Austin, April 26, 1837, *EL*, p. 334. In writing of what Molesworth "wrote and did," Mill refers to Molesworth's speech at the Bath dinner, Jan. 5, 1837, and to his article, "Terms of Alliance," which appeared that month.

16. Mill to Fonblanque, n.d. [Feb. 7, 1838]; Mill to Roberston, n.d. [Jan. 30 or early Feb. 1838]; *EL*, pp. 376–77, 371–72.

17. "Lord Durham and the Canadians," *LWR, 28,* 503.

could ground their criticism on a defense of the colonists' constitutional rights. In addition, Roebuck's experience in Canada and his radical views made him sympathetic to the rebel cause and, still more important, while a Member for Bath, he had become a paid agent of the Assembly of Lower Canada, which was the body that provided inspiration and leadership for the rebellion. Already in April 1837 the Philosophic Radicals with a few sympathizers had opposed the government's Canadian policy. Later (Jan. 1838), when the government proposed the suspension of the Canadian constitution for four years and the establishment of authority to send a high commissioner (who turned out to be Durham), the parliamentary Radicals vigorously opposed the abrogation of the constitution. In response to the government, John Temple Leader, who shared with Roebuck the position of parliamentary leader of the Radicals on the Canadian question, announced that "it was the intention of those with whom he acted to divide upon every resolution, and to discuss the question on every occasion possible." Despite this, however, the government, with Tory support, gained overwhelming majorities, and the Radicals were left with minorities ranging from 6 to 39 votes. They were even taunted with having a "dwindling minority." Each time it included Leader, Buller, Molesworth, Grote, Col. Thompson, W. Ewart, Hume, and C. P. Villiers; more than ever they appeared to be a small, rigid, disgruntled minority.[18]

The defense of the Canadian insurgents by the small faction of extreme Radicals, in addition to isolating them from some reformers, also attracted the enmity of the moderates. This of course magnified the threat to Mill's hopes. Baines, for example, the liberal Dissenter who edited the *Leeds Mercury,* was opposed to the government's Canadian policy, but he thought it "exceedingly desirable that Mr. Leader, Sir Wm. Molesworth, and the other speakers [at a forthcoming public meeting on Canada] should be less violent and less bitter against the Government, than they were during the late debate in the House of Commons;

18. *Hansard, 37,* 137–44; *38,* 211, 216–48. Buller did not vote with the minority in one of the divisions. For Mill's defense of their position see "Lord Durham and the Canadians," *LWR, 28,* 532–33.

for I assure you that their tone has considerably prejudiced the cause they so ably and so justly espouse." [19] Parkes also regretted this development: "unluckily the advocates of the Lower Canadians here have damaged the cause. Leader and Molesworth hailed the break out for its insurrectionary spirit and home effect—an ignorant and absurd rejoicing." [20] This judgment was also to be found in that section of liberal opinion represented by George Cornwall Lewis, who also thought the Radicals had "acted very ill"; however bad the government's position, "it afforded no reason for inciting to rebellion, or for approving it when it had taken place." [21]

Even more discouraging was the hostility that came from such prominent spokesmen for the moderate reformers as Bulwer and Fonblanque. Mill's solicitation of support from Edward Bulwer was so unsuccessful that Bulwer openly attacked in Parliament "those who were called philosophical Radicals." He said:

> It was the same small and isolated knot of Gentlemen, who, on the first day of this session declared so much contempt of the Reform Bill, and so much hostility to the Government, who now differed also from the whole people of England in their sympathy for a guilty and absurd revolt. . . . the great body of Liberal politicians neither agreed with them in their policy for Canada nor their principles for England.

This provoked Grote to reply that "the words 'philosophical Radical' . . . were at least as respectable as the terms 'literary Whig.' " [22]

Fonblanque's hostility in the *Examiner* was even more discouraging, for the paper continued to be liberal in tone, even

19. Baines to Place, Jan. 2, 1838; Place to Baines, Jan. 4, 1838: Add. MSS 35, 151, ff. 51–53, 57. Place defended Leader and Molesworth.

20. Parkes to Cobden, Jan. 17, 1838, SRO, Cobden Papers.

21. G. C. Lewis to his father, Feb. 22, 1838: *Letters of Sir George Cornwall Lewis,* ed. G. F. Lewis, (London, 1870), p. 99.

22. *Hansard, 40* (Jan. 23, 1838), 398–99; Fonblanque commented on this incident: "Mr. Grote in applying the nickname slipped into the fallacy of vituperation, and sinned against Bentham": *Examiner,* Jan. 28, 1838, p. 50.

quite Radical in the legislative reforms it demanded; but it supported the Whig ministry on the ground that it was the only
viable alternative to the Tories. Fonblanque published a long
leader ridiculing the Radical position, and particularly Roebuck's, in the Canada debate. He labeled the parliamentary Radicals Detrimentals and Wrongheads and identified the *London
and Westminster Review* with the "Grote conclave." He accused
the *Review* of proposing a plan

> to vote with the Tories to turn out the Whigs, and then to
> vote with the Whigs to turn out the Tories, and thus to turn
> in themselves . . . the plan of the *London Review* would
> only end in establishing the Tories in power. . . . The Lon-
> don Reviewer asserts that the alliance between the Ministry
> and the Radicals is at an end; but how many members out
> of the Radical minority of little less than 200 have spoken
> or acted as if the alliance was at an end, or as if they desired
> it to be at an end?

And Fonblanque went on to suggest a

> policy of toleration, and the substitution of amicable con-
> troversy for the attempt to discredit, disparage, and destroy
> those who are not prepared to subscribe to every article of
> the radical creed, as settled in the last * * * * * conclave.
> We abjure Popery in politics. We deny the infallability of
> Mr. Grote. . . . Neither will we obey the bulls of excom-
> munication, or the interdicts fulminated in the *London
> Review*.[23]

Mill denied that the *Review* spoke for the Grote coterie; indeed,
he tried to disassociate himself from them, though not from their
political cause. He told Fonblanque that these observations put
"the last seal to your ministerialism by espousing the enmities
of the ministry, and displaying personal hostility to old friends
whom your new friends wish to hunt down." [24]

23. *Examiner*, Jan. 28, 1838, p. 49; Feb. 4, 1838, pp. 65–66. Having
been defeated in the 1837 election, Roebuck spoke at the bar as an
agent of the Canadian legislature, not as an M.P.

24. Mill to Fonblanque, Jan. 30, 1838, *EL*, p. 369; also see pp.
370–77 and above p. 109. In contrast to Mill's suspended judgment in

Mill was distressed by the way the Canadian rebellion brought to the surface the alienation of the Philosophic Radicals from the large but amorphous body of reformers in Parliament, for his only purpose was to see "the moderate Radicals . . . form themselves openly and avowedly into a distinct body from the Whigs." He said, in fact, "I have never had any other notion of practical policy since the Radicals were numerous enough to form a party, than that of resting on the *whole body* of Radical opinion, from the Whig–Radicals at one extreme to the more reasonable and practical of the working classes, and the Benthamites, at the other." Therefore, in the face of hostility from Fonblanque and Bulwer and the moderate reformers generally, Mill complained that the Canadian question "suspends all united action among Radicals, . . . sets one portion of the friends of popular institutions at variance with another, and . . . interrupts for the time all movements and all discussions tending to the great objects of domestic policy." The split between the Philosophic Radicals and other reformers made it difficult for him to determine his position, so that, as the April 1838 publication of the *Review* approached, he postponed writing the political article, since he was waiting, he said, until he had made up his mind what the relations of the *Review* were likely to be to parties in Parliament.[25] Apparently he could not decide, for the April number appeared without the usual political article commenting on the state of parties and the immediate issues before Parliament. This uncertainty continued; the number scheduled for July was delayed a month, when it again appeared without a political article.[26] The scheduled October number did not ap-

----

1837 (see above p. 203), he now formed what became a final judgment of Fonblanque: "After 1834 he sank into little better than their [Whigs] supporter and panegyrist": *Early Draft*, p. 156.

25. Mill to E. L. Bulwer, March 3, 5, 1838, *EL*, pp. 380, 383; "Lord Durham and the Canadians," *LWR*, *28*, 504.

26. An exception was the 5-page article "Lord Durham and His Assistants," which appeared only in the second edition of this number (pp. 507–12). Since Mill complained that his Canadian views had an adverse effect on sales of the *LWR*, the need for a second edition must be attributed to interest in the article "Bentham," which appeared in this number.

pear; Mill confessed that he was "thinking very little about the review but a good deal about my Logic." Mill was justified in feeling that the Canada question "in an evil hour crossed the path of Radicalism." [27]

MILL'S HOPES REVIVED

Throughout much of 1838 the other Philosophic Radicals shared Mill's discouragement. The Radical group in Parliament remained small and isolated, with little hope for concessions from the Melbourne government. The distant hope that Lord Durham would assume the leadership of a Radical party had been nourished but held in abeyance after 1834. Suddenly, however, when the already strained relations between Durham and the Whig government reached a crisis, Durham resigned as Governor-General of Canada. News of Durham's resignation and intention to return from Canada reawakened Mill's hope for a Durham party and stirred him to excitement and activity.

Durham's resignation created an opportunity for Philosophic Radical plans only because Durham, who had always been far to the left of even the most liberal Whigs, returned furiously hostile to Melbourne and the entire Whig ministry. This created the hope that he would assume leadership of the Radicals—moderates and Philosophic alike—and thus become the catalyst that would bring the realignment of parties that Mill and the other Philosophic Radicals had been seeking. Durham already felt enmity for the Melbourne government when he departed for Canada in May 1838. He felt estranged from them on the basis of political opinion, and he also was angered by the government's reluctance to approve his appointments to the staff he wished to take to Canada. Although Buller was unobjectionable, Turton and Wakefield invited criticism. Turton had been convicted for adultery, and Wakefield had spent three years in Newgate for abducting an heiress. As it was, Wakefield accompanied Durham without a formal appointment and at his own expense; Turton did not receive a formal appointment until he arrived

27. Mill to Robertson, Oct. 2, 1838; Mill to Bulwer, March 5, 1838: *EL*, pp. 388, 382. Cf. Packe, *Life of Mill*, pp. 229–30, where optimism is attributed to Mill at this stage.

in Canada. Durham was offended; "the way Lord Melbourne has given me up in the affair of Turton," he wrote, "leads me to expect any thing but support." [28] The event that touched off the resignation was the government's disapproval of Durham's policy in Canada. On his arrival he found he was in charge of prisoners, including some of the leaders of the rebellion. He issued an ordinance granting amnesty to most of them and ordered transportation to Bermuda for a few of the leaders, intending this as a lenient sentence. But his authority did not extend to Bermuda, and this became a pretext for criticism at home that was led by Brougham, his old rival for popularity among reformers. The criticism mounted, both in the press and in Parliament, and Melbourne failed to defend Durham, who thus felt betrayed. When he heard that the government would not sanction the ordinance he resigned on September 25, 1838, just four months after his arrival in Canada.[29]

The opportunity to turn this event to Radical party advantage was greatly facilitated by the presence in Canada of Wakefield and Buller, both said to possess considerable influence on Durham and both in touch with other Philosophic Radicals at home.[30] After the resignation, Wakefield was quick to report to Molesworth that Durham "is mortally but coolly and unmovably offended at everything Whig," and he invited the Radicals to be "men enough to enjoy the prospect: For my part," he said, "I would not exchange the present prospect for any that could have arisen from the quiet completion of his work *here*." [31] Buller wrote to Mill to say that he "read with great interest your views on the general state of politics," and he explained the relevance of Durham's resignation to those views:

28. Durham to Ellice, Aug. 9, 1838, NLS, EP, E 30, f. 57. Chester New, *Lord Durham* (Oxford, Clarendon, 1929), pp. 366–74.

29. Ibid., pp. 429–48.

30. "Lord D. goes chiefly by Buller's advice. . . . Wakefield . . . can get Lord D. to do anything he chooses": Edward Ellice, Jr. (who accompanied Durham as a secretary) to his father, Aug. 28, 1838, NLS, EP, E 64, f. 58.

31. Wakefield to Molesworth, Sept. 29, 1838; Fawcett, *Molesworth*, p. 201. Wakefield predicted that Durham's return "will be a great occasion in English politics."

You will see what attitude the Radicals ought to assume with respect to his returning now at open defiance with Whigs and Tories. . . . Circumstances seem to be approaching, in which it will be perfectly possible for us to force him into power. The cue of all Radicals then is to receive him not as having failed, but as having done great things —as having kept Canada quiet—disposed of the prisoners with unexampled vigor and lenity—restored amicable relations with America—set about reforming abuses, and changing the defective civil laws—and above all prepared a Constitution for Canada. . . . But you know best what is to be done.[32]

Mill did know what was to be done. This was the turn of events for which he had been waiting. All along he had looked for a Durham-led reform party, for he thought Durham's moderate radicalism (ballot, triennial parliaments, and household rather than universal suffrage) could serve as the basis of the compromise policy that would unite the entire phalanx of natural Radicals that were analyzed in the article "Reorganization of the Reform Party." He called it the Durham policy and said that "under its banner we hope to see gathered together the whole movement party of the empire." Such a party depended for its existence on a leader of the Durham type. It was presumed that attitudes and opinions of the populace, like the various factions, coteries, and sections of parties, were radical; to bring them together into a popularly supported, powerful party "only requires a popular leader." [33]

Mill's depressed mood now quickly changed. Durham's resignation, he said, "has awakened me out of a period of torpor about politics." With obvious enthusiasm, he wrote to Molesworth:

The present turn in Canada affairs brings Lord Durham home, incensed to the utmost (as Buller writes me) with

32. Buller to Mill, Oct. 13, 1838: *Report of the Public Archives for the Year 1928* (Ottawa, 1929), pp. 74–76.
33. "Reorganization of the Reform Party," *LWR, 32,* 476, 489; also see 483, 491–92.

both Whigs and Tories—Whigs especially, and in the best possible mood for setting up for himself; and if so, the formation of an efficient party of moderate Radicals, of which our Review will be the organ, is certain—the Whigs will be kicked out never more to rise, and Lord D. will be head of the Liberal party, and ultimately Prime Minister.[34]

In his *Autobiography* Mill observed that "any one who had the most elementary notions of party tactics, must have attempted to make something of such an opportunity." [35]

Durham sailed for England on November 1 and was due to arrive about a month later. Mill felt there was "a great game" to play in the coming session of Parliament. He knew Durham's course of action was uncertain, but he thought chances were equal that Durham would cooperate in the formation of a Radical party. Mill saw himself (with Buller, Wakefield, Molesworth, and a few others) as a force that could, despite its small size, tip a delicately balanced situation in the Radical direction. The result, Mill said, "will wholly depend upon whether Wakefield, we ourselves, and probably Buller and his own resentment," on the one hand, "or Bulwer, Fonblanque, Edward Ellice, the herd of professing Liberals, and the indecision and cowardice indigenous to English noblemen," on the other, "have the greatest influence in his counsels." And Mill added, "Give us access to him *early* and I will be d———d if we do not make a hard fight for it." [36]

Mill wrote an article in which he acted on Buller's advice to show Durham not as having failed, but as having done great things, and the article was quickly published in an unscheduled issue of the *Review*.[37] Although most of the article was a defense of Durham's conduct and policy in Canada, Mill carefully combined it with an account of the significance of Durham's resigna-

34. Mill to Molesworth, Oct. 19, 1838, *EL,* p. 390. Mill apparently referred to an earlier letter than the one quoted above, p. 229.

35. *Auto.,* p. 182.

36. Mill to Robertson [Nov. 1838], *EL,* pp. 391–92.

37. Buller to Mill, Oct. 13, 1838. Mill closely followed Buller's proposed agenda for such an article, not only describing Durham's achievements as Buller listed them but even using some of Buller's terminology.

tion for domestic politics. When he told Molesworth that Durham "comes home fully prepared . . . to set up for himself," Mill explained that it was "for the purpose of acting at once upon him and upon the country in that *sens* I have written an elaborate defence of him." [38] He could only have been thinking of the Radical party when he wrote, in beginning the article:

> There were consequences dependent upon Lord Durham's mission to Canada, calculated to make it the turning point of English politics for years to come, and to raise every incident connected with it, however secondary in appearance, to the character of an event in history.[39]

Not only did it involve all the important affairs of Canada, but also

> something greater than this, because involving, in its remoter consequences, these and all other national interests: the prospects of the popular cause in England; the possibility of an effective popular party, and of a Liberal ministry worthy of the name.

He held out the hope that this popular Liberal–Radical party (the name he gave it varied) could be made "the predominant party" that would "break the power of the artistocratic faction, and this time provide more effectually that the dead might not be able to revive" [40]; and finally, that realignment of parties for which he and the Philosophic Radicals had striven might be achieved.

In order to persuade Durham that he could successfully mobilize the forces of radicalism, an effort was made to create evidence of popular support for him and his Canadian policy despite official criticism. Wakefield, who arrived in England ahead of Durham, persuaded the editor of the *Spectator* to take

38. Mill to Molesworth, Nov. 14, 1838, *EL*, p. 391.

39. Mill, "Lord Durham's Return," *LWR, 32* (Dec. 1838), 241. Cf. New, *Durham,* pp. 477, n. 3, 478, where Mill's motive is misconceived; New asserts, "Mill had no political ambition. This was a work of pure patriotism."

40. "Lord Durham's Return," pp. 242–43.

up Durham's defense. Extracts from Mill's article, which could not appear until the following month, were printed in the *Spectator* from Mill's page proofs, and it was probably in this form that Durham first became acquainted with Mill's defense.[41] Wakefield and Molesworth went to Plymouth to meet Durham, apparently in the hope of persuading him to act on his resentments and to stage-manage his reception. Wakefield had already written to Durham to say that the coming fortnight after his arrival would be "far and far away, the most important occasion of your life; not to yourself alone, but to your country." Wakefield went on to say that, "If anything should induce you to take part in an attempt (which must fail) to bolster up the present state of government, you would fall to nothing in public estimation." On the other hand, Durham was told, if "you would set up for yourself and *act* on the principles of 1834 [i.e. organic reform]," then a great deal of Radical support would be attracted.[42]

Wakefield kept up a continuous barrage of warnings and exhortations. He tried to paint a picture of growing public enthusiasm for Durham that would continue only if Durham acted on Radical principles. Wakefield's first letter had said that, had he written earlier, the letter "would have been in very gloomy terms. The whole press, without exception of a single paper, seemed to be against you." Indeed, he would have had to say "that you were ruined as a politician unless some great change of feeling toward you should immediately take place." Now, however, Wakefield could "rejoice in being able to assure

41. Wakefield to Durham, Nov. 27, 1838, CPA, Durham Papers, 2, 477; New, *Durham,* p. 478; *Spectator, 11* (Nov. 24, 1838), 1108–09. Wakefield carried a letter from Buller recommending to Mill a course of action on which Wakefield himself now embarked: "Go before [Durham] and make his way ready. . . . [Wakefield] knows all, and will inform you exactly of all. You may speak with him in perfect confidence. . . . keep Ld. Durham up to the mark": Buller to Mill, Oct. 19, 1838, BL, Mill-Taylor Collection. Rintoul, editor of the *Spectator,* attended the meeting at which, according to Mill, the Radicals resolved to form a party: *EL,* p. 365.

42. Wakefield to Durham, Nov. 27, Dec. 3, 1838, CPA, Durham Papers, *2, 477, 503.

you that *the tide has turned.*" Knowing that Mill's article would appear in the *Spectator* and then in the *Review,* he predicted to Durham that he would "not at first see the evidence of it, but you will before a week has passed." They were trying to create in Durham's mind an image of an enthusiastic public opinion that would support him in the course the Radicals were anxious that he follow. As Wakefield got nearer to Plymouth, public interest in Durham's plans with respect to domestic politics seemed to mount. At first, "the anxiety what you will do, is universal and great." Then, some days later, Radical opinion was characterized as saying: "Now we have got a man who can, and will, go through with Reform." Wakefield added that those reformers "who are in earnest—who are not content that the Reform Bill should be a final and *fruitless* measure—are roused. They have been made apathetic by the Melbourne policy of submission to the Tories." Durham was told that his return in circumstances which led reformers to hope that he would act independently of the Melbourne Whigs had "given them heart; and they will support you through thick and thin if you are true to yourself. . . . I begin to be pretty confident that the spirit of Reform will revive all over the country." In the midst of this letter Wakefield reported that Woollcombe (Molesworth's election agent) "comes to tell me—that all is right here [Exeter],—that you must go to the Town Hall, and will be enthusiastically received." A couple of days later, Wakefield again wrote: "Nothing could be better than the state of things. . . . The general feeling is in your favour. . . . It is now clear to me that the stream is with you and running apace."[43]

Molesworth arranged and chaired a meeting for Durham on his first day ashore, and the journey to London was marked by similar arrangements. Throughout there was a hope that Durham would forthrightly speak his mind and encourage the formation of Radical sentiment. At the very least, there was concern that he might make a "declaration of Melbournism, which, if pub-

43. Wakefield to Durham, Nov. 24, 27, Dec. 3, 5, 1838, CPA, Durham Papers, *2,* 466, 477, 503, 523. "We have noticed symptoms of an inclination . . . to greet Lord Durham . . . as a Leader of the Liberal Party": *Spectator, 11* (Nov. 24, 1838), 1110.

lished, would ruin you with those—the great majority—upon whom alone you can rely for earnest and thorough-going support." [44]

The Collapse of Mill's Hopes

Durham did not immediately commit himself and, before he did, Ellice urged him to step cautiously. Ellice was a liberal, reforming Whig, a personal friend of Durham's and sympathetic with his domestic program. But on this occasion he was moved by a wish to prevent Durham from doing anything that would lead to the fall of the Melbourne government, for he doubted the possibility of organizing a viable reform party to the left of the existing government.

Durham had given Ellice a warning of his feelings, for he had written to say the attempt to ruin him had failed, and that he would return to England as "the plaintiff and not the defendant." Ellice also was aware of the way the Radicals would try to use Durham. To his son, who accompanied Durham as a private secretary, Ellice wrote that the public, though not satisfied, "are not prepared for a Durham, Wakefield, and Buller Cabinet, and mark my words, that if they come home with that expectation, they will be laughed at." [45] Therefore he urged "temperate conduct and safe counsel" on Durham, and warned that "neither the one or the other are to be found in the recommendations of the writer in the Westmr. Review!" [46] He also warned about Buller, who was "an intelligent, handy, and most amiable fellow; but he has neither experience, or prudence, and is in the hands of the younger Mill (I wish it were the elder one) a person very much of his own character—with considerable learning, and critical talent—but also a 'denisen of Utopia.' " [47]

Mill's hopes for the organization of a Durham party were

44. New, *Durham*, p. 480; Wakefield to Durham, Durham Papers, Dec. 5, 1838. Durham's speech at Devenport was hailed as a sign that he was for reform, as in 1834, and that the Bowlby policy had been dropped: *Spectator, 11* (Dec. 8, 1838), 1159. On Bowlby, see p. 235.

45. Durham to Ellice, Oct. 11, 1838; Ellice to his son, Oct. 23, 1838, NLS, EP, E 30, f. 63.

46. New, *Durham*, p. 479.

47. Ellice to Durham n.d. [c. Dec. 1838], LP.

shared by only a few other Philosophic Radicals—notably
Buller, Molesworth, and Wakefield. Others such as Place, Roebuck, and the Grotes were unwilling to cooperate, and this was
one of the obstacles to success. To them Durham was suspect
because of an incident during the elections in 1837. Many (not
only the Philosophic) Radicals had looked upon Durham as a
potential leader ever since 1834 when he resigned from the
Cabinet and went on a northern tour to advocate the ballot,
household suffrage, and triennial parliaments.[48] But the high
esteem in which he was held by Radicals was challenged in 1837
when his political credo was again exposed to public examination. In a letter of support he wrote for a candidate in County
Durham he did not deny any of the opinions he shared with the
Radicals; yet the statement had a moderate, conciliatory tone
that made it difficult for them to look on him as a possible leader,
while some of the statements could be interpreted as criticisms
of Radical tactics. He criticized those who would reform institutions "on fanciful and untried principles," and he announced
his determination "never to force them [his principles] peremp-
torily or dogmatically on the consideration of the Government
or the Parliament." [49] Durham's return in 1837 after serving as
ambassador in Russia led to speculation about his political
course, but this letter, and the wide publicity it received, ended
most Radicals' hopes that he might assume leadership of their
embryonic party. Place saw it as Durham's "going over" to the
ministers and hopefully thought it would "cause the people to see

48. "Warburton gave 12 of us a dinner . . . last night, all . . . true to
you and *our* principles. This seemed to me the unanimous opinion, and
one formed after a long and highly complimentary discussion of you and
the Future": Parkes to Durham, May 1, 1836, LP; *Spectator, 10* (Feb.
25, 1837), 181, urged a "Durham Policy" as a way of uniting all non-
Whig reformers. Mrs. Grote looked for a "Durham party" in 1834:
Buckley, *Parkes,* p. 159. There were recurring rumors concerning such
a party: New, *Durham,* pp. 224, 233–34.
49. Durham to Bowlby, July 8, 1837, CPA, Durham Papers, *1,* 186.
The letter was released to the press; Fonblanque printed it and included
long excerpts in a leader that called it a "statesmanlike manifesto" that
should be "generally adopted as the chart of all sincere and sensible
reformers": *Examiner,* July 16, 1837, p. 449.

that no lord can really be their friend." Molesworth called it infamous and Mrs. Grote, in retrospect, explained that the ill-advised letter "had the effect of entirely dissipating such hopes as his previous connexion with the Radicals had given birth to, of his willingness to put himself at the head of that party." [50] These suspicions were not overcome. After learning of Durham's resignation, Mrs. Grote, unlike Mill, was unmoved. "Lord Durham may take up his old cast off opinions again, and go for 'Rad' leadership . . . but D. has too long trifled with the earnest reformers, and I hope he will live to learn that he has 'let the tide go by,' never to be recovered." [51]

The Philosophic Radicals were also divided over the proper remedy for the Canadian rebellion, and this added to the difficulties Mill faced. Most of them evaluated Canadian policy by its consequences for domestic politics. Roebuck, however, because of his special connections with Canada, was prevented from forming opinions about it solely in terms of domestic party considerations. As a result, while Mill (with Buller, Wakefield, and Molesworth) was defending Durham's conduct and policy, Roebuck was becoming increasingly hostile to it. His initial judgment had been extravagantly favorable; at first he thought Durham's conduct in Canada, even if unconstitutional, "wise, prudent and humane," a view qualified only because of the "utter folly" in appointing Turton and Wakefield.[52] But the basic shift in his attitude came in response to Durham's ordinance that exiled the prisoners. Roebuck, who six weeks before called Durham humane and wise, now decided that his policy was tyrannical. Yet this ordinance was defended by Mill in a brief article added to a second edition of the *Review* issued in August 1838. Mill justified the ordinance on the ground that it was probably necessary to prevent the few leaders from being present where they would have a disturbing influence and thus have prevented Durham from playing the peace-making role he

50. Place to L. G. Jones, July 20, 1837; quoted in New, *Durham,* p. 316. H. Grote, *Philosophical Radicals of 1832,* pp. 33–34.

51. Mrs. Grote to Place, Oct. 27, 1838, Add. MSS 35,151, f. 107.

52. Roebuck to Brougham, July 8, 10, 23, Aug. 14, 1838, UCL, BrP.

was to perform. Mill made it clear that his sympathies were with the Canadians, but his wish to defend Durham led him to show little concern for both the possibility that Durham had exceeded his authority and the fate of the leaders of the rebellion, including Papineau whom he mentioned alone among the twenty-three proscribed prisoners.[53] Since Roebuck was strongly opposed to Durham's ordinance, he attacked Mill's defense of it. Mill's argument, he said, justified "an act of undisguised tyranny." If valid, it also justified the repressive policies of Castlereagh, Peter, and Napoleon. Such a position, Roebuck claimed, was not the result of calm reflection, but naiveté. Inexperienced in the world of action, "persons around him lead his opinions to what point they please. . . . Mill has doubtless been beset by Buller's friends . . . Having the faculty of finding irrefragable arguments for every side of every question, it was not difficult to trump up a defense for Lord Durham." [54]

This disagreement was carried on in the press. Wakefield defended Durham, and Roebuck's criticisms of Mill were repeated by his brother-in-law Falconer, who until recently had been

53. "Lord Durham and His Assailants," *LWR, 29,* 507–12. Durham, Mill said (pp. 511–12), is "the very last man whom any one in earnest for Reform should permit himself, at the present time, to be betrayed into any act of hostility not called for by an imperious duty." Buller wrote that Durham "feels most grateful to you for your article . . . and is prepared to listen to your councils": Buller to Mill, Oct. 19, 1838. Mill also defended Durham's ordinance in the *Morning Chronicle,* Aug. 13, 1838, p. 2, where he indiscreetly identified Buller as the writer of a letter (of June 30) which he quoted at length. Buller's letter may have been the source of facts and arguments used in the *LWR* article. On Mill's authorship, see Buller to Mill, Oct. 13, 1838, in *Report of the Public Archives . . . 1928,* p. 74; Buller to Ellice, Sept. 29, 1838, NLS, EP, E 5, f. 16.

54. Roebuck to Brougham, Aug. 31, 1838, UCL, BrP. Also, "Give him premises and he will reason logically—farther, he will go through an inductive process with singular acumen and *singular inaccuracy*. . . . He is wonderfully wise—but wonderfully prone to error. . . . If Mill's father were alive, I think he would be startled by this doctrine of passive obedience." Buller agreed: the ordinance "will appear to you horribly unconstitutional and despotic, but it is really mild": quoted by Mill, see n. 53 above.

employed by Mill on the *Review*.[55] Roebuck denied Mill's claim
that Durham had conciliated all parties in Canada; he even
thought Durham had seized the opportunity to resign because
the remedy he preferred was not workable. Thus he ridiculed
Buller for writing "as if they were returning in triumph, trumpets
blowing, drums beating, and colours flying." Now, moved by
considerations of Canadian policy, Roebuck expressed indifference to Durham's future and called him "a mere tool in the
hands of a few designing rogues."[56] This disarray among the
Philosophic Radicals was an obstacle against which Mill appealed, but which he could hardly overcome.

Finally Durham himself was unwilling to cooperate. He continued to feel hostile to the Whig leadership but, he said, "the
'difference' between me and the Government is *personal* not
political." He felt alienated from them, but he would make no
effort to topple the government. "The Ministers have behaved so
infamously to me that I have none but official communication
with them. . . . I belong to no party. I do not support—I do not
attack the Ministry. If they fall it will be from their own weakness, and must crumble to pieces, but I will have nothing to do
with the operation."[57] Although he may have been influenced

55. Richard Garnett, *Edward Gibbon Wakefield* (London, 1898), pp.
173, 244. *Spectator, 11* (Nov. 3, 1838), 1039–40; (Nov. 10), 1061–62;
(Nov. 17), 1084–85; (Nov. 24), 1109. Falconer to Place, Sept. 1, 1838:
Add. MSS 35,151, ff. 83–84, on his review of Mill's first Canadian article.
After Falconer's and Roebuck's criticisms of Durham, the *Spectator*, in
view of its shift in policy, was accused of being "re-Durhamized"; actually,
it was cautiously pro-Durham: *Spectator, 11* (Nov. 24), 1110; (Dec. 15),
1184–85.

56. Roebuck to Brougham, Oct. 23, 25, 1838, UCL, BrP; H. Grote,
Philosophical Radicals of 1832, pp. 46–47; Hyde, "Utility and Radicalism," *Economic History Review, 16* (1946), 43, n. 7.

57. Durham to Ellice, Dec. 26, 1838, NLS, EP, E 30, f. 70; Durham to
H. Lambton, Dec. 21, 1838, CPA, Durham Papers, 2, 542. The Cabinet
was just as furious with Durham: Hobhouse, *Recollections, 5,* 166;
Russell said, "his leaving his post at Quebec to boast of his success at
Plymouth, just when the rebellion broke out afresh, has lowered him in
the eyes of all men of sense. . . . If however he thinks Molesworth can
carry a party to back him, he will find himself mistaken": Russell to
Ellice, Dec. 10, 1838, NLS, EP, E 49, f. 20.

by the divisions among the Radicals and their estrangement from the moderate reformers—both circumstances that would have made it difficult for a party rebellion to succeed—his attitude was mainly determined by a tactical position already revealed in the Bowlby letter. Even though he was somewhat radical in his opinions, he showed himself to be less than radical when it came to party tactics.[58]

The Radicals were left uncertain as to Durham's intentions during the few weeks immediately following his return, as he devoted himself to preparing his report on Canada. He remained aloof from public meetings and other political activities. But he did show his hand even when he tried to prevent an interruption to his isolation, for he refused to receive a deputation from the Westminster Reform Association, an organization which, according to Fonblanque, included many Chartists. In explaining his refusal, he held that they hampered the achievement of "efficient reform" and were "destructive" and that their "ulterior designs" were incompatible with his own principles. The Philosophic Radicals do not appear to have been connected with the Association, yet Durham's criticism of it was taken as an indication of how he felt about cooperation with all Radicals. Fonblanque, anxious to preserve the Whig ministry for the sake of what he thought to be the Liberal party, interpreted Durham's reply to be a rejection of all extreme Radicals, "whence may be plainly inferred the course which his Lordship intends to pursue." [59] Leader saw it in this light, remarking that "there was no sort of necessity" for Durham's response, and "that he had evidently seized the opportunity of addressing *them* in that shape"; and he concluded, "of course there was an end of any possibility of a connection between him [Durham] and them." Place now

58. Durham to Parkes, Nov. 11, 1836, LP. Also, "Durham thinks the Radicals great fools": Stanley to Parkes, Jan. 20, 1837, UCL, JPP. Durham might also have been moved by his resentment against the Radicals, and specifically those connected with Grote, for having been insufficiently enthusiastic about his conduct in 1834: Durham to Parkes, Aug. 20, 1836, LP.

59. Reid, *Durham, 2,* 310; on his avoidance of domestic politics in speeches made after his return, *Spectator,* Dec. 8, 1838, p. 1154; *Examiner,* Dec. 23, 1838, p. 801.

called Durham "a lost mutton" and said he "had a chance such as few men have had, but he was all a Lord and none a man." [60]

Mill, still slow to accept failure, at first showed no sign of discouragement. At least there is no evidence of his reaction to Durham's rebuff to the Westminster Reform Association. In late December, because of seriously bad health, he left England on a six-month leave from India House. When he left there were plans for Robertson to see Durham, apparently to establish a direct connection between Durham and the *Review*. Mill, just beginning his journey, urged Robertson to send many letters; "I expect from them the particulars of a game well played in which I have a deep stake." [61] But Robertson's report of the interview finally destroyed Mill's hopes of realizing the ambitious plans that had stirred him a few months before. Mill at last recognized that Durham's course

> cannot lead to the organization of a radical party, or the placing the radicals at the head of the movement,—it leaves them as they are already, a mere appendage of the Whigs; and if there is to be no radical party there need be no Westminster Review, for there is no position for it to take, distinguishing it from the Edinburgh. . . . In short, it is one thing to support Lord Durham in *forming* a party; another to follow him when he is only joining one, and that one which I have so long been crying out against.

He added that, "if the time is come when a radical review should support the Whigs, the time is come when I should withdraw from politics." [62] And this is what he proceeded to do.

There was a fleeting opportunity to revive hope in May 1839 when the Melbourne government resigned because of Radical votes on the Jamaica question. Peel was asked to form a government but felt unable to do so because of the Queen's opposition to his appointments to her household. The Whigs momentarily

60. Greville *Memoirs, 4,* 111–12; Place to Mrs. Grote, Jan. 2, 1839, H. Grote, *Philosophical Radicals of 1832,* p. 33.
61. Mill to Robertson, Dec. 28, 1838, *EL,* p. 394. Mill probably had an interview with Durham: *Auto.,* p. 183.
62. Mill to Robertson, April 6, 1839, *EL,* pp. 396–97.

resisted the temptation to stay in office, and there were rumors
that Durham would be sent for. However, Mill, in Italy at the
time, probably did not even know of these events.[63]

When his article "Reorganization of the Reform Party,"
planned for publication in January 1838, finally appeared in
April 1839, it could serve only as an epitaph to Radical hopes,
and Mill regretted its appearance "in a posture of affairs so
unsuitable to it." After his return to England in July he published two more numbers and contributed only one major article
(on Coleridge), and in March 1840 he terminated his ownership
of the *Review*. Before he began the negotiations that led to the
severance of his connection with it there was an offer, apparently,
to make it a ministerial organ, financed by a Whig patron. Mill
had been losing money on it but refused whatever offer had been
made. He was anxious that the *Review* avoid getting "a character like Fonblanque's." Once he was satisfied that it would
be continued on Radical lines, Mill ended his connection with it.
He now concluded, "it is no part of my vocation to be a party
leader." [64]

63. "I have been unusually long without English news having neither
had any letters nor seen any newspapers but of very old date." Mill to
Mrs. James Mill, May 19, 1839: *EL,* p. 398.
64. Mill to Robertson, April 6, May 31, 1839; and [March 1840(?)];
Mill to Cole [Feb. or March (?) 1840]; Mill to Sterling, Sept. 28, 1839,
EL, pp. 397, 400, 419, 421, 423, 406. The *Review* was turned over to
Henry Cole and William Hickson in March 1840.

9. Disillusionment

> Every Party, when they find a Maxim for their turn, they
> presently call it a Fundamental, they think they nail it with
> a Peg of Iron, whereas in truth they only tie it with a wisp
> of Straw.
>
> —HALIFAX [1]

Now in 1839, little more than a decade after the dreams of
establishing a powerful parliamentary party first took shape,
John Mill began to share a sense of failure with the other
Philosophic Radicals. The moderate reformers continued to
resist the aggressive tactics designed to force the Whigs to
coalesce with their "natural" aristocratic allies the Tories. The
Melbourne government's existence became increasingly tenuous,
and the moderate reformers became more and more critical of
those on their left who threatened it. Edward Bulwer, for example, described them as "a small, conceited, and headstrong
party" that should be called "the sect of the Impracticables." [2]
The cleavage between the Radicals and the moderate reformers
remained, and the expected merger of Whigs and Tories into an
aristocratic party never occurred. On the contrary, the Whigs
continued to look upon the Tories as their strongest long-run
enemy, whereas the Radicals were regarded merely as an annoying faction. Both in public opinion and in electoral organization,
the Tories increased their strength throughout the decade. By
1839, far from having merged into an aristocratic party, the
Whigs and Tories were poised against one another in a fairly
even struggle for power. The two aristocratic factions that
James Mill had opposed twenty years before continued to dominate the political scene.

1. *The Complete Works of George Savile, First Marquess of Halifax,*
ed. W. Raleigh (Oxford, Clarendon, 1912), p. 209.
2. "Present State and Conduct of Parties," *Edin. Rev.,* 71 (April 1840),
282–83.

Decline of Parliamentary Radicalism

On the surface the conduct of the Radicals appeared to be much the same. If anything, they were more aggressive than ever in dealing with the government. They began the session with a vigorous attack on the ministry; later there were persistent demands for a "reform of the Reform Bill," and they became more insistent as the government's majority narrowed and as the Chartist agitation grew. By and large, however, it was not the Philosophic Radicals who took the initiative in these moves; leadership had passed to other Radicals, such as Dunscombe, Wakley, and Harvey. These men had been on the periphery of Grote's coterie during previous sessions, but they were coming to the fore now that the Philosophic Radicals were losing heart. Hume, Grote, Ward, Molesworth, and Buller continued to complain about the finality doctrine and called for organic reforms; Grote again proposed the ballot, and Hume called for household suffrage.[3] Despite the appearance of continuity, the Philosophic Radicals felt depressed about politics. This was perhaps best revealed in their unenthusiastic, even indifferent, responses to developments which a couple of years earlier would have provoked excitement and great hope.

There were two such events—the resignation of the government in May 1839 and the decision to make the ballot an open question. The government resigned after it carried a bill for the suspension of the constitution of Jamaica by a majority of only five. Radical votes played the key role: ten Radicals (including Grote, Hume, Leader, Molesworth, Dunscombe, and Wakley) voted with the Tories, and some ten others stayed away, thereby denying the government the margin it thought necessary to remain in office. This was just the situation they had looked forward to a few years earlier. But now there was little satisfaction at finding themselves in a position to bring down the government, for they were so few in number and so isolated from the mod-

3. *Hansard, 45* (Feb. 5, 1839), 79–83; *46* (March 21, 27, 1839), 1055, 1078, 1090–92, 1235; *47* (June 4, 1839), 1366; *50* (Aug. 13, 1839), 256; *51* (Feb. 4, 1840), 1238. On the emergence of other Radical leaders: ibid., *45* (Feb. 5, 1839), 64, 72–74, 79–82; *47* (June 4, 1839), 1360–66; *50* (Aug. 7, 9, 13, 1839), 9, 158–63, 258.

erate reformers that they could not entertain hopes that the government's fall would lead to either realignment of parties or a considerable infusion of radicalism into the government party. If the considerable number of moderate reformers (the "nominal Whigs," the "200 ballot men") had been willing to join the Philosophic Radicals in an anti-Whig revolt, the situation might have been exploited. But in fact the moderate Radicals were "very anxious . . . to prop up the concern. They are very angry with their more violent compeers (Grote, Leader, etc.)" [4] for having threatened to desert the government. Faced with such an attitude, the Philosophic Radicals could not expect to implement their old fantasy of realignment. Indeed, even some of their close associates voted with the government and provided it with the slim majority it managed to achieve (Buller, H. G. Ward, Warburton).[5]

It must have been an awareness of that attitude that led the *Spectator*, the newspaper most sympathetic to Philosophic Radical views at this time, to deny that the few Radical votes against the government were responsible for its defeat. Rintoul argued that Melbourne would have resigned even if the Radicals had voted with him instead of with Peel.[6] The unpopularity of the Radicals' desertion of the government was also reflected in the action of Hume's constituents, who had met before the critical vote to declare their wish that he support the government. He cited Blackstone, Burke, and Bailey by way of justifying his failure to comply with their wish, but they informally declared that by his disobedience "his representative office ceases." [7] Only

4. *Greville Memoirs, 4,* 154–55, 160; *Hansard, 47* (May 6, 1839), 972.

5. Mill, away on the Continent at the time, was uncertain: "I cannot judge whether [Buller] or the ten radicals who voted against the ministry were in the right. I think it likely that I should have done as he did. . . . Buller's remarks on the general state of politics seem to me sensible and right; whether his practical views are right or not will depend very much on the conduct of the ministry, which I feel persuaded will entirely disappoint . . . him": Mill to Robertson, May 31, 1839, *EL,* p. 400.

6. *Spectator,* May 11, 1839, p. 429.

7. Ibid., May 25, 1839, p. 488; also, Hume *"sits* for Kilkenny, but, as the constituents say, represents it not." Fonblanque blamed the "Tory-Radicals" for Melbourne's fall: "Faction had done its work. . . . [They]

a few, like Molesworth, could say, "I do not regret, but rejoice in, the consequence of my vote." All the same, he sensed that his constituents at Leeds might not be pleased, and he renewed his offer to resign his seat if they were not satisfied with his parliamentary conduct.[8]

When the Whig government, a week after its resignation, was restored to office as a result of the Bedchamber crisis, the Radicals again found themselves in a situation they would have welcomed a couple years before. The two aristocratic factions were now more nearly balanced; if Melbourne was to maintain himself in office, he was more dependent than ever on Radical votes. There was pressure from moderate Radicals for concessions, and there even were rumors that concessions would be forthcoming.[9] Aware of the opportunity, the Philosophic Radicals tried to bargain, and they met at Molesworth's house (May 12) to consider their course of action. They had little hope of success. Place, of course, was skeptical. The *Spectator* was "doubtful whether Ministers will do—can do—any thing to appease their Radical allies." [10] Melbourne received a delegation from the "Molesworth clique" which threatened to withhold support unless he made concessions, and Warburton also sought to negotiate with Russell. The immediate response from the ministers was negative. Melbourne uttered "cautious ambiguities" and "intimated . . . that he was resolved to make none [i.e. concessions] whatever"; and Russell reaffirmed his finality doctrine. Radical reactions varied. Some wished to support the government on almost any terms and said so. For example,

---

went over to the enemy. . . . Mr. Grote [was] the ringleader and spokesman of the section that colaesced with the Tories": *Examiner*, May 12, 1839, p. 289.

8. *Spectator, 12* (May 11, 1839), 434. Leader also was unrepentant: ibid. (May 18, 1839), 461.

9. *Greville Memoirs, 4,* 154, 176. Hobhouse wrote in his diary, "nothing was thought of but parliamentary numbers . . . when Poulett Thompson's brother was drowned in the Thames . . . the only reflection which that catastrophe called for from our Secretary of the Treasury was, 'and so we shall lose two votes' ": *Recollections, 5,* 188.

10. Place to Hume, Feb. 9, 1839; Place's Memorandum, May 11, 1839: Add. MSS 35,151, ff. 132, 168, 171. *Spectator, 12* (May 25, 1839), p. 477.

Warburton said, "if there was the smallest encouragement on the part of the government to lead them to believe that they would take the Amendments of the Reform Act under their patronage, there would be the greatest forbearance by the liberal party." This attitude led Greville to observe that the Radicals "catch (as dying men at straws), at a vague expression about 'progressive reforms,' and try (or pretend) to think that this promises something, though they know not what." Warburton was not typical, however; others, where they still took an interest, responded to the ministerial rejection with disappointment but not surprise. Hume and Ward accepted Whig conservatism with regret, but no longer with anger.[11]

Actually, the government was not quite so unresponsive as the Radicals thought. Two days after Russell had reaffirmed his opposition to alteration of the Reform Bill a divided Cabinet finally agreed to make the ballot an open question. They established no fixed policy on the ballot; they only agreed to disagree and not require resignations as a result of such disagreement.[12] In doing this the Whig leaders were responding to many pressures and probably least of all to the pressure from their extreme left. The Philosophic Radicals had looked for this as a minimum concession back in 1836–37 but were disappointed. In yielding now, two years later, Melbourne was probably less concerned to conciliate the extreme Radicals than to insure himself against the crumbling of the large but varied group of moderate reformers on whom he depended for his slim majority. Back in 1837 when this concession might have pacified the Philosophic and other extreme Radicals, he enjoyed a majority of perhaps sixty to eighty. Now, however, with his majority almost gone, and facing pressure from some of the moderates, he finally yielded.

---

11. Attwood, May 16, 1839: C. M. Wakefield, *Life of Thomas Att-wood* (London, 1885), p. 369; *Greville Memoirs, 4,* 174–75; *Hansard, 47* (June 4, 1839), 1349–55, 1362–73. From Munich Mill wrote, "The radicals will not insist on any conditions, and if they did the ministry would reject them": Mill to Robertson, May 31, 1839, *EL,* p. 400.

12. *Hansard, 50* (Aug. 23, 1839), 523; *51* (Jan. 29, 31, 1840), 816, 1063–65. *Greville Memoirs, 4,* 177. *Spectator, 12* (June 8, 1839), 525, 532.

Fonblanque, who may be seen as a spokesman for this group, thought the moderate Radicals "would take the slightest concessions, the least thing that would satisfy their constituencies, but that *something* they must have." An indication that there were converts to the ballot among the moderates who yet supported the ministry was to be found in the enlarged minority of two hundred who had supported Grote's motion in 1838 and in the fact that Macaulay, who was soon to enter the Cabinet, was a firm supporter of it. So were some others of Melbourne's Cabinet colleagues.[13]

Making the ballot an open question raised quite a storm, but the excitement was confined to the Tories (and some conservative Whigs), who were outraged that the government leaned so far toward democratic radicalism.[14] (The Ballot Act was not passed until 1872.) Among the Philosophic Radicals this concession caused none of the excitement that it would have evoked in 1837. The *Spectator* accused the Whigs of political immorality for using the question for selfish party purposes. It was confident that nothing would be gained by it, and it claimed justification for this evaluation when an increase of only seventeen was added to the vote supporting Grote's motion later that month. Grote was so little pleased that he was reluctant to introduce what previously had been considered his annual motion; according to Parkes, he had to be "prevailed on." The Philosophic Radicals were so little interested that hardly anyone called on Mrs. Grote after the debate, "a melancholy contrast with previous occasions, when the whole corps of Radicals were wont to come and pour out their congratulations in Eccleston Street [Grote's residence]." [15]

13. Ibid., June 22, 1839, p. 585. On Fonblanque, *Greville Memoirs, 4*, 154. Even the *Morning Chronicle* advocated the ballot (as well as household suffrage), though without intending that such measures should bring party realignment.

14. *Hansard, 50*, 509; *51*, 799, 802, 906, 1026.

15. *Spectator, 12* (June 15, 1839), pp. 559–60; June 22, p. 573. Parkes to Cobden, June 7, 1839, SRO, Cobden Papers; H. Grote, *Life of Grote*, p. 131. When Greville says the Radicals "are full of exultation," he is referring to the moderate reformers: *Memoirs, 4*, 177. Buller was offered a minor office in August, but refused.

The events of 1839 had the effect of making the Philosophic Radicals feel as if they had been squeezed off the political stage. Not only were they reduced to a handful, but the points of doctrine by which they had distinguished themselves from other Radicals and Liberals no longer served as boundaries. Mill had made the ballot the distinguishing principle of Philosophic Radicalism, assuming that once it was adopted it would be an effective instrument for bringing realignment of parties. Yet they now found the Whig Macaulay eloquently defending Grote's favorite proposal during the debate in 1839. This led Mill to complain that the ballot "is passing from a radical doctrine into a Whig one," and he called it "essentially a juste milieu, middle class doctrine." [16] There also was a challenge from outside Parliament where the growing prominence of Chartism in 1839 challenged the Philosophic Radicals' claim to be the political and intellectual leaders of the democratic movement.

The Philosophic Radicals again were reminded of their isolation, for the moderates continued to criticize them for being (despite their small numbers) a threat to the government. One such attack came in an anonymous pamphlet, addressed as an open letter to Grote, in which the author identified himself as a Radical member of Parliament. "The Radicals have done almost all that they should have avoided doing, and omitted to do almost all that they ought to have done." Among their sins was to "have brought forward, or threatened to bring forward motions for the wildest, and most sweeping changes in our institutions." Furthermore, they "quarrelled with the Ministers— for not doing that which it was impossible they should do. . . . And now, to crown all, they, or a portion of them, sufficient it is said for all the purposes of mischief, threaten finally to desert to the Tory camp—unless Ministers will subscribe to the precise

16. Mill to Kemble, Oct. 14, 1839, *EL,* p. 410. "The fact is notorious here that every year more and more of the Whigs are converted *to* the ballot, and none have ever been converted *from* it. . . . So hostile to the ballot were all the Whigs [before 1832] that the Ballot was considered ultra-Radicalism, the very *n[on] plus ultra* of Democracy. A few rational persons . . . alone saw that it was not so": Mill to Beaumont, Oct. 18, 1839; Yale Univ. Library, Tocqueville-Beaumont MSS, C. XI. c.

view they are pleased to take of the further reform of our representative system. Some ten or fifteen Honourable Gentlemen . . . presume to dictate the course to be taken by the whole of the Liberal party." [17]

Another symptom of the moderate reformers' allegiance to the Whig government came from a point closer to the center of the political spectrum. Edward Lytton Bulwer, who was courted by Mill only a year before, again in 1839 employed his pen to attack "the most impatient of the Ultra-Radicals." He expressed surprise that they "profess at once to be friends of reform and opponents of the Ministry." It was the simple fact, he said, "that no liberal politician . . . can honestly contend that there is no distinction, except that of office, between Whigs and Tories." It was necessary, he argued, that the party produce "a certain practical compromise of theory and action." It was impossible for Lord Melbourne to "govern England on the principles of Sir William Molesworth. . . . If Sir William Molesworth succeeded to Lord Melbourne, there would be a million Molesworths to condemn him for not going far enough. It is easy for the speculative to outbid the practical man." [18]

The moderate reformers' persistent allegiance to the Whigs was to eliminate the Radical party. The Philosophic Radical coterie had considered itself the core of an expanding party, for it looked on the 200 ballot men as latent Radicals. Now with the ballot more popular, yet without affecting party allegiances, the Philosophic Radicals could no longer see themselves as the seed from which a great party would soon grow. Grote "felt indisposed to remain as one of so very small a number as now constituted the Radical cluster." Macaulay had said in 1839 that

17. *Shall We Overturn the Coach? or, What Ought the Radicals To Do? Discussed in A Letter to George Grote, Esq., M.P. from a Radical Member of the House of Commons* (London, 1839), pp. 36–37.

18. "Defence of the Whigs," *Edin. Rev., 70* (Oct. 1839), 258, 260, 264. Bulwer had consulted ministers about the article and begged the editor to preserve his anonymity: Bulwer to Napier, Sept. 14, 1839, Add. MSS 34,620, ff. 371–72. The Radical John Wade had also softened in his attitude to the Whigs, who now deserved "national gratitude and confidence": *Glances at the Times, and Reform Government* (5th ed. London, 1840), p. 30.

he considered the Radical party to be reduced to Grote and his wife.[19] Mill was most poignantly aware that the party, both as it existed and as he had envisioned it, had dissolved. "Even I," he said, "who have been for some years attempting it must be owned with very little success, to induce the Radicals to maintain an independent position, am compelled to acknowledge that there is not room for a fourth political party in this country—reckoning the Conservatives, the Whig–Radicals, and the Chartists as the other three." [20]

DISILLUSIONMENT: WORKING CLASSES AND MIDDLE CLASSES

The Philosophic Radicals' depression turned to disillusionment. Although their earlier frustration as politicians had dejected them, their confidence as philosophers had not been undermined. As spokesmen for a doctrine, up to now they had felt undaunted, and therefore, as politicians, they had looked on their frustration as temporary: political victory was postponed, but it was still conceivable, indeed, in optimistic moods, it was foreseeable. But now at the end of the decade the Philosophic Radicals experienced doubts about their doctrine, which originated in their recognizing a discrepancy between the realities of social and political life and the image of reality that was derived from their doctrine.

According to Philosophic Radical doctrine, the only legitimate

19. H. Grote, *Philosophical Radicals of 1832,* p. 63; *Greville Memoirs, 4,* 176; Sydney Smith, who was close to the Grotes, reported (1840) that the Radicals were "discouraged, no longer sanguine of their future. They had persuaded themselves that they should change everything. The sound common sense of the public paralyzes them": F. Guizot, *An Embassy to the Court of St. James in 1840* (3d ed. London, 1863), p. 174.

20. Mill to Napier, April 22, 1840, *EL,* p. 430. Molesworth and Leader moved from their Eaton Square residence that had served as Philosophic Radical meeting place to smaller quarters more "suitable . . . to [their] diminished political dimensions": Parkes to Stanley, Dec. 24, 1839, JPP, UCL. "Our political world here is fallen into a state of the most profound degradation and apathy. Every thing like rational or instructed Radicalism is well nigh extinct: those who used to be called Radicals are absorbed into the Whigs": Grote to Beaumont, Aug. 1, 1839; Yale Univ. Library, Tocqueville-Beaumont MSS, C. XI. c.

affiliation was with "the People," for only they comprehended the universal interest. In contrast, the interest of any segment of the people was by definition partial and therefore sinister. Identification with the middle or working class, therefore, was a "false consciousness," for both those classes were constituent parts of the people. The only significant conflict was between universal and sinister interests, between people and aristocracy. The Philosophic Radicals' aspirations rested on the two assumptions that "the People" had real existence and that the antagonism between the aristocratic factions was trivial and impermanent.

Toward 1840 there were certain prominent social and political developments that challenged continued belief in these assumptions. The challenge came from the Chartist and the Anti-Corn Law movements, which gave evidence of class consciousness among both working and middle classes, as well as conflict between them. This made it difficult to go on believing that a viable, large Radical party based on the People, among whom there were neither class conflicts nor any significant class divisions, could be established. Chartism and the Anti-Corn Law movement punctured the Philosophic Radicals' confidence in the image of reality derived from their doctrine.

The emergence of Chartism as a prominent working-class movement demanding organic reform made it necessary for the Philosophic Radicals to define their attitude toward it. In the end they became unequivocally hostile; but initially they had mixed feelings. On the one hand, they were sympathetic with the six points of the Charter as a program for Radicalism. Yet Chartism, by the character of its support and its unstated goals, made the Philosophic Radicals aware of deficiencies in their own philosophy and politics.

Chartist advocacy of organic reform should have attracted the Philosophic Radicals. There also was the Chartists' success in mobilizing popular support for organic reform, providing a notable exception to the prevailing apathy. Even though the Chartist leaders achieved most of their successes among only certain segments of the working classes, at least they could provide some evidence of popular demand for changes in the constitution. The Chartists advocated reforms that were crucial to

Philosophic Radical doctrine—universal suffrage, secret ballot, annual parliaments, payment of M.P.s, equal electoral districts, and abolition of property qualifications for M.P.s. The Philosophic Radicals approved of all six points, though they placed greatest emphasis on the first two. It was only because they were seeking reform by Parliamentary means and through parliamentary initiative that they had modified their demands in the hope of broadening their basis of support within Parliament. But they did not conceal their belief that in time the Charter ought to be incorporated into the Constitution. However, for the present they spoke of household rather than universal suffrage and triennial rather than annual parliaments. Despite this concession to what appeared to be immediately possible, there was an affinity between the Chartist and the Philosophic Radical program of reform.[21]

This similarity was not mere coincidence. Place and Roebuck had a hand in the original formulation of the Charter. Place, who had been an advocate of aggressive tactics and a severe critic of the Philosophic Radicals' timidity, was quicker than the other Radicals to assume that their goals would not be immediately achieved by means of a realignment of parties. Therefore, as early as 1836–37 he diverted some of his energies to working-class organization. He renewed his acquaintance with William Lovett, who had organized the London Working Men's Association in 1836. This organization was not the only source of Chart-

21. Mill said of the Radicals, "They look forward to a time . . . when the whole adult population shall be qualified to give an equal voice in the election of members of Parliament. . . . they anxiously desire . . . to hasten this progress. . . . Their principle of government is, until Universal Suffrage shall be possible, to do everything for the good of the working classes, which it would be necessary to do if there were Universal Suffrage": "Parties and the Ministry," *LWR, 28* (Oct. 1837), 18. Also see Hume, *Hansard, 46* (March 21, 1839), 1049; see above, pp. 30, 37–38, 90–93. Mill advocated payment of MPs: *LWR, 30,* 359–60. Chapman, describing the program advocated in Roebuck's *Pamphlets,* included abolition of property qualifications, ballot, equal electoral districts, shortened parliaments, and extension of suffrage to all occupants: "Preliminary Reforms.—Being a Summary of the Principles Advocated in these Pamphlets," *Pamph. P.* [No. 22, Nov. 5, 1835], p. 14. *Constitutional,* Feb. 25, 1837, p. 3, approved the six points of the Charter.

ism, but it did produce the document that gave the movement its name, and Place and Roebuck helped Lovett in the drafting of it. Of course, the working-class spokesmen had advocated universal suffrage, ballot, and annual parliaments before Place took part in their deliberations, and this program had become part of the Radical tradition. But Place had an important influence on the Chartist movement. The working-class politicians were inclined to emphasize the economic and industrial grievances, but they accepted Place's terms—that their economic views be left out, making the Charter an exclusively political document. During this period (1836–37) Place thought the working classes receptive to sound teaching. They were "to a great extent free from sinister interests," and this meant that false views of their interest could be removed.[22] With this optimistic diagnosis of the possibility of persuading the working classes to adopt orthodox radicalism, Place initially thought Chartism could provide the basis for a Radical movement that would be exclusively political.[23]

Despite their agreement on the necessity of organic reform, there were facets of Chartism that made the Philosophic Radicals suspicious of it. One of these concerned the Chartist attitude to violence. Committed to the achievement of reform by parliamentary means, the Philosophic Radicals were bound to look askance at Chartist allusions to physical force, the Birmingham riots of mid-1839, and the insurrection led by Frost later that year. It is true that they themselves had used the language of menace during the Reform Bill agitation in 1831–32, but whether they seriously intended to carry out their threats remains very doubtful. In contrast, the Chartists appeared to have meant what they said, and there were outbreaks of violence that seemed to give credence to their words. Place complained of the illegality of some of the Chartists' proceedings, and even Roebuck was intimidated by their allusions to violence. "Force is the ultima ratio, but fools are ever talking of appealing to force,

22. He also was impressed with "Their readiness to receive instruction": Place to Brougham, July 1, 1837, UCL, BrP.

23. Wallas, *Place,* pp. 360–62, 365–67, 370–71; Henry Solly, *Woodford, 1,* 55–59; Hovell, *The Chartist Movement,* p. 73.

just as if the use of force did not of itself even at the best retard advance." [24] However, this was no more than a minor source of their alienation from Chartism.

The Philosophic Radicals from the beginning were opposed to the class basis of the Chartist movement. This class basis was made evident in Chartist rhetoric which sought to justify organic reform as a means of conferring benefits on the working classes exclusively. It also was evident in the virulent hostility Chartist orators and writers directed to the middle classes. Chartist pre-occupation with class was incompatible with the Philosophic Radicals' postulate that a Radical party could be legitimately based only on the whole people. It also would have left the middle classes in alliance with the aristocracy or it would have produced a three-way conflict. Neither of these alternatives was compatible with the Philosophic Radicals' vision of the way the Radical party would take shape. This had nothing to do with the Philosophic Radicals being "middle class radicals"; they opposed exclusively middle-class political groups on the same grounds. Both middle- and working-class parties implicitly acknowledged inherent conflict within the populace and thus denied the validity of the conception of universal interests and the social reality of "the People." Consequently they challenged the ideas that gave legitimacy to the Philosophic Radicals' ambitions.

The Chartists would have been welcomed into the Radical movement if they had been willing to give up their identification with one class of the people. Place "refused to have any thing to do with the proposed charter bill unless they made it the base of a general Union of all persons without exception who were willing to repose themselves on that base." [25] Not that Place failed to recognize class differences; they clearly existed, but he assumed that fundamental political interests were common to all classes. Therefore, now as in 1831–32, Place sought "the junction of the middle and working classes" as the only legitimate way of engaging the people in day-to-day politics. Mill also would have welcomed Chartist support of radicalism, but on the

24. Place to Hume, Jan. 13, 1841, Add. MSS 35,151, f. 295; Roebuck to Brougham, Aug. 31, 1838, UCL, BrP. Hume, *Hansard, 51* (Feb. 4, 1840), 1238–39.

25. Place to Falconer, Sept. 2, 1838, Add. MSS 35,151, f. 85.

same terms as Place. He also recognized the existence of divergent class interests; but the working classes, as "natural Radicals," were also a constituent part of the body of the people. In calling on the working class along with all the other natural Radicals "to knit themselves together into one compact body [Mill said], we are not seeking to build a party on a mere combination of classes for the promotion of separate interests, however legitimate. We are appealing in behalf of the general interest of all, to those whose particular interests have opened their eyes. It is not for themselves, it is for a principle, that we would summon them into the field." [26]

With this outlook there could only be increased opposition to the Chartists as they persisted in making their claims solely on behalf of the working class and as they continued to show hostility to the middle classes. Place complained that the proposal for a Chartist convention was a plan for "a general war upon all who are not of their own class." And he protested that the Chartists spoke in this vein—"the middle class Tyrants, our Oppressors, the murderers of the people have set up Corn Law agitation for the purpose of misleading and cheating the working people, as they have always done whenever the people have been led by them, have nothing to do with them, oppose them every where." The Chartists were seen as men who mistakenly sought to alienate the working class from the larger entity of which they were but one part. The result, according to Place, was to make Chartism "anomalous," to put it in a "false position" from which no progress could be made. The Chartists should have recognized that "the only real enemy [is] the Aristocracy" and that cooperation with the middle classes was essential. Until this happened, the Chartists would "have no power at all, not even a particle of power in a National sense." [27]

26. Mill, "Reorganization of the Reform Party," *LWR, 32*, 488. Also, "let the working classes learn to know the Parliamentary Radicals. . . . They are the only party in politics who have, to any great degree, common objects with the working classes": Mill, "Parties and the Ministry," *LWR, 28*, 17.

27. Place to Hume, Jan. 13, Feb. 10, 1841; Place to Warburton, May 5, 1839, and April 7, 1840; Place to W. Carpenter, Oct. 14, 1839: Add. MSS 35,151, ff. 161, 181, 251, 295, 309. Place overcame his objection to chartism when it broadened its social basis; in 1842 he supported

The Chartists' views of class in relation to politics were reflected in their economic doctrines, which also were objectionable to the Philosophic Radicals. Parkes called them "poison of
every anti social description instilled into the minds of the
Labouring Classes." [28] Their belief in the labor theory of value
was tied to the exaggerated significance they gave to the working
class. And their hostility to private property and their opposition
to repeal of the Corn Laws was seen as part of their misguided
hostility to the middle class. The initial assumption that the
Chartist leaders could be persuaded to give up some of these
economic views was to fade, but not before Place somewhat
condescendingly tried to persuade Lovett, Vincent, and other
London Chartists that the economic doctrines they saw as devices to justify working-class subordination to the middle classes
were in fact intellectual tools that correctly explained the laboring classes' severe conditions. He expounded the logic of the
Poor Law, the operation of supply and demand as it affected
wages, and the Malthusian position. Plaintively he asked, "Do,
pray, consider the case and see without prejudice, if you can,
whether what I have written, be, or, be not the simple truth." [29]

Chartist hostility to the anti-Corn Law agitation exemplified
to the Philosophic Radicals the way that ignorance and prejudice
led the Chartists to pursue narrow class goals. The Chartists
considered the agitation for repeal of the Corn Laws as an
exclusively middle-class effort in which they had no interest, and

---

Sturge's Complete Suffrage Union, which was committed to "reconciliation between the Middle and Labouring Classes"; thus it was the narrow
class basis and not the endorsement of universal suffrage that usually was
objectionable in Chartism: Norman McCord, *The Anti-Corn Law League
1838–1846* (London, Allen and Unwin, 1958), p. 114; Henry Richard,
Memoirs of Joseph Sturge (London, 1864), p. 297.

28. Parkes to Cobden, Nov. 23, 1839, SRO, Cobden Papers.

29. Place to Lovett, Dec. 8, 1838, Add. MSS 35,151, ff. 110–11. At
first Mill also reacted to Chartist economic views without despair; in an
article drafted in late 1837, though not published till 1839, he denied
that the working classes' Owenite views were hostile to private property;
he eulogized politically active working-class leaders; and he thought it
possible that they would postpone making some of their demands: "Reorganization of the Reform Party," *LWR, 32,* 494–98.

Chartist mobs attacked Anti-Corn Law meetings.[30] From the Philosophic Radical point of view, there was no need for the agitation of the Corn Law question to become an issue dividing the people. They saw no incompatibility between Corn Law repeal and the Charter. Both would confer benefits on all classes. If they were to rank them in order of importance, organic reform took precedence over Corn Law repeal.[31] However, on practical grounds they thought Corn Law repeal might be given priority by reformers, for universal suffrage did seem to be a more radical departure than repeal and, whereas the middle class opposition to universal suffrage arose from genuine fear, working class opposition to Corn Law repeal seemed to the Radicals to rest on intellectual error, which therefore could be overcome more easily.[32] Not that the Philosophic Radicals had a prominent

30. McCord, *Anti-Corn Law League,* pp. 56–58. Also see Lucy Brown, "The Chartists and the Anti-Corn Law League," in Asa Briggs, ed. *Chartist Studies* (London, Macmillan, 1959), pp. 342–54.

31. Mill: "The Corn Laws may be got rid of; but it can only be through a further Parliamentary Reform. . . . the manufacturers and merchants will have to learn what the working classes have already learnt— that they must combine to agitate, not against the Corn Laws, but against the source of the Corn Laws, as well as of every other grievance —the vicious constitution of the legislature": "Reorganization of the Reform Party," *LWR, 32,* 485. Also Place: "He who is desirous to have the corn laws repealed should have impressed on him the necessity of promoting the adoption of the Charter as the means of (carrying?) the repeal of all the laws which embarrass Trade and Commerce and are in any way inimical to the welfare of the people." Place to Lovett, n.d. [1838], Add. MSS 35,151, ff. 86–87. Also see above p. 74; *Spectator, 12* (Feb. 2, 1839), 98–99. Thompson was an exception: *Letters of a Representative . . . Second Series,* p. 35.

32. Hume, *Hansard, 46* (March 15, 1839), 729; (March 21), 1075; Mill, "Reorganization of Reform Party," pp. 492–93, 499. Believing that working class agitation was economic in origin, Mill (pp. 496–97) thought it would be easy to persuade working class politicians to compromise their demand for universal suffrage, providing their economic grievances (not their theoretical economic views) were dealt with. "Their minds are engrossed with one subject—the relation between labourers and employers. It is for the sake of benefiting themselves in that relation, that they desire Universal Suffrage. . . . They would be much more easily satisfied than is supposed by those who are unacquainted with the state of their minds." In addition to erroneous judgment, the Chartist opposi-

part in agitation for repeal; if anything, they found the Corn
Law agitation an embarrassment because it led to conflict between working and middle classes. But the agitation was there,
and they were irritated with the Chartists for using it as an excuse
for expressing hostility to the middle class. Thus Place said of the
Chartists, "If wise they would see that the attempt to repeal the
Corn Laws is a war with the Aristocracy, and if more wise still
they would see that the Aristocracy is, as it must be, their only
real enemy." [33]

Still another facet of the Philosophic Radical objection to the
exclusively working-class basis of Chartism concerned claims to
leadership. Representatives of the working classes or any other
segment of the populace were to have a subordinate place in the
coalition of groups that was to make up the party based on the
universal interest of all the people. Mill assumed this in his vision
of the party of natural Radicals. This was also Place's assumption when he tried to reconcile Chartists and other reformers by
proposing alterations in the language and amendments to the
provisions of the Charter. And it was in Hume's mind when he
speculated about the "chance of the Chartists now acting more
moderately if we were to put ourselves at their head." [34]

It was soon discovered that the Chartists had no intention of
playing such a subordinate role—that (despite the prominence of
their appeals to the working class) they also claimed to speak for

tion to repeal also was ascribed (at least by Place) to bribery by the
Tories: George Jacob Holyoake, *Bygones Worth Remembering* (London,
1905), *1,* 112–14.

33. Place to Thompson, Jan. 2, 1841, Add. MSS 35, 151, f. 290. Also
see above, p. 73; McCord, pp. 75–79, 178. Several of the Philosophic
Radicals were members of the Metropolitan Anti-Corn Law Association,
organized in 1836, but it had little direct connection with the Anti-Corn
Law League, which dominated when the agitation became national in
scope. However, the few Philosophic Radicals that were affiliated with
the League had only minor roles. Of course, C. P. Villiers, who was
marginally associated with the Philosophic Radicals, was the most prominent advocate of repeal in Parliament before the League agitation got
under way, but even he pressed for democratization as a prerequisite of
necessary legislation. *Hansard 50* (Aug. 9, 1839) 174–75.

34. Hume to Place, Feb. 9, 1840; Hume to Place, Jan. 13, Feb. 10,
1841: Add. MSS 35,151, ff. 208, 295, 309.

the people. Thus they challenged the Philosophic Radicals' implicit claim to leadership of a broadly based Radical party. Faced with this rival claim, the Philosophic Radicals' hostility reflected their resentment at the implied usurpation of the leadership role they had assumed for themselves. Molesworth called the Chartists the "pretended leaders of the working classes" and complained that they "have assumed to themselves the title, and I believe most falsely, of the leaders of the working classes." Roebuck lamented the absence of "true and honest guides" among the working people.[35] Place was still more explicit:

> [The Chartists] misinterpret to the many the actions and opinions of those who may have become more enlightened and will represent them as enemies of the people whom they would be the best qualified and best disposed to serve. The people will continue to be misled and will look upon their best friends as their worst enemies.[36]

Place also called the Chartist Convention, known as the People's Parliament, a "fraud," and Roebuck described the author of the Petition of 1842 (probably Feargus O'Connor) as a "malignant demagogue." [37]

Chartism also made it difficult for the Philosophic Radicals to appeal to the people in order to justify their claim on behalf of the Radical party. The evidence of working-class consciousness provided by the Chartists cast doubt on the very existence of "the People," for it emphasized the cleavages among the populace and prevented the coalescence of those various nonaristocratic classes that were to provide the social basis of a Radical party. By encouraging conflict among the natural Radicals the Chartists "have done grievous injury to the popular cause . . .

35. Roebuck to Brougham, March 21, 1839, UCL, BrP. *State of the Nation. Condition of the People. Speech of Sir William Molesworth, Bart., M.P., Delivered Feb. 5, 1840* (London, 1840), p. 15.

36. Wallas, *Place*, p. 384. However, to the Chartists, Place was a "rascally Whig" and a Malthusian: ibid., pp. 373, 378.

37. Jephson, *Platform*, 2, 263; Leader, *Roebuck*, p. 143. Referring to a Chartist mob of 150, Place said they "call themselves *the people*, and their impudence and tyranny is without example": Place to Roebuck, Dec. 23, 1840, Add. MSS 35,151, f. 288.

they have been the worst enemies of progressive reform." [38]
O'Connor and his *Northern Star* "were the worst enemies the
working people had." Place thought O'Connor "knew that he
could only hold the people to himself by increasing the enmity
between the working and all other classes of the people." Place
was rarely more bitter than when he passed judgment on most of
the Chartist leaders. He thought Stephens "a fanatic," also a
"malignant, crazy man"; Bronterre O'Brien "a three-parts insane
and savage man"; Hetherington "was an honest man, with too
little brains to guide him"; O'Connor, "the most reckless of them
all"; and collectively they were "the misleaders of the people."
He even damned them with the aristocrats as having "sinister
objects to accomplish." [39]

The Philosophic Radicals also turned against the middle
classes and for the same reason, though these classes, not being
very actively engaged in extraparliamentary politics at this time,
occupied less of their time and emotional energies than did the
working classes. Parkes reported that the middle classes "are tired
of the agitations and electoral struggles of the last ten years." [40]
This in itself was objectionable; but still more serious was the
fact that when they did express political opinions they only
demonstrated a sense of separateness from the working classes.
Mill and Roebuck lamented this development: "A large part of
the middle class . . . has already [in 1835] gone over to the Tories
[and] one section of the middle class, which is nearest to the
people, is daily going over." [41] This shift was accompanied by a

38. Molesworth, *State of the Nation,* p. 14.

39. Place to Hume, Feb. 10, 1841, Add. MSS 35,151, f. 309; Jephson,
Platform 2, 200, 254–57; Wallas, *Place,* p. 384. However, it should be said
that Place and Parkes tried to save Frost after his conviction, and Roebuck defended some Chartists.

40. Parkes to Ellice, Sept. 16, 1841, NLS, EP, E 38, f. 30. Also, Place
wrote: "Had a very considerable portion of the middle class [in Leeds]
been prepared to associate at once for reform, they might have proceeded in spite of . . . the working people, but they were not, and had
not any reason to expect they would be supported by any considerable
portion of their own class": Place to Hume, Jan. 13, 1841, Add. MSS
35,151, f. 293.

41. Conversation with Tocqueville, May 29, 1835: *Journey to England,*
p. 86. Mill also condemned "the middle classes for that apathy towards

growing fear of the working class, which more and more came to be focused on the Chartist demand for universal suffrage. A Radical party, based on both middle and working classes, had the task of finding a compromise agreeable to both. Yet middle-classes' fear of the working classes prevented them from playing their part.

> If ever democratic institutions are to be obtained quietly [Mill wrote], a great change in the sentiments of the two great classes towards one another must precede the concession; at present there is hardly a person possessed of the smallest property . . . who would not prefer almost any evils to those which they would expect from the political ascendancy of the working classes.[42]

Mill thought they would even risk civil conflict. "The middle classes are still very far indeed from the time when they will cry *Concede*—they will be much more likely to cry *Resist!*" [43]

This divisive effect of the middle classes provoked the Philosophic Radicals' hostility. The Philosophic Radicals were inclined, in any case, to be critical of "bourgeois" life. Mill complained that "the energies of the middle classes are almost confined to money-getting," and he accused the middle classes of "a general indifference to those kinds of knowledge and mental culture which cannot be immediately converted into pounds, shillings, and pence." [44] And Mrs. Grote had complained that

---

the political rights and peculiar interests of the labouring classes, which they have to a considerable extent manifested": "On the Defence of the House and Window Tax," *Mo. Rep.*, 7, 577.

42. "Reorganization of the Reform Party," *LWR, 32,* 500.

43. Mill to Robertson, Oct. 2, 1838, *EL*, p. 389.

44. Mill, "Civilization," *LWR, 25* (April 1836), 12; Mill, "State of Society in America," *Lond. Rev.,* 2 (Jan. 1836), 375. There is a passage in which Mill appears to express a preference for middle-class leadership: "The motto of a Radical politician should be, government *by means of* the middle for the working classes": "Reorganization of the Reform Party," *LWR, 32,* 494. However, the context of this article clearly shows that Mill wished to appease middle-class fear of the working class, and this passage should be seen in that light. See above, n. 21, for a formulation of the same idea in a way that more accurately reflects Mill's beliefs.

"the whole frame of social life in Eng[lan]d is . . . perverted by
the admira[tio]n for wealth and its appendages." [45] As a result
of both apathy and fearfulness, the middle classes refused to
play the part assigned them in the Philosophic Radicals' image
of political reality. There was an angry reaction. Place deplored
their "quiescence and abject submission." Roebuck called them
the "shopocracy." [46] Mrs. Grote cried out against the *epicier* and
asked, "who *can* do any good with such a pack of rotten quacks
and a stupid middle class who dream only of shop." [47]

Having experienced disappointment with both the working and
the middle classes, the Philosophic Radicals also expressed their
anger at the People. The body that would have taken on reality
had the middle and working classes assumed their proper roles
now had no real existence. As the Philosophic Radicals realized
that their image of reality was a mirage they became angry.
Place spoke of "the misled, ill-judging multitude," and Roebuck
decried popular ignorance:

45. Mrs. Grote to Place, Aug. 16, 1837, Add. MSS 35,150, f. 279.
46. Place quoted in Jephson, *Platform, 2*, 214-15. Roebuck quoted in
Examiner, Nov. 22, 1837, p. 762. Place also thought they were "among
the most despicable people in the nation in a public point of view":
quoted in O. F. Christie, *The Transition from Aristocracy 1832–1867*
(London, Seeley, 1927), p. 64.
47. Mrs. Grote to Place, March 11, 1840, Add. MSS 35,151, f. 241. "I
see no hope for England or France whilst the '*Epicier*' predominates as
he does in both countries. All Governments seem to be secured by the
fears of the timid trader": Mrs. Grote to Leon Faucher, Aug. 27, 1839:
Lady Eastlake, *Mrs. Grote* (London, 1880), pp. 76–77. The degree of
Mill's disapproval of the middle class is also revealed in his second (1840)
reveiw of Tocqueville. Sharing Tocqueville's concern about those moral
and intellectual characteristics that create a risk of tyranny, Mill disputes Tocqueville's ascription of these to democracy and attributes them
instead to "commercial civilization." The middle class is the agent by
which this is introduced. "America is *all* middle class . . . [it is] in a condition, both as to education and pecuniary means, corresponding to the
middle class here." "The American Many, and our middle class, agree
in being commercial classes." "All the intellectual effects which M. de
Tocqueville ascribes to Democracy, are taking place under the democracy
of the middle classes." "Democracy in America," *DD, 2*, 21, 64, 68, 71;
also see 19–20, 25, 65–67, 71–73, 77.

Take the masses separately and talk with them, what do you find—why, a profound ignorance and necessarily inveterate prejudice. How then can the compound mass differ from its component ingredients. There is no chemical fusion to make a hundred ignorant individuals, one instructed body.

He was angry with the people for failing to recognize their real interest. He resented their rejection of him at the 1837 election when, had he "joined the Ministry, and sold the people," he said, "my seat would have been safe for life." His resentment grew, and later he said of them, if "they desire to be well governed, let them, but I am not going to crawl to them in order to persuade them to their own good." [48]

The real cause of the Philosophic Radicals' anger was recognized by Fonblanque. He compared them to the painter who visited the menagerie:

to see in the flesh the quadruped he had spent his days in painting . . . and, in answer to his eager inquiries for the lions, when the noble beasts were shown to him he flew into a violent passion, charged the keeper with cheating the public, and insisted the lions were no lions, for, said he, "I have been painting lions all my life, and should know pretty well what they are like." [49]

They had assumed the People existed, yet finally Chartism and middle-class apathy and fear of the working classes showed them that the People was not a unitary body. It was assumed that the people would recognize their true interest in organic reform, yet their indifference to it, and their greater interest in erroneous

48. Wallas, *Place,* p. 384; Roebuck to Place, Sept. 18, 1837: Add. MSS 35, 151, f. 18; Leader, *Roebuck,* pp. 118–19. "The people must go through another probation, before men of my decided opinions can be of use": Roebuck to Place, Jan. 29, 1838: Add. MSS 35,151, f. 73.

49. *Examiner,* Dec. 16, 1838, p. 785. Fonblanque was pointing to the unreality of their expectations and its origins in doctrinairism; but the occasion for this observation was their reaction on discovering Durham's unwillingness to cooperate.

reforms was not easily denied. The Philosophic Radicals had counted on the realignment of parties to conform with the underlying, real struggle between people and aristocracy, yet the Tories increased in strength, and enmity between Whig and Tory "factions" continued. Meanwhile, efforts to form a party separate from the Whigs were unsuccessful. The obvious inapplicability of the doctrine in which the Philosophic Radicals had so much faith could produce only disillusionment.

WITHDRAWAL AND APOSTASY

There are degrees of despondency, and the Philosophic Radicals experienced several of them. Back in 1837 they were disappointed with their failure to achieve realignment and angry with the moderate reformers for not identifying themselves as Radicals. In 1838, as they saw how intractable the politicians of all parties were going to be, they directed their anger against the political system. At that time they already were disposed to give up politics but, had they given up then, they would have departed with their faith unaltered. However, during the very last years of the decade they could not avoid noticing the evidence of class consciousness and class conflict as well as the signs of viability in the party system they had previously thought obsolete; as a result, they experienced doubt about the validity of their doctrine. Consequently, they withdrew from politics with disillusionment and bitterness and a sense of having wasted their efforts.

There was, on the whole, more bitterness on the part of those who had advocated aggressive tactics than among those who were disposed to compromise. Mrs. Grote exemplified this. She was "pained by the spectacle of wreck and ruin in the field of Politics at home." [50] Surveying the situation, she felt obliged to admit that "the full measure of humiliation and contempt has now been reached in the persons of the Radical party in Parlt." The Whigs, still blameworthy in her eyes, "ought to have the full weight of the public hate" for (and here she alludes to her husband and the other Philosophic Radicals) "having defiled and destroyed all our contemporary leaders . . . of education and

50. Mrs. Grote to C. Babbage, n.d. [May 13, 1840 or '41], Add. MSS 37,200, f. 264.

knowledge." [51] She was not alone in such feelings. Everybody, she said, "is sick and weary of the name of politics," and she and Mr. Grote "now tacitly agree to avoid the subject." Roebuck reported "much despondency" among the radicals,[52] and Charles Austin, who, it was rumored, would have been Attorney-General or Lord Chancellor had Durham come to power in 1839, now confessed to a disappointment so bitter that he thought he would "never . . . take an interest in them again." [53] Mrs. Grote bemoaned their wasted efforts. "Thus at times I sigh," she said, "over those ten years of infructuous devotion to the public service; unrequited even by [Grote's] constituents . . . and only compensated by the esteem and admiration of some dozen high-minded men." [54] John Mill joined this chorus, as Caroline Fox reveals in a report of his conversation:

> 'No one,' he said with deep feeling, 'should attempt anything intended to benefit his age, without at first making a stern resolution to take up his cross and to bear it. If he does not begin by counting the cost, all his schemes must end in disappointment.' [55]

51. Mrs. Grote to Roebuck, Feb. 28, 1840: James M. Osborn Collection, Yale Univ. Also, "Sulk and apathy are at present the order of the day. . . . we are cankered at the core. . . . my distaste for the worldlings strengthens with experience."

52. Mrs. Grote to Leon Faucher, Aug. 27, 1839, Eastlake, *Mrs. Grote,* pp. 75–77; Roebuck to Tait, Nov. 28, 1840, Leader, *Roebuck,* p. 131.

53. Pierce, *Sumner, 2,* 58; C. Austin to Mrs. Grote, 1843, H. Grote, *Philosophical Radicals of 1832,* p. 66. Austin refused an offer to be Solicitor-General in 1841: Mrs. Grote to Sumner, Jan. 31, 1841, Harvard College Library, Sumner Papers.

54. Mrs. Grote to R. Currie, Nov. 1842, Grote, *Posthumous Papers,* pp. 70–71.

55. Caroline Fox, *Memories of Old Friends* (3d ed., London, 1882), *1,* 138 (entry of March 20, 1840). She added, "This was evidently a process through which he (Mill) had passed, as is sufficiently attested by his care-worn and anxious, though most beautiful and refined countenance." She also described a walk with Sterling and Mill: "They talked on politics. I asked if they would really wish for a Radical Government. . . . John Mill sighed out, 'I have long done what I could to prepare them for it, but in vain; so I have given them up, and in fact they have given me up' " (p. 151, entry of March 27, 1840).

Mill also confessed being "out of heart about public affairs as much as I ever suffer myself to be," and soon he had "almost given up thinking of the subject." [56]

The election in 1841 forced the Philosophic Radicals to decide whether they would seek to remain in Parliament. Grote and Molesworth refused to seek re-election. Grote explained to his constituents his unwillingness to remain in the absence of any effective, really Liberal party with which he could identify himself. He repeatedly refused offers to stand as candidate in the years that followed.[57] Roebuck had been out of Parliament since 1837, and now in 1841 he was returned once again for Bath. However, once in the House he felt isolated from "the so called radicals" and only reluctantly took part in proceedings from which he expected little.[58] Buller had intended to leave Parliament and attempt to get an appointment as a judge in Calcutta; but in the end he sought re-election and was successful.[59] After losing his seat in 1841, Hume was returned, though he claimed that he was disgusted with Parliament and wished to take his leave. Parkes, however, gave up his ambition to enter Parliament (though this may have been connected with the death of Lord Durham, whom he had hoped to serve).[60] Warburton was re-elected at Bridport but soon resigned his seat when he could not avoid acknowledgment of his involvement in the extensive bribery that had occurred.[61] Already during the mid-thirties Place had stopped expecting that Parliament would be an instru-

56. Mill to d'Eichthal, Dec. 25, 1840; Mill to R. B. Fox, Sept. 9, 1842: *EL*, pp. 456, 543.

57. H. Grote, *Life of Grote*, p. 140; G. Grote, *Posthumous Papers*, pp. 79–80, 121.

58. Roebuck to Brougham, Oct. 16, 1841, UCL, BrP.

59. Henry Cole, "Diary, 1841, 1842," entry of Feb. 2, 1841, Victoria and Albert Museum.

60. Grote, *Posthumous Papers*, pp. 79–80; Buckley, *Parkes*, p. 168.

61. Parkes' obituary described Warburton's petition that revealed "the gross costs and corruptions of all his six successive returns for Bridport": *Times*, Sept. 21, 1858, p. 7 (on Parkes' authorship, see Parkes to Brougham, Sept. 23, 1858, UCL, BrP. Warburton returned to Parliament in 1843. Also see Parkes to Stanley, Sept. 8 and [n.d. but c. Sept. 12] 1841, UCL, JPP.

ment of further organic reform, and he refused to waste his time "by having it occupied by any of the paltry measures likely to be entertained by the house of Commons." [62] Those who returned to Parliament did so as representatives of other causes. Philosophic Radicalism as a political movement, after ten years of struggle to form a new party, was now ended.

Despairing of politics, they took to scholarship. Mill had been working on his *Logic* at intervals throughout the previous decade, and he now returned to it with renewed interest. Molesworth began work for his edition of Hobbes in 1838, when his gloomy views of politics were germinating. Now in 1841, no longer in Parliament, he traveled on the Continent and worked on the edition. He also reported living "a life of the most tranquil repose: reading mathematics, studying the undulatory theory of light," and being "delighted at being free from the turmoil of politics." Grote returned to his Greek history, and began, with G. C. Lewis, a new classical journal. His wife reported that politics "are dead and buried," and "desiring to mix no more therein we relapse into letters, Philosophy and projects for rational enjoyment of our lives—we all mean to visit Italy some day." She added that Grote had been "getting up matter for his great work." A couple of years later he wrote to John Austin that the "prospect of public matters, as far as present progress is concerned, presents little which interests me," the History being his "greatest object of interest and delight." [63] Mill announced a preference for doing reviews of histories, and even Place and Roebuck took to writing on that subject. Place continued his narrative accounts of working-class political organization which,

62. Place to Hume, Feb. 9, 1839, Add. MSS 35,151, f. 132. Ewart was returned; Thompson was defeated. Stephen, *English Utilitarians, 3,* 39.

63. Molesworth to Mrs. Grote, Sept. 1841, Fawcett, *Molesworth,* p. 233; Grote, *Posthumous Papers,* p. 77; Mrs. Grote to Charles Sumner, Jan. 31, 1841, Harvard Coll. Library, Sumner Papers; Grote to J. Austin, Feb. 1843: Janet Ross, *Three Generations of Englishwomen* (London, 1888), *1,* 178–79. "Such times only make me wish to get back to my books and my thoughts, which I hope I shall before very long be enabled to do": Grote to Beaumont, Aug. 1, 1839; Yale Univ. Library, Tocqueville-Beaumont MSS, C. XI. c.

with his histories of manners and of reform movements, had
been a refuge for him at other times during the thirties when he
despaired of achieving anything through political action. Roebuck also turned to history and now began a book he called
Ten Years of Whig Administration. It was to vindicate Radicalism: "the book will live as a testimony; and if I tell the truth I
think some of our Whig people will be handsomely damned to
posterity." [64]

Once they acknowledged the defeat of their ambitions, their
attitude to the Whigs in some cases softened. Mill, Buller, and
even Roebuck began contributing to the *Edinburgh Review.*
Mill appears to have been the intermediary between Napier, its
editor, and some of the former contributors to the *Westminster.*
They wrote to Napier assuring him of their moderation and
willingness to avoid attacking the Whigs. Roebuck thought he
could write an article on Jefferson "without at all departing from
the views generally put forth by the Review." He also managed
to let Napier know that "Bentham had some views on the subject
of judicature, which experience has made me think erroneous,
though formerly I thought him right." [65] Buller intimated to
Macaulay that he would like to become a contributor. When the
editor responded favorably, Buller rather heavily (and presumably with irony) expressed his gratitude that his contributions
were not regarded "as unworthy of a place in that most efficient
organ of sound political and critical reviews." After his first
contribution appeared (in 1841) he reassuringly told Napier
that he "need not have specified 'moderation' and 'hesitation':
for if there are any two qualities in the world that I excel in,
these are the very two." Buller accepted a ministerial appointment in 1841, although two years earlier he had spurned Melbourne's offer of the secretaryship of the Board of Control on
"the true ground that that was not an office, for which I would

64. Mill to Napier, April 27, Sept. 21, 1840, *EL,* pp. 431, 444; Hayek,
John Stuart Mill and Harriet Taylor (London, Routledge, 1951), p. 111;
Leader, *Roebuck,* pp. 132–33.
65. Roebuck to Napier, Nov. 4, 25, 1841, Napier Papers, Add. MSS
34,622, ff. 249, 283.

be tongue-tied in Parliament." However, with the Radicals' effort and failure receding into the past, the post was offered again, and even though it was obvious that the government could not long remain in office, he accepted.[66] By 1844 he admitted that "he had grown out of being a Utilitarian." [67]

This mellowing attitude to the Whigs went farther with John Mill than it did with the other Radicals. Still committed to liberal goals, yet faced with the failure of his own brand of radicalism, Mill looked to the Whigs as the political agency through which those goals would be achieved. Recognizing that the Radicals as a party did not exist, he provided a rationale for this new attitude to the Whigs by noting that if there was "hope to do any good, it can only be by merging in one of the existing great bodies of opinion." As a result, he tended to identify himself with the fortunes of the Whig party, as if it now incorporated radicalism. He bent far—much farther than he would have two years before—to see them as a party with which a Radical could be honestly affiliated. They had "to some extent reanimated radical feeling, which will now again resume its upward movement and the Whigs having put themselves really at the head of the popular party, will have an opportunity . . . of making themselves again popular." To this he added, "they have quite converted me to them,"; indeed, he even called their speeches during a debate on the Corn Laws (the occasion for these statements) "the speeches of philosophers"! This attitude did not hinge on the Corn Law question, for he had already told the editor of the

66. Buller to Napier, Aug. 8, 1839, Napier Papers, Add. MSS 34,620, f. 321; Buller to Napier, Nov. 22, 1841: *Selections from the Correspondence of the Late Macvey Napier* (London, 1879), p. 370; Buller to Durham, Aug. 29, 1839, CPA, Durham Papers, *3*, 389; Wrong, *Buller*, pp. 40–41. Even Mrs. Grote now admitted "that great benefit has accrued from ten years of Whig ascendancy": H. Grote to Senior, Sept. 14, 1841, *Life of Grote*, p. 145.

67. Henry Cole, *Fifty Years of Public Work* (London, 1884), *1*, 16, n. 1. When the London Debating Society discussed the question, "That the Utilitarian System of Philosophy is pernicious and absurd," it was Buller who was present to defend Utilitarianism: *Fourth Supplement to the Laws and Transactions of the London Debating Society*, pp. 12–13.

Whig review that his "adhesion to the Edinburgh is in a certain sense political as well as literary." [68] As a result, he was now able to tell Fonblanque that "there is nothing in practical politics in which we now differ, for I am quite as warm a supporter of the present [Whig] Government as you are." [69]

The significance of the discrepancy between these views and those he had held not long before was reduced for Mill by virtue of his altered belief about the relation between thought and action. Now that his plan for a parliamentary party devoted to fundamental changes in the constitution had failed, his interest in politics, with its emphasis on institutions, diminished, and he turned to the realm of thought. Having failed as a politician, he now downgraded that role and looked for improvement through philosophy. He seems to have consoled himself that he was entering an era when "the progress of liberal opinions will again, as formerly, depend upon what is *said* and *written*, and no longer upon what is *done*." This shift of emphasis is similar to the shift that took place in 1829–31 when he temporarily rejected his father's "constitution mongering." Using language that was reminiscent of that St. Simonian episode, Mill once more held that "the mental regeneration of Europe must precede its social regeneration." He regarded his *Logic* as a contribution to the process by which this was to be achieved. Now that his intensive efforts on behalf of a specific doctrine had failed, he saw the speculative realm as one in which a variety of intellectual themes mingled to form guiding principles for the future. He again admired eclecticism as peculiarly appropriate to "the present great transitional movement of opinion and society." Against this background Mill again (as in 1830–31) tried to fashion a role for himself as a philosopher whose task was to synthesize

68. Mill to Napier, April 22, Sept. 21, 1840; to R. B. Fox, July 24, 1841: *EL*, pp. 430, 444, 481. Just before the fall of the Whig government Mill predicted a long tenure of office for the Whigs and said that, "except our Chartists all the radicals will now be one with the Whigs": Mill to d'Eichthal, n.d. [*c*. May, 1841]. Mill did not hold this view for long: *EL*, p. 472; Cf. 572.

69. Mill to Fonblanque, June 17, 1841, *EL*, pp. 478–79; also, "They have conformed to my programme, they have come up to my terms, so it is no wonder that I am heart and soul with them."

the various themes current in a transitional era in order to prepare for the future.[70]

Mrs. Grote made her peace with the Whigs in her own way. She accepted an invitation to Holland House. Charles Buller was sent to arrange it—"there should remain on record," he said, "some memorial . . . of the very most arduous negotiations ever entrusted to human diplomacy"—and he explained to Mrs. Grote that Lady Holland "wants to know whether, if she asks you to dinner you will go?" Since Lord and Lady Holland had "made a great point of it," using Sydney Smith as well as Charles Buller as ambassadors, Mrs. Grote felt her "dignity quite safe in accepting their advances." So Grote, who ten years earlier avoided aristocratic company on principle, now went to Holland House "without any twinges of conscience on his part." [71] This was the occasion on which Sydney Smith is said to have whispered in Mrs. Grote's ear, "Now that you have been seduced, my dear, I may tell you that your virtue was sometimes uncommonly disagreeable." Soon afterward Parkes wrote to Sumner in America that "Mrs. Grote was presented at Court . . . has lately dined at Holland House; and subsequently soireed at Lansdowne House!!! I tell her I who have avoided and declined all Whig brothels shall soon be the last of English Republicans." These episodes brought her to write her sister in Norway that she had "made a number of new acquaintances among fine folks" which, she said, "I think to follow up now that Radicalism is extinct and politics no longer absorb my energies." [72]

The Philosophic Radical group now dispersed. Although there had been misunderstandings between some of them during the

70. Mill to Napier, July 30, 1841; to R. B. Fox, Dec. 19, 1842, *EL*, pp. 483, 563–64. He now saw himself as one who has "to make new trains of thought intelligible": Mill to Chadwick, April, 1842, *EL*, p. 516. See pp. 110–12.

71. Buller to Mrs. Grote, April 21, 1840, *Posthumous Papers*, p. 57; Mrs. Grote to Mrs. C. Lewin, April 22, 1840, *Lewin Letters, 1,* 365; *Life of Grote*, pp. 43, 132.

72. Reeve, "Personal Memoir of Mr. Grote," *Edin. Rev., 138* (July 1873), 235; Parkes to Sumner, June 2, 1840, Harvard Coll. Library, Sumner Papers; Mrs. Grote to Mme. von Koch, Feb. 14, 1841, *Lewin Letters, 2,* 6.

thirties, relationships now became acrimonious. Roebuck and Molesworth had been particularly intimate with the Grotes, with whom they now quarreled. Shared beliefs and hopes in politics had been some bond of union, but, as Mrs. Grote explained, she "ceased to hold much intercourse with those individuals who formed the circle of our friendships in relation to politics." [73] With the dispersal of the group there no longer was occasion to talk of a "Grote conclave." In 1843 Mill took part in a conversation about "Jeremy Bentham and his influence, with some question whether there could then be a muster in London of Bentham's remaining disciples in sufficient number, and of sufficient mark, to attest the permanence of his influence." The company offered the names of "one or two persons" who would be "conspicuous in such a muster." [74]

73. Mrs. Grote to L. Faucher, Aug. 27, 1839, Eastlake, *Mrs. Grote,* pp. 76–77. Mrs. Grote, *Philosophical Radicals,* pp. 75–76.

74. David Masson, *Memories of London in the 'Forties* (Edinburgh, 1908), pp. 34–35.

10. *Aftermath*

There is no limit to the chimeras which a man may persuade himself of, whose mind has never had anything to do but to form conceptions, without ever measuring itself and them with realities.

—JOHN MILL [1]

"See how everybody and every thing has fallen asunder, and how little of name, fame and achievement is left,—except for those who have quitted politics for another ground." Thus Harriet Martineau felt in the eighteen sixties, after reading Mrs. Grote's *Philosophical Radicals of 1832*. Having begun with high hope, the embryonic movement collapsed, and the disappointment was proportionate to the considerable abilities and aspirations that had gone into it. Although most of the Philosophic Radicals achieved prominence later in the mid-Victorian era, they had indeed fallen asunder, and they never again cooperated for a political purpose. Back in the thirties Harriet Martineau had known several of the Radicals and had looked with sympathy on their efforts, and she was saddened, reflecting on the outcome:

I do not remember that I have ever before felt as I do today the dreariness of the tale of the people and the circumstances. Think of your personages as we must think of them now! Poor Roebuck! and the wretched figure he cuts as the credulous dupe of old Brougham! . . . Charles Buller [died 1848]—gone so early . . . Joe Parkes (my favourite aversion) always a blemish on the party. . . . The Austins accomplishing nothing at all corresponding to their known abilities, and the consequent general expectation. And Molesworth himself,—more creditable as having really accomplished something (put an end to Transportation, and opened Kew Gardens on Sundays)—dying so early, and

1. "Armand Carrel," *LWR, 28* (Oct. 1837), 70.

leaving a general impression of a wild and uncomfortable life. J. S. Mill only now entering upon such a political career [as an M.P.] as he longed for before he was half his present age (which I believe to have been that woman's doing, with much other mischief). Really,—Mr. Grote's History etc. and J. S. Mill's present activity and daily rising influence seem almost the only comfortable and cheering aspects in the history of the Philosl. Radicals. . . . Mournful is it now to read this narrative of yours.[2]

Radical ideas survived and spread, but through other spokesmen. The Philosophic Radicals were at most only marginally connected with the prominent Radical and Liberal movements for Parliamentary reform during the forties and later. They were unenthusiastic and sometimes even critical when new advocates for their former views appeared on the scene. When the agitation for shorter parliaments was revived in the sixties, Mill had lost interest in the question, and he shifted his position on the secret ballot. Although it was a "justifiable demand when originally made, [it] would at present, and still more in time to come, produce far greater evil than good." [3] (Place said, "If James Mill could have anticipated that his son John Stuart should preach so abominable a heresy . . . he would have cracked his skull." [4]) Grote, whose popular fame originated in his frequent motions on behalf of the ballot, said in 1867: "Since the wide expansion of the voting element, I confess that the value of the ballot has sunk in my estimation." [5]

2. Harriet Martineau to Mrs. Grote, Feb. 23, 1867, Add. MSS 46,691, unfol.

3. *Thoughts on Parliamentary Reform* (2d ed. London, 1859), p. 29; Packe, *Mill*, pp. 370, 415, where his shift on the ballot is attributed to Mrs. Taylor; Bertrand and Patricia Russell, *The Amberley Papers. The Letters and Diaries of Bertrand Russell's Parents* (New York, Norton, 1937), *1*, 370.

4. Reported in Bowring to Chadwick, Dec. 23, 1868, UCL, Chadwick Papers.

5. In a conversation of 1870 he also said "I have come to perceive that the choice between one man and another, among the English people, signifies less than I formerly used to think it did": Peter Anton, *Masters*

A democratic suffrage also became less attractive with the passage of time. Roebuck, depressed by popular apathy, thought universal suffrage would bring little change. "We shall some day have this extended suffrage, and things will remain exactly as they are, and the fools who now [1848] rave about it, will find some other topic for idle talk." [6] Mill, of course, continued to advocate universal suffrage, but with qualifications, such as his proposal for a graduated suffrage (and thus plural voting), which made him something of an equivocal democrat. His uneasiness about the influence of a prejudiced, unthinking multitude is shown in the ambivalence of his position.[7] The whole tone of the Grotes' approach to politics also changed. In 1869 Grote said he had outlived his faith in republican views, and his wife clearly indicated that she had. The country needed someone, she said, "to get up and say he will *not* consent to place the govt. of this old country in the hands of the 'greatest number,' i.e., represent[ation] by numerical majority." [8] And when there was a loud demand for an extension of the suffrage during the sixties, she advised a young enthusiast for democracy, Lord Amberley, to "avoid committing himself to sentimental democratic views . . . lest he should one day have to recede from positions taken

---

in History (Edinburgh, 1880), pp. 115–16. After the ballot was adopted and used, Grote's widow said, I "lean to the notion that open voting would have given much the same verdict"; H. Grote to A. Hayward, Feb. 9, 1874, Yale Univ. Library. Molesworth never altered his opinion on the ballot: *Hansard, 134* (June 13, 1854), 89–109.

6. Roebuck to Brougham, n.d. [1848], UCL, BrP.

7. *Considerations on Representative Government* (London, 1861), pp. 168–69, 174–75. Also see Sir Henry Maine, *Popular Government* (3d ed. London, 1886), p. 33: "universal suffrage has greatly declined in the estimation . . . of philosophers who follow Bentham."

8. Fonblanque, *Life and Labours*, pp. 21–22; H. Grote to Ellice, Jan. 30, 1859, NLS, EP. In 1852 she complained that "the moment anyone begins to 'bum bum' on the big drum, about 'the masses,' and so forth, the 'aristos' takes fright. . . . Why will nobody venture to say that the working classes are only a part, and not the whole, of a civilized community, and that the 'leisure classes' have an equal claim to be considered, in framing institutions": H. Grote to Ellice, (Jan.?) 10, 1852, NLS, EP, E 23, ff. 89, 119. Grote, however, refused the offer of a peerage in later years.

up in the warmth of his popular sympathies." [9] It was sentiments such as these that brought Henry Reeve to remark that the Benthamite school "perished with its first disciples: no such thing as a Benthamite of the second generation is known to exist, and even the survivors of the original sect no longer belong to it." [10]

Their contemporaries often saw the Philosophic Radicals as sectarian, doctrinaire—what today would be called ideological. The ideological approach to politics has been endemic in modern and modernizing nations since the eighteenth century, though some countries seem to have been more prone to it than others.[11] The Philosophic Radicals exemplify many of the characteristics of this approach, but they are a much less extreme and less pure example than those usually cited.

One of the characteristics of the ideological approach is a disposition to form judgments and act in terms of a doctrine that provides standards for condemning the entire political system.[12] The purpose of such a doctrine (or ideology) is to furnish

9. H. Grote to Lady Amberley, Dec. 11, 1866: *Amberley Papers, 1*, 545. Cf. Henry Taylor, *The Statesman* (London, 1836), pp. 124–25: "A young man . . . sometimes . . . declaims with a moral earnestness and solemnity as one who is in it head and heart, [but] then he cannot change . . . without incurring the reproach of corrupt motives or of a volatile understanding."

10. Reeve, "Autobiography of John Stuart Mill," *Edin. Rev., 139* (Jan. 1874), 117. Place seems to have been the only one to retain complete optimism about the usefulness of democratic reform. At 78, in response to a skeptical observation by Grote, he wrote, "I hope yet to see . . . a very large portion of the working people capable of . . . discreetly exercising the right of suffrage under the ballot, and with these improvements [others had been mentioned] a multitude of smaller matters all tending to promote human happiness": Place to Grote, Feb. 28, 1850, Add. MSS 35,151, f. 407.

11. It has had antecedents, of course, especially in movements of protest that have been inspired (if not caused) by religious prophecies and visions. See Norman Cohn, *The Pursuit of the Millennium* (London, Secker and Warburg, 1957), esp. Chap. 10–12 and pp. 307–14; John J. Ign. von Dollinger, *Prophecies and the Prophetic Spirit in the Christian Era*, Eng. trans. Alfred Plummer (London, 1873); Karl Mannheim, *Ideology and Utopia*, Eng. trans. L. Wirth and E. Shils (New York, Harcourt Brace, 1946), pp. 190–97.

12. Some of the most illuminating observations about the ideological

a blueprint for large-scale change. Toward this end, the doctrine provides both a vision of the kind of regime that is to come and a description of the path by which the goal can be reached. The envisioned end is sometimes a millennium or a utopia, the result (according to Matthew Arnold) of the way men, "by help of their imagination, take short cuts to what they ardently desire." [13] It need not encompass an entirely new social order or a fundamental change in human nature, but it must be sufficiently comprehensive to involve the transformation of an institution or some large segment of society. In the case of Philosophic Radical doctrine the purpose was to transform the existing aristocratic regime into a democracy. As it happened, their vision of democracy was vague, for Philosophic Radical doctrine emphasized the means by which existing society would be transformed but neglected the regime of the future. However, the future regime, as they envisioned it, had a characteristic in common with such regimes as portrayed in many other ideological doctrines, including those that are more emphatically utopian. It would be apolitical; on the assumption that the universal interest would prevail, interest groups, which were sinister, would not exist, nor would there be party conflict. With the establishment of institutions that allowed for the implementation of the universal interest, politics (which assumes conflict) would be unnecessary.

Since the Philosophic Radicals were committed to a doctrine that discredited the existing system and sought its transformation, they participated in it without a full commitment to its values and traditions. This approach to politics separated them from other politicians and publicists (including many Radicals).

approach are to be found in analyses of particular cases; for example, see Raymond Aron, *The Opium of the Intellectuals* (London, Secker and Warburg, 1957); J. L. Talmon, *The Origins of Totalitarian Democracy* and *Political Messianism* (London, Secker and Warburg, 1952, 1960). For general observations on this approach, see Daniel Bell, *The End of Ideology* (Glencoe, Ill., Free Press, 1960), pp. 369–75; Edward Shils, "Ideology and Civility: On the Politics of the Intellectual," *Sewanee Review*, 66 (1958), 450–53, 465–69; Lewis S. Feuer, *Psychoanalysis and Ethics* (Springfield, Ill., Thomas, 1955), pp. 126–30.

13. Quoted by Alfred Plummer, "Introduction," p. vii, in Dollinger, *Prophecies*.

Most others took their cues from sentiments and attitudes and beliefs that were a by-product of loyalties to particular groups and institutions—family, university, church, and party. Such persons would have responded favorably to Monmouth's exhortation (in *Coningsby*); "You go with your family, sir, like a gentleman; you are not to consider your opinions, like a philosopher or a political adventurer." Whereas other politicians acted with ease within the existing system, the Philosophic Radicals condemned that system because it provided only for small changes—"piddling domestic detail ameliora[tion]s," Mrs. Grote called them.[14] They felt political activity was worthwhile only if it was related to that comprehensive end formulated in their doctrine. Then politics would be properly conducted—the extremes would be engaged. Those seeking that end would battle those resisting it. All others, that is, all the nonideological politicians, were condemned as irrelevant, trivial, or worse. This included the Tories (all but the Ultras), the Whigs, and the moderate reformers who were to the left of the Whigs but who looked to Whig leadership of the reform movement. Although all these were thought to be unworthy, the Philosophic Radicals, as spokesmen for the Left, typically directed their greatest animus against the moderate left-center. Its resistance seemed to be the immediate obstacle to realignment, and that resistance seemed all the more irrational since it came from men who called themselves reformers.[15]

The Philosophic Radicals also exemplified the ideological

14. B. Disraeli, *Coningsby* (London, 1881), p. 410 (Book 8, Chap. 3). H. Grote to Place, May 2, 1841, Add. MSS 35,151, f. 337.

15. Grote (1838) complained that "the degeneracy of the Liberal party and their passive acquiescence in everything, good or bad, which emanates from the present Ministry, puts the accomplishment of any political good out of the question": H. Grote, *Philosophical Radicals of 1832*, p. 41. To Place the moderate reformers were "so called liberals"; to Rintoul they were "pseudo Radicals"; referring to "the whole tribe of Marshalls and Baines," Roebuck said, "were [the Whigs] out of office every man of this sort would be really and heartily . . . radical": Roebuck to Brougham, Nov. 16, 1840, UCL, BrP; *Spectator, 12* (May 25, 1839), 477; Place to Roebuck, Jan. 24, 1838, Add. MSS 35,151, f. 71. See pp. 67, n. 83; 206–07.

approach in their attitude to compromise. Since all the non-ideological politicians were seen as unworthy, compromise with any of them was regarded with great distaste. Power would be worth possessing only if it was acquired by "a strict, a severe, rigid adherence to acknowledged principles, by unflinching courage, by a determination never to shift, to truckle either to one party or another." Mrs. Grote expressed fear of "a shuffling dirty compromise" with the Whigs and called on the Radicals to "stand clear of 'expediency gabble'" that would only bring degradation. Compromise with the Whigs involved sacrifice of principle. Thus Molesworth felt "contaminated by the Whigs; with them I feel most anxious to be at war, convinced as I am that their influence over our party is of the most demoralising description." [16] Such feelings were the source of a disposition among some of the more doctrinaire Philosophic Radicals to prefer being in a "virtuous minority" rather than appear to be affiliated with the Whigs.[17] When they found themselves drawn into cooperation with the Whigs they felt as if they had betrayed their cause (for example, see pp. 154,196). On such an occasion Mrs. Grote condemned "their sheepish conduct" and "cried at their desertion." At the end of the decade when Hume found himself sitting with the Whigs, and in the absence of a Radical opposition with which he could associate himself, he felt torn: "As a Reformer he was in a false position, and though very

16. Roebuck to Brougham, Aug. 31, 1838, UCL, BrP; H. Grote to Place, June 2, [1836], Add. MSS 35,144, f. 378; Molesworth to Place, Oct. 5, 1836, Add. MSS 35,150, f. 167.

17. See p. 171. Moleworth said the Radicals' "servile union with the Whigs [has] disgusted me, and I felt no strong inclination to appear again in the ranks of their followers: not that I . . . care how often I am in the smallest minority": Molesworth to Place, Sept. 5, 1836, Add. MSS 35,150, f. 145. The phrase "virtuous minority" is Parkes', who was not one of the more doctrinaire members, though he considered adopting the tactics implied in the phrase; see Parkes to Durham, Aug. 7, 1836; LP. Cf. R. H. S. Crossman on the dispute between the Traditionalists and Revisionists within the Labor Party: "Our heresy consisted in a stubborn determination, despite the three successive electoral defeats, to stick to our 'irrelevant' socialist principles until another crisis made them relevant—even if this meant a long sojourn in the wilderness": "Scientists in Whitehall," *Encounter, 23* (July 1964), 3.

unwilling to change sides, his duty almost forced him to do it."
The country, he said, was "in a wretched state." With the approaching end of the Whig government in 1841 Mrs. Grote felt
relieved: "we shall be freed from the irksome duty of figuring in
the same section with these miserable quacks." [18]

Since the political system was dominated by nonideological
politicians, the Philosophic Radicals were critical of the political
and social system that denied the intelligentsia a political role and
even an audience. John Stuart Mill was especially severe. He
regarded his countrymen as being almost exclusively concerned
with religion and "worldly advancement," especially the latter.[19]
This created an excess of practicalness:

> There is a practicalness which comes by nature, to those
> who know nothing and aspire to nothing; exactly this is the
> sort which the vulgar form of the English mind exemplifies,
> and which all the English institutions of education, what-
> ever else they may teach, are studiously conservative of
> . . . [This is] the atmosphere which kills so much thought
> [and] sobers what it spares.[20]

As a result, the English excelled as businessmen, but they were
anti-intellectual. "Our people are not ripe for any generalizations
of . . . [a] wide and ambitious kind. . . . This is not a place for

18. H. Grote to Place, March 27 [1838]; May 2, [1841], Add. MSS
35,151, ff. 79–80, 337. *Hansard, 46* (March 27, 1839), 1235.

19. "Writings of Alfred de Vigny" (1838), *DD, 1,* 290. Also Place: "In
this country of arbitrary classifications and distinctions where a large part
of life is occupied in the endeavour to ascend into the class above . . .
where all such persons consider it a bounden duty to treat every one beneath them with the contumely with which they themselves are treated
by every one above them, no one thinks it needful . . . to do justice to
the common people": Add. MSS 27,790, f. 115 (c. 1834–36). Also see
James Mill, "Education," pp. 45–46, in *Essays.* Cf. S. M. Lipset, *Political Man* (New York, Doubleday, 1960), pp. 322–23, 336, for a discussion
of the way perceptions of social structure are shaped by the intellectuals'
need to justify their feeling of alienation from society.

20. Mill, "Armand Carrel," *LWR, 28* (Oct. 1837), 70. "Mill had acquired something like prejudice and even contempt not only for English
society, which he little knew, but also for contemporary development of
English thought": Hayek, p. vii, in Mill, *Spirit of the Age.*

speculative men." [21] This was especially serious for its political consequences. Since the English were "very inattentive to any thing that cannot be carried instantly into practice," they would attend only to those politicians dealing in small, incremental changes. The advocates of large-scale change would be dismissed: "The English people have never had their political feelings called out by abstractions. They have fought for particular laws, but never for a *principle* of legislation." This attitude made them cautiously shrink from extremes, making it "an age without earnestness . . . [a] natural era of compromises and half-convictions." [22] Finally, and worst of all, the English were not serious about politics; that is, they did not see all facets of life as having a political dimension. For politics (and art too) the Englishman "keeps only bye-corners of his mind."

> It is but a small minority among Englishmen who can comprehend, that there are nations among whom Politics, or the pursuit of social well-being, and Poetry . . . are passions as intense, as absorbing—influencing as much the whole tendencies of the character, and constituting as large a part of the objects in life of a considerable portion of the cultivated classes, as either the religious feelings, or those of worldly interest. . . . politics . . . instead of being either a trade or a pastime, [is] taken completely *au serieux*.[23]

The absence of such an attitude in England was at once a sign

21. Mill to d'Eichthal, Nov. 12, 1839, *EL*, p. 413. He added the qualification, "except (at most) within the limits of ancient and traditional Christianity."

22. Mill, "Comparison of the Tendencies of French and English Intellect," *Mo. Rep., 7* (Nov. 1833), 802; "Coleridge," *DD, 1,* 429–30. Consequently, Mill tried to avoid the appearance of being devoted to abstract principles; e.g. *EL*, p. 360. However, this does not mean that he was not a spokesman for them. Cf. J. P. Mayer, Introduction, p. 15, in Tocqueville, *Oeuvres Complètes*, vol. 6, *Correspondance Anglaise* (Paris, Gallimard, 1954).

23. Mill, "Writings of Alfred de Vigny," *DD, 1,* 290. Cf. Bagehot: "The *too clever by half* people, who live in *Bohemia,* ought to have no more influence in Parliament, than they have in England, and they can scarcely have less": quoted in Norman St. John-Stevas, *Walter Bagehot* (Bloomington, Indiana Univ. Press, 1959), p. 52.

of the need for an intelligentsia and an obstacle to its establishment.

In order to be plausible an ideology must make assumptions about human nature and society, for it must show that the envisioned society can function; and (what was more important for the Philosophic Radicals) it must make assumptions about the process of change to show that it is possible for the transformation to take place. Toward this end the Philosophic Radicals assumed that the political world had two dimensions, one of them "more real" than the other. Thus, regardless of appearances, it was held that the conflict between populace and aristocracy was in some sense more real than any of the other conflicts that existed, including those within the existing party system and within parties and social classes. This outlook made it possible to condemn existing institutions, such as the party system, as illegitimate; and thus it justified attacks upon that system. More important, since the party system was not in accord with "reality," it was possible to believe that it was weak and vulnerable to attack; therefore this outlook nourished the expectation that the party system could be made to disappear, no matter how healthy it might seem. This assumption also allowed the Philosophic Radicals to believe that new social formations could emerge—hence their expectation that the two aristocratic factions would unite into a new aristocratic party and that a new Radical party would take shape. These parties, unlike those in the existing system, would be in accord with the underlying reality. Believing that they were attuned to fundamental (even if not fully visible) social forces, the Philosophic Radicals could feel optimistic and believe in the importance of their mission. Unlike the Whigs, they were "fighting for *realities*." [24]

Believing that there was an underlying reality that provided the foundations for proper political action, it was easily assumed that there was no great difficulty in transforming institutions so they would faithfully reflect that reality. There were certain basic

24. H. Grote to Parkes, Jan. 22, [1835]: LP. Cf. Talmon, *Totalitarian Democracy*, p. 136; R. J. Lifton, *Thought Reform and the Psychology of Totalism* (New York, Norton, 1961), p. 421, on the conviction of those who believe "that reality is their exclusive possession."

motivations that had a tendency to make men cooperate to promote their fundamental interests and thus to coalesce as members of an aristocratic party or a popular, Radical party. False information or traditionally held misconceptions might prevent them from recognizing where they really belonged, but once they were forced to recognize the realities, the party system would be transformed. Those with an understanding of the underlying reality could force the issues that would cause men to redefine their positions. For example, the ballot issue was especially important for the Philosophic Radicals because they thought it would serve this purpose (see pp. 69–71). Aggressive tactics thus seemed rational (see pp. 170–74). They were to provide the catalytic agent that would suddenly bring the underlying reality to the surface where it would be evident to all. This outlook also gave plausibility to the continuing complaints against Grote for failing to take the initiative. To Mill it seemed that circumstances were favorable, even inviting, and that only bold leadership was wanting. If Grote's "courage and energy had been equal to the circumstances, or to his knowledge and abilities, the history of these ten years of relapse into Toryism might have been very different. His standing and social position would have enabled him to create a real Radical party, for which the materials then existed." [25] This expectation that great changes could be suddenly accomplished seemed reasonable to them because they thought their tactics were grounded in reality. Thus John Mill could believe in "the practicability of Utopianism." [26]

The Philosophic Radicals exemplify another characteristic that is sometimes attributed to ideologically-oriented intellectuals. Since they were not entirely untainted by a worldly wish for power, their doctrine contained within it the seeds of conflict

25. *Early Draft*, pp. 155–56. Mill added, "All this would probably have happened if my father had been in Parliament." He softened this judgment of Grote in the later version and admitted having had "an exaggerated sense of the possibilities": *Auto.*, pp. 165–66.

26. Mill, "Rationale of Representation," *Lond. Rev.*, *30* (July 1835), 367. Cf. Bell, who says that spokesmen for 19th century ideologies "embarked upon what William James called 'the faith ladder,' which in its vision of the future cannot distinguish possibilities from probabilities, and converts the latter into certainties": *The End of Ideology*, p. 372.

between their desire for power and their wish for reform—a
conflict which was neither inevitable nor necessary. But the
possibility of such conflict was a consequence of the particular
way they visualized the path to reform. They chose to see it in
terms of realignment. However, in addition to leading to democratic reform, realignment would have established a place for
their party in a two-party system, and hopefully it would have
led to the exercise of power. Since they were committed to realignment tactics, they were reluctant to cooperate with the
Whigs, even though such cooperation was a condition of achieving incremental reform. Such cooperation also would have
separated the Whigs from the other aristocratic faction, whereas
realignment required that they merge; and it would have involved
compromise and the end of the Radicals as an independent body
and the loss of a sense of identity with it. However, by fighting
the Whigs and resisting cooperation with them the Philosophic
Radicals could sustain the hope that their party would become
fully established and thus be eligible to form a government. By
visualizing the achievement of reform in a way that also would
necessarily have made them the sole agents by which it could be
gained, they created in their own minds an inhibition about the
kind of political activity that contributes to the gradual accumu-
lation of partial reforms. This was the source of tension and even
conflict between incremental reform and their quest for power.
The desire for power penetrated their fantasies (see pp. 175–
77), it sometimes affected their conduct, and it can be discerned
in their doctrine, giving it that "all or nothing" character which
was at the heart of the doctrinairism that contemporaries either
complained of or ridiculed.[27] Tocqueville recognized this facet
of their outlook; having described in his diary the argument for

27. Referring to the Philosophic Radicals' reaction to the Municipal
Corporations Bill, Sydney Smith asked, "Who, but the idiots of the earth,
would fling a country like this into confusion, because a Bill (in its mutilated state a great improvement) is not carried as far, and does not em-
brace as much, as the best men could wish? Is political happiness so
cheap, and political improvement so easy, that the one can be sported
with, and the other demanded, in this style?": Smith to Mrs. Austin,
Sept. 7, 1835, *Letters of Sydney Smith,* ed. N. C. Smith (Oxford, Clarendon, 1953), 2, 624.

realignment (as presented in conversation by Roebuck and Mill), he noted that the argument was "more subtle than true; the reasoning of a man in a hurry to enjoy, rather than of men whose first care is to make enjoyment sure." [28]

There are occasions when the ideological approach to politics is effective, but England in the early and mid-nineteenth century provided few of them. Fundamental change in the economy and social structure created a need for constitutional adjustments. But the ensuing political changes were adaptive, incremental, evolutionary. Everything in the political system seemed to conspire to create obstacles to the kind of change demanded by doctrinaires. Bagehot, looking back to the time of the Reform Bill and Althorp's performance, saw "all the characteristic virtues which enable Englishmen to effect well and easily great changes in politics," including the disposition to compromise—"rather to give up something than to take the uttermost farthing"; and the pragmatic approach to a problem—"their hand-to-mouth readiness to take what solves it without thinking of other consequences." [29] Tocqueville, visiting in 1833, also recognized the nondoctrinaire approach to change. Individuals had grievances, but they were not generalized. "Talk with a man of the people. . . . He will complain of such-and-such a Lord, or the course which the House of Lords had adopted, but it does not seem to have entered his head that one could do without Lords. . . . So, too, if you speak to a member of the middle classes; you will find he hates some aristocrats but not the aristocracy." This kind of attitude was an obstacle to the spread of general principles that would mobilize support for ideological politicians. Thus grievances were taken up, "one small thing after another, and [reformers] have not in any way conceived one of those general principles which announce the approach of the total subversion of the existing order." [30] George Cornwall Lewis also observed

28. Tocqueville, *Journeys*, p. 86, n. 2. On the so-called "double role of the intellectuals," see Bell, *End of Ideology*, pp. 335–37, 392–93 (n. 147).

29. "Lord Althorp and the Reform Act of 1832" (1877), *The Works and Life of Walter Bagehot*, ed. Mrs. Russell Barrington (London, Longmans, 1915), 7, 38–39.

30. Tocqueville, *Journeys to England and Ireland*, pp. 69–70.

that "no principle of that [experimental] sort is ever carried to its full extent at one blow in England. Both in our wise and foolish acts we generally do things by halves." Consequently there was a "perpetual drag chain" on those seeking to innovate.[31]

In such a political system the majority of politicians of all parties were nondoctrinaire. As Bagehot put it, they "are not eager to press the tenets of their party to impossible conclusions. On the contrary, the way to lead them—the best and acknowledged way—is to affect a studied and illogical moderation." [32] He thought the Whigs exemplified this approach: their doctrine defied abstraction.

> In truth Whiggism is not a creed, it is a character. Perhaps as long as there has been a political history in this country there have been certain men of a cool, moderate, resolute firmness, not gifted with high imagination, little prone to enthusiastic sentiment, heedless of large theories and speculations . . . with a clear view of the next step.[33]

On the Tory side there were doctrinaires (the so-called Ultras), but they were a small minority. Most Tories (now calling themselves Conservatives) responded, though grudgingly, to Macaulay's appeal when he urged reverence to ancestors, "not by superstitiously adhering to what they, in other circumstances, did, but by doing what they, in our circumstances, would have done." [34] The bulk of the Radicals also shied away from extremist leadership, as the allegiance of the moderate reformers—the "200 ballot men," for whom Fonblanque was spokesman—made clear.[35] As a result, extremist factions tended to go into

31. Lewis to Mrs. Austin, March 4, 1848: *Letters of G. C. Lewis,* p. 169.

32. Bagehot, *English Constitution,* p. 126.

33. Bagehot, "The First Edinburgh Reviewers" (1855), *Works, 2, 62.* Cf. Macaulay: "I would not take the trouble of lifting up my hand to get rid of an anomaly that was not also a grievance": *Speeches,* p. 31.

34. Ibid., p. 8.

35. John Wade, former editor of *The Black Book,* represented one facet of moderate radicalism. By 1840 he complained of the "two extremes of politics, between which lies the great mass of intelligence and moderation . . . [They are] equally impracticable in their aims, equally

opposition, leaving a majority of moderates to support the government. Bagehot pointed out that a cabinet's success depended on gaining a hold on "the great middle part of Parliament." [36]

Most other politicians took their cues from many sources but not from doctrinal beliefs such as Philosophic Radicalism. Yet the Philosophic Radicals thought they knew what forces were "really" operating. Their expectations were based on their understanding of these forces, and to the extent that there was a discrepancy between the reality and their image of it, disappointment should have followed. Yet it is a measure of their faith that, despite much evidence, they continued to act as if that image was in fact correct. They used it as a guide in a nonideological environment where other politicians did not behave in accordance with any single principle, and certainly not in accordance with Philosophic Radical doctrine. The Philosophic Radicals placed the blame for their failure on poor leadership, lack of organization, apathy.[37] But their doctrinairism was much more important, for it gave them preconceived beliefs about the way men would act and the way the political system would develop, and these led to false perceptions and misleading expectations. It also led them to adopt tactics that isolated them from their intended allies and failed to provoke the realignment of parties they were seeking.

... bigoted ... One of these is mainly composed of anti-Catholic zealots, Orangeists ... As the Conservatives are bigoted to the past, their antipodes, or the movement party, are infatuated with the future. Both dwell much in the extremes of fancy, differing only in the tenses of their ideality": *Glances at the Times*, p. 5.

36. Bagehot, *English Constitution*, p. 143. Also see Norman Gash, *Mr. Secretary Peel* (London, Longmans, 1961), p. 457.

37. "Their lot was cast in the ten years of inevitable reaction ... when the public mind desired rest": Mill, *Auto.*, pp. 165–66. Place said much the same thing: "The time has passed away when the 'Man of the People' was run after by the ignorant mob composed of all classes who shouted 'the Cause the Cause' without having a definite idea of the meaning of the words they used": Place to Warburton, April 7, 1840, Add. MSS 35,151, f. 251. On inadequacy of leadership, see p. 283. On lack of organization and disagreement about tactics, see *Hansard, 41* (March 7, 1838), 582; *47* (May 3, 1839), 832, 840.

A major source of false and misleading cues was an assumption that was one of the foundations of their realignment strategy —that "the People" really existed as a viable group on which a political party could be based. They assumed that politicians and other citizens would feel a sense of identity with the people in preference to other groups and that they would define their interests in terms of that identification. This led the Philosophical Radicals to expect that the middle and working classes would cooperate politically; and it led to their failure to correctly estimate the intensity of class consciousness among the Chartists, the degree of concern with economic rather than political problems among the working classes, and the extent to which hostility and suspicion between middle and working classes would obscure perceptions of the universal interest that comprehended both. As a consequence, they ineffectively made pleas for tolerance and harmony when faced with the strong emotions of class enmity. Molesworth recommended that the working classes "cordially" unite with the middle classes. The "chief object" of radical endeavor, Roebuck advised, "should be to heal the differences now existing between the middle and the working classes, and to unite them. . . . with common interests, feelings, and sympathies." He meant to achieve this by "laying down a principle to which both parties [i.e. classes] will adhere." But there was no issue on which they could agree. The Philosophic Radicals were so far out of touch with the people on behalf of whom they spoke that they failed to perceive the true state of popular opinion. Molesworth could only suggest as a counter to Chartism that the people demand education.[38] Carlyle, with an instinctive understanding of the people's felt needs that the Philosophic Radicals lacked, asked what radicalism had obtained for the people—"what other than shadows of things has it so much as asked for . . . Cheap Justice . . . Poor-Rate . . . Ballot-Question 'open' or shut: not things but shadows of things; Benthamee formulas; barren as the east-wind!" Carlyle found nothing mysterious in the history of Chartism, "especially if that of Radical-

38. Molesworth, *State of the Nation . . . Feb. 5, 1840*, p. 15; Leader, *Roebuck*, pp. 123–24, 133.

ism be looked at. All along, for the last five-and-twenty years, it was curious to note how the internal discontent of England struggled to find vent for itself through *any* orifice. . . . How Parliamentary Radicalism has fulfilled this mission, entrusted to its management these eight years now, is known to all men." [39]

Another major source of false perceptions and misleading expectations was the assumption that the Whigs and Tories would coalesce into a single aristocratic party and, as a prelude to this, the moderate reformers would separate from the Whigs to join the Radicals. Despite the persistence of the traditional antagonism between Whigs and Tories, the Philosophic Radicals pointed to what they saw as signs of merger. To Molesworth "the Whigs are but the remains of a dying faction. . . . Their only adherents are a few of the landed gentry . . . most of whose offspring are Tories." [40] Mill said "the Whig *coterie* is not renewed. There are no young Whigs. . . . Nor does anyone doubt that were a general election to take place just now [1836], whether the Tories were reduced in number or not, the Radicals would gain still further upon the Whigs." There also was an expectation that the moderate reformers (the 200 ballot men) would assert their latent radicalism and desert Whig leadership. [41]

An ideological approach can be effective when a political system disintegrates and other politicians lose confidence and fail to exercise leadership and when the citizenry becomes apathetic and vulnerable to manipulation. In these circumstances doctrinaire politicians can reshape the political order and give the ap-

39. Thomas Carlyle, *Chartism* [1839] (London, 1858), pp. 54–56. Also see, A. Seth Pringle-Pattison, *The Philosophical Radicals and Other Essays* (Edinburgh, 1907), p. 45: "The reason they invoked with so much confidence was abstract and unhistorical, and, as a consequence, their insight failed them when they had to deal in any way with the unseen foundations of society or the hidden springs of national life."

40. Molesworth, "Terms of Alliance," *LWR, 26,* 291.

41. Mill, "Tories, Whigs, and Radicals," *LWR, 25,* 296. When Grote introduced his ballot motion after it had been made an open question in 1839 the minority supporting him was increased by only 17 votes and the plurality against him was increased by 1 vote. Yet compare the expectations with regard to making the ballot an open question, above, pp. 174–75.

pearance of having been accurate in their diagnosis and successful in their prophecies. But this was not the kind of situation
the Philosophic Radicals faced and, consequently, from a
mistaken diagnosis they proceeded to adopt an unrealistic
strategy. Yet for a decade they persisted in believing that it was
possible, even probable, that their tactics would lead to the
establishment of a Radical party. They did not recognize the
difficulty, because their rigid attachment to a doctrine prevented
them from perceiving the varied forces that moved other men,
and it made them insensitive to the alternative paths of development that lay before the political system. Using the doctrine as
a guide, they acted in relation to a "people" and a disintegrating
party system that hardly existed except in their preconceived
image of reality. This image was (as Tolstoy used the word)
"brain-spun," and it remained with them as long as they were
politicians, indeed, it helped sustain them in that role. It was
given up only when disillusionment set in. But by that time they
were too embittered to act. Joseph Parkes was an exception. Too
much of a realist ever to be disillusioned, he recognized the
brain-spun character of his doctrinaire friends: "what Condorcet
dreamed political society *would be,* Molesworth and Co. dream
it *is.*" [42]

Of course, to say they failed is to judge them by the standard
they set for themselves. They failed to transform the party system and establish the Radical party called for in their doctrine.
By any other standards their achievements were considerable.
But it was not as parliamentary politicians that they were influential. Rather, it was as administrators and, to a lesser degree,
in extraparliamentary politics that they exercised this influence.
This is not to say that they had no impact on the course of
parliamentary politics. Apart from the fact that their faction

42. Parkes to Ellice, Jan. 8, 1837, LP. "Mr. Grote is a very worthy,
honest, and able man; and, if the world were a chess-board, would be
an important politician": Sydney Smith, *Ballot* (London, 1839), p. 17, n.
"With a power of analytical reasoning unsurpassed by the wisest philosophers, he [Mill] combined an infirmity of judgment which not infrequently
led him to mistake Utopian dreams for established truths": Reeve,
"Autobiography of John Stuart Mill," *Edin. Rev.* (Jan. 1874), *139,* 91.

often was a source of anxiety and sometimes a threat to Melbourne's government, one can point to Buller's part in getting the Public Records Office established; to Warburton's Bill (1838) that made it possible to use personal as well as real property in establishing the property qualification for Members of Parliament; and to Molesworth's report on transportation (1838), which contributed to the abolition of this kind of punishment. But their influence from within Parliament was negligible by comparison with what they achieved in various quasi-administrative roles. Parkes drafted the report that was the basis of the Municipal Corporations Bill, and he was the driving force on the Commission. Buller, as secretary to the Durham mission in Canada, played an infinitely larger part than he did as a Member of Parliament. Of even greater significance is the role played by the Mills as officials of the East India Company, which had a large measure of the responsibility for ruling India. As Examiners, whose duty it was to draft dispatches that carried instructions to the Company's agents in India, they helped fulfill Bentham's prophecy that after his death he would be "the dead legislative of British India." Of course, the gradual settlement of the major lines of policy reduced John Mill's opportunity to exercise influence, and their distance from India restricted his father as well. Nevertheless, as members of a small group of permanent officials holding office comparable to that of a permanent undersecretary in the civil service, they had opportunities to direct and shape policy, and their influence on Indian developments dwarfs their achievements in cooperation with their friends in Parliament.[43] Finally, there is Chadwick. He did not help the Philosophic Radicals in trying to establish a Radical party, but he was a spokesman for Bentham's administrative principles, and in this role he became a major architect of extensive reforms and the expansion of the machinery of government during the nineteenth century.[44]

43. Eric Stokes, *The English Utilitarians and India* (Oxford, Clarendon, 1959), pp. 49–50 and Chap. 2–4.

44. Chadwick is an extreme example of the extensive Benthamite influence that was unconnected with radicalism as a parliamentary phenomenon. According to R. K. Webb, "The men who carried out this

They were aware of these achievements but felt little pride in them, for their ambitions were directed to the establishment of the Radical party. For the same reason they would not have found much consolation in being told that their politics and their journalism, in combination with the impact of Benthamism generally, would have in the long run a pervasive effect on many facets of life. Yet many observers testified to this. For example, during the 1850s Whewell described how Bentham had been "kept in a peculiar manner present to our minds as a contemporary." [45] In the seventies Sidgwick felt that Bentham's political ideas were still relevant to contemporary problems. They were not "a matter of merely historical interest," but rather "an important element of our current political thought; hardly a decade . . . has elapsed since it might almost have been called a predominant element." [46] By the end of the century it was even thought that "utilitarianism forms the popular philosophy of the day." [47] However, their ambition was to achieve a sudden transformation of the party system; their doctrine seemed to justify the belief that it could be done; and their tactics were designed to do it. Although their contemporaries and observers who followed have seen evidence of widespread influence—some of it hardly the kind that the original Benthamites would have wished

Benthamite revolution were by no means all or even in very large part, radicals. In many an office in Whitehall or Pall Mall the Benthamite lion lay down with the Whiggish lamb": "A Whig Inspector," *Journal of Modern History, 27* (Dec. 1955), 352.

45. William Whewell, *Lectures on the History of Moral Philosophy in England* (London, 1852), pp. 188–89. Roebuck was an exception in that he was consoled by signs of indirect influence. Although the Radicals were not successful in "converting and bringing over large numbers of political partisans," they had a profound effect on public opinion by inducing men "to reason after a new fashion": *History of the Whig Ministry* (1852), *1,* 343–44.

46. Henry Sidgwick, "Bentham and Benthamism in Politics and Ethics" (1877), *Miscellaneous Essays and Addresses* (London, 1904), p. 135.

47. T. H. S. Escott, *England: Its People, Polity, and Pursuits* (London, [1905]), *2,* 328–29. Also see Leslie Stephen, *The English Utilitarians* (London, 1900), *2, 42:* as the men who "formulated and deliberately defended the principles which were beginning to conquer the world," the Philosophic Radicals achieved intellectual leadership among all types of reformers.

for [48]—the Philosophic Radicals in their disillusionment felt too embittered to hope for the success that was still to come.

When there is a discrepancy between reality and the image one has of it, the doctrine that gave birth to the misleading image may be blamed. As an alternative, the blame may be shifted onto society for not allowing the image to be actualized. This encourages anger, but not complete disillusionment, for it allows one to assume that the image might have been realistic and that the tactics might have worked. Society was at fault. Thus a sense of alienation allows for the maintenance of faith. In some moods the Philosophic Radicals responded in this way. After the elections in 1837 Mrs. Grote wrote from Switzerland that her "thoughts never turn upon Eng[lan]d but with regret and distaste, in connection with our diseased social and pol[itica]l system." [49] Her admiration for Switzerland was similar to John Stuart Mill's feeling that Germany and especially France were more congenial than England. In France there were people with "determinate views on all the subjects most interesting to mankind; and [they] keep none of these back, but state them to the public on every fitting occasion." And this was especially true for political philosophy, whereas in England anyone for whom that was a vocation was stifled.[50] Mill seems never to have tired

48. Fabian socialists have been described as (and also thought themselves) intellectual heirs to Bentham and his disciples. Beatrice Webb thought Bentham "was certainly Sydney's intellectual godfather": *Our Partnership* (London, Longmans, 1948), p. 210. Also see, Dicey, *Law and Opinion;* G. D. H. Cole, *British Working Class Politics, 1832–1914* (London, Routledge, 1941), pp. 122–23; Fabian Tracts nos. 165, 168, 221. Engels was the first to claim this line of descent for the socialists: *The Condition of the Working Class in England in 1844,* Eng. trans. F. K. Wischnewetzky (London, Allen and Unwin, 1950), p. 240.

49. Also, "the whole frame of social life in Engd. is so perverted by the admira[tio]n for wealth and its appendages that what we see here shames us": H. Grote to Place, Aug. 16, 1837, Add. MSS 35,150, f. 279. In later years such was Grote's "aversion and contempt for the senseless chatter usually going on in Ho. of C. . . . that he will hardly ever look at a 'debate' ": H. Grote to 3rd earl Grey, Feb. 20, 1860: Univ. of Durham, Grey Papers.

50. Also, "I come to you as *littérateurs* and artists come to Europe from that country of pure *industrialism,* the United States of America; because there is no call in their own country for the kind of labour which

of expressing disdain for his own country. General society in England was "thoroughly insipid"; there was a "low moral tone" and an "absence of high feelings" evident in "the habit of, not indeed professing, but taking for granted in all modes of implication, that conduct is of course always directed towards low and petty objects." He was contemptuous of "the mean and cramped externals of English middle class life" and "wearied with discontented struggling (Benthamicè) devil-by-the-tail-pulling England." He even went so far as to attribute the defects of his early family life to the pattern prevailing in the nation at large. Having recalled his mother's deficiencies, his father's despotic character, and the general absence of affection in his home, Mill explained, "I give my father's family not as peculiar in this respect but only as a too faithful exemplification of the ordinary fact." [51]

The Philosophic Radicals' approach to politics is part of the tradition of ideological thinking that has flourished since the late eighteenth century; but it is a faint reflection of what this mode

---

is their vocation. . . . in political philosophy, the initiative belongs to France . . . [because of] the far more elevated *terrain* on which the discussion is engaged": Mill, "Comparison of the Tendencies of French and English Intellect," *Mo. Rep., 7,* (Nov. 1833), 803–04. On Germany, see Mill to Mrs. Austin, May 22, 1842, *EL,* p. 522; "Taylor's Statesman," *LWR, 27* (April 1837), 3 (both Grote and Mill wrote parts of this article).

51. Mill to Mrs. Austin, Aug. 22, 1842, *EL,* p. 543; *Early Draft,* pp. 68, 71, 170, 184; also, among Rejected Leaves, pp. 183–84: "My father . . . resembled almost all Englishmen in being ashamed of the signs of feeling, and by the absence of demonstration, starving the feelings themselves. In an atmosphere of tenderness and affection he would have been tender and affectionate; but his ill assorted marriage and his asperities of temper disabled him from making such an atmosphere. . . . my father's children neither loved him, nor, with any warmth of affection, any one else. I do not mean that things were worse in this respect than they are in most English families. . . . there is less personal affection in England than in any other country. . . . That rarity in England, a really warm hearted mother." Cf. Solly's description of a visit to the Mill household: "accustomed as I was to my father's behaviour to my mother, and that of other gentlemen whom I had observed in similar relations, I could not help being rather pained at his [James Mill's] manner occasionally to Mrs. Mill. She was a tall, handsome lady, sweet-tempered, with pleasant manners, fond of her children; but I think not much interested in what the elder ones and their father read and talked about": *Eighty Years, 1,* 147.

of thought and action can be, and therefore it is on the periphery of this tradition. Of course, some of their doctrinairism was temperamental, but it also had an intellectual component that derives from that tradition. After all, Mill called his father the Voltaire of England and had himself found a model in the *philosophes*. The Philosophic Radicals had a measure of that abstraction in their theorizing that led them to base their actions on a level of reality which most other political observers did not recognize. This was the kind of abstract theorizing that had provoked Burke's criticisms, though its substance was quite different. They also had a rationalist skepticism about religion and a suspicion of tradition that has attracted the enmity of anti-ideological critics. Furthermore, their ideas were invested with populist assumptions similar to those found among the revolutionary intelligentsia of the late eighteenth century. Like the *philosophes,* they also made historicistic assumptions that not only made it possible to see politics in terms of Left and Right but also encouraged a doctrinaire version of this outlook in which politics becomes most pure when the engagement of extreme Left and Right dominates the political arena.

On the other hand, despite the affinities, they do not fit the description of fanatic ideologues described by such critics as Burke and Tocqueville and, among contemporaries, by Talmon, Aron, and Hoffer. They did not hold abstract theories that discredited all the values and beliefs that upheld the established society, nor were they disposed to use philosophy as a means of justifying a new despotism; and their sectarian attitudes never brought them near to an affiliation with an organization that could even potentially have become a mass movement. Whereas other ideologues dreamed of benevolent despotisms that would demand conformity to what they were sure was the fundamental order of reality, the Philosophic Radicals were doctrinaire politicians whose faith was revealed in nothing worse than dogmatism.[52] The difference can be traced in part to the substance of their ideas, which were never sufficiently comprehensive to

52. Cf. Eric Hoffer, *The True Believer* (New York, New American Library, 1960), pp. 76–81, 119–33; Tocqueville, *L'Ancién Regime,* Book 3, Chap. 1; Talmon, *Origins,* pp. 135–43, 249–55.

entail a risk that the entire social and moral order would be subjected to the manipulations of doctrinaire purposes. But the difference can also be attributed to the fact that the Philosophic Radicals worked in an alien environment. There was little in the British political tradition that encouraged the elaboration of ideological views, and the system held out few rewards for politicians who held such views. This environment was not only an external obstacle; in varying degrees, as their ambivalence about the aggressive tactics indicates (see pp. 194–99), its values were internalized by the Philosophic Radicals.

For these reasons the Philosophic Radicals were somewhat removed from the tradition of modern ideological thinking. They had the makings of "true believers" (a phrase that may have originated with John Stuart Mill).[53] Yet their fantasies of new worlds never became grotesque, and their efforts to transform their own world always remained within the ground rules accepted by their contemporaries. Tocqueville, who knew several of them, tried to place them in relation to the French Radical, who typified to him the ideologue. He acknowledged the similarities: "There are a great many enthusiastic sectarians among English Radicals. One also finds a fair number of men who have been won over by French philosophic ideas." Yet he emphasized the differences. Unlike their French counterparts, they respected legality and principles of legitimacy: "I have never caught them showing signs of wishing to impose on the Nation (even for its own good) a political condition not of its own choosing. The whole question is to win a majority: and I have never seen that they had any idea of doing so otherwise than by legal means." In addition, the English Radical leaders recognized the role of religion and property as conditions of civilized society. Whereas the French Radical would "violate [property] in practice, [as] he attacks it in theory" and goes in for "the flaunting not only of anti-Christian opinions, but also of the most anti-social philosophical ideas," the English Radicals, in contrast, acknowledge

53. Mill to Carlyle, March 9, 1833, *EL,* p. 144. Mill's meaning is not obvious; he refers to persons capable of responding to Carlyle's thoughts and being changed by them, suggesting a person who takes seriously intellectual problems.

that "respect [for property] is the essential basis for a civilized society" and are "convinced of the political necessity for religion." Thus Tocqueville, even though he was especially sensitive to the threat of ideologues to a political system, could say that "at present [1835] I think that an enlightened man of good sense and good will would be a Radical in England." [54]

54. Tocqueville, *Journeys to England and Ireland,* pp. 86–87. It seems clear that Tocqueville had the Philosophic Radicals in mind, for this passage follows and is part of the entry in which he records a conversation with Roebuck and Mill; also, he refers to the Radical "leaders" and to their knowledge of political economy. On the significance of Tocqueville's contacts with English Radicals for the development of his thought, see Seymour Drescher, *Tocqueville and England* (Cambridge, Harvard, 1964), pp. 97–98.

Index

Yale Studies in Political Science